ROMANS 1-8
A Commentary in the Wesleyan Tradition

William M. Greathouse
with George Lyons

BEACON HILL PRESS
OF KANSAS CITY

ISBN 978-0-8341-2362-5

Printed in the United States of America

Library of Congress Cataloging-in-Publication Data
Greathouse, William M.
    Romans 1-8 / William M. Greathouse with George Lyons.
        p. cm. — (New Beacon Bible Commentary)
    Includes bibliographical references.
    ISBN 978-0-8341-2362-5 (pbk.)
    1. Bible. N.T. Romans I-VIII—Commentaries. I. Lyons, George. II. Title.

    BS2665.53.G74 2007
    227'.1077—dc22

                                                                    2007046444

10 9 8 7 6 5 4 3

DEDICATION

For Becky, Mark, and Beth,
who walk in "the truth of the gospel" (Gal 2:5, 14)

Lovingly,
Your father
William M. Greathouse

COMMENTARY EDITORS

General Editors

Alex Varughese
  Ph.D., Drew University
  Professor of Biblical Literature
  Mount Vernon Nazarene University
  Mount Vernon, Ohio

George Lyons
  Ph.D., Emory University
  Professor of New Testament
  Northwest Nazarene University
  Nampa, Idaho

Roger Hahn
  Ph.D., Duke University
  Dean of the Faculty
  Professor of New Testament
  Nazarene Theological Seminary
  Kansas City, Missouri

Section Editors

Joseph Coleson
  Ph.D., Brandeis University
  Professor of Old Testament
  Nazarene Theological Seminary
  Kansas City, Missouri

Kent Brower
  Ph.D., The University of Manchester
  Vice Principal
  Senior Lecturer in Biblical Studies
  Nazarene Theological College
  Manchester, England

Robert Branson
  Ph.D., Boston University
  Professor of Biblical Literature
  Olivet Nazarene University
  Bourbonnais, Illinois

George Lyons
  Ph.D., Emory University
  Professor of New Testament
  Northwest Nazarene University
  Nampa, Idaho

Alex Varughese
  Ph.D., Drew University
  Professor of Biblical Literature
  Mount Vernon Nazarene University
  Mount Vernon, Ohio

Jeanne Serrão
  Ph.D., Claremont Graduate University
  Dean of the School of Theology and
    Philosophy
  Professor of Biblical Literature
  Mount Vernon Nazarene University
  Mount Vernon, Ohio

Jim Edlin
  Ph.D., Southern Baptist Theological
    Seminary
  Professor of Biblical Literature and
    Languages
  Chair of the Division of Religion and
    Philosophy
  MidAmerica Nazarene University
  Olathe, Kansas

CONTENTS

GENERAL EDITORS' PREFACE

The purpose of the New Beacon Bible Commentary is to make available to pastors and students in the twenty-first century a biblical commentary that reflects the best scholarship in the Wesleyan theological tradition. The commentary project aims to make this scholarship accessible to a wider audience to assist them in their understanding and proclamation of Scripture as God's Word.

Writers of the volumes in this series not only are scholars within the Wesleyan theological tradition and experts in their field but also have special interest in the books assigned to them. Their task is to communicate clearly the critical consensus and the full range of other credible voices who have commented on the Scriptures. Though scholarship and scholarly contribution to the understanding of the Scriptures are key concerns of this series, it is not intended as an academic dialogue within the scholarly community. Commentators of this series constantly aim to demonstrate in their work the significance of the Bible as the church's book and the contemporary relevance and application of the biblical message. The project's overall goal is to make available to the church and for her service the fruits of the labors of scholars who are committed to their Christian faith.

The *New International Version* (NIV) is the reference version of the Bible used in this series; however, the focus of exegetical study and comments is the biblical text in its original language. When the commentary uses the NIV, it is printed in bold. The text printed in bold italics is the translation of the author. Commentators also refer to other translations where the text may be difficult or ambiguous.

The structure and organization of the commentaries in this series seeks to facilitate the study of the biblical text in a systematic and methodical way. Study of each biblical book begins with an **Introduction** section that gives an overview of authorship, date, provenance, audience, occasion, purpose, sociological/cultural issues, textual history, literary features, hermeneutical issues, and theological themes necessary to understand the book. This section also includes a brief outline of the book and a list of general works and standard commentaries.

The commentary section for each biblical book follows the outline of the book presented in the introduction. In some volumes, readers will find section **overviews** of large portions of scripture with general comments on their overall literary structure and other literary features. A consistent feature of the commentary is the paragraph by paragraph study of biblical texts. This section has three parts: **Behind the Text**, **In the Text**, and **From the Text**.

The goal of the **Behind the Text** section is to provide the reader with all the relevant information necessary to understand the text. This includes specific historical situations reflected in the text, the literary context of the text, sociological and cultural issues, and literary features of the text.

In the Text explores what the text says, following its verse-by-verse structure. This section includes a discussion of grammatical details, word studies, and the connectedness of the text to other biblical books/passages or other parts of the book being studied (the canonical relationship). This section provides transliterations of key words in Hebrew and Greek and their literal meanings. The goal here is to explain what the author would have meant and/or what the audience would have understood as the meaning of the text. This is the largest section of the commentary.

The *From the Text* section examines the text in relation to the following areas: theological significance, intertextuality, the history of interpretation, use of the Old Testament scriptures in the New Testament, interpretation in later church history, actualization, and application.

The commentary provides *sidebars* on topics of interest that are important but not necessarily part of an explanation of the biblical text. These topics are informational items and may cover archaeological, historical, literary, cultural, and theological matters that have relevance to the biblical text. Occasionally, longer detailed discussions of special topics are included as *excurses.*

We offer this series with our hope and prayer that readers will find it a valuable resource for their understanding of God's Word and an indispensable tool for their critical engagement with the biblical texts.

Roger Hahn, Centennial Initiative General Editor
Alex Varughese, General Editor (Old Testament)
George Lyons, General Editor (New Testament)

AUTHOR'S PREFACE

Romans has become a familiar friend. In 1968 my first commentary, "Romans," was published as 275 pages of volume eight of the ten-volume *Beacon Bible Commentary*. In 1975 my devotional commentary in *Beacon Bible Expositions* was published. This third effort is not a revision of either. It is a fresh commentary, coming after monumental developments in Romans scholarship in the intervening years. Two publications sparked what has become known as the "new perspective" on Romans: *The Romans Debate*, edited by Karl P. Donfried (rev. ed., 1991) and Ernst Käsemann's *Commentary on Romans* (1980). Fine summaries of the new perspective appeared in the July 2004 edition of the journal *Interpretation*.

One notable effect of the new perspective is a significant loss of confidence in the objectivity and certainty of Reformed Protestant readings of Romans, emphasizing personal redemption and the Lutheran understanding of justification. This pessimistic understanding of Christian living had prevailed in Western Christianity from the time of the Reformation. In brief, it viewed God's righteousness as simply the gift of justifying faith, understood mainly as a change of relationship and status for believers. In this view, justified believers remain *simul justus et peccator* ("at once righteous and sinful") until death. Christians, therefore, remain the sin-victimized "wretched man" of Rom 7:24. The gracious gift of justification, however, does relieve the *angst* of guilt and the fear of death, producing in the believer a peaceful conscience. Any talk of true ethical righteousness or sanctification in this present life, however, is ruled out by definition. Any "righteousness" or "holiness" ascribed to Christians is only "imputed." This pessimism served to widen the gap between Protestantism and Roman Catholicism.

Ironically, it was Lutheran Ernst Käsemann's 1980 *Commentary on Romans* that first seriously challenged the Lutheran consensus that God's righteousness was simply the gift of justifying faith. He argues that God's righteousness is

> primarily a power rather than a gift. . . . The phrase "the righteousness of God" in Paul . . . speaks of the God who brings back the fallen world into the sphere of his legitimate claim . . . [in] the Son of God . . . as our Kyrios, the one eschatological gift of God to us. (28-29)

God's righteousness is both God's *gift* and his *demand*; the Giver always unfailingly accompanies the Gift. Käsemann thereby opens the way for a real doctrine of Christian ethical righteousness and sanctification—precisely Paul's doctrine in Rom 6—8 and 12—15.

It was this understanding of Romans that the Oxford don turned itinerate Anglican evangelist, John Wesley, vigorously defended during the eighteenth century. More recently, it is the view supported by Anglican bishop N. T. Wright's treatments of Paul's theology (see, e.g., his 1993 *Climax of the Covenant*). All these developments are good news for Wesleyan scholars, whose approach to Romans was regarded with jaded eyes as special pleading motivated by dogmatic considerations. Today, NT scholars of every stripe, many of them highly regarded Romans scholars, espouse an "optimism of grace" much like Wesley proclaimed. Such grace promises Christians a righteousness and holiness that are genuinely ethical and realizable in the life of the Spirit now (see July 2004 *Interpretation*).

The Romans debate of the 1970s further illuminates the nature of the Roman letter, restoring as it does confidence in the unity and integrity of Romans. Jewish in its origin (and in its continuing struggle with the Torah), the Roman community, by A.D. 57-58 had become predominantly Gentile in the interim following Claudius's A.D. 48 edict, which evicted all Jews from Rome (see Acts 18:2). Upon returning, Jewish Christians found a totally new situation developing, a mixed Gentile-Jewish community. These facts illuminate chs 14—15 and support ch 16 as integral of Paul's letter.

The forty-year span between the BBC and the NBBC, I spent preaching, lecturing, serving my denomination as a general superintendent, and most recently in retirement. It was also my privilege during those years to teach classes on Romans at both Nazarene Theological Seminary and Trevecca Nazarene University. These assignments necessitated the joyful task of keeping abreast on Romans scholarship in new commentaries and professional journals.

Admittedly, writing a verse-by-verse commentary from the Greek is another matter. It is here that the assistance of my editor, George Lyons, has been invaluable. His Emory University Ph.D. in NT studies and his proficiency in Greek, sharpened by daily classes at Northwest Nazarene University, have enabled him to give this commentary a scholarly quality and authority it would not otherwise possess. Both the author and the readers, therefore, stand in special debt to George Lyons.

I would be unforgivably delinquent not to express appreciation also for my wife Judy's unfailing encouragement for me to give the best hours each day for the past three years to the grueling work of writing, rewriting, and then e-mailing daily offerings to Dr. Lyons. Most of all, I am indebted to the illumination of the Spirit, flickering as it sometimes was, as I sought divine guidance and strength for the task of writing. *Soli Deo Gloria*.

William M. Greathouse

ABBREVIATIONS

With a few exceptions, these abbreviations follow those in *The SBL Handbook of Style* (Alexander 1999).

General

A.D.	anno Domini (precedes date) (equivalent to C.E.)
B.C.	before Christ (follows date) (equivalent to B.C.E.)
B.C.E.	before the Common Era
C.E.	Common Era
cf.	compare
ch	chapter
chs	chapters
e.g.	*exempli gratia*, for example
esp.	especially
etc.	*et cetera*, and the rest
f(f).	and the following one(s)
i.e.	*id est*, that is
lit.	literally
LXX	Septuagint
MS	manuscript
MSS	manuscripts
MT	Masoretic Text (of the OT)
n.	note
n.d.	no date
n.p.	no place; no publisher; no page
nn.	notes
NT	New Testament
OT	Old Testament
s.v.	*sub verbo*, under the word
v	verse
vv	verses

Modern English Versions

ASV	American Standard Version
ESV	English Standard Version
HCSB	Holman Christian Standard Bible
JB	Jerusalem Bible
KJV	King James Version
MOFFATT	*The Bible: A New Translation*, James A. R. Moffatt
NAB	New American Bible
NASB	New American Standard Bible
NCV	New Century Version
NEB	New English Bible
NIV	New International Version
NJB	New Jerusalem Bible
NLT	New Living Translation
NRSV	New Revised Standard Version
PHILLIPS	*The New Testament in Modern English*, J. B. Phillips
REB	Revised English Bible
RSV	Revised Standard Version
TEV	Good News Bible: Today's English Version

Print Conventions for Translations

Bold font	NIV (bold without quotation marks in the text under study; elsewhere in the regular font, with quotation marks and no further identification)
Bold italic font	Author's translation (without quotation marks)
Behind the Text:	Literary or historical background information average readers might not know from reading the biblical text alone
In the Text:	Comments on the biblical text, words, phrases, grammar, and so forth

From the Text:	The use of the text by later interpreters, contemporary relevance, theological and ethical implications of the text, with particular emphasis on Wesleyan concerns

Apocrypha

APOT	*The Apocrypha and Pseudepigrapha of the Old Testament.* Edited by R. H. Charles. 2 vols. Oxford, 1913
Bar	Baruch
Add Dan	Additions to Daniel
Pr Azar	Prayer of Azariah
Bel	Bel and the Dragon
Sg Three	Song of the Three Young Men
Sus	Susanna
1-2 Esd	1-2 Esdras
Add Esth	Additions to Esther
Ep Jer	Epistle of Jeremiah
Jdt	Judith
1-2 Macc	1-2 Maccabees
3-4 Macc	3-4 Maccabees
Pr Man	Prayer of Manasseh
Ps 151	Psalm 151
Sir	Sirach/Ecclesiasticus
Tob	Tobit
Wis	Wisdom of Solomon

OT Pseudepigrapha

Ahiqar	*Ahiqar*
Apoc. Ab.	*Apocalypse of Abraham*
Apoc. Adam	*Apocalypse of Adam*
Apoc. Dan.	*Apocalypse of Daniel*
Apoc. El. (H)	Hebrew *Apocalypse of Elijah*
Apoc. El. (C)	Coptic *Apocalypse of Elijah*
Apoc. Mos.	*Apocalypse of Moses*
Apoc. Sedr.	*Apocalypse of Sedrach*
Apoc. Zeph.	*Apocalypse of Zephaniah*
Apocr. Ezek.	*Apocrypon of Ezekiel*
Aris. Ex.	Aristeas the Exegete
Aristob.	Aristobulus
Artap.	Artapanus
As. Mos.	*Assumption of Moses*
2 Bar.	*2 Baruch (Syriac Apocalypse)*
3 Bar.	*3 Baruch (Greek Apocalypse)*
4 Bar.	*4 Baruch (Paraleipomena Jeremiou)*
Bk. Noah	*Book of Noah*
Cav. Tr.	*Cave of Treasures*
Cl. Mal.	Cleodemus Malchus
Dem.	Demetrius (the Chronographer)
El. Mod.	*Eldad and Modad*
1 En.	*1 Enoch (Ethiopic Apocalypse)*
2 En.	*2 Enoch (Slavonic Apocalypse)*
3 En.	*3 Enoch (Hebrew Apocalypse)*
Eup.	Eupolemus
Ezek. Trag.	Ezekiel the Tragedian
4 Ezra	*4 Ezra*
5 Apoc. Syr. Pss.	*Five Apocryphal Syriac Psalms*

Dead Sea Scrolls and Related Texts

Q	Qumran
Gk. Apoc. Ezra	*Greek Apocalypse of Ezra*
Hec. Ab.	Hecataeus of Abdera
Hel. Syn. Pr.	*Hellenistic Synagogal Prayers*
Hist. Jos.	*History of Joseph*
Hist. Rech.	*History of the Rechabites*
Jan. Jam.	*Jannes and Jambres*

Jos. Asen.	*Joseph and Aseneth*
Jub.	*Jubilees*
L.A.B.	*Liber antiquitatum biblicarum* (Pseudo-Philo)
L.A.E.	*Life of Adam and Eve*
Lad. Jac.	*Ladder of Jacob*
Let. Aris.	*Letter of Aristeas*
Liv. Pro.	*Lives of the Prophets*
Lost Tr.	*The Lost Tribes*
3 Macc.	*3 Maccabees*
4 Macc.	*4 Maccabees*
5 Macc.	*5 Maccabees* (Arabic)
Mart. Ascen. Isa.	*Martyrdom and Ascension of Isaiah*
Odes Sol.	*Odes of Solomon*
Ph. E. Poet	Philo the Epic Poet
Pr. Jac.	*Prayer of Jacob*
Pr. Jos.	*Prayer of Joseph*
Pr. Man.	*Prayer of Manasseh*
Pr. Mos.	*Prayer of Moses*
Ps.-Eup.	Pseudo-Eupolemus
Ps.-Hec.	Pseudo-Hecataeus
Ps.-Orph.	Pseudo-Orpheus
Ps.-Phoc.	Pseudo-Phocylides
Pss. Sol.	*Psalms of Solomon*
Ques. Ezra	*Questions of Ezra*
Rev. Ezra	*Revelation of Ezra*
Sib. Or.	*Sibylline Oracles*
Syr. Men.	*Sentences of the Syriac Menander*
T. 12 Patr.	*Testaments of the Twelve Patriarchs*
T. Ash.	*Testament of Asher*
T. Benj.	*Testament of Benjamin*
T. Dan	*Testament of Dan*
T. Gad	*Testament of Gad*
T. Iss.	*Testament of Issachar*
T. Jos.	*Testament of Joseph*
T. Jud.	*Testament of Judah*
T. Levi	*Testament of Levi*
T. Naph.	*Testament of Naphtali*
T. Reu.	*Testament of Reuben*
T. Sim.	*Testament of Simeon*
T. Zeb.	*Testament of Zebulun*
T. 3 Patr.	*Testaments of the Three Patriarchs*
T. Ab.	*Testament of Abraham*
T. Isaac	*Testament of Isaac*
T. Jac.	*Testament of Jacob*
T. Adam	*Testament of Adam*
T. Hez.	*Testament of Hezekiah*
T. Job	*Testament of Job*
T. Mos.	*Testament of Moses*
T. Sol.	*Testament of Solomon*
Theod.	Theodotus, *On the Jews*
Treat. Shem	*Treatise of Shem*
Vis. Ezra	*Vision of Ezra*

Josephus

Vita	*Vita*
Life	*The Life*
C. Ap.	*Contra Apionem*
Ag. Ap.	*Against Apion*
A.J.	*Antiquitates judaicae*
Ant.	*Jewish Antiquities*
B.J.	*Bellum judaicum*
J.W.	*Jewish War*

Apostolic Fathers

Barn.	*Barnabas*
1-2 Clem.	*1-2 Clement*
Did.	*Didache*
Diogn.	*Diognetus*
Herm. *Mand.*	Shepherd of Hermas, *Mandate*
Herm. *Sim.*	Shepherd of Hermas, *Similitude*
Herm. *Vis.*	Shepherd of Hermas, *Vision*
Ign. *Eph.*	Ignatius, *To the Ephesians*
Ign. *Magn.*	Ignatius, *To the Magnesians*
Ign. *Smyrn.*	Ignatius, *To the Smyrnaeans*
Ign. *Phld.*	Ignatius, *To the Philadelphians*
Ign. *Rom.*	Ignatius, *To the Romans*
Ign. *Pol.*	Ignatius, *To Polycarp*
Ign. *Trall.*	Ignatius, *To the Trallians*
Mart. Pol.	*Martyrdom of Polycarp*
Pol. *Phil.*	Polycarp, *To the Philippians*

Greek Transliteration

Greek	*Letter*	*English*
α	*alpha*	*a*
β	*bēta*	*b*
γ	*gamma*	*g*
γ	*gamma nasal*	*n* (before γ, κ, ξ, χ)
δ	*delta*	*d*
ε	*epsilon*	*e*
ζ	*zēta*	*z*
η	*ēta*	*ē*
θ	*thēta*	*th*
ι	*iōta*	*i*
κ	*kappa*	*k*
λ	*lambda*	*l*
μ	*my*	*m*
ν	*ny*	*n*
ξ	*xi*	*x*
ο	*omicron*	*o*
π	*pi*	*p*
ρ	*rhō*	*r*
ρ	initial *rhō*	*rh*
σ/ς	*sigma*	*s*
τ	*tau*	*t*
υ	*upsilon*	*y*
υ	*upsilon*	*u* (in diphthongs: *au, eu, ēu, ou, ui*)
φ	*phi*	*ph*
χ	*chi*	*ch*
ψ	*psi*	*ps*
ω	*ōmega*	*ō*
῾	rough breathing	*h* (before initial vowels or diphthongs)

Hebrew Consonant Transliteration

Hebrew/ Aramaic	*Letter*	*English*
א	*alef*	'
ב	*bet*	*b*
ג	*gimel*	*g*
ד	*dalet*	*d*
ה	*he*	*h*
ו	*vav*	*v* or *w*
ז	*zayin*	*z*
ח	*khet*	*ḥ*
ט	*tet*	*ṭ*
י	*yod*	*y*
כ/ך	*kaf*	*k*
ל	*lamed*	*l*
מ/ם	*mem*	*m*
נ/ן	*nun*	*n*
ס	*samek*	*s*
ע	*ayin*	'
פ/ף	*pe*	*p*
צ/ץ	*tsade*	*ṣ*
ק	*qof*	*q*
ר	*resh*	*r*
שׂ	*sin*	*ś*
שׁ	*shin*	*š*
ת	*tav*	*t*

BIBLIOGRAPHY

1944. *The Book of Common Prayer.* New York: Oxford University Press.

Achtemeir, Paul J. 1985. *Romans.* Interpretation. A Bible Commentary for Teaching and Preaching. Atlanta: John Knox.

Alexander, Patrick H., and others, eds. 1999. *The SBL Handbook of Style for Ancient Near Eastern, Biblical, and Early Christian Studies.* Peabody, Mass.: Hendrickson.

Allchin, A. M. 1991. "The Epworth-Canterbury-Constantinople-Axis." *Wesleyan Theological Journal* 26, 1:23-37.

Augsburger, Myron. 1961. *Quench Not the Spirit.* Scottdale, Pa.: Herald.

Augustine. 1955. *Confessions and Enchiridion.* Trans. and ed. Albert C. Outler. Vol. 7 of Library of Christian Classics. Philadelphia: Westminster.

Bangs, Carl. 1971. *Arminius: A Study of the Dutch Reformation.* Nashville: Abingdon.

Barclay, William. 1957. *The Letter to the Romans.* The Daily Study Bible. Philadelphia: Westminster.

Barrett, C. K. 1957. *The Epistle to the Romans* in Harper's New Testament Commentaries. New York: Harper and Brothers.

———. 1963. *Reading Through Romans.* London: Epworth.

Barth, Karl. 1933. *The Epistle to the Romans.* Trans. from the 6th ed., Edwin C. Hoskyns. London: Oxford University Press.

———. 1959. *A Shorter Commentary on Romans.* Trans. Edwin C. Hoskyns. Richmond, Va.: John Knox.

———. 1993. *The Holy Spirit and the Christian Life: The Theological Basis of Ethics.* Trans. R. Birch Hoyle. Library of Theological Ethics. Louisville, Ky.: Westminster/John Knox.

———. 2004. *Church Dogmatics.* 14 vols. Ed. and trans. Geoffrey W. Bromiley and others. Edinburgh: T&T Clark.

Bassett, Paul M., and William M. Greathouse. 1985. *The Historical Development.* Vol. 2 of *Exploring Christian Holiness.* Kansas City: Beacon Hill Press of Kansas City.

Bauer, Walter. 1979. *A Greek-English Lexicon of the New Testament and Other Early Christian Literature.* Trans. and adapted William Arndt, F. Wilbur Gingrich, and Frederick W. Danker. Chicago: University of Chicago Press.

Beet, Joseph Agar. 1885. *St. Paul's Epistle to the Romans.* London: Hodder and Stoughton.

Benoit, Pierre. 1973. *Jesus and the Gospel.* Trans. Benet Weatherhead. Bristol: Herder and Herder.

Benson, Bob, Jr., and Michael W. Benson. 1989. *Disciplines for the Inner Life.* Hendersonville, Tenn.: Deeper Life.

Beyer, Hermann Wolfgang. 1964. *"eulogeō, ktl."* Pages 754-63 in vol. 2 of *The Theological Dictionary of the New Testament.* Ed. Gerhard Kittel and Gerhard Friedrich. Trans. Geoffrey W. Bromiley. Grand Rapids: Eerdmans. 1964-76.

Bietenhard, Hans. 1976. "Please." Pages 814-20 in vol. 2 of *The New International Dictionary of New Testament Theology.* 3 vols. Trans. with additions and revisions from *Theologisches Begriffslexikon zum Neuen Testament,* ed. by Lothar Coenen and others by a team of translators. Grand Rapids: Zondervan, 1971-78.

Black, Matthew. 1973. *Romans* in *New Century Bible Commentary.* London: Oliphants.

Blass, Friedrich, Albert Debrunner, and Robert W. Funk. 1961. *A Greek Grammar of the New Testament and Other Early Christian Literature.* Trans. Robert W. Funk. Chicago: University of Chicago Press.

Blue, B. B. 1997. "Food, Food Laws, Table Fellowship." Pages 376-79 in *Dictionary of the Later New Testament and Its Developments.* Ed. Ralph P. Martin and Peter H. Davids. Downers Grove, Ill.: InterVarsity.

Bonhoeffer, Dietrich. 1995. *The Cost of Discipleship.* Trans. R. H. Fuller. New York: Simon and Schuster.

Bray, Gerald, ed. 1998. *Romans.* Vol. 6 of *Ancient Christian Commentary on Scripture: New Testament.* Ed. Thomas C. Oden. Downers Grove, Ill.: InterVarsity.

Briscoe, D. Stuart. 1982. *Romans.* Vol. 6 of The Communicator's Commentary. Ed. Lloyd J. Ogilvie. Waco, Tex.: Word Books.

Brooke, George J. 1992. "Testimonia." Pages 391-92 in vol. 6 of the *Anchor Bible Dictionary*. New York: Doubleday.

Bruce, F. F. 1963. *The Epistle of Paul to the Romans: An Introduction and Commentary*. Vol. 6 in The Tyndale Bible Commentaries. Grand Rapids: Eerdmans.

Brunner, Emil. 1959. *The Letter to the Romans*. Trans. H. A. Kennedy. Philadelphia: Westminster.

Bullinger, E. W. 1898. *Figures of Speech Used in the Bible*. London: Eyre and Spottiswoode.

Bultmann, Rudolf. 1970. *Theology of the New Testament: Complete in One Volume*. Trans. Kendrick Grobel. New York: Harper.

Byrne, Brendan. 1996. *Romans*. Vol. 6 of Sacra Pagina. Ed. Daniel J. Harrington. Collegeville, Minn.: Liturgical Press.

———. 2004. "Interpreting Romans: The New Perspective and Beyond." *Interpretation* 58, 3:241-52.

Calvin, John. 1960. *The Epistles of Paul to the Romans and Thessalonians*. Trans. Ross Mackenzie. Repr. Grand Rapids: Eerdmans.

———. 1970. *Institutes of the Christian Religion*. 2 vols. in one. Trans. Henry Beveridge. Repr. Grand Rapids: Eerdmans.

Cell, George Croft. 1935. *The Rediscovery of John Wesley*. New York: Henry Holt.

Cerfaux, Lucien. 1959. *The Church in the Theology of St. Paul*. Trans. Geoffrey Webb and Adrian Walker. Freiburg: Herder and Herder.

Chilton, Bruce D., and Jacob Neusner. 1995. *Judaism in the New Testament*. London: Routledge.

———. 2004. *Classical Christianity and Rabbinic Judaism: Comparing Theologies*. Grand Rapids: Baker Academic.

Clarke, Adam. n.d. *The New Testament of Our Lord and Saviour Jesus Christ*. Vol. 2. New York: Abingdon-Cokesbury.

Collins, Kenneth J. 1997. *The Scripture Way of Salvation*. Nashville: Abingdon.

———. 2005. *The Evangelical Moment: The Promise of an American Religion*. Grand Rapids: Baker Academic.

———. 2007. *The Theology of John Wesley: Holy Love and the Shape of Grace*. Nashville: Abingdon.

Cragg, Gerald. 1951. "The Epistle to the Romans" (Exposition). Pages 353-668 in vol. 9 in *The Interpreter's Bible*. Ed. George A. Buttrick and others. New York: Abingdon-Cokesbury.

Cranfield, C. E. B. 1975. *The Epistle to the Romans*. Vol. 1 of The International Critical Commentary. Edinburgh: T&T Clark.

———. 1979. *The Epistle to the Romans*. Vol. 2 of The International Critical Commentary. Edinburgh: T&T Clark.

———. 1985. *Romans: A Shorter Commentary*. Grand Rapids: Eerdmans.

Cullmann, Oscar. 1953. *Peter: Disciple, Apostle, Martyr: A Historical and Theological Study*. Trans. Floyd V. Filson. London: SCM.

Denney, James. 1970. "St. Paul's Epistle to the Romans." Pages 555-725 in vol. 2 of *The Expositor's Greek New Testament*. Ed. W. Robertson Nicoll. Repr. Grand Rapids: Eerdmans. 1897—1910.

Dodd, C. H. 1932. *The Epistle to the Romans* in The Moffatt New Testament Commentary. New York: Harper and Brothers.

Donfried, Karl P. 1976. "Justification and Last Judgment in Paul," in *Zeitschrift für die neutestamentliche Wissenschaft und die Kunde der Alteren Kirche* 67:90-110.

———. 1987. "The Kingdom of God in Paul." Pages 175-90 in *The Kingdom of God in Twentieth Century Interpretation*. Ed. W. Willis. Peabody, Mass.: Hendrickson.

———. 1991. *The Romans Debate*. Rev. ed. Peabody, Mass.: Hendrickson.

Dunn, James D. G. 2002a. *Romans 1-8*. Vol. 38A. Word Biblical Commentary. Dallas: Word.

———. 2002b. *Romans 9-16*. Vol. 38B. Word Biblical Commentary. Dallas: Word.

Erdman, Charles R. 1925. *The Epistle of Paul to the Romans*. Philadelphia: Westminster.

Fitzmyer, Joseph. 1993. *Romans. A New Translation with Introduction and Commentary*. Vol. 33 of the Anchor Bible. Ed. William Foxwell Albright and David Noel Freedman. New York: Doubleday.

Gamble, Harry, Jr. 1979. *The Textual History of the Letter to the Romans: A Study in Textual and Literary Criticism*. Grand Rapids: Eerdmans.

Garlington, Don B. 1990. *"The Obedience of Faith": A Pauline Phrase in Historical Context*.

Wissenschaftliche Untersuchungen zum Neuen Testament 38. Tübingen: Mohr Siebeck.

Gaventa, Beverly Roberts. 2004. "The Cosmic Power of Sin in Paul's Letter to the Romans: Toward a Widescreen Edition." *Interpretation* 58, 3:229-40.

Godet, F. 1883. *St. Paul's Epistle to the Romans.* Trans. A. Cusin. New York: Funk and Wagnalls.

Goppelt, Leonard. 1964. *Jesus, Paul and Judaism.* Trans. Edward Schroeder. New York: Nelson.

Greathouse, William M. 1968. "Romans." Pages 18-292 in vol. 8 of *Beacon Bible Commentary.* Kansas City: Beacon Hill Press of Kansas City.

———. 1975. *Romans.* Vol. 6 of Beacon Bible Expositions. Kansas City: Beacon Hill Press of Kansas City.

———. 1998. *Wholeness in Christ: Toward a Biblical Theology of Holiness.* Kansas City: Beacon Hill Press of Kansas City.

———. n.d. *Romans.* Vol. 6 of Search the Scriptures. Kansas City: Nazarene Publishing House.

Greathouse, William, and H. Ray Dunning. 1989. *An Introduction to Wesleyan Theology.* Rev. ed. Kansas City: Beacon Hill Press of Kansas City.

Grieb, A. Katherine. 2002. *The Story of Romans: A Narrative Defense of God's Righteousness.* Louisville, Ky.: Westminster/John Knox.

Hardy, Edward Rochie. 1954. *Christology of the Later Fathers.* Vol. 3 of *The Library of Christian Classics.* Ed. Cyril C. Richardson. Philadelphia: Westminster.

Hays, Richard B. 1983. *The Faith of Jesus Christ.* Society of Biblical Literature Dissertation Series, 56. Chico, Calif.: Scholars Press.

———. 1993. *Echoes of Scripture in the Letters of Paul.* New Haven, Conn.: Yale University Press.

———. 1996. *The Moral Vision of the New Testament: Community, Cross, New Creation, A Contemporary Introduction to New Testament Ethics.* San Francisco: HarperSanFrancisco.

Heitzenrater, Richard. 1995. *Wesley and the People Called Methodists.* Nashville: Abingdon.

Hill, Craig. 2003. *In God's Time: The Bible and the Future.* Grand Rapids: Eerdmans.

Hodge, Charles. 1950. *Commentary on the Epistle to the Romans.* Grand Rapids: Eerdmans.

Jewett, Robert. 1971. *Paul's Anthropological Terms: A Study of Their Use in Conflict Settings.* Vol. 10 of Arbeiten zur Geschichte des antiken Judentums und des Urchristentums. Leiden: Brill.

———. 2007. *Romans: A Commentary.* Hermeneia. Minneapolis: Fortress.

Jones, E. Stanley. 1942. *Abundant Living.* New York: Abingdon-Cokesbury.

Kallas, James. 1964. "Romans XIII.1-7: An Interpolation." *New Testament Studies* 11/4:365-74.

Kallistos, Bishop. 1976. *The Deification of Man.* Minneapolis: Light and Life.

Karkkainen, Veli-Matti. 2004. *One with God: Salvation as Deification and Justification.* Unitas. Collegeville, Minn.: Liturgical Press.

Käsemann, Ernst. 1969a. "On the Subject of Primitive Christian Apocalyptic." Pages 108-37 in *New Testament Questions of Today.* Trans. W. J. Montague. Philadelphia: Fortress.

———. 1969b. "'The Righteousness of God' in Paul." Pages 168-82 in *New Testament Questions of Today.* Trans. W. J. Montague. Philadelphia: Fortress.

———. 1980. *Commentary on Romans.* Trans. and ed. Geoffrey W. Bromiley. Grand Rapids: Eerdmans.

Keck, Leander E. 1995. "What Makes Romans Tick?" Pages 3-29 in *Pauline Theology.* Vol. 3: Romans. Ed. David M. Hay and E. Elizabeth Johnson. Society of Biblical Literature Symposium Series, 23. Minneapolis: Fortress.

———. 2005. *Romans.* Abingdon New Testament Commentaries. Ed. Victor Paul Furnish. Nashville: Abingdon.

Kirk, K. E. 1937. *The Epistle to the Romans in the Revised Version with Introduction and Commentary.* Clarendon Bible. Oxford: Clarendon.

Knox, John. 1951. "The Epistle to the Romans" (Exegesis). Pages 353-668 in vol. 9 of *The Interpreter's Bible.* Ed. George A. Buttrick and others. New York: Abingdon-Cokesbury.

Koperski, Veronica. 2001. *What Are They Saying About Paul and the Law?* Mahwah, N.J.: Paulist Press.

Kuhn, Karl Georg. 1964. *"Israël, Ioudaios, Hebraios* in Jewish Literature after the OT." Pages 359-68 in vol. 3 of *The Theological Dictionary of New Testament Theology.* Ed. Gerhard

Kittel and Gerhard Friedrich. Trans. Geoffrey W. Bromiley. Grand Rapids: Eerdmans. 1964-76.

Leenhardt, Franz J. 1957. *The Epistle to the Romans.* Cleveland and New York: World Publishing.

Leith, John H. 1973. *Creeds of the Churches: A Reader in Christian Doctrine from the Bible to the Present.* Rev. ed. Richmond, Va.: John Knox.

Liddell, Henry George, Robert Scott, Henry Stuart Jones, and Roderick McKenzie. 1996. *A Greek-English Lexicon.* Rev. and aug. throughout. New York: Oxford University Press.

Lightfoot, J. B. 1913. *St. Paul's Epistle to the Philippians.* London: Macmillan.

Lincoln, Andrew T. 2002. *Ephesians.* Vol. 42 in Word Biblical Commentary. Dallas: Word.

Long, Thomas T. 2004. "Preaching Romans Today." *Interpretation* 58, 3:265-75.

Lossky, V. 1973. *The Vision of God.* Crestwood, N.Y.: St. Vladimir's Seminary Press.

Luther, Martin. 1961. *Lectures on Romans.* Trans. and ed. Wilhelm Pauck. Vol. 14 of The Library of Christian Classics. Philadelphia: Westminster.

Luthi, Walter. 1961. *The Letter to the Romans.* Richmond, Va.: John Knox.

Lyons, George. 1985. *Pauline Autobiography: Toward a New Understanding.* Society of Biblical Literature Dissertation Series, 73. Atlanta: Scholars Press.

Malina, Bruce J., and John J. Pilch. 2006. *Social Science Commentary on the Letters of Paul.* Minneapolis: Fortress.

McCant, Jerry. 1981. "The Wesleyan Interpretation of Romans 5—8." *Wesleyan Theological Journal* 16, 1:68-84.

McComiskey, Thomas E. 1980. "*(qadash)* be hallowed, holy, sanctified; to consecrate, sanctify, prepare, dedicate" in vol. 2 of *Theological Wordbook of the Old Testament.* Ed. R. Laird Harris, Gleason L. Archer Jr., and Bruce K. Waltke. Chicago: Moody.

McCormick, K. Steve. 1991. "Theosis in Chrysostom and Wesley: An Eastern Paradigm on Faith and Love." *Wesleyan Theological Journal* 14, 1:38-103.

McGonigle, Herbert Boyd. 2001. *Sufficient Saving Grace: John Wesley's Evangelical Arminianism.* Carlisle, U.K.: Paternoster.

McGrath, Alister E. 2003. *A Brief History of Heaven.* Blackwell Brief Histories of Religion. London: Blackwell.

Metzger, Bruce Manning, and United Bible Societies. 1994. *A Textual Commentary on the Greek New Testament, Second Edition: A Companion Volume to the United Bible Societies' Greek New Testament.* 4th rev. ed. New York: United Bible Societies.

Meyer, Heinrich August Wilhelm. 1889. *Critical and Exegetical Hand-Book to the Epistle to the Romans.* Trans. John C. Moore and others. New York: Funk and Wagnalls.

Mitton, C. Leslie. 1953-54. "Romans—vii. Reconsidered," *The Expository Times.* 65:78-81, 99-103, 132-35.

Moo, Douglas J. 1996. *The Epistle to the Romans.* Grand Rapids: Eerdmans.

Morris, Leon. 1988. *The Epistle to the Romans.* Pillar New Testament Commentary. Grand Rapids: Eerdmans.

Moule, H. C. G. n.d. *Ephesian Studies.* London: Pickering and Inglis.

Moulton, James Hope. 1978. *Prolegomena.* Vol. 1 of *A Grammar of New Testament Greek.* 3rd ed. Edinburgh: T&T Clark.

Munck, Johannes. 1967. *Christ and Israel. An Interpretation of Romans 9—11.* Trans. Ingeborg Nixon. Philadelphia: Fortress Press.

Murray, John. 1959. *The Epistle to the Romans.* Vol. 1. Grand Rapids: Eerdmans.

Nanos, Mark D. 1996. *The Mystery of Romans: The Jewish Context of Paul's Letter.* Minneapolis: Fortress.

Noble, T. A. 1999. *The Foundation of Christian Holiness.*Unpublished. Private circulation.

Nygren, Anders. 1949. *Commentary on Romans.* Trans. Carl C. Rasmussen. Philadelphia: Fortress.

O'Keefe, John J., and R. R. Reno. 2005. *Sanctified Vision: An Introduction to Early Christian Interpretation of the Bible.* Baltimore: Johns Hopkins University Press.

O'Neill, J. C. 1975. *Paul's Letter to the Romans.* London: Pelican.

Oord, Thomas J., and Michael Lodahl. 2005. *Relational Holiness: Responding to God's Call.* Kansas City: Beacon Hill Press of Kansas City.

Pelikan, Jaroslav. 1971. *The Emergence of the Catholic Tradition.* The Christian Tradition, vol. 1. Chicago: University of Chicago Press.

———. 1974. *The Spirit of Eastern Orthodoxy.* The Christian Tradition, vol. 2. Chicago: University of Chicago Press.

Peters, John L. 1956. *Christian Perfection in American Methodism.* Nashville: Abingdon-Cokesbury.

Polkinghorne, John, and Michael Welker, eds. 2000. *The End of the World and the Ends of God: Science and Theology on Eschatology.* Harrisburg, Pa.: Trinity Press International.

Purkiser, W. T. 1983. *The Biblical Foundations.* Vol. 1 of *Exploring Christian Holiness.* Kansas City: Beacon Hill Press of Kansas City.

Purkiser, W. T., Richard S. Taylor, and Willard H. Taylor. 1977. *God, Man, and Salvation: A Biblical Theology.* Kansas City: Beacon Hill Press of Kansas City.

Quimby, Chester Warren. 1950. *The Great Redemption.* New York: Macmillan.

Rack, Henry D. 2006. "Some Recent Trends in Wesley Scholarship." *Wesleyan Theological Journal* 41, 2:182-99.

Räisänen, Heikki. 1986. *Paul and the Law.* Philadelphia: Fortress.

Reed, Millard C. 2005. *From a Pastor's Heart.* Nashville: Trevecca Nazarene University Press.

Reumann, John. 1966. "The Gospel of the Righteousness of God." *Interpretation* 20, 4:432-52.

Ridderbos, Herman. 1975. *Paul: An Outline of His Theology.* Trans. John Richard DeWitt. Grand Rapids: Eerdmans.

Robinson, J. A. T. 1952. *The Body.* London: SCM Press.

Royo, Antonio, and Jordan Aumann. 1962. *The Theology of Christian Perfection.* Dubuque, Iowa: Priory Press.

Russell, Jeffrey Burton. 1998. *A History of Heaven.* New ed. Princeton, N.J.: Princeton University Press.

Sanday, W., and A. C. Headlam. 1929. *A Critical and Exegetical Commentary on the Epistle to the Romans.* The International Critical Commentary. New York: Charles Scribner's Sons.

Sanders, E. P. 1977. *Paul and Palestinian Judaism: A Comparison of Patterns of Religion.* Minneapolis: Augsburg/Fortress.

———. 1985. *Jesus and Judaism.* Philadelphia: Fortress.

Sangster, W. E. 1954. *The Pure in Heart.* New York: Abingdon.

Schleiermacher, Friedrich D. 1956. *The Christian Faith.* Trans. and ed. H. R. Mackintosh and J. S. Stewart. Edinburgh: T&T Clark.

Schnackenburg, Rudolf. 1965. *The Church in the New Testament.* Trans. W. J. O'Hara. New York: Herder and Herder.

Schreiner, Thomas R. 1998. *The Law and Its Fulfillment: A Pauline Theology of Law.* Grand Rapids: Baker Academic.

Schrenk, Gottlob. 1964. *"patēr, ktl."* Pages 945-1022. TDNT. Pages 359-68 in vol. 5 in *The Theological Dictionary of New Testament Theology.* Ed. Gerhard Kittel and Gerhard Friedrich. Trans. Geoffrey W. Bromiley. Grand Rapids: Eerdmans. 1964-76.

Scobie, Charles H. H. 2003. *The Ways of Our God: An Approach to Biblical Theology.* Grand Rapids: Eerdmans.

Scott, E. F. 1947. *Paul's Epistle to the Romans.* London: SCM Press.

Seesemann, Heinrich. 1964. *"pateō, ktl."* Pages 940-45 in vol. 5 in *The Theological Dictionary of New Testament Theology.* Ed. Gerhard Kittel and Gerhard Friedrich. Trans. Geoffrey W. Bromiley. Grand Rapids: Eerdmans. 1964-76.

Spross, Daniel B. 1985. "The Doctrine of Sanctification in Karl Barth." *Wesleyan Theological Journal* 20, 2:54-76.

Stählin, Gustav. 1968. *"prokopē, prokoptō."* Pages 703-19 in vol. 6 in *The Theological Dictionary of New Testament Theology.* Ed. Gerhard Kittel and Gerhard Friedrich. Trans. Geoffrey W. Bromiley. Grand Rapids: Eerdmans. 1964-76.

Stein, Robert H. 1989. "The Argument of Romans 13:1-7." NTOA 31/4:325-43.

Stendahl, Krister. 1963. "The Apostle Paul and the Introspective Conscience of the West." *Harvard Theological Review* 56, 3 (July 1963): 199-215. Republished in 1976 in *Paul Among Jews and Gentiles.* Philadelphia: Fortress.

Stirewalt, M. Luther. 1991. "The Form and Function of the Greek Letter-Essay." Pages 147-74 in *The Romans Debate.* Rev. and expanded ed. Ed. Karl P. Donfried. Peabody, Mass.: Hendrickson.

Stowers, Stanley K. 1981. *The Diatribe and Paul's Letter to the Romans.* Society of Biblical Literature Dissertation Series, 57. Chico, Calif.: Scholars Press.

Stuhlmacher, Peter. 1994. *Paul's Letter to the Romans: A Commentary*. Trans. Scott J. Haffeman. Louisville, Ky.: Westminster/John Knox.

Stuhlmacher, Peter, and Donald A. Hagner. 2002. *Revisiting Paul's Doctrine of Justification: A Challenge to the New Perspective*. Downers Grove, Ill.: InterVarsity.

Tannehill, Robert C. 1967. *Dying and Rising with Christ: A Study in Pauline Theology*. Beihefte zur Zeitschrift für die neutestamentliche Wissenschaft 32. Berlin: Töpelmann.

Thielman, Frank. 1994. *Paul and the Law: A Contextual Approach*. Downers Grove, Ill.: InterVarsity.

Thomas, W. Griffith. 1947. *St. Paul's Epistle to the Romans*. Grand Rapids: Eerdmans.

Tyerman, L. 1882. *Wesley's Designated Successor*. London: Hodder and Stoughton.

Watson, Francis. 1991. "The Two Roman Congregations: Romans 14:1—15:13." Pages 203-15 in *The Romans Debate*. Rev. and expanded ed. Ed. Karl P. Donfried. Peabody, Mass.: Hendrickson.

Welch, Reuben R. 1988. *Our Freedom in Christ*. A Bible Study in Romans. Grand Rapids: Francis Asbury Press of Zondervan.

Wesley, John. 1931. *The Letters of the Rev. John Wesley, A.M.* 8 vols. Ed. John Telford. London: Epworth.

———. 1950. *Explanatory Notes upon the New Testament*. Reprint. London: Epworth.

———. 1979. *The Works of John Wesley*. 3rd ed. 10 vols. Ed. Thomas Jackson. Repr. Grand Rapids: Baker, 1872.

Wesley, John, and Charles Wesley. 1870. *The Poetical Works*. Ed. G. Osborn. London: Wesleyan-Methodist Conference Office.

Westerholm, Stephen. 2003. *Perspectives Old and New on Paul: The "Lutheran" Paul and His Critics*. Grand Rapids: Eerdmans.

———. 2004. "The Righteousness of the Law and the Righteousness of Faith in Romans." *Interpretation* 58, 3:253-64.

Wiles, Gordon P. 1974. *Paul's Intercessory Prayers: The Significance of the Intercessory Prayer Passages in the Letters of St. Paul*. Studiorum Novi Testamenti Societas Monograph Series, 24. Cambridge: Cambridge University Press.

Wiley, H. Orton. 1959. *The Epistle to the Hebrews*. Kansas City: Beacon Hill.

Williams, Colin. 1960. *John Wesley's Theology Today*. Nashville: Abingdon.

Winger, M. 1999. "From Grace to Sin: Names and Abstractions in Paul's Letters." *Novum Testamentum* 41, 2:145-75.

Wink, Walter. 1983. *Naming the Powers: The Language of Power in the New Testament*. Minneapolis: Augsburg/Fortress.

———. 1986. *Unmasking the Powers: The Invisible Forces That Determine Human Existence*. Minneapolis: Augsburg/Fortress.

———. 1992. *Engaging the Powers: Discernment and Resistance in a World of Domination*. Minneapolis: Augsburg/Fortress.

Wood, A. Skevington. 1963. *Life by the Spirit*. Grand Rapids: Eerdmans.

Wood, Lawrence W. 1996. "Third Wave of the Spirit in the Pentecostalization of American Christianity: A Wesleyan Critique." *Wesleyan Theological Journal* 31, 1:110-40.

Wright, J. Edward. 2003. *Early History of Heaven*. Oxford: Oxford University Press.

Wright, N. T. 1991. *The Climax of the Covenant: Christ and the Law in Pauline Theology*. Minneapolis: Fortress.

———. 1995. "Romans in the Theology of Paul." Pages 30-67 in *Pauline Theology*. Vol. 3: Romans. Ed. David M. Hay and E. Elizabeth Johnson. Society of Biblical Literature Symposium Series, 23. Minneapolis: Fortress.

———. 1999. *The Challenge of Jesus*. Downers Grove, Ill.: InterVarsity.

———. 2002. "The Letter to the Romans: Introduction, Commentary, and Reflections." Pages 393-770 in vol. 10 in *The New Interpreter's Bible*. Ed. Leander E. Keck. Nashville: Abingdon.

———. 2006. *Paul in Fresh Perspective*. Minneapolis: Fortress.

Wuest, Kenneth S. 1945. *Romans in the Greek New Testament*. Grand Rapids: Eerdmans.

Yoder, John Howard. 1972. *The Politics of Jesus*. Grand Rapids: Eerdmans.

Yoder, Perry B. 1987. *Shalom, the Bible's Word for Salvation, Justice, and Peace*. Newton, Kans.: Faith and Life.

Young, Richard A. 1994. *Intermediate New Testament Greek: A Linguistic and Exegetical Approach*. Nashville: Broadman and Holman.

INTRODUCTION

A. The Importance of Romans

Of Romans, Martin Luther wrote:

> This letter is the principal part of the New Testament and the purest gospel, which surely deserves the honor that a Christian man should not merely know it by heart word for word, but that he should be occupied with it daily as the daily bread of his soul. For it can never be read too often or too well. And the more it is used the more delicious it becomes and the better it tastes. (Quoted in Brunner 1959, 9)

Scholars have disputed the claim that Romans is "the principal part of the New Testament." There are strong reasons for maintaining that the Gospels hold this distinction since they constitute the primary historical witness to Christ, but we must agree with the judgment that "what the gospel is, what the content of the Christian faith is, one learns to know in the Epistle to the Romans as in no other place in the New Testament" (Nygren 1949, 3).

Throughout the centuries this Epistle has in a peculiar way been able to furnish an impulse for spiritual renewal. When the church had drifted away from the gospel, a deep study of Romans has repeatedly been the means by which the loss has been recovered. Who can estimate the far-reaching effects upon the church and the world of the conversion of Augustine through the prayers of his godly mother Monica, Bishop Ambrose of Milan, and his reading of Rom 13:11-14 (see From the Text on this passage).

In November 1515, Martin Luther, Augustinian monk and doctor of sacred theology at the University of Wittenberg, began his expositions of Romans. As he prepared his lectures he came to see more clearly the meaning of Paul's gospel of justification by faith. The phrase the "righteousness of God" he had once hated as demanding what he could not deliver. Now in his study he came to see righteousness as a gift of God by which a person came to live, by faith. And he felt himself reborn. The consequence of this new insight the world knows. The Protestant Reformation had been born.

Under the date of May 24, 1738, John Wesley noted in his *Journal:*

In the evening I went very unwillingly to a society in Aldersgate Street, where one was reading Luther's preface to the Epistle to the Romans. About a quarter before nine, while he was describing the change which God works in the heart through faith in Christ, I felt my heart strangely warmed. I felt I did trust in Christ, Christ alone, for salvation: And an assurance was given me, that he had taken away *my* sins, even *mine*, and saved *me* from the law of sin and death. (1979, 1:103)

In that moment the Evangelical Revival of the eighteenth century was born.

In August 1918, Karl Barth, pastor of Safenwil in Canton Aargau, Switzerland, published an exposition of the Epistle to the Romans. "The reader," he said in the preface,

will detect for himself that it has been written with a joyful sense of discovery. The mighty voice of Paul was new to me: and if to me, no doubt to many others also. And yet, now that my work is finished, I perceive that much remains which I have not yet heard. (1933, 2)

But what Barth heard he wrote down—and that first edition of his *Romerbrief* fell "like a bombshell on the theologians' playground" (Catholic theologian Karl Adam, in *Das Hochland*, June 1926, as quoted in J. McConnachie. 1926-27. "The Teaching of Karl Barth," *Hibbert Journal* 25:385). That bombshell exploded the liberal humanistic theology that prevailed in the early twentieth century and gave birth to the Evangelical movement that has subsequently revolutionized Protestantism (Collins 2005).

What happened to Augustine, Luther, Wesley, and Barth has turned the tide of Western civilization and culture. On a smaller scale similar things happen to us as we let the words of this Epistle come alive to our minds and hearts in the power of the Holy Spirit.

B. The Place and Date of Writing

In none of Paul's letters are the place and time of writing so clearly indicated in the letter itself as in the case of Romans. In 15:19-32 the apostle makes it clear that he is nearing the culmination of his ministry in the East. He had preached the gospel "from Jerusalem all the way around to Illyricum" (v 19). Curiously, Acts does not mention Paul's mission in Illyricum—including all or parts of today's Albania, Bosnia and Herzegovina, Croatia, Kosovo, Macedonia, Serbia and Montenegro, and Slovenia. It, like Spain, today's Spain and Portugal, was Latin-speaking territory in Paul's day (but see Jewett 2007, 75-77).

Paul felt that he had completed his mission in the East. As he wrote, he was making plans to go West—to barbarian Spain, and, since Rome was already evangelized, to visit the Roman church on the way. But first, he had to perform a special task in behalf of Jerusalem. For some time he has been engaged in gathering a collection among the churches of Macedonia and Greece "for the poor among the saints" (v 26) there. That offering now virtually complete, Paul awaited only the opportunity to deliver it.

Paul planned to end his work on the collection in Corinth and to depart from there for Jerusalem (1 Cor 16:3-4). While he wrote 2 Corinthians (see 2 Cor 9:3-5), Paul was carrying out that plan and was on his way to Corinth.

That the letter was delivered by the deacon Phoebe from Cenchrea, the eastern port of Corinth (Rom 16:1), adds plausibility to the supposition that he wrote Romans from Corinth. This was the apostle's final visit to Corinth, since soon after this in Jerusalem his long imprisonment began (Acts 20:2-3). The dating of this final visit to Corinth depends on which overall chronology of Paul's ministry one adopts. The earliest date suggested is January—March, A.D. 53, and the latest, January—March, A.D. 59, in either case barely a quarter century after the death and resurrection of Jesus (see Jewett 2007, 18-21).

C. The Occasion and Purpose for Romans

For a long time Paul had planned to visit the Roman church (Rom 1:8-15; 15:22). With this prospect in sight, Paul hopes to realize his plan as soon as he has delivered the collection to the mother church in Jerusalem. "So after I have completed this task and have made sure that they have received this fruit, I will go to Spain and visit you on the way" (15:28). This statement eloquently demonstrates that he conceived his work to be as an evangelist, not as a pastor. His calling was to plant, not to water. His mission was not to build on another's foundation but to lay his own (15:18-21). He hoped that the collection—so important that Paul intended to deliver it even in the face of threatened death (Acts 21:10-14)—would heal the breach between his Gentile converts and the Jewish believers in Jerusalem. With the presentation of this gift the work he began from Antioch (Acts 13:1-4) would be culminated and he would be free to move westward with his gospel.

The so-called *Romans Debate* (Donfried 1991, first edition published in 1977) is particularly concerned with answering the question: Why did Paul write this kind of letter to the Romans? Scholarly answers are inevitably circular, often telling more about their theology than their competence as historians. Beyond scholarly reconstructions of the alleged opponents and accusations Paul hoped to refute (Acts 28:21-22 denies that false rumors about Paul had reached Rome that he had to clarify), what Paul explicitly claims is that he hoped to recruit the assistance of the Roman church for his plan for evangelizing Spain (Rom 15:22-33). He prayed that the Romans would give him a warm welcome when he arrived and be in a mood to help him with his work in the western part of the empire.

Robert Jewett's recent commentary identifies Romans as "a unique fusion of the 'ambassadorial letter' with several of the other subtypes in the genre: the parenetic letter, the hortatory letter, and the philosophical diatribe" (2007, 44). Paul writes as a spokesman for the foreign policy of God. He writes to persuade the Roman Christian community to join him in a cooperative mission to evangelize Spain (for "The Cultural Situation in Spain," see Jewett 2007, 74-79). His theological arguments identify the message they would proclaim as the "power of God." His "ethical admonitions show how the gospel is to be lived out in a manner that would ensure the success of this mission" (Jewett 2007, 44; see 42-46).

> If the Roman house and tenement churches can overcome their conflicts and accept one another as honorable servants of the same master (14:4), they would be able to participate in a credible manner in the mission to extend the gospel to the end of the known world. (Jewett 2007, 88; see 79-90)

D. Christianity in Rome

We have no direct information about the origin of Christianity in Rome (see Jewett 2007, 59-74). Its beginnings are shrouded in obscurity. The tradition that Peter was its founder has no historical support. He was still in Jerusalem as late as A.D. 39 (see Gal 1:18), but there are no references in Acts or any of Paul's letters to Peter's presence in Rome. It is generally agreed, however, that Peter did eventually go to Rome and that he was martyred there (see Cullmann 1953).

Acts 2:10-11 refers to "visitors from Rome (both Jews and converts to Judaism)" present for the first Christian Pentecost. It is possible that these converts took the new faith back to the Eternal City. We know that travel was widespread at this time and that there was a steady migration to the capital from all over the empire. Romans 16 bears testimony to the fact that many of the Christians in the Roman congregations had come to the capital from other areas.

The fourth-century writer Ambrosiaster gives what is the most probable account of Christian beginnings in Rome.

> It is established that there were Jews living in Rome in the times of the apostles, and that those Jews who had believed passed on to the Romans the tradition that they ought to profess Christ and keep the law. . . . One ought not condemn the Romans, but to praise their faith; because without seeing any signs or miracles and without seeing any of the apostles, they nevertheless accepted faith in Christ, although according to a Jewish rite. (Knox 1951, 9:362)

This account accords well with a note in Suetonius' *Life of Claudius*, to the effect that Claudius "expelled Jews from Rome because they kept rioting at the instigation of Chrestus" (Knox 1951, 9:362). NT scholars widely assume that Suetonius confused the common Greek slave-name *Chrestus* with *Christos* (Fitzmyer 1993, 31). The riot Suetonius mentioned probably referred to trouble that arose in the synagogues of Rome when Christianity was introduced. In any event, Christian Jews as well as Jewish unbelievers would have been banished by Claudius's edict in A.D. 49. Acts 18:2 refers to that edict as the reason for the presence in Corinth of Priscilla and Aquila.

Therefore, by A.D. 49 Christianity had been introduced to the Jewish community of Rome. But by the time Paul wrote Romans the church was predominantly Gentile (Rom 1:4-6, 13; 11:13-24; 15:15-16). In the Jewish synagogues of Rome, there would have been, in addition to believing Jews, many "God-fearers," Gentile half-converts who had been attracted to the monotheism and ethical teachings of Judaism. This mixture of Jews and God-fearers (and perhaps some Gentile proselytes) would have made up the majority of Christians until Claudius's banishment of "Jews" in A.D. 49.

These Jewish Christians, on their return to Rome, apparently found a Christian situation quite different from the one they left. They were now in the minority in the church that they had shaped earlier (Fitzmyer 1993, 31). Both the returning Jewish Christians and the Gentile Christian majority found themselves under a prohibition against all quasi-political agitation (Stuhlmacher 1994, 7).

We should not be surprised that the central issue of Romans is the relationship of the Christian gospel to the Mosaic law. In its original setting, this letter to the Romans was Paul's attempt to address the problem created by the events sketched above and the resulting divisions between Jewish and Gentile Christians that threatened Roman Christianity ca. A.D. 57.

In getting at the historical "reasons" for Romans, these issues are important. From the wider canonical perspective, however, Romans stands as an ecumenical theology designed to show and insure the *true meaning* of the Torah in light of God's final word in Christ, and to liberate the message of Christ from its Jewish trappings in order "to win obedience from the Gentiles" (15:18 RSV; see also v 19; 1:1-6; 16:26). Romans does not simply address the Jewish problem—it addresses the *human* problem.

E. The Unifying Theology of Romans

Romans 1—8 constitute the heart of the letter. Leander E. Keck provides an intriguing analysis of these chapters as they address the human problem:

> Paul states the gospel in such a way that its scope reaches from Eden to the eschaton, from the "fall" to the redemption of the world. . . . The gospel is God's saving power for every being, albeit for the Jew first. There is one gospel and only one, for all. . . . But if the gospel is God's saving power for *all* who believe, the one gospel must bring one solution for the one condition in which all find themselves. However important are the election of Israel, the promise to Abraham, the gift of the Law, the Davidic ancestry of God's Son, in no way do these exempt "the Jews" from solidarity with the Gentiles in the human condition. It is the *human* problem that the gospel addresses.

> In developing the foregoing theme, Paul inevitably "goes back to Adam" and "unpacks the Adamic situation three times," with an argument that moves "in a spiral fashion, each time going deeper into the human condition, each time finding the gospel the appropriate antidote." (Keck 1995, 3:24-26)

Paul's exposition of the human situation (1:18—4:25) indicts both Gentiles and Jews as guilty before God and under the power of sin (3:9). This indictment reaches its climax in 3:19-20. The indictment is followed by the good news of God's righteousness now manifest in Christ Jesus, which provides justification by faith (3:21-26). Keck prefers to call it rectification by faith. On the basis of *the faithfulness of Christ* (*pisteos Christou*, 3:22) as God's atoning sacrifice, a rectified relationship to God is now open to all people (3:30). Those who respond in faithfulness to God's free offer of participation in the saving benefits of what Christ has done not only enter into a right relationship with God but also are empowered to live in the way God considers right.

In 5:12-21, the human condition calls for more than a rectified relationship to God; humanity needs liberation from the sin that rules our Adamic condition. For Paul there are two, and only two, alternate realms: that of Adam (the rule of sin and death) and that of Christ (the rule of grace and eternal life through justification). As Paul develops this theme in 6:1—7:6, he argues that freedom from sin and death is possible only through *participation* in Christ's death and resurrection, which promises "newness of life" (6:4 KJV), that is, the "new life of the Spirit" (7:6 RSV).

In 7:7—8:17 we are taken deeper into the human situation. As fallen in Adam (7:7-25), Jew and Gentile alike discover that an alien power has so usurped control of their existence and enslaved them that they achieve the exact opposite of what they intend. This alien resident is the "sin that dwells in me" (7:17, 20 NKJV), against which the Law is powerless. But what the Law could not do, God has done through Christ—he has won a decisive victory over sin that sets "free from the law of sin and death" all those who "do not live according to the sinful nature but according to the Spirit" (8:2, 4) whom they have received through Christ (8:1-17).

To identify the unifying theology of Romans is more difficult than casual readers might suspect. Romans is, after all, a sent letter, not a systematic theology. Certainly, Paul writes with deep theological convictions, but he does not write here or elsewhere anything that might pass for a theological treatise. Even his theological convictions emerge indirectly, not as theoretical abstractions. His is pastoral and practical theology. Any truly biblical theology must be as timely and relevant as the biblical books it attempts to represent. And, thus, it must be redone in every generation. Romans comes closest to being "theology" of any book in the Bible. But it does not seem to be either the product or the presentation of a coherent theological system. It grew out of everyday life issues and is concerned with Christian living.

The discipline of "biblical theology" attempts to discern the theological convictions underlying, unifying, and arising from the anthology of books we call the Bible. It takes for granted that the community of faith that brought these diverse books together into the canon of Scripture found within them a coherent unity. Biblical theologians seek to discover and demonstrate the internal theo-logic that unifies the Bible's witness to the triune God—creator of the universe, redeemer of Israel, king of the mundane, incarnate Word, powerfully weak, mother and lord of the church, and grand designer of history's consummation (to be overly brief and deliberately provocative).

So what is the unique contribution to biblical theology of Paul's letter to the Romans? Romans does not stand as a monument to the genius of the Apostle Paul alone. As the heir of the OT traditions of Israel, Paul's thought was significantly shaped by first-century Pharisaism, apocalyptic Judaism, the cultural assumptions of the Mediterranean world of the Hellenistic age, the church's lived experience of the Christ event, and the universal gift of the Holy Spirit.

In turn, Romans has significantly influenced the Protestant tradition, which returned the complement and read Romans in ways that reflected its own emerging sense of identity. Careful research into Romans may help us distinguish which of our cherished theological convictions may actually be traced back to Romans and which arise from other sources.

The key concept of Romans is *the righteousness of God*—God's righteousness manifest in the death of Messiah Jesus, whom he put forward as an atoning sacrifice, to be received by faith—the eschatological (end time) salvation that irrupted into history with the death and resurrection of Jesus and the gift of the Spirit. This divine activity created a new humanity in the likeness of Jesus, which is destined to include chosen Israel. In the end, God's righteousness promises the renewal of creation itself.

The righteousness of God is his *saving activity* in Christ: "God was reconciling the world to himself in Christ" (2 Cor 5:19). In Christ we have a glimpse of God as Sovereign Love, who gives his creatures the freedom to receive or spurn his proffered love. As Creator of heaven and earth, he yearns to be worshipped by grateful creatures (Rom 1:18-21a).

In his foreknowledge he has in love predestined all humans—both Gentiles and Jews (1:21b—2:29)—"to be conformed to the image of his Son, in order that he might be the firstborn within a large family" (8:29 NRSV). Such is the gospel in a nutshell: the Creator's self-unveiling in his Son Jesus the Messiah.

This story Paul weaves in with that of the people Israel whom God had chosen as a witness to him as saving Lord of all nations. To this end God called Abraham, giving him the promise of Gen 12:1-3. Israel, however, inadequately understood and seldom faithfully pursued their mission, choosing to bask in their election (see Isa 40—53).

At a critical moment of salvation history Jesus was born, suffered, died, and arose—as the promised Servant of the Lord (see Gal 4:1-7; Isa 52:13—53:12). In retrospect the birth of the nation Israel was the birth of the church, destined to fulfill God's call to Abraham, to declare to the world the gospel as the "the power of God for the salvation of everyone who believes" (Rom 1:16).

The gospel proclamation created a "new Israel" primarily of Gentiles, with only a remnant of believing Jews, but with a hope firmly in view that finally "all Israel will be saved." This is the gospel Paul declares in Romans, but which we "see in a mirror, dimly" (1 Cor 13:12 NRSV). But what we see is true and trustworthy: that which God has made visible to human eyes in Christ.

This, however, is not the final story. In the end, Messiah Jesus will return, not only to save all Israel, but also to redeem the created order! This indeed is a mystery. "However, as it is written: 'No eye has seen, no ear has heard, no mind has conceived what God has prepared for those who love him'—but God has revealed it to us by the Spirit. The Spirit searches all things, even the deep things of God" (1 Cor 2:9-10).

Before going further, we must take account of another fundamental aspect of Paul's theology in Romans: the corporate nature of *"man."* The word must be italicized because "man" in Romans is the *'adam* of the OT—"humankind." Few biblical texts are more important for grasping the biblical understanding of humanity as moral beings than Gen 1:26-27:

> Then God said, "Let us make humankind in our image, according to our likeness; and let them have dominion over the fish of the sea, and over the birds of the air, and over the cattle, and over all the wild animals of the earth, and over every creeping thing that creeps upon the earth." So God created humankind in his image, in the image of God he created them; male and female he created them. (NRSV)

The Hebrew word for "humankind" is *'adam,* a generic term that embraces not only male and female but also all humanity. The transition from the generic *'adam* to the personal "Adam" does not occur until 4:25: "Adam knew his wife again, and she bore a son and named him Seth" (NRSV). In ch 5 we find the corporate significance of the term: "This is the list of the descendants of [*'adam*]. When God created humankind, he made them in the likeness of God. Male and female he created them, and he blessed them and named them 'Humankind' when they were created" (vv 1-2 NRSV).

The dual sense of Adam is preserved in Rom 5:12-21. The first Adam is the *man* of Gen 3 who disobeyed his Creator and fell; but Adam was also the corporate *'adam* of Gen 1:26-27. In the fall of the first Adam, "humankind" became depraved and sinful. The last Adam is the *man* Jesus, conceived sinless by the Holy Spirit in the Virgin's womb, who in his own person coped with the power of the flesh and sin—not by some innate conditioning as divine Son of God but as a human whose Spirit-empowered obedience to God, even to death, "condemned sin in the flesh" (Rom 8:4 NRSV). "The first man Adam became a living being," whose disobedience set the race on the course of sin and death. "The last Adam, a life-giving spirit," whose obedience potentially sanctified all humankind (1 Cor 15:45; see 2 Cor 3:18). Romans 5:12-21, thus, offers us at least a partial glimpse of Paul's doctrines of sin and salvation.

Romans defines "sin" as *hē hamartia*—"the Sin" that entered the race at the fall, a personified power that tyrannizes all unbelievers, both "outside" and "under" the Law (5:13-14; 7:7-25), until the end. Sin and Death are vanquished at the Second Advent (see 1 Cor 15:22-27). "The sting of death is sin, and the power of sin is the law. But . . . God . . . gives us the victory through our Lord Jesus Christ" (1 Cor 15:56-57).

Romans further defines "flesh" (*sarx*) and "Spirit" (*pneuma*). *Pneuma* translates the Hebrew term *ruach,* used in the OT for the "power" and "presence" of God, who enabled Israel's champions to throw off the yoke of their oppressors. In Romans *pneuma* is the personal power of the Holy Spirit, who transforms sinners into saints (see 2 Cor 3:18).

Sarx is humanity in its weakness (see Rom 8:3 NRSV; see *basar* in Isa 31:3). *Sarx* is the humanity of Jesus (Rom 1:3), in which he by the power of the Spirit "condemned sin in the flesh" (8:4 NRSV). *Sarx* is unregenerate human nature (7:18). As believers, we were formerly "in the flesh," dependent on human resources alone.

But now we are "in the Spirit," liberated from the oppressive power of sin (8:9-10). As renewed believers we serve God in the spirit (*pneumati mou*, "my spirit," 1:9 NRSV). The Spirit of God = Spirit of Christ = Spirit imparts life to believers (8:2, 4, 5, 6, 10), frees them from the law, sin, and death (8:1-17), so that they possess "the new life of the Spirit" (7:6 NRSV); supplies directive power to "the sons [and daughters] of God" (8:14); intercedes for the children of God (8:26-27), is the sanctifying agent of believers (8:1-17), witnesses to their adoption, and pledges the certainty of their future glory (8:16-17, 22-25).

Romans also defines the Law (*nomos*). While the term *nomos* identifies the first division of the Hebrew canon (3:21), in salvation history it signifies the covenant that God made with Israel at Mount Sinai (Exod 19:4-6). But *nomos* can also mean "principle" (Rom 3:27; 7:21; 8:2). As covenant, by *nomos* Romans means the Law that was fulfilled by Christ (8:1-4). In yet another sense, by *nomos* Paul means the requirements of the moral law written on the human heart (2:14-15); in this sense it is also the requirements of the Law fulfilled by the Spirit in the heart, making one a true Jew (2:25-29).

Finally, Romans firmly defines the "works of the law" that nullify salvation for unbelievers. "Works of the law" are not "good deeds done to merit God's favor" (as Luther thought), nor are they the works of *individuals* seeking to *enter into* relationship with God. Such individualism is foreign to Paul's thought. Unbelieving Jews erroneously *presume* they are the Israel of God, even as they reject Jesus as Messiah. Their sin thus is a *corporate* refusal to acknowledge Christ as the "end" (*telos*) of the Law (10:4; see 9:24—10:4, with commentary).

Most recent interpreters have adopted E. P. Sanders' explanation of "covenantal nomism" concerning the relation between works and law in the Judaism of Paul's day. According to Sanders, the "pattern" or "structure" of covenantal nomism is this:

> (1) God has chosen Israel and (2) given the law. The law implies both (3) God's promise to maintain the election and (4) the requirement to obey. (5) God rewards obedience and punishes transgression. (6) The law provides the means of atonement, and atonement results in (7) maintenance of the covenantal relationship. (8) All those who are maintained in the covenant by obedience, atonement and God's mercy belong to the group which will be saved. An important interpretation of the first and last points is that election and ultimately salvation are considered to be by God's mercy rather than human achievement. (Sanders 1977, 130)

Throughout Romans, as in all Paul's letters, salvation's frame of reference is corporate. This corporate understanding governs both Israel and the church. The *old* Israel is the Israel of the law that rejects Jesus as the Christ. Those who believe—both Jews and Greeks—are the *new* Israel of God (until *all* Israel is saved, 11:25-32). Also, employing a different metaphor, Paul writes, "We were all baptized by one Spirit into one body—whether Jews or Greeks, slave of free—and we were all given the one Spirit to drink" (1 Cor 12:13). It is within these two images that the Pauline *kerygma* functions.

F. The Rhetorical Genre and Logical Organization of Romans

The use of a thesis statement to introduce the body of Paul's letter to the Romans (1:16-17) is unique among his letters. This gives it something of the character of a treatise within a letter frame (1:1-15 and 15:14—16:27). M. Luther Stirewalt overemphasizes this, identifying Romans as a "letter-essay" (1991). The almost systematic-theological character of Romans arises from its use of the demonstrative (epideictic) genre, here in praise of the gospel. Consistent with this rhetorical goal is Paul's repeated use of the diatribe style to advance his argument. Among the prominent features of diatribe is Paul's repeated use of imaginary interlocutors to clarify and solidify his presentation of the gospel (Stowers 1981).

Paul writes this letter not primarily as a theologian but as a missionary, with ambitious plans to evangelize Spain (15:22-29) with the good news that is "the power of God for the salvation of everyone who believes" (1:16). His exposition of the gospel is not ivory-tower theory but is intended to deepen the level of his readers' existing commitment to the implications of the righteousness of God revealed in the gospel. If he is to gain the support of a divided Roman audience for his missionary venture to the western, barbarian region of the Roman Empire, he must bring them together around their common gospel.

Romans begins much as Paul's earlier letters, with a salutation identifying its sender, intended recipients, and his characteristic greeting (1:1-7). It differs from the others primarily in being far more expansive in each of these three concerns.

The thanksgiving section customary in Pauline letters appears (1:8-15), distinguished here by the unusual circumstance of Paul writing to a Christian community he had neither founded nor previously visited. As in Paul's other letters, the thanksgiving doubles as a rhetorical exordium, formally introducing the purpose (*causa*) he intends to achieve in the body of the letter (1:16—15:13).

Within the thanksgiving, Paul announces his plans to visit Rome but delays divulging the details until the conclusion (*peroration*) of the letter (in 15:14—16:23). He does not postpone his "eagerness to proclaim the gospel to . . . Rome" (1:15 NRSV) until his arrival, however. The body of the letter preaches the message he identifies indiscriminately as "the gospel" (1:15, 16, 17; 11:28; 15:20), "the gospel of God" (1:1; 15:16), "the gospel of his Son" (1:9), "the gospel of Christ" (15:19), or "my gospel" (2:16; 16:25).

31

In the letter thesis (1:16-17), Paul insists that the gospel he preaches is the message of God's righteousness (see also 3:5, 21, 22, 25), which is "the power of God for the salvation of everyone who believes: first for the Jew, then for the [Greek]" (1:16). Throughout the letter, Paul will insist upon these themes: the universal scope of the gospel, the faithfulness of God and the necessity of the human response of faith, and the distinction within salvation history of Jews and non-Jews. The gospel recounts the powerfully transforming activity of God within communities of faith.

The message of God's righteousness is universally needed because all human beings without exception are hopeless slaves of sin (1:18—3:20). This is true whether that sin takes the baser form of Gentile idolatry and depravity (1:18-32) or the more sophisticated self-righteous delusion of Jews (2:1-29). But sinful humanity first encounters God's righteousness revealed as divine wrath (1:18). God abandons his rebellious creatures to suffer the consequences of their self-destructive refusal to honor God as God (1:19-23), which only leads them deeper and deeper into the darkness of moral depravity (1:24-32).

Paul is convinced that God is not indifferent about what humans do. The wrath that for the present expresses itself as divine abandonment (1:19-23) will only be confirmed in the final judgment, based on deeds—righteous or unrighteous (2:1-16). That is, apart from the gospel.

The gospel that came first to Jews (1:16) makes them first in judgment (2:9) and reward (2:10). Jews will not be exempt from judgment simply because of their privileges as God's people (2:17-24). To be truly a Jew is not a matter of name and ethnic identity, but "a matter of the heart" (2:29 NRSV; see 2:25-29).

Paul grants that Jews enjoy considerable advantages as God's people, particularly the gift of the Law. But their unfaithfulness only increases their accountability (3:1-8). Paul demonstrates that all humanity is under the power of sin (3:9) by appealing to scripture to show that what is true of Jews is all the more true of Gentiles (3:9-20). The Law points out sin but is powerless to prevent it (3:20).

In the new age inaugurated by the coming of Jesus Christ, God has revealed his righteousness apart from Law but not inconsistent with it (3:21). In the faithfulness of Christ God has provided the means of freeing enslaved humanity from sin and its consequences, while maintaining his integrity (3:21-26). He offers his righteousness as a gift to all who are not too proud to accept it (3:27-31).

The new thing God has done in Christ, offering justification by faith, is consistent with OT teaching. Paul presents Abraham as the prototype of all who are put right with God on the basis of faith in his promise (4:1-25).

The gospel that puts believers right with God has the power to enable them to live right through the sanctifying gift of the Holy Spirit (5:1—8:39). The power of grace brings with it the possibility of peace and reconciliation with God in this age and hope for final salvation in the age to come, even in the face of present suffering (5:1-11).

Contrary to how it has classically been used, Paul does not appeal to the original sin of Adam to account for human sinfulness (in 5:12-21). Instead, he shows how the obedience of Christ, which eventuated in his saving death, offers fallen humanity a new alternative. Adam and Christ are each the head of a human family. But human destiny depends on its lord, not on heredity alone. Grace more than compensates for the damage sin has done (5:20-21).

Thus, Paul urges believers to live out of the resources of grace under the lordship of Christ (6:1-14). By offering themselves freely as instruments of righteousness, Christians may be freed from the shame of sin to enjoy the gift of sanctification and its end, eternal life (6:15-23).

The same justifying act of God that sets believers free from slavery to the power of sin and its consequences frees them to live "in the new way of the Spirit" (7:6; see 7:1-6). Human strength alone is incapable of fulfilling the demands of Law, because Law itself has been victimized by sin (7:7-25).

Only by Christ's gift of the indwelling Holy Spirit are believers set free from sin and empowered to fulfill the Law (8:1-11). That same Spirit sustains believers as they await final redemption (8:12-17). He assists them to pray as they should and works in their lives to accomplish God's saving purpose for all humanity—"to be conformed to the likeness of his Son" (8:29; see 8:18-30).

Paul concludes his exposition of the provision of the gospel of righteousness with the confident assertion that nothing in the universe "will be able to separate [believers] from the love of God that is in Christ Jesus" (8:39; see 8:18-39). But this leads the Jewish apostle to the Gentiles to address a potential objection to this confidence—the current general lost state of most of God's historical people, Israel (9:1—11:36).

Paul approaches this delicate problem from several perspectives. He insists that ethnic descent alone was never sufficient to determine the identity of God's people. God acts with sovereign mercy, apart from human claims or supposed rights (9:1-29). Israel is presently resistant to the gospel because it refused to acknowledge Christ as its Messiah, although it should have known better (9:30—10:21).

Israel's present lost state is not an indication that God is done with them (11:1-32). A remnant of believing Israel is root and trunk of the new Israel, consisting of believing Jews and Gentiles (11:1-10). Israel's unbelief has provided the unexpected opportunity for the gospel to be proclaimed to the Gentiles, whose response of faith has made them to become honorary Israelites (11:11-24). They in turn will provoke Israel to come to faith.

Paul warns his mostly Gentile audience that if pride and unbelief excluded unbelieving Israel from the people of God, honorary members should not be presumptuous (11:13-14).

Paul is confident that within God's mysterious plan to have mercy on all people (11:32), "the full number of the Gentiles" (11:25) and "all Israel" (11:26) will come to faith in Christ and final salvation (11:15-32). He concludes his exposition of the gospel as the righteousness of God in history with a doxological praise for the incomprehensible wisdom of God (11:33-36).

The final section of the body of the letter to the Romans is an exposition of God's righteousness in practice (12:1—15:13). Repeating the sacrificial imagery of 6:13 and 19, Paul urges his readers to offer themselves collectively as a living sacrifice to God (12:1). This will allow God to transform them completely—through sanctification, renewing their corporate mind "to test and approve" God's will. This is the worship God expects of his holy church (12:2).

Among the dramatic changes that will mark the practice of the Christian community, Paul mentions the mutuality of humble believers who use their gifts for the benefit of the entire community (12:3-8). Such a church will put unpretentious love into practice, both inside and outside the community (12:9-21). They will not complicate the church's ability to preach the gospel by defying the government or refusing to pay taxes (13:1-7). Instead, by loving both fellow believers and unbelievers they will fulfill what the Law demands (13:8-10).

Aware that the full day of final salvation is rapidly approaching, Paul urges his audience to reject the evil done under cover of darkness and live already as people of the day. This they can do under the lordship of Jesus Christ (13:11-14).

If Paul's mission to Spain is to be successful, he will need the assistance of a united Roman church (15:14-33). Therefore, he urges Jewish and Gentile believers to put aside the petty differences that divide them (14:1-23). They must refuse to treat one another as competitors—strong vs. weak. Rather than judging and despising one another because of such differences, they are to accept one another as God in Christ accepted them (15:1-13).

Paul does not ask the Roman churches to agree on the cultural differences that divide them. But he does expect them to agree on this: "with one heart and mouth" to "glorify the God and Father of our Lord Jesus Christ" (15:6). This means they will join a universal chorus of praise for God's faithfulness to Jews and his mercy to Gentiles and "overflow with hope by the power of the Holy Spirit" (15:13; see 15:7-13).

Paul concludes his lengthy celebration of the gospel of the righteousness of God (1:16—15:13) with an account of his travel plans, including an intermediate stop in Jerusalem en route to Rome and, with the assistance of the Roman Christians, on to Spain (15:14-33).

In the process Paul demonstrates how intimately his self-understanding is tied to the gospel. He identifies himself as "a minister of Christ Jesus to the Gentiles with the priestly duty of proclaiming the gospel of God, so that the Gentiles might become an offering acceptable to God, sanctified by the Holy Spirit" (15:16).

The letter closes with an expanded version of the customary formalities of ancient letters. Paul recommends his patroness, Phoebe, who is delivering the letter to Rome in his behalf (16:1-2), sends greetings to significant known individuals in the churches of Rome (16:3-16a) and greeting from his companions (16:16b, 21-24).

Warnings against false teachers interrupt his greetings (16:17-20). The letter ends with a doxology "to God who is able to strengthen you according to my gospel" (16:25 NRSV; see 16:25-27).

G. The Different Text Forms of Romans

Robert Jewett notes that "text critics have discovered fifteen different forms of Romans, including one no longer extant that is described by the church fathers" (2007, 4). The church fathers report that in the second century Marcion "removed entirely" the last two chapters from his version of the letter.

The most troublesome feature of the different textual traditions of Romans concerns the so-called wandering doxology—16:25-27. In various manuscripts it appears after 14:23; 15:33; 16:20b; 16:23; 16:24; in other manuscripts it appears twice, after 14:23; 15:33, or 16:23; in others, it is absent entirely.

On this basis, many critical scholars speculated that Rom 16 was not an original part of Paul's letter to Rome. They conjectured that it originated as Paul sent a copy of the letter to Rome with greetings to his friends in Ephesus. Harry Gamble effectively exploded this theory with his 1979 *Textual History of the Letter to the Romans*.

Recent scholars have argued that the original Romans may have lacked the benediction, 16:25-27, and that 16:17-20 may have been "a very early interpolation inserted at the time of the publication of the letter corpus" (Jewett 2007, 6). Although a case may be made for such conjectures, this commentary interprets the canonical form of the letter, which includes both passages.

I. LETTER PRESCRIPT: ROMANS 1:1-15

A. The Apostolic Greeting (1:1-7)

BEHIND THE TEXT

Born *Saul* of Hebrew parents (Phil 3:4-6), *Paul* was his Roman name. He was both a Roman citizen and a Diaspora Jew of the sect of the Pharisees. The former placed him in the elite category of Greco-Roman society, the latter potentially among the elite of Jewish society (Acts 16:37-39; 22:22-29). Acts indicates that Paul received his elementary education in Jerusalem, not in Tarsus—"I am a Jew, born in Tarsus of Cilicia, but brought up in this city. Under Gamaliel I was thoroughly trained in the law of our fathers" (22:3). Admittedly, Paul's claim in Gal 1:22 that he was unknown to the Judean church complicates this traditional view.

37

As a child from a well-connected Jewish family, Paul would have learned to speak, read, and write in Greek, Hebrew, and Aramaic. His ministry in Illyricum (Rom 15:19) and his plans to evangelize in Spain (v 28), both Latin-speaking regions, suggests that he also spoke that language. Under Herod the Great, Jerusalem had become a cosmopolitan and Hellenistic city, with both a hippodrome and a Greek theater. It was an important city to Greek-speaking Jews of the Diaspora like Paul's parents as well as a great pilgrimage destination for pious Jews from all over the Mediterranean.

Formal education began at age six for both Jewish and pagan boys. Jews of both Palestine and the Diaspora were early grounded in Jewish traditions. Paul would have been thoroughly grounded in Holy Scripture. Paul's OT citations indicate that he regularly consulted and followed the Septuagint (LXX: "seventy," designating a Greek translation of the Hebrew Bible begun in the third century B.C.), as well as the Hebrew text. Paul's theological education would have been comparable to that of today's seminary students (Gal 1:14; Acts 5:33-39).

Paul embraced the eschatology of the Pharisees, but his understanding of it was radically altered by his conversion to Christ (see Gal 1:3-5). Pharisees divided salvation history into two epochs: the old age before the coming of the Messiah was considered evil and unredeemable due to Adam's fall; the new age would inaugurate the future rule of God that was to be good and incorruptible. Because of his encounter with the risen Christ, Paul came to share the Christian view that the future age had broken into history in the person and work of Jesus Christ, while the present age persisted. Thus, there was an overlapping of the ages, referred to in the NT as "the last days" (see Acts 2:16-21). In this "time between the times," those who have been "rescue[d] . . . from the present evil age" (Gal 1:4) may experience the blessings of the future here and now (Heb 6:5), as they await the final consummation at Christ's return in glory (Rom 8:18-25).

Paul would also have learned methods of debate and persuasion from his teachers, such as argument from current experience to scriptural proof in midrashic fashion (1 Cor 9:7-14) and the use of allegory (Gal 4:21-31). In his oral culture, rhetoric was a fundamental staple of ancient education. Paul's oratorical skills suggest influences from both Jewish and pagan rhetoricians. In addressing a church he had neither founded nor visited, Paul introduced himself and his gospel with obvious rhetorical sensitivities. His apostolic greeting in Rom 1:1-7, one sentence in Greek, is the longest salutation in the Pauline letters.

Paul claims that his gospel was promised long ago but gives no hint as to where the promise is found in the OT. Paul's summary of his gospel seems to incorporate a fragment of early Palestinian proclamation, handed down to the Roman community (see Acts 2:22-36). Joseph Fitzmyer (1993, 229-30) reconstructs the kerygmatic formula as a two-pronged affirmation (italics indicate Paul's additions):

his Son	
born	established
of David's stock	as Son of God *with power*
according to the flesh	according to the spirit of holiness
by his resurrection from the dead	Jesus Christ our Lord.

The basic formula in Rom 1:3-4 is probably pre-Pauline; it contains the only reference in Paul's letters to Jesus as the Son of David, the only use of the verb *horizein* ("to declare"), and the Semitic phrase **Spirit of holiness** rather than "the Holy Spirit." This confessional formula summarizing **the gospel . . . regarding his Son,** quotes Jewish Christian tradition that Paul believes will establish his faith-identity with the Romans.

Paul regards his hearers as predominantly Gentile (see 1:6, 13; 11:13; 15:15-19), although their community contained Jewish Christians as well. The apostle understood his commission to be the fulfillment of God's ancient promise to Abraham in Gen 12:1-4, that through him "all peoples on earth will be blessed" (v 3) with the salvation that provides the obedience of faith that eluded ancient Israel but is now gloriously possible for the new Israel of God composed of "everyone [both Jews and Gentiles] who believes" (Rom 1:16; see 9:6-8) **in Jesus Christ our Lord** (1:4).

IN THE TEXT

■ **I** Ancient Greco-Romans letters followed the pattern: "Sender to Recipient, Greetings." Paul adapts the customary form—**Paul . . . to all in Rome,** expanding and giving it a Christian emphasis throughout. Because he had not founded nor yet visited the Roman church, the letter's lengthy salutation allowed him to present his credentials (Jewett 2007, 97) and the salient points of the argument to follow. His opening words are more than a formal introduction; they anticipate the theme of the letter.

Paul introduces himself as a **servant** (*doulos,* "slave") **of Christ Jesus** (v 1). This is more than an expression of feigned humility; Paul is completely at his Master's disposal. "The essential theme of his mission is not within him but above him" (Barth 1933, 27). Abraham (Gen 26:24; Ps 105:6, 42), Moses (Num 12:7-8), David (2 Sam 7:5, 8), and the prophets (Isa 20:3; Jer 7:25; Amos 3:7) were all called servants of the Lord. This is the first instance of this usage in the NT. Paul quietly replaces "the prophets and leaders of the Old Covenant, and . . . substitutes the name of his own Master . . . for that of Jehovah" (Sanday and Headlam 1929, 3). Paul's Roman audience may have heard his self-description as *a slave of Christ Jesus* as comparable to the title "slave of Caesar," proudly borne by those in the emperor's service (Jewett 2007, 99).

By identifying himself as **called to be an apostle** (*klētos apostolos, a called apostle*), Paul insists that he is "an apostle *by way of a call*" (Godet 1883, 74). *Klētos* has its roots in the OT: Abraham (Gen 12:1-3), Moses (Exod 3:10), and the prophets were God's servants by way of a divine summons. In Gal 1:14-16 Paul describes his call, echoing the language of Isa 49:1 and Jer 1:5.

Apostolos means literally an "envoy" or "missionary" ("one sent out"; note the Latin equivalent *missus*). Apostle has two applications in the NT. In the narrow sense it applied only to the Twelve (Mark 3:14; Luke 6:13; Acts 1:21-26). But in the broader Pauline sense it included Barnabas (14:4, 14), James the brother of Jesus (Gal 1:19), and others (Rom 16:7; see Luke 24:10; assuming Joanna = Junia [see the commentary on 16:7]), whose call derived from their personal encounter with the risen Christ (1 Cor 9:1-2; 15:8-9; Gal 1:1, 15-16). Paul's summons to be an apostle came directly from "Jesus Christ and God the Father" (Gal 1:1), who laid on him the responsibility of proclaiming the gospel to the Gentile world (Rom 1:16).

Set apart for the gospel thus parallels *klētos apostolos*. **Set apart** (*aphōrismenos*) has the same root meaning as *Pharisee* (*pharisaios*). As a fulfilled Pharisee (see Jewett 2007, 101-2), he was "separated" **for the gospel of God. The gospel** is the good news of God's saving intervention in human history in his Son, **Christ Jesus** our Lord.

Submission is the human response to the divine act of separation. God separates his servants; they make themselves available to him (see Rom 12:1). Human acceptance of the divine act of separation, faithful cooperation with the plan of God, is not inevitable. "I pommel my body and subdue it," Paul writes as a *klētos apostolos,* "lest after preaching to others I myself should be disqualified" (1 Cor 9:27 RSV; see Matt 24:13).

■ **2** Paul emphasizes the continuity of the gospel dispensation with the old covenant. The good news had been **promised beforehand through the prophets in the Holy Scriptures** (Rom 1:2). Although, the thought of God's promising activity is "deeply rooted in the OT . . . , it is not expressed there" explicitly (Cranfield 1975, 55 n. 3). NT authors do not limit the term **prophets** to those we normally think of; they include all the inspired authors of the OT, such as Moses (Acts 3:22) and David (Acts 2:30-31; Jewett 2007, 103). It is unusual that they are designated here *"his* prophets" (emphasis added; *tōn prophētōn autou*). This is the only place in the NT where the expression **the Holy Scriptures** (*graphais hagias*) appears (in 2 Tim. 3:15, "holy Scriptures" translates *hiera grammata*). The term *hagios* ("holy") modifies the usual designation for *hai graphai* ("the writings")—what we call the OT.

It is impossible to determine with certainty which passages Paul has in mind as he refers to the OT precedents for the **gospel**. Dunn suggests that "they would already include at least some of the texts cited or alluded to later on (see, e.g., on 4:25) and in the sermons in Acts, and here particularly 2 Sam 7:12-16 and Ps 2:7 (see on 1:3)" (2002a, 38A:10). Many NT scholars speculate that the earliest Christians had compiled *testimonia*, collections of Christian proof texts, used to validate their reading of the OT in light of the crucifixion and resurrection of Christ (see 1 Cor 15:3-4). There is evidence corroborating this in "the sequence of Isa 28:16, Ps 117, 118:22, and Isa 8:14 repeated in Matt 21:42, Rom 9:33, and 1 Pet 2:6-8" (Brooke 1992, 6:391) and the existence of such collections among the Dead Sea Scrolls.

Promised in the OT

Cranfield (1975, 55 n. 3) notes that the two-preposition (*pro* and *epi*) compound form of the verb translated **promised beforehand** (from *proepangellō*) occurs only here and in 2 Cor 9:5. The *pro-* prefix particularly emphasizes the priority of the promise. The one-preposition verb form (from *epangellomai*) occurs fifteen times in the NT, notably in Rom 4:21 and Gal 3:19. The noun *epangelia* ("promise") occurs nearly fifty times, including eight in Romans (4:13, 14, 16, 20; 9:4, 8, 9; 15:8) and nine in Galatians. Paul may have appropriated the Greek terms applied to God's promises in the earlier pseudepigraphal Psalms of Solomon (7:9 [10]; 12:7 [6]; and 17:6 [5]).

The gospel represents not a break with the past, but the consummation of it. Thus, Paul writes in 1 Cor 15:3-4 that "Christ died for our sins according to the Scriptures" and that "he was raised on the third day according to the Scriptures." The repeated insistence that these things happened in accordance with the Scriptures shows how vital this was to Paul. "The words of the prophets, long fastened under lock and key, are now set free. . . . Now we can see and understand what was written, for we have an 'entrance into the Old Testament'" (Barth 1933, 28; quoting Luther; see 2 Cor 3:14-16).

1:2-3

■ **3** Although the gospel has its *source* in God, the *content* of the good news is **regarding his Son** (Rom 1:3), in whom all the OT promises are fulfilled (2 Cor 1:20) and the saving acts of God performed (2 Cor 5:18-19). "The gospel is the center around which it all revolves. From beginning to end it treats of the Son of God" (Nygren 1949, 47).

Many scholars agree that Rom 1:3-4 seems to cite a brief creedal formula expounding on the nature of the Son of God. Paul diplomatically "selects a credo that bears the marks of both . . . the Gentile and Jewish branches of the early church" (Jewett 2007, 107; see 103-8). The key to understanding this christological formula is to grasp its antithetical character. The Greek term translated **human nature** (*sarx*) here is the same one frequently (mis-)translated **sinful nature** elsewhere in the NIV (see the sidebar "Flesh" with the commentary on Rom 7). **As to his human nature,** Jesus was descended from David.

Paul's point is not merely that God's Son shares our common humanity or that he was a Jew, although he takes both for granted. If his point were merely to insist that Jesus was human, any ancestor would do. He does not speak of him here as "born of a woman," as in Gal 4:4. If his point had been to emphasize Jesus' Jewishness, he would surely have mentioned his descent from Abraham (see Matt 1:1). That Jesus was a **descendant of David** reflects Jewish messianic expectation, that the Messiah would be the Son of David.

■ **4 Through the Spirit of holiness** (Rom 1:4), he who in his human existence belonged to the royal line of David was **declared with power to be the Son of God by his resurrection from the dead.**

> It is implied that there are two things to be said about Christ, not indeed contradictory but complementary to and different from each other. Christ belongs to two spheres or orders of existence, denoted respectively by flesh and Spirit. (Barrett 1957, 36)

An even more basic truth, however, underlies the twofold formula. He who was *from the beginning Son of God* was manifested first in weakness, then in power. The preexistent Son of God became incarnate, "sent" in the flesh (8:3; see 8:32; Gal 4:4).

The participle translated **was** (*genomenou*) in the phrase **was a descendant of David** (Rom 1:3) properly denotes "transition from one state or mode of existence to another. . . . '[Who] was born' . . . is practically equivalent to the Johannine *'elthontos eis ton kosmon'* ('coming into the world')" (Sanday and Headlam 1929, 6). If this passage alone supported the doctrine of Christ's preexistence, it would be difficult to sustain, but its canonical context—alongside John 1, Phil 2, and Col 1—certainly makes this a plausible reading.

Jesus, as a human **descendant of David** was **declared with power to be the Son of God.** His prior divine status was recognized **by his resurrection from the dead** (Rom 1:4); it did not make one who was merely human divine. **Declared** (*horisthentos*) is elsewhere translated "decreed" (Luke 22:22), "determined" (Acts 17:26), and "appointed" (v 31).

> There is neither need nor warrant to resort to any other rendering than that provided by the other New Testament instances, namely, that Jesus was "appointed" or "constituted" Son of God with power and points therefore to an investiture which had an historical beginning parallel to the historical beginning mentioned in verse 3. (Murray 1959, 36)

Paul's point is similar to that expressed in Heb 1:5, on which H. Orton Wiley comments:

> The words, "This day have I begotten thee," (1:5a) are applied by St. Paul to the Resurrection in Acts 13:33, and by St. John in Rev. 1:5. The Son is indeed the "only begotten of the Father" before all worlds, and the deity of the Son necessarily underlies the Incarnation and the Resurrection;

otherwise, it would exclude His work as Mediator. *But the Son was also begotten again in the Resurrection, which marked the full out-birth of the humanity of Jesus from a state of humiliation to that of glorification and exaltation.* (1959, 52-53; emphasis added. Wiley quotes Rom 1:3-4 as parallel to Heb 1:5.)

Whether *horisthentos* means **declared,** "designated" (RSV), or "proclaimed" (REB) does not threaten belief in Christ's essential deity. The debated issue is whether the resurrection confirmed an existing status or conferred a new one.

What does the phrase **with power** modify? Should it be translated **declared with power to be the Son of God** (NIV) or designated "the Son of God with power" (KJV)? The Greek allows either rendering. The majority of modern versions follow the KJV. The phrase *en dynamei* (**with power**) elsewhere in the NT (see Mark 9:1; 1 Cor 15:43, 56; and 1 Thess 1:5) is used in the sense of "invested with power."

> The meaning of the first six words of this clause then is probably "who was appointed Son-of-God-in-power" (that is, in contrast with His being Son of God in apparent weakness and poverty in the period of his earthly existence). (Cranfield 1975, 1:62)

"The divine glory, which formerly was hidden, was manifest after the resurrection" (Nygren 1949, 48).

The most difficult phrase in the formula is rendered literally and accurately **the Spirit of holiness.** Is this a reference to Jesus' human spirit or to the Holy Spirit? Is a contrast between Jesus' flesh and spirit intended? Is his human nature ("the sphere of flesh") contrasted with his heavenly nature ("the sphere of the Holy Spirit")? By capitalizing **Spirit of holiness** the NIV correctly identifies the phrase with "the Holy Spirit." Although Paul nowhere else refers to the Holy Spirit in this way, the Semitic expression probably quotes a Palestinian formula (as in the Dead Sea Scrolls), accounting for the unique terminology. Romans 8:11 similarly mentions the activity of the Holy Spirit in the resurrection.

A second surprising phrase, **by his resurrection from the dead,** in Greek is literally "by resurrection of those who are dead." Nygren understands Paul to mean, "Through Christ the resurrection age has burst upon us" (1949, 50). Ephesians 1:19—2:7 notes that the same power that raised Christ from the dead has resurrected *us* from the death of sin. So also in 1 Cor 15:19-58, Paul insists that

> *the resurrection is the turning point in the existence of the Son of God.* Before this the whole race was under the sovereign sway of death; but in the resurrection of Christ life burst forth victoriously, and a new aeon began, the aeon of the resurrection and life. (Nygren 1949, 51)

The phrase **Jesus Christ our Lord** presumes the primitive Christian confession, "Jesus is Lord" (1 Cor 12:3; see Phil 2:11). God designated Jesus Son of God with power by the resurrection and assigned him the name and authority implied in the name **Lord**. The name **Jesus** identifies the person, the incarnate Son. The title **Christ** speaks of him as the promised, Spirit-anointed Messiah of Israel (see John 1:33-34). **Lord** was used of human masters as well as divine beings in Greco-Roman practice. But the LXX use of *kyrios* to translate the divine name of Israel's God Yahweh expedited the church's exalted Christology. **Lord** identifies Jesus with the ineffable name of God (Phil 2:9-11 and Rom 14:9-11 echo Isa 45:23). The Aramaic prayer, *Marana tha*, "Come, O Lord!" (1 Cor 16:22), suggests that Jesus was first addressed as Lord among Jewish, not Greek-speaking Gentile Christians.

■ **5** The revelation of the lordship of Jesus rounds out the christological formula Paul quotes, while it amplifies and explains the nature of the apostle's commission to preach the gospel in Rome. From the exalted and glorified Lord Paul **received grace and apostleship** (Rom 1:5). Paul did not receive two gifts. As an example of hendiadys, the two expressions are mutually interpretive. For Paul, grace was the undeserved privilege and responsibility of being a spokesman for Christ. Not everyone who receives grace is made an apostle, but for Paul the two were inseparable. He was not first converted and later called to be an apostle. Rather, he received the double call on the Damascus Road (see Acts 9:15; Gal 1:15-16).

Paul was commissioned at his conversion **to call people from among all the Gentiles** **to the obedience that comes from faith.** Paul's fourfold use of the word **all** (from *pas*) in the introduction to Romans (1:5, 7, 8, and 16) emphasizes the inclusive scope of his message to the fractured Christian community there (Jewett 2007, 113). Before the letter is complete Paul will have used the word *pas* more than seventy times.

The phrase **to the obedience that comes from faith** (*eis hypakoēn pisteōs*; see 16:26; Acts 6:7) is translated literally in the margin of the KJV: "to the obedience of faith." Those who accept Jesus as Lord are expected to obey him. *Lordship* and *obedience* are correlative terms. J. A. Beet comments aptly, "The act of faith is submission to God" (1885, 33). Since sin means making self the end and rule of life, faith means the abdication of self and the exaltation of Jesus Christ as Lord. "The expression here used by Paul defines admirably the goal at which Christian apostleship aims: to bring men back into a state of obedience, since the present state is essentially one of disobedience (5:19)" (Leenhardt 1957, 40). The formula **for his name's sake** (Acts 5:41; 9:16; 15:26; 21:13; 3 John 7) emphasizes that "Jesus Christ is 'the foundation and theme of proclamation' in missionary contexts" (see Rom 15:20; Jewett 2007, 111).

■ **6** The apostle addresses the Roman Christians as **among those who are called to belong to Jesus Christ** [*klētoi Iēsou Christou*: *called of Jesus Christ*] (v 6). Their call to be the people of Christ, to be **saints** (see v 7), is exactly parallel to his call to be an apostle (v 1; Jewett 2007, 112).

How does one come to belong to Christ? Despite contemporary Christian usage emphasizing human volition and choice, the NT insists that people come to him by invitation only. Believers, as *hoi klētoi,* the **called,** come to God wholly "by grace" (Eph 2:8). The Synoptic Gospels refer to *klētoi* as "all who are invited to enter Christ's kingdom, whether or not they accept the invitation." Thus, the *eklektoi,* "the elect," are a smaller, select group within "the called" (see Matt 22:14; Keck 1995, 24-26). In Paul, however, "both words are applied to the same persons; *klētos* implies that the call has been not only given but obeyed" (Sanday and Headlam 1929, 4). Romans 8:28 validates Karl Barth's claim that Jesus Christ is the Elect One, with *all* believers "elect in Christ."

■ **7** Paul emphasizes that all the Roman Christians—Jews and Gentiles—are loved by God (v 7). Here Paul employs the great NT word for love—*agapē.* This is God's own love for all humanity revealed supremely in the cross, where Christ died for "sinners" (5:8), even while they were still his "enemies" (5:10). His love is personally experienced through the Holy Spirit "poured" into human hearts by the gift of his Holy Spirit (5:5). His love entirely encompasses the lives of believers. Henceforth, no power whatever can separate them from the love God has given them in Christ Jesus (8:35-39). When Paul addresses the Roman Christians as **loved by God,** he uses the word in this profound and inclusive sense. To be God's beloved, his friends, characterizes the existence of all Christians.

Finally, they are ***called saints*** (*kletois hagiois*), not simply **called to be saints,** as if they were not already. They are really "saints" by virtue of God's call (Godet 1883, 74). The NT understands all believers to be "saints," i.e., "holy" or "sanctified" (*hagioi;* see 15:25-26, 31; 16:2, 15). The basic idea of sainthood is separation. The saints are those people God has separated "from all the people on earth to be his very own" (Deut 7:6 NCV; see 1 Kgs 8:53; 1 Pet 2:9-10). In this sense the Roman Christians were "holy." They were no longer simply Gentiles or Jews; they had been **called to belong to Jesus Christ** (Rom 1:6). God had claimed them for himself.

Paul's opening greeting, **Grace and peace to you from God our Father and from the Lord Jesus Christ,** is similar to that found in all his letters. The Pauline greeting has been explained as the combination of the Greek *charein,* "greetings," for which Paul substitutes *charis,* "grace," and a translation of the standard Jewish greeting *shalom,* "peace"—*eireinē* in Greek.

But the combination of "grace and peace" also echoes the Aaronic blessing: "The LORD bless you and keep you: The LORD make his face to shine upon you, and be gracious to you: The LORD lift up his countenance upon you, and give you peace" (Num 6:24-26 RSV). If so, then "grace" would represent God's merciful bounty or covenantal favor revealed in Christ Jesus, and "peace" would connote the fullness of prosperity and well-being characteristic of God's goodness to Israel of old. For all of this Paul prays: that it may come to the Christians of Rome from God our Father and our Lord Jesus Christ as the sum of evangelical blessings. (Fitzmyer 1993, 228)

FROM THE TEXT

Paul's understanding of **the gospel of God . . . regarding his Son** (Rom 1:1, 3), and of himself as an apostle set apart for the proclamation of that gospel **among all the Gentiles** (v 5) is the central theme of this passage. At least four theologically significant assertions arise naturally from the introduction to Romans.

First, the christological formula defining the gospel in 1:3-4 stands at the center of orthodox Christian faith. In the early years the church fathers wrote learned treatises on the subject, emphasizing the meaning of Christ's deity and incarnation. The church condemned the Jewish teaching that Jesus was a man who *became* the Son of God, either by the Spirit coming upon him at his baptism or by his resurrection from the dead. This doctrinal error became known later in history as adoptionism, a denial of the incarnation (John 1:14).

On the other extreme, the church condemned the error, arising from the gnostic notion that matter is essentially evil. Gnostics held that Jesus was a phantom, having only the *appearance* of human flesh. This doctrine became known as Docetism, from the Greek word *dokein*, meaning to "seem" or "appear."

Another heresy, known as Sabellianism, is more properly a Trinitarian error, but it does affect Christology. Sabellius taught that there was but one God, who manifested himself, first as Father, then as Son, and finally as the Holy Spirit. This error, also called modalism, has been popularized in recent history by the "Jesus only" doctrine, which denies the Trinity, insisting that Jesus alone is truly God.

As the christological discussions of the church continued, a very serious challenge to Christ's essential deity arose, which threatened the Christian faith. It was fostered by Arius (256-336), a Greek theologian. Arius taught that while Christ was divine, and was incarnate, there was a time when he was not. Arius's Christ was a demigod, not the *eternal* Son of God.

The triumph of orthodox Christian faith over Arianism was accomplished chiefly by the skillful biblical argumentation of Athanasius (293-373). The issue was officially settled by the Council of Constantinople in 381 and enshrined in the Nicene Creed, to which all orthodox Christian churches subscribe.

A close examination of the christological formulas in Rom 1:3-4 reveals that the essential elements of the creed are confessed there in germinal form. But Paul's concerns in Romans go well beyond confessional considerations. Not only faith as opinions, but also faith as obedience matters.

Second, to obey the gospel requires that believers must live obediently as those who belong to Jesus Christ (vv 5-7). To obey fully means not only to hear but also to hearken to God. It requires "submission" to his lordship and purposes (Fitzmyer 1993, 137). *TRUST & OBEY*

To understand the gospel and proclaim it with saving power, we must be convinced and thoroughly changed by the Holy Spirit (1 Cor 2:12-14). As important as theological education and ministerial training may be, the power of Paul's ministry (and ours) is not human but supernatural—by "the Spirit who is from God" (see 1 Cor 2:4). Paul's ministry embodies and models this primal truth (Gal 1:11-16; see 2 Cor 3:7-18), applicable to all (see 2 Cor 3:3-6).

The intermediate goal of the gospel is ongoing moral *transformation* into the likeness of Christ—to be saints (Rom 1:7). John Wesley calls this process *sanctification*, by which he means renewal in the image of God (see Col 3:10). Believers as **saints** are not only *separated* from the rest of humanity but also *purified*.

> Since all sin is the erection of self into the end and rule of life, sin is utterly opposed to holiness. God's holiness makes Him intolerant of sin, because sin robs Him of that which His holiness demands. Only the holy are pure, only the pure are holy. (Beet 1885, 39)

Purification begins in conversion. John Wesley expected this cleansing to deal with both *outward* and *inward* sin (1979, 5:150; commenting on 1 Cor 6:9-11). Conversion purifies from sin as God breaks the *rule* of sin in the lives of the saints—his people. Having received the sanctifying Spirit, they yearn to be cleansed from the *root* of sin that remains—to be transformed, ruled, renewed, and used unreservedly by God (see 6:13, 19; 12:1-12; 2 Cor 7:1)—to be entirely sanctified (1 Thess 5:23-24).

Wesley was convinced that God justifies us in order to sanctify us. Sanctification begins a lifelong process of transformation, marked by certain specific stages on the way. Wesley often described this process in terms of Gal 5:6—"faith expressing itself through love." In his sermon "On Patience" he describes the distinction between the various phases of the process as ever-increasing degrees of love.

Third, what the Lord called Israel to become at Sinai, he makes universally possible through Christ and the church: "a priestly kingdom and a holy nation" (Exod 19:6 NRSV; see Gen 12:1-4; Exod 19:5-8). God's concerns extend well beyond salvaging random individuals to the creating of a holy community. "Although the whole earth is mine, you will be for me a kingdom of priests and a holy nation" (Exod 19:5-6).

God's covenant with Israel promised the people they would be "a priestly kingdom and a holy nation" (NRSV). Now, in the end time of salvation history, God made his people "priests of the Lord" and "ministers of our God." God never wavered in his purpose (see 1 Pet 2:9-11 and Rev 1:6 NRSV). Old Testament priests brought Israel before God to worship and experience the glory of his holiness. Their two key functions were to represent God to the people and to represent the people to God. God expected Israel to perform these two functions in relation to the nations (see Exod 19; Isa 42:6-7; 43:10-12; 49:6), but Israel failed in its mission (see 42:19-20).

Fourth, Paul is confident that his gospel is no novelty. It was **promised beforehand through his prophets in the Holy Scriptures** (Rom 1:2). If he explains this claim in Gal 3:6-9, the gospel merely continues what God set out to do in Israel. Paul appeals to Abraham, the father of Israel, in Gen 12 (esp. vv 1-3) and 15 (esp. vv 4-6), on whom he will elaborate at length in Rom 4.

The gospel was not an unexpected irruption into history; it was the culmination and fulfillment of God's redemptive plan for humanity. The multiplied millions transformed by the power of the gospel seal the truth of God's promise to Abraham. "For no matter how many promises God has made, they are 'Yes' in Christ. And so through him the 'Amen' is spoken by us to the glory of God" (2 Cor 1:20).

The God of Abraham is the God and Father of our Lord Jesus Christ. To understand what God is doing in our world, we must come back to this central point: God is determined to fulfill the promises he made to father Abraham. The very essence of God's character—his holiness, righteousness, justice, power, and love—hangs on his faithfulness to the covenant promises he made to Abraham.

The God of history invites his people to join him in carrying out his ultimate goal: "that at the name of Jesus every knee should bow, in heaven and on earth and under the earth, and every tongue confess that Jesus Christ is Lord, to the glory of God the Father" (Phil 2:10-11).

B. Paul's Interest in the Roman Church (1:8-15)

BEHIND THE TEXT

The first sentence of an ancient Greek letter, after the salutation, was often of a religious nature, informing the recipients of the writer's prayer to the gods on their behalf. The prayer was usually a thanksgiving (or petition), typically concerned with the recipients' health. Romans follows this practice, although the character and content of Paul's thanksgiving are far from conventional. His prayer is not for the physical welfare of those to whom he writes, but a prayer of thanksgiving that their faith was widely reported. Paul assures them of his unceasing prayers for them, including the prayer that God may permit him to visit them.

Epistolary thanksgivings in ancient letters also typically serve as a rhetorical exordium. That is, they introduce and anticipate the key concerns that will be developed in the letter. Paul explains that he desires to see them so that they may be mutually strengthened by their fellowship together. And he assures the Roman community that he had long planned to visit them, but he had been previously prevented by circumstances beyond his control. Jewett notes the rhetorical interplay between "me" and "you" (plural) developed in vv 8-12 that Paul uses to establish "the relationship between himself and his audience within the framework of the inclusive gospel" outlined in vv 1-7 (2007, 117).

Verses 13-15 solemnly express Paul's sense of the obligation laid upon him as apostle to the Gentiles and his particular eagerness to preach the gospel to the Christians in Rome as in the rest of the Gentile world. Paul felt obliged to preach the gospel as if he were constantly discharging a debt owed to all humankind—"a debt which he will never fully discharge so long as he lives" (Bruce 1963, 75).

The letter to the Romans stands as a stopgap measure to preach the gospel to the Romans until Paul arrives and is able to do so in person. Only at the close of the letter does Paul disclose his ambitious scheme to recruit the Romans to assist him in taking the gospel to Spain, the western extremes of the empire (15:22-29).

Since Paul has never been to Rome and had no part in founding the Roman church, his thanksgiving must overcome the barrier of strangeness that separates him from his mostly unknown readers (see ch 16). Barclay is typical of the interpreters who imagine that Paul also feels obliged to break down their suspicions (Barclay 1957, 5). What many see as a strategy to overcome suspicions is actually a normal feature of ancient rhetoric—establishing one's trustworthy ethos with an audience. Since effective persuasion requires all the rhetorical resources available, ancient authors characteristically appeal to ethos (character), logos (reason), and pathos (emotion) to make their case. Paul is no exception. He is not on the defensive, but on the offensive, as he seeks to persuade the Romans to become partners in the gospel.

IN THE TEXT

I. Paul's Prayer (1:8-12)

■ **8** Paul begins his thanksgiving with a sincere compliment: **First, I thank my God through Jesus Christ for all of you, because your faith is being reported all over the world** (v 8). **First** probably intends no more than *From the very outset* or *Above all;* not that he meant to make a further point but did not. This is Paul's "main point," his reason for writing (Jewett 2007, 118).

My God is an OT phrase Paul would naturally use (see Pss 3:7; 5:2; 7:1, 3, etc.), which expresses the intimacy and reality of his present relationship to God **through Jesus Christ**. "The gifts of God," Wesley observes, "all pass through Christ to us, and all our petitions and thanksgivings pass through Christ to God" (1950, 517; on Rom 1:8).

Paul's prayer was **for all** of the Roman Christians without exception (see vv 5, 7, 16). He is thankful that there is a church of Jesus Christ in the imperial capital. His claim that their faith is *universally* known—**is being reported** [*katangelletai*] **all over the world**—is an obvious example of hyperbole (see 1 Thess 1:8). His gratitude is not for their strategic location or splendid reputation but simply that they *believe* (Cranfield 1975, 1:75). Their faith, like the gospel itself, is *being proclaimed* (see 1 Cor 9:14; 11:26; Phil 1:18; Jewett 2007, 119).

Paul does not use **your faith** as we sometimes do, to refer to the particular doctrinal content of Roman Christianity. His thanksgiving is occasioned by the fact that they, like other Christians, are believers who have staked their eternal salvation on the conviction that Jesus is the Christ (see Rom 1:17; see 1 Cor 1:5-7; Eph 1:15-16; Col 1:3-7; 1 Thess 1:2-3, 7-8; 2 Thess 1:2-4; Phlm 5). At their best, Christians incarnate the gospel and represent their Lord.

■ **9** Paul frequently calls upon God to vouch for the truth of claims only God can validate. Here he writes, **God, whom I serve with my whole heart in preaching the gospel of his Son, is my witness how constantly I remember you in my prayers at all times** (Rom 1:9-10a). The verb *latreuō* translated **serve** is used in classical Greek for the service of a deity; in the LXX it regularly refers to the worship of Israel's God Yahweh (see the noun *latreia* in 12:1). In 15:30-32, Paul will invite the Romans to intercede in prayer in his behalf, as he has been doing in theirs for some time.

The Greek phrase translated **with my whole heart** is literally "with my spirit" (KJV). Paul does not mean that his worship of God was only a subjective or purely spiritual act. His service to God not only takes the form of a continuous attitude of prayer but also comes to expression in evangelical

ROMANS

1:8-9

preaching, of necessity, something externally observable and objective. **Preaching the gospel of his Son** is for Paul an act of worship directed from his inner self as an expression of praise to God himself (Käsemann 1980, 18; Fitzmyer 1993, 244, 245; Moo 1996, 58).

■ **10** Paul's prayers for the Romans are an integral expression of his worship (see Phil 3:3). But his **prayers at all times** (Rom 1:10*a*) for all his churches are "one part of Paul's service to God, . . . which he fulfils inwardly and secretly" (Cranfield 1975, 77).

Paul's Oath and Hyperbole

Paul frequently calls upon God to witness to the truth of his claims (see 2 Cor 1:23; 11:31; Gal 1:20; Phil 1:8; 1 Thess 2:5, 10; see also Rom 9:1; 2 Cor 2:17; 12:19). How such implicit *oaths* before God stand in relation to Matt 5:33-37 and Jas 5:12 is a question that has, naturally, often been asked. That the canon includes Paul's oaths is one indication that Matt 5:33-37 and Jas 5:12 may not be understood as forbidding all oaths without exception (Cranfield 1975, 1:75).

But why does Paul make oaths at all? It is not that he is usually a liar who can be trusted only if he solemnly swears to tell the truth. It seems to be rather that the claims he makes under oath are impossible to validate: Only God knows the truth.

That the faith of the Roman Christians was universally proclaimed may be innocent flattery intended to win the favor of his unknown audience. Paul's repeated claims to pray unceasingly for his readers are certainly hyperbolic. Both claims deliberately exaggerate the truth to make their truthful point more forcefully. That there were Christians in the capital of the empire was a significant milestone in the Christian mission to reach the whole world (Matt 26:13; 28:19-20; Jewett 2007, 120).

In more than half a dozen passages in Paul's letters, he claims to pray constantly (Rom 1:9; 12:12; Eph 1:16; Col 1:9; 1 Thess 1:2-3; 2:13; 2 Tim 1:3). Certainly, for example, he cannot literally spend all his time in thanksgiving for the Romans and for the Thessalonians. He also prays for other congregations. And he obviously spends time in other activities as well—plying his trade, preaching, and teaching. Some of his time must be spent eating, drinking, sleeping, traveling, writing pastoral letters, and other mundane tasks.

Paul's hyperbolic point is to claim that intercessory prayer is not only an interruption in his normal activities but also his normal activity. Worship is not something Paul does only at scheduled intervals. He practices a variety of prayer that is unceasing, fervent, and comprehensive of all of life (see Luke 18:1; 21:36; and Heb 5:7). And whenever he prays, he asks God to enable him to come to Rome. And God alone can vouch for this.

Paul finally gets to the object of his longstanding prayers: **I pray that now at last by God's will the way may be opened for me to come to you** (Rom 1:10*b*). His plan to visit Rome is no lately conceived plot. The expression *ēdē pote,* **now at last,** expresses Paul's sense that he has spent enough time waiting (see Phil 4:10). He is persuaded that finally it is **God's will** for him to make his long proposed visit to Rome (see Rom 15:32).

Paul takes seriously that his plans are subject to the sovereign *will of God* (see 12:2; 15:32; 1 Cor 1:1; 2 Cor 1:1; 8:5; Gal 1:4; Eph 1:1; 6:6; Col 1:1; 4:12; 1 Thess 4:3; 5:18). Throughout the NT, writers recognize that "man proposes, God disposes" (see Acts 18:21; 1 Cor 4:19; 16:7; Heb 6:3; Jas 4:15). Paul could not have known how God's purposes for his visit would be affected by the leaders of the Jerusalem church, by the scheming of his opponents, and by corrupt Roman politicians. Thus, it was years, not months, before Paul was able to visit Rome, and then not as a missionary, but as a prisoner (see Acts 21—28).

■ **11** Paul's claim, **I long** [*epipothō*] **to see you** (Rom 1:11), employs terminology sometimes used to express "familial feelings or personal friendship," but "nowhere outside early Christianity does it appear in reference to bonds among group members" (see Rom 15:23; 2 Cor 9:14; Jewett 2007, 123).

The apostle explains the motive of his visit: **that** [*hina*] **I may impart to you some spiritual gift** [*charisma . . . pneumatikon*] **to make you strong.** Evidently the Romans will miss this spiritual endowment if they remain personally unacquainted with him. Precisely what Paul meant by this *charisma* may only be guessed from descriptions in his other letters. He would, of course, come to Rome endowed with the "fruit" of divine love (*agapē*—1 Cor 13; Gal 5:16, 22-25) and empowered with "gifts" (*charismata*) to serve the body of Christ (1 Cor 12:4-31; 14:1-40).

> But here, the "particular gift of the Spirit" Paul had in mind
> is simply the Gospel, which according to i.5 had been entrusted to him. Other men have other gifts. . . . This particular gift, the proclamation of the Gospel, is the gift of the apostolic office bestowed on him. (Barth 1959, 18)

If this is what Paul means, he assumes that the Spirit would empower his preaching in Rome so that by hearing the gospel in faith, the Romans would experience the *charisma* (see Acts 19:1-6; Gal 3:2).

Paul's express reason for desiring to visit the Romans is **to make you strong** (lit. *for you to be established*). He does not say, "that I may establish you." The modesty of the passive omits Paul's personal part in the process. He notes later that it is God "who is able to establish you by my gospel and the proclamation of Jesus Christ" (Rom 16:25).

Precisely how Paul expects the Roman house and tenement churches to be strengthened will become clear only in the course of the letter. Paul hopes to enrich their understanding of and deepen their commitment to the gospel (chs 1—11), to consolidate them as a community characterized by love (chs 12—13), to resolve the conflicts separating the weak and the strong (chs 14—15), and to enlist them for his mission to Spain (ch 15).

■ **12** But the fact that Paul's relationship to Rome is not like that to the churches he founded causes him to reformulate his aspirations. He continues, **that** [*touto de estin,* **but that is** + an infinitive of purpose] **you and I may be mutually encouraged by each other's faith** (v 12). The stress falls on the mutuality of what will take place when he visits them. The Romans will have something to give him too (see 15:24, 30-32).

2. Paul's Plans (1:13-15)

■ **13** Paul is a stranger to Rome; and the church there was founded by others. But as an apostle to the Gentiles (see 11:13; 15:14-21) he can write, **I do not want you to be unaware** [*agnoein*], **brothers [and sisters], that I planned many times to come to you . . . in order that** [*hina*] **I might have a harvest among you, just as I have among the other Gentiles** (1:13). This epistolary disclosure formula (see 11:25; 1 Cor 10:1; 11:3; 12:1; 2 Cor 1:8; 1 Thess 4:13) suggests that Paul begins a new section here. He turns from his prayer report concerning his forthcoming Roman visit to introduce its evangelistic purpose [*hina*]. He does not disclose the details of his plans until Rom 15:22-29.

The familial address heightens the sense of intimacy between Paul and his readers (see 7:1, 4; 8:12; 10:1; 11:25; 15:14, 30; 16:17). The term **brothers,** of course, does not refer to Paul's biological male siblings or even more broadly to his fellow Jews. The bond that unites them is not gender or ethnicity but their shared faith in Christ. He addresses them as fellow Christians.

Although Paul considers his readers fully evangelized, not all in Rome are believers. Thus, Paul anticipates winning converts (**a harvest:** *tina karpon, some fruit*) as a result of his preaching in Rome—**among you . . . as . . . among the other Gentiles.** But more importantly, he looks beyond Rome to more distant harvest fields of Spain awaiting the gospel, which he hopes the Roman Christians will help him evangelize. This and other passages (see 11:13, 25-28; 15:15-16) in the letter indicate the dominantly Gentile character of the Roman church. The **brothers** Paul addresses include "sisters" (see ch 16). And most of them are apparently non-Jews (see e.g., 11:13-24).

There is no question of Paul's right, or his desire, to preach in Rome. The reason he has not already visited them is that he had been **prevented from doing so until now** (1:13). Barrett comments:

> Paul does not here (as at I Thess. 2:18) speak of a hindering of Satan; indeed the use of the passive may (in Semitic fashion) conceal a reference to God—it had not been God's will that Paul should come (see Acts 16:6f. and perhaps I Cor. xiv.12). This should probably be understood to

mean that urgent tasks (only recently completed, xv. 18f., 22 f.) had kept him in the East. (1957, 26)

■ 14 Paul wants to make it clear that the purpose for his longed-for visit is greater than his own wish; it is his inescapable duty. Accordingly, his announced purposes for visiting Rome reach their climax in the declaration, I am obligated both to Greeks and to non-Greeks [lit. *barbarians*], both to the wise and the foolish (Rom 1:14). Jewett identifies this verse as "in several respects the 'key to Romans'" (2007, 130).

■ 15 Paul here as elsewhere (see the commentary on 4:4; 8:12; 13:7, 8; 15:1, 27) uses the economic term obligated (*opheiletēs*, "a debtor," v 14 NRSV) in an extended, metaphorical sense. Paul does not preach the gospel (v 15) as a volunteer. His divine calling compels him to consider preaching to all a moral obligation, but one he is eager to discharge (see 2 Cor 8:11, 12, 19; 9:2).

> If I proclaim the gospel, this gives me no ground for boasting, for an obligation [*ananke*, "necessity" or "pressure"] is laid on me, and woe to me if I do not proclaim the gospel! For if I do this of my own will, I have a reward; but if not of my own will, I am entrusted with a commission. (1 Cor 9:16-17 NRSV)

Jews typically divided the world between Jews and non-Jews, "Gentiles" (*ta ethnē*, lit. "the nations"; see Acts 14:5; 26:17; Rom 3:29; 9:24; 1 Cor 1:23; 2:15). Rather than ethnicity, language was the basis Greco-Romans used to divide the world between "us" and "them." Greek speakers typically distinguished themselves from non-Greek speakers, whom they designated with the derogatory term of contempt *barbarians* (*barbaroi*; v 14). Such people were not only uncivilized but also subhuman.

Barbaroi is a meaningless onomatopoeia word that attempts to represent the strange, unintelligible sounds foreign speakers make (*"bar, bar"*), comparable to our colloquial "blah, blah." Although Paul certainly speaks Greek, he does not accept the assumptions underlying this linguistic dualism. He simply adopts the standard terminology of "the imperial worldview" his Roman audience readily understands. He certainly knew that "Spaniards were viewed as barbarians par excellence" (Jewett 2007, 130). But he is convinced that the gospel is for all.

The educational dualism classifying all humanity as either wise or foolish (see Titus 3:3) was essentially synonymous in the minds of most Greeks, who considered their language, culture, and worldview superior to that of the rest of the world. Dunn observes:

> That Paul should be thus prepared to designate the Gentile world in categories of culture and rationality (rather than of races or geographical areas) is striking; it indicates his confidence in the power of his message even in the face of hellenistic sophistication. (2002a, 38A:32)

Thus, when Paul refers to **Greeks** and "barbarians" he means practically "the cultured and the uncultured" or "the sophisticated and unsophisticated." Similarly, **the wise and the foolish** signify "the educated and the uneducated" (Dodd 1932, 8). Paul acknowledges the inclusive character of his obligation to preach the gospel to the entire Gentile world. His task as an apostle to the Gentiles is to bring all men and women everywhere under the lordship of Jesus Christ and "to the obedience that comes from faith" (1:5; see 11:13; 15:18; and Gal 2:8). And he is resolved to pursue this mission with passion, fervor, and enthusiasm (Jewett 2007, 133).

FROM THE TEXT

Those called to full-time professional Christian ministry would do well to emulate the apostle Paul as he reveals his mission-passion in this passage.

His ministry was *eucharistic:* The thought of standing before the Romans and proclaiming the gospel filled Paul with *thanksgiving.* He felt compelled to thank God for the privilege and obligation to preach the gospel (see 1 Cor 9:16; 2 Cor 5:14-20). Paul's ministry was sustained through constant *prayer.*

Not only prayer but also preaching was an integral expression of Paul's *worship.* Preaching in the power of the Spirit allowed Christ to take human words and communicate through them his living word to the hearts of all who would listen. It is a characteristic Pauline tendency to conceive of acts of mundane service as expressions of worship. Those who occupy the pulpit, as well as those who sit in the pews, must get over the notion that worship involves primarily singing praise songs to Jesus.

Paul's was an appropriately *contextualized* ministry. Despite his Jewish upbringing, his confidence in the power of the gospel allowed him to understand the cultural assumptions of his Gentile audience in order to communicate the good news intelligibly and effectively. He understood his world well enough to speak in categories it understood; and he understood the gospel well enough to communicate it faithfully, without accommodating its truth to the culture in the process.

II. THE GOSPEL OF GOD'S RIGHTEOUSNESS: ROMANS 1:16—15:13

The Thesis of the Letter (1:16-17)

BEHIND THE TEXT

Romans 1:16-17 serves a significant transitional role in the letter. In some respects it brings the opening remarks in the letter prescript to a conclusion. But more importantly, it introduces all Paul has to say in the body of the letter. It is difficult to decide whether a hinge belongs to the door or to the door frame. Just so, Paul's announcement of the letter theme in these verses facilitates the movement from the letter frame into the flow of his argument concerning the gospel of God's righteousness.

To understand Paul's usage of the term "righteousness of God" (v 17 NRSV) we must examine the use of the phrase in the OT. There, in the Hebrew Scriptures, two great theological words tower above all others: *qodesh* ("holiness") and *tsedaqah* ("righteousness"). Holiness is the *inner nature* of God; righteousness is God's *saving activity*. God's holiness and God's righteousness are both key concepts to a right interpretation of v 17, since the eighth-century B.C. prophets gave new content to both by closely associating the two ideas.

All four prophets are unanimous in reiterating that Yahweh by his very nature demands righteous conduct from worshippers and will be content with nothing less (see Isa 1:15-18; Hos 6:6; Amos 5:21-24; Mic 6:6-8). If we were to choose a passage of Scripture that indicates the new content of *qodesh*, it would be Isa 5:16: "The Holy God shows himself holy by righteousness" (NRSV). The novel content of righteousness found in the eighth-century prophets is more than a demand for right conduct on the part of Yahweh's worshippers; it is the sanctifying or hallowing to be done in righteousness by the exaltation of the holiness of the Lord in their midst (see Isa 6:1-8).

The OT evidence suggests that God's righteousness is not only a *status* or *gift* to be enjoyed by Israel as God's elect; it is *the salvation of God*. The righteousness of God shows itself in his saving deeds. While the ethical content of righteousness must by no means be discounted, the emphasis is on God's mighty work in saving the humble, those who devotedly trust in and serve the Lord, even in the face of suffering. In the Prophets and in the Psalms this motif becomes supreme (see Ps 71; Isa 42:7; 49:6; 52:13—53:12).

In Psalms and Isaiah the words "righteousness" and "salvation" are often used in synonymous parallelism. These correlative terms provide an immediate background for understanding Rom 1:16-17. See Isa 51:5:

——   My righteousness draws near speedily,
        my salvation is on the way.

Or Ps 71:15:

—— My mouth will tell of your righteousness,
        of your salvation all day long.

—— In Isa 45 the Lord is called "a righteous God and a Savior" (v 21). The passage continues:

Turn to me and be saved,
all you ends of the earth. . . .
Before me every knee will bow;
by me every tongue will swear.
They will say of me, "In the LORD alone
are righteousness and strength." (vv 22-24)

Psalm 98:2 closely resembles Paul's words in Rom 1:16-17:

58

The LORD has made his salvation known
and revealed his righteousness to the nations.

See Dunn (2002a, 38A:40-43) for an exhaustive treatment of the range of interpretive options for the crucial phrase "righteousness of God" in v 17 (NRSV).

The roots of the Pauline doctrine of **salvation** (v 16) all spring from the OT. There the word has at least three meanings. (1) It signifies deliverance from physical evil (1 Sam 11:9, 13). In this sense Paul himself speaks of salvation in Phil 1:19 as release from imprisonment. (2) Salvation also describes the deliverance of the people of God (a) from slavery at the Red Sea (Exod 14:13; 15:2) and (b) from Babylonian Exile (Isa 45:17; 46:13, etc.). (3) The OT also prophesies messianic salvation in Jer 31:31-34; Ezek 36:24-32; Joel 2:28-32; Zech 13:1. This latter view is the primary concern of the NT doctrine (Matt 1:21; Luke 1:69, 71, 73, 77; 7:50).

"The righteous will live by faith" quotes Hab 2:4. The word rendered **faith** is the Hebrew *emunah*, from a verb originally meaning "to be firm." It is used in the OT in the physical sense of steadfastness. Thus, the better rendering is "faithfulness." "Faith" is a word for which, in the NT active sense of the Greek noun *pistis*, the Hebrew has no simple equivalent, although the term "believe" (Greek *pisteō*) is derived from the same root as *emunah*.

The Hebrew refers to faithfulness in terms of reliability; the Greek, in terms of relying. *Emunah* is the word used to describe the uplifted hands of Moses, which were steady (Exod 17:12). It is also used of men in charge of money who "acted with complete honesty" (2 Kgs 12:15). It is closely akin, if not identical, to the English idiomatic statement, "Hold steady," implying that if we do not "bolt," the circumstances that surround us will change. Righteous Israelites, those who remain loyal to the Law, will survive, despite their present suffering. However, the wicked, despite their present comfort, will be destroyed in the end.

The Septuagint translated the Hebrew *emunah* using the Greek *pistis* ("faith"). It was this translation that Paul made use of and thus incorporated the vision of Habakkuk into the very heart of his proclamation of the gospel. By it he means that single act of faith by which the sinner is "justified," restored to a rectified relationship to God.

IN THE TEXT

■ **16** These transitional verses define in Paul's own terms the gospel he intends to preach in Rome. Here the apostle begins to present the purpose for which the letter was written—an exposition of Paul's gospel of deliverance from sin and the grace needed to sustain a right relationship with God. The transition from what precedes, however, is hardly noticeable. Romans 1:16-17 announces the theme of the letter—**the gospel,** the thesis (called the *propositio* in rhetoric) he will develop in the formal body of the letter (1:18—15:13).

Paul begins by assuring the Romans that he is **not ashamed of the gospel** (v 16). His delay in coming to Rome is not due to any misgivings on his part about the gospel.

> No one should think that he could not come because he shunned the challenge which Rome especially, as the impressive centre of the Gentile world, would mean to his message. He is not afraid that the Gospel might not be equal to its encounter with the accumulated culture and vulgarity of the metropolis, that the spiritual and unspiritual powers, the culture and banality prevailing there might confound the Gospel and stultify him as well. (Barth 1959, 20)

Paul's shamelessness is not based on any reliance on his own spiritual resources, eloquence, or the like. His confidence rests solely upon the **power** of the **gospel,** despite the opinions of those who consider its message of the cross shameful, scandalous, and foolish (see 1 Cor 1:18—2:5). Paul's negation (**not ashamed**) illustrates the figure of speech known as litotes or meiosis. Such deliberate understatement affirms its opposite: He is prepared to confess the gospel (see Mark 8:38) in the capital of the empire with boldness. (See the sidebar "Further Reading on Honor and Shame in Mediterranean Society" with the commentary on Rom 6:1-23.)

Paul does not say that the **gospel** *has* saving **power.** It *is* the **power** of God to save—God's own power, unique, incomparable, omnipotent, and personal (Hab 3:18-19). The word **gospel** is not to be equated simply with Paul's preaching. It is not simply the articulation of the story that is powerful to save. It is the events his preaching proclaims that are saving. Paul's preaching is merely a witness to these events. Nonetheless, when the gospel is proclaimed in the power of the Spirit, God's **power** (*dynamis*) is at work in the preaching. "The gospel is God's means of restoring righteous control over a disobedient creation" (Jewett 2007, 138).

Paul might have used *energeia* here, but his choice of *dynamis* puts the stress upon the Source rather than the process of God's power (Sanday and Headlam 1929, 23). God is the Source of our salvation, but he saves through the message of the gospel (see 1 Cor 1:18-25).

> And the implication is that God's power as it is operative unto salvation is through the gospel alone. It is the *gospel* which is God's power unto salvation. The message is God's word, and the word of God is living and powerful (see Heb 4:12). (Murray 1959, 27)

Those who attempt to exegete Rom 1:16-17 would do well to heed the warning of Ernst Käsemann: "The message of the NT soon would no longer be recognizable if exegesis were allowed to exploit every linguistic possibility" (1980, 282). Accordingly, in navigating through the swirling waters of these two verses, we would do well to permit the governing words in the passage to guide us: **salvation** (*sotēria*), **righteousness from God** (*dikaiosynē theou*), and **faith** (*pistis*). As we do, we must keep in mind Paul's understanding of his mission "to call people from among all the Gentiles to the obedience that comes from faith" (1:5).

Salvation is the clear emphasis of the passage. The salvation, which is the effect the gospel produces, is messianic salvation of the eschaton (= end time). It was inaugurated by the life, death, resurrection, and exaltation of Christ. As eschatological salvation, it was from the beginning marked by **power:** in Christ's miracles, in his victory over death, and subsequently in the work of the Holy Spirit (John 7:37-39; Acts 2:32-33). The gospel Paul preaches has the power to transform individuals and communities who hear and believe it. It is the "powers of the age to come" (Heb 6:5 NRSV) invading the present. Salvation means "deliverance from the present evil age and the restoration of wholeness . . . along with preservation from the wrath to come and the fulfillment of salvation when the new age is fully present" (Jewett 2007, 138).

Christ vs. Caesar

In contrast to the Roman imperial cult, which fancied the Caesars as saviors and benefactors of the universe, Paul offers a counterclaim. The gospel shatters the unrighteous precedence given to the strong over the weak, the free and well-educated over slaves and the ill-educated, the Greeks and Romans over the barbarians. If what the world considers dishonorable has power, it will prevail and achieve a new form of honor to those who have not earned it, an honor consistent with divine righteousness. All who place their faith in this gospel will be set right, that is, be placed in the right relation to the most significant arena in which honor is dispensed: divine judgment. Thus the triumph of divine righteousness through the gospel of Christ crucified and resurrected is achieved by transforming the system in which shame and honor are dispensed. The thesis of Romans therefore effectively turns the social value system of the Roman Empire upside down. (Jewett 2007, 139)

It is the anticipatory enjoyment of future salvation in the power of the gospel that is the key to Paul's thought. **The power of God for . . . salvation** is already at work in **everyone who believes.** In the strict sense of the Greek terms, believers are not finally saved; they are in the process of being saved. Paul's certainty of final salvation rests on the conviction that "Christ died for us" (Rom 5:8; see vv 9-10). In the meantime believers groan and travail as they await the redemption of their bodies, since they *were saved in hope* (8:24) only. But they have the help of the Spirit (8:26-27) until the final consummation of the work of salvation (13:11).

■ **17** The gospel is God's saving power for salvation, *because* in it **a righteousness from God** (*dikaiosynē theou*) **is** being **revealed** (1:17). A correct understanding is the key not only to this Epistle but to the gospel itself. Paul announces the apocalyptic and revelatory (Greek *apocalyptein*, "to reveal") character of the gospel: it has disclosed God's sovereign plan of end-time salvation for all humanity, proceeding from his righteousness and realized in the gospel Paul has been proclaiming.

Paul uses the verb *apocalyptetai* again in 1:18 with a different connotation: God reveals both his righteousness and his wrath in the gospel. The phrase *dikaiosynē theou* reappears in 3:5, 21-22. The genitive *theou*, "of God," is a possessive or subjective genitive, describing God's upright or righteous character or his righteous activity. When *dikaiosynē* is called a quality or attribute, nothing static is implied; it is an aspect of God's **power** (1:16), from which proceeds his saving activity (Fitzmyer 1993, 257).

In Romans *dikaiosynē* has the same range of meanings as "the righteousness of God" in the OT. In 3:21-22 and 10:3 it is used in the comprehensive sense of 1:17. In 2:5 it means the justly deserved punishment God will mete out on the day of judgment. In 3:5 it is the fidelity with which God keeps his promises. In 3:25-26 it describes the culminating exhibition of divine judgment on sin. The death of Christ is at once the proof of God's wrath against sin and the means by which his righteousness "goes forth" to justify the person who trusts in Jesus. In the death of his Son, God's righteousness becomes his saving mercy extended to all humanity. The way in which Paul speaks of the righteousness of God being revealed (*apocalyptetai*) in 1:17 requires that the genitive "of God" (NRSV) should be taken in the same way in 1:18, which refers to **the wrath of God . . . being revealed** [*Apocalyptetai*].

The **righteousness of God** certainly emphasizes that God is the author of this righteousness and believers its recipients. The genitive of author or origin is the obvious point of Phil 3:9, where Paul contrasts "a righteousness of my own that comes from the law" with "the righteousness that comes from God and is by faith. The gift character of "righteousness" seems also to be stressed in 1 Cor 1:30. Paul's use of *dikaiosynē theou* in 2 Cor 5:21 is unique and has no precedent in either the OT or the intertestamental literature (Fitzmyer 1993, 258).

But Käsemann insists that interpreters "can no longer be content to take Phil 3:9 as the normative key" to understanding the righteousness of God (1980, 26). God's righteousness indeed is his *gift* to us in Christ, but it is also his *demand* (see Rom 6:15-23; Greathouse 1998, 94-101). "Standing in salvation is both here and everywhere standing in obedience, that is, in the presence and under the power of Christ" (Käsemann 1980, 28-29). Otherwise we "separate the gift from the Giver."

The apostle's concern is not with sinlessness as freedom from guilt, but with freedom from the power of sin. . . . Righteousness is the power of God which has come on the scene in Christ and with justification, which effects new life in anticipation of bodily resurrection, and which sets us in its service. (Käsemann 1980, 172-77)

There can be no final justification apart from sanctification.

The third emphasis of Paul's gospel is that the saving power of God includes **all who have faith** (1:16; see 3:22; 4:11; 10:4, 11). That the gospel is for **all** does not ignore the history of salvation—**first to the Jew, then to the Greek** (1:16). "Salvation is a matter of faith, to which all of the Christian groups in Rome have equal access" (Jewett 2007, 140).

Although Käsemann properly grasped the cosmic dimensions of Paul's usage, he did not take account of the establishment of new forms of communalism in faith communities formed by those who accepted this message about being set right in Christ. It is the inclusive gospel of Christ that equalizes the status of Greeks and barbarians, wise and uneducated, Jews and Gentiles, which offers new relationships in communal settings to all on precisely the same terms. . . . The goal of divine righteousness is to establish salvation, which in the context of the expression "to all who have faith," implies the establishment of faith communities where righteous relationships are maintained. (Jewett 2007, 142)

The gospel transforms individuals within holy communities.

The gospel proclaims **a righteousness that is by faith from first to last** (1:17). The Greek expression *ek pisteōs eis pistin* (lit. *from faith to faith*), might be understood to modify the phrase **righteousness of God** (Cranfield 1975, 1:100). On this interpretation the sentence might be translated: ***In the gospel the righteousness of God is revealed—and that righteousness is from faith to faith.*** If it modifies the verb **revealed,** the translation would be: . . . ***the righteousness of God is revealed from faith to faith*** (Jewett 2007, 144).

From Faith to Faith

Jewett (2007, 143) calls attention to parallel expressions in the LXX and other Pauline letters:

- Ps 84:7a—The righteous "go from strength to strength" (NASB).
- Jer 9:3c—The unrighteous "proceed from evil to evil" (NASB).
- 2 Cor 2:15-16—"We are a fragrance of Christ to God among those who are being saved . . . an aroma from life to life," but to "those who are perishing . . . an aroma from death to death" (NASB).

- 2 Cor 3:18—Believers "are being transformed into the same image from glory to glory" (NASB).

Jewett takes *from faith to faith* to refer to "the missionary expansion of the gospel, which relies on the contagion of faith" (2007, 143). But it might equally be taken to refer to the progressive transformation God's righteousness effects within communities of faith.

The Greek expression might be translated *through faith for faith.* The gospel discloses a righteousness that is *based on faith and addressed to faith.* That is, the gospel presupposes that God is faithful to his covenant promises and calls for humans to respond in faithfulness to his saving initiative.

Nygren understands the expression "from faith to faith" as suggesting something like the Protestant formula *sola fide*—"faith alone." "When the righteousness of God is revealed in the gospel, it is to faith and faith alone" (1949, 78-79).

Faith is an attitude toward God which involves an attitude toward self—all trust in one's own deserving is shut out. This attitude of faith, Paul is going to insist in this letter, is the sole condition of salvation. (Knox 1951, 9:392)

To have faith is to accept the gospel, to open one's life to God's saving power. In support of this thesis Paul appeals to Hab 2:4: **The righteous will live by faith.** Curiously, Paul's citation is not identical to any surviving manuscript of the LXX nor to the standard Massoretic (MT) text of the Hebrew OT. All of these use a personal pronoun, which Paul omits in Rom 1:17 and Gal 3:11. The MT has *"his* faith." Most LXX manuscripts have *"my* faith." Some have *"my* righteous one," as does Heb 10:38.

Paul's quotation has been variously understood. Scholars debate whether Paul takes Habakkuk to mean "the righteous (one) shall live by faith" (Catholic) or "the one-who-is righteous-by-faith shall live" (Reformed). Richard B. Hays contends that the debate is pointless, since "no one seriously supposes that Paul reckons with the possibility of some hypothetical person who is *dikaios apart from* faith" (1983, 150).

The future tense verb, **will live,** is a logical, not a predictive future. It refers to the present experience of eschatological salvation (see Hab 3:18-19; Gal 3:11). "The phrase *ek pisteōs* ['by faith'] specifies the manner in which *ho dikaios* ['the righteous one'] shall find life (= be justified)" (Hays 1983, 151).

Hays considers two crucial questions: First, who is "the righteous one"? Interpreters typically take "the righteous" generically to refer to all who are justified by faith (e.g., Jewett 2007, 145). But a number of "new perspective" interpreters consider "the righteous one" a designation for the Messiah, as in Acts 3:14; 7:52; 22:14; 1 Pet 3:18; and 1 John 2:1 following Isa 53:10-12 (see Hays 1983, 151-54).

Second, by whose faith or faithfulness shall the righteous one live? Hays insists that the word **faith,** translating the Hebrew *emunah*, conveys the idea of steadfastness or fidelity. Likewise, the Greek *pistis* may mean both "fidelity" and "faith."

Paul's omission of the pronouns in his quotation of Hab 2:4 allows that salvation life comes because of God's faithfulness, the faithfulness of the Messiah, and the faith God's people place in him. Hays suggests that Paul held all of these at once.

Paul's gospel is founded upon the story of a Messiah who is vindicated (= "justified") by God through faith. This Messiah (Jesus Christ) is not, however, a solitary individual whose triumph accrues only to his own benefit, he is a representative figure in whom the destiny of all God's elect is embodied. Thus, all are justified through *his* faith. Their response to him, however, is also one of faith. (1983, 156-57)

In the light Christ sheds upon the prophet's statement, Paul understands Habakkuk to be speaking about righteousness by faith. "The Scripture foresaw that God would justify the Gentiles by faith, and announced the gospel in advance to Abraham: 'All nations will be blessed through you'" (Gal 3:8). Paul spills considerable exegetical ink in Gal 3 and 4 to prove that God's promised blessing of the Spirit was made to Abraham and to his offspring Jesus Christ and applied to all who by faith participate in him.

Paul quotes Habakkuk to establish his central thesis: The gospel reveals the righteousness of God through faith. Salvation depends entirely on the grace of God in Christ. It is Paul's purpose in this letter to show that we can neither justify nor sanctify ourselves. The words "He who through faith is righteous" (Rom 1:17 RSV) summarize and anticipate the message of 3:21—4:25. The words "shall live" (RSV) prepare for 5:1—8:39.

The closing words of 1:16, **first for the Jew, then for the Gentile** prepare for chs 9—11. This significant qualification underscores the truth that God's free gift of salvation, which makes possible "the obedience that comes from faith" (1:5), is promised to the *entire world!* "Everyone who calls on the name of the Lord will be saved" (10:13, citing Joel 2:32). Paul refuses to ignore the history of salvation, as if all God had done in Israel before the coming of Christ was inconsequential. One cannot simply obliterate the distinction between Jews and Gentiles without falling victim to the error of Marcionism.

FROM THE TEXT

Until the emergence of the "new perspective" on Romans, the prevailing Protestant understanding of Paul's gospel was an expression in one form or another of Luther's teaching that believers remain *simul justus et peccator*—"at the same time righteous and a sinner." While offering Christians freedom from paralyzing feelings of guilt and the sure hope of heaven, such a gospel leaves believers in the ethical predicament of Rom 7, crying out to the very end, "What a wretched man I am! Who will rescue me from this body of death?" (v 24). The implication is that Christ saves believers not *from* but *in* their sin! Roman Catholic scholars generally insisted that justification included moral renewal, as did Wesleyans, but with significant differences (see Greathouse and Dunning 1989, 82-83).

Luther also clearly taught the promise of new birth by the Spirit. It was this message found in Luther's *Preface to the Epistle to the Romans* that Wesley heard the night his heart was "strangely warmed" on Aldersgate Street. Luther's "Preface" was God's word to John Wesley and enabled him to "trust in Christ, Christ alone for salvation" and experience the new birth and the beginnings of sanctification. Yet, Luther had no *doctrine* of sanctification. He believed that original sin remained in Christians until they died. His personal pursuit of holiness and constant self-examination convinced him that he did not possess perfect love for either neighbor or God. Instead, he found himself consumed by self-love.

Calvin generally agrees with Luther on this point, pointing out that while for Paul "to justify" means simply to "acquit," or "confer a righteous status on," it cannot be separated from sanctification: "To 'imagine that Christ bestows free justification upon us without imparting newness of life' is shamefully to 'rend Christ asunder.'" Justification is indeed basic for Paul, Calvin continues, but "we cannot receive righteousness in Christ without at the same time laying hold on sanctification" (quoted in Cranfield 1975, 1:95).

Luther and Calvin agree that justification can never be separated from the new birth (or from *sanctification*, for Calvin). But both see believers helplessly locked in concupiscence. For both Reformers, *entire* sanctification awaits death or the return of Christ.

In his sermon "On God's Vineyard" Wesley summarizes how the doctrines of justification and sanctification as typically understood by Catholics and Protestants compare to the views of the people called Methodists.

They [Methodists] know, indeed, that at the same time a man is justified, sanctification properly begins. For when he is justified, he is "born again," "born from above," "born of the Spirit"; which, although it is not (as some suppose) the whole process of sanctification, is doubtless the gate of it. Of this, likewise, God has given them a full view. They know, the new birth implies a great change in the soul, in him that is "born of the Spirit," as was wrought in his body when he was born of a woman: Not an outward change only . . . but an inward change from all unholy, to all holy tempers, . . . from an earthly, sensual, devilish mind, to the mind that was in Christ Jesus. . . .

It is, then, a great blessing given to this people, that as they do not think or speak of justification so as to supersede sanctification, so neither do they think or speak of sanctification to supersede justification. They take care to keep each in its own place, laying equal stress on one and the other. They know God has joined these together, and it is not for man to put them asunder: Therefore they maintain, with equal zeal and diligence, the doctrine of free, full, present justification, on the one hand, and of entire sanctification both of heart and life, on the other; being as tenacious of inward holiness as any Mystic, and of outward, as any Pharisee. (Wesley 1979, 7:205)

A. God's Righteousness Needed (1:18—3:20)

1. The Human Predicament (1:18-32)

BEHIND THE TEXT

This first major subdivision of Romans is basic to the development of Paul's main theme. Humans have no claim to divine favor; the whole race of unbelievers exists under the wrath of God. Because they have turned from the Creator to the creature, all have become morally depraved. **Jews and Gentiles alike are all under sin. . . . "There is no one righteous, not even one"** (3:9-10). Consequently, no one is excused; the entire world stands guilty before God (vv 19-20). The whole of humanity is morally bankrupt, unable to claim a favorable verdict at the judgment bar of God, and desperately in need of his mercy, pardon, and healing.

It is possible to understand this passage merely as a description of the contemporary Gentile world in its idolatry and gross iniquity. But to limit this penetrating discussion to one period or segment of humankind is to miss God's word to us. Human **godlessness and wickedness** (1:18) permeate every age and culture. Paul's purpose is not to inform the Roman Christians about their pagan contemporaries; it is to show the sinful predicament of all of fallen humanity. This is the human situation apart from the redemptive power of God. "Humanity, as a result of its disobedience to God, has involved itself in a desperate and morally sick situation" (Leenhardt 1957, 60). "This section of the epistle speaks of human guilt and divine judgment in relation to Gentiles and Jews, who are viewed as representatives of humanity . . . as such, and not just with representatives of religious groupings" (Käsemann 1980, 33).

Humanity Under the Wrath of God

In his indictment of the world under **the wrath of God,** Paul begins, not with Moses, but with Adam. This concerns all of humanity in general. Genesis 1:27 literally reads: "So God created man ['ādam] in his own image, in the image of God created he him; male and female created he them ['ādam = him = them]" (KJV). The designation 'ādam is not singled out as an individual until 4:25.

Immediately thereafter, however, in 5:1-2, the narrative returns to ch 1: "When God created man ['ādam], he made him in the likeness of God. He created them *male and female* and blessed them. And when they were created, he called them 'man' ['ādam]" (emphasis added). This complex use of Adam is present throughout Romans. In one sense, "Each of us has become his own Adam" (*2 Bar.* 54:19, quoted in Käsemann 1980, 47).

Yet we are always in the continuity of the history initiated by Adam, which from Paul's standpoint does not atomize into moments. . . . For the apostle, history is governed by the primal sin of rebellion against the Creator, which finds repeated and universal expression. It is thus governed by the wrath of God, which throws the creature back on itself, corresponding to its own will, and abandons it to the world. (Käsemann 1980, 47)

This Hebraic understanding of 'ādam informs Paul's use of the Greek *anthrōpos* in Rom 1:18. Thus, the word translated "man" throughout refers to the figure called Adam in Gen 1. But both in Genesis and Romans, "man" = "Adam" refers to humanity rather than to a solitary individual.

God's judgment of all humanity in Rom 1:18—3:20 describes humanity as it appears in the light of the cross of Christ. It is not a description of especially wicked persons only, but the innermost truth of all of us, as we are in ourselves. That Paul in 1:18-32 has in mind primarily the Gentiles is certainly true. But we cannot do justice to the apostle's intention if we assume—as many interpreters seem inclined to do—that these verses refer exclusively to them.

In v 18 Paul uses the general term *anthrōpōn* ("of humanity") and nowhere speaks of either "Gentiles" or "Greeks." Paul's description of the human propensity for idolatry in v 23 echoes the language of the Old Testament, particularly Ps 106:20 and Jer 2:11. Both passages refer to *Israel's* idolatry— the first, to the golden calf incident; the second, to later unfaithfulness to God in favor of other gods. Clearly, Paul presumes that what he says about all humanity applies to Israel as well (so Jewett 2007, 152).

The main point of Rom 2:1—3:20 is precisely that the Jews, who think themselves entitled to sit in judgment on the Gentiles, are doing the very same things for which they condemn them. It follows, then, that, by describing the obvious sinfulness of the heathen, Paul was, in fact, describing the basic sinfulness of fallen humanity as such—"the inner reality of Israel no less than that of the Gentiles" (Cranfield 1975, 1:104). The correctness of this view is confirmed by the "therefore" at the beginning of 2:1. "If 1:18-32 does indeed declare the truth about *all* men, then it really does follow from it that the man who sets himself up to judge his fellows is without excuse" (Cranfield 1975, 1:105-6). So we understand the above verses to be the gospel's revelation of the idolatry ensconced in Israel as well as in paganism.

Paul's description of the symbiotic relationship between pagan idolatry and immorality is heavily indebted to the polemic against idolatry found in the Jewish-Hellenistic apocryphal Wisdom of Solomon (chs 11—15). Serious students would do well to read these chapters to appreciate how thoroughly Jewish Paul's understanding of human unrighteousness is.

IN THE TEXT

a. Introduction: The Wrath of God (1:18)

■ **18** The postpositive conjunction *gar*, **For,** introduces this section of the letter as a substantiation of the theme stated in 1:16-17. Here we have a description of "the deplorable state of human affairs" apart from the gospel (Jewett 2007, 151). Humanity's situation in sin is an existence under **the wrath of God**, which is **being revealed from heaven.** Sinful existence is characterized as attempting to **suppress the truth** about God.

The repetition of the present tense verb **revealed** (*apokalyptetai*) is proof of a double revelation—of "righteousness" (v 17) and of **wrath** (v 18). Just as "the righteousness of God" (NRSV) means the whole situation that exists when humans are right with God, so **the wrath of God** means the total situation that exists when humanity turns away from the Creator. This perspective must be widened to embrace the entire human race. Every person, without exception, knows either God's righteousness or God's wrath—his love or his displeasure, his saving power or his judgment. "In Christ," Luther once remarked, "'God is love.' Outside Christ, 'Our God is a consuming fire'" (citing 1 John 4:8 and Heb 12:29).

What is meant by **the wrath of God** (*orgē theou*)? The answer will not become clear until we answer the further question, What is meant by God's wrath **being revealed**? In only two other passages does Paul add to the word **wrath** the genitive qualifier **of God,** and he never uses the verb "to be angry" with God as the subject.

This has led some interpreters, among them C. H. Dodd, to define **wrath** in a wholly impersonal sense. Dodd claims that "to Paul, 'the wrath' meant, not a certain feeling or attitude of God towards us but the process or effect in the realm of objective facts" (1932, 20). Elsewhere the apostle warns that "a man reaps what he sows" (Gal 6:7), and that "the wages of sin is death" (Rom 6:23). Dodd and likeminded interpreters take this to mean that God has created a moral order in which sin is its own punishment and destruction. In this chapter divine wrath means that God gives sinners up to the consequences of their own rebellion and misdeeds (1:24-32). Thus, God's wrath is not his active intervention to add evil consequences as punishment for human rebellion and disobedience. The unpleasant results of sin are the "natural" consequence of choosing to live at odds with God's design for the universe. It is a bit like the consequences one suffers for spitting into the wind or attempting to defy the law of gravity. God does not have to intervene. Sin is its own punishment. "One is punished by the very things by which one sins" (Wis 11:16 NRSV).

Calvin comments here that "the word *wrath*, referring to God in human terms as is usual in scripture . . . implies no emotion in God, but has reference only to the feelings of the sinner who is punished" (1960, 30). God's wrath should not be misunderstood as a divine temper tantrum. God's wrath in the present is his unremitting resolve to reclaim his rightful reign over a race in rebellion and on the road to ruin. It is not about an emotion at all; it is about God's personal reaction against sin. Its present revelation is not to be seen in fire and brimstone falling on hapless sinners. Remarkably enough, Rom 1:24-32 insist that God's wrath is expressed in permissiveness, not peevishness. He lets his rebellious creatures have their own way and suffer the consequences. The punishment for sin is sin. Human law exacts no punishment of those who leap from skyscrapers. Like sin, its certain consequence is death—its own punishment.

Like salvation, wrath has present and future dimensions. The present revelation of wrath is not God's last word to unrepentant rebels, as we shall see in 2:5-11. In the meantime, sinners continue their free fall to doom, becoming more depraved on the way. Their only hope is repentance and rescue.

God's wrath is the dark side of his faithfulness to his creatures. For him to excuse sin would make him untrue to his own nature as God. For God to spare them the consequences of their choice of unworthy lords would be to encourage them in self-destructive folly. God loves his creation too much to be an enabler.

When creatures refuse to acknowledge God as Creator and Lord, they remove themselves from his lordship. Creatures *will* devote themselves to some lord. The only question is, Who or what will it be? Our lordship determines our character, the quality of our lives, and our destiny. Thus, in a sense, sinners experience **the wrath of God** as the apparently "natural" consequence of attempting to live at odds with the reality that the Creator exists and that creatures owe him their gratitude and worship. God's wrath is expressed in his refusal to spare sinners from the consequences of their self-destructive folly.

This is certainly true so far as it goes, but does it do justice the idea of *orgē theou* in our text? The manner in which Paul places **the wrath of God** against his "righteousness" in v 17 and uses the dynamic term **being revealed** in both cases suggests that **wrath** represents something in the attitude and purpose of God. In v 17 he has stated that God's righteousness is being revealed in the gospel, i.e., in the ongoing proclamation of the gospel. In view of the parallelism between vv 17 and 18, the most natural way of taking v 18 is to understand Paul to mean that **the wrath of God is being revealed** *in the gospel.*

But what is **being revealed** and where? What does one witness in this revelation? and, Where does one see it? Paul might mean by the revelation of **the wrath of God** in the gospel the visual portrayal of God's willingness to accept the awful consequences of sin witnessed historically in the violent death of Christ on the cross. Or, he might mean the vivid portrayal of this, which was "seen" in the preaching of the gospel (see Gal 3:1). Or, he might mean that the faithful preaching of the gospel must announce God's judgment on sin as well as his grace extended to sinners. Perhaps these possible meanings are not mutually exclusive.

The two revelations—of the righteousness and the wrath of God—in these verses are really two aspects of the same process. The preaching of Christ crucified, risen, ascended, and coming again is at the same time both the offer of God's righteousness to believers and the revelation of God's wrath against sin. In the gospel, divine mercy and divine judgment are inseparable from each other; the mercy offered us is no cheap grace or superficial pardon, but God's costly redemption. The reality of God's wrath is not truly known until it is seen in its revelation in Gethsemane and on Golgotha (see also Rom 3:24-26; Cranfield 1975, 1:110).

By revelation Paul does not refer to some private visionary experience, comparable to a waking dream, of divine origin. He simply refers to the making visible and known within the context of human history what was previously invisible and known only to God.

Since both "righteousness" and "wrath" are abstract verbal nouns, we must ask, What kind of visible or knowable activity underlies these terms? Paul does not think of the revelation of wrath as the unpleasant, tangible symptoms of human suffering inflicted by or permitted by God as punishment for sinning. Nor does he think of the revelation of righteousness as the visible rewards God showers upon believers in the form of, say, health and prosperity.

Simply put, for Paul this twofold revelation is witnessed in the Christ event. His life, death, and resurrection simultaneously demonstrate the righteousness of God and the wrath of God. This is what Paul means when he insists that the wrath as the well as the righteousness of God are **being revealed** in the gospel.

But God's wrath is also revealed **from heaven** (*ap' ouranou*). Paul employs the phrase **from heaven** in order to emphasize the utter seriousness of *orgē theou* as being really *God's* wrath (Cranfield 1975, 1:111). The expression **from heaven** repeats and emphasizes the point of the descriptive genitive—this display of wrath is **from God.** Paul's emphasis on the divine source of wrath undermines any notion of its impersonal character—this is no *natural* disaster.

God's wrath is no outburst of divine fury; it is the reaction of the holy and merciful God called forth by and directed against human **godlessness** and **wickedness.** In this disclosure, which takes place again and again in the preaching of the gospel, sin is unmasked and brought to light, while at the same time needy sinners are led to faith in the Crucified (see Gal 3:1-2).

The terms **godlessness** (*asebeia*) and **wickedness** (*adikia*) are better translated as *"un*godliness" and "unrighteousness," since each is preceded by the negative Greek *a*, which corresponds to the English "un": (*a-seibeia, a-dikia*). *Asebeia* derives from *sebomai*, which means, "I stand in awe," "worship," or "adore" and expresses itself as idolatry, the worship of the creature rather than the Creator (Rom 1:19-23).

Adikia means moral perversity and is illustrated by immorality—living at odds with what is right (vv 24-32). Both terms refer to the immoral lifestyle of those who live contrary to proper religious beliefs and practices. From the Jewish and Christian perspective, this would include the practice of idolatry. And from the Hellenistic-Jewish background (reflected in the apocryphal Wisdom of Solomon), idolatry is always associated with immorality.

Both sins express the willfulness of persons **who suppress the truth by their wickedness** (v 18; see v 25), i.e., the stubborn, self-willed thinking that insists on their own way. This is the lifestyle of lawless rebels who refuse to accept instruction. Suppressing the truth carries the notion of "holding back." Human immorality is due to willful ignorance, a rejection of revealed truth. This implies, as Paul will show, that all people have the truth and that by their unrighteousness they refuse to act upon it. Thus, all sin is positive resistance to God—rebellion.

The announcement of God's outpoured wrath on sinners lays the theological groundwork for the declaration of God's righteousness that follows in 3:21—8:39. Paul begins with a description of the human predicament in 1:18—3:20, before he offers its solution in the plan of God that rescues us in Christ.

Protestant interpreters generally equate Paul's theological logic with the order of salvation. If sinners are to seek divine help, it is not enough that they know such help is available; they must be convinced they desperately need it. Before God can save sinners, he must first pronounce them guilty. They must know themselves condemned in order to be saved. Condemnation is the first phase of salvation. Only those who know they are lost truly realize their desperate need of grace. And only those rescued from this extremity may be properly grateful to God for his undeserved deliverance. The "good news" implies the prerequisite proclamation of the "bad news" of **the wrath of God.**

But interpreters from the "new perspective" have challenged this Reformed consensus. E. P. Sanders (1985) insists that Paul did not know his plight until he encountered its solution in his encounter with the risen Christ. Some similarly "raised in the church" may come to appreciate the seriousness of the problem of sin only after they have been delivered from it and understand what this rescue exacted of God.

In Paul's case at least, there seems to be no indication that he first experienced a moral collapse before coming to faith in Christ. His "robust conscience" (Stendahl 1963) did not inflict him with guilt as a precondition for the Damascus Road event. It seems that only after his experience of deliverance did he come to appreciate the theological implications of it. Thus, his experience moved from solution to plight, despite the theological movement of Romans. It is dangerous to assume that Romans' exposition of the bad news first requires that this is necessarily the way the gospel must be preached and experienced.

b. Humanity's Original Sin (1:19-23)

Paul now tells us *how* sinful humans suppress the truth and *why* God's wrath is outpoured on them. Those who practice "wickedness" (1:18) are not the particularly reprehensible humans as distinguished from the masses. All humans apart from God's saving grace are wicked by definition. God's wrath is outpoured because humans refuse the knowledge of God offered by the Creator. Unrighteousness and wickedness are but symptoms of a more basic fault.

> All the perversions of life can be traced back to one fundamental cause, and this original sin is not to be found in the field of morals but in the soil of religion: perversion of life arises from perversion of faith. (Luthi 1961, 22)

■ **19** Humans have violated divine truth, Paul begins, **since what may be known about God is plain to them** [*phaneron estin en autois* = **is manifest in them**], **because God has made it plain to them** (v 19). The Greek expression means simply that any revelation must pass through human consciousness (Sanday and Headlam 1929, 42). "Divine truth" should not be thought of as an abstract body of useful information. That is, **what may be known about God** is simply that there is only one God and that he is the Creator of all that exists (see Ps 19 vs. Wis 13:1). The crime humans uniformly commit is idolatry—treating created things as if they were God. God **may be known** only because he *makes himself* known. Human discovery must be understood within the framework of divine disclosure; human realization of the truth that is God depends on divine revelation. But God has manifested himself plainly to all without exception.

■ **20** The **invisible** God has made himself known **since the creation of the world** (Rom 1:20). Although the phrase *apo ktiseōs kosmou* may be rendered "from the created universe," it is generally agreed that Paul's thought is temporal: *since the creation of the universe.* Ever since its origin, creation has revealed the mind of God.

Although God cannot be known directly through reason (1 Cor 1:21), he is knowable. This knowledge, however, is not forced upon a passive subject; to learn about God we must adopt a positive and receptive attitude. Creation exists as an invitation to dialogue with God. Certain things may be **clearly seen,** but only if we are willing to see.

Our contemplation of the world considered as a work of God has two objects: **his eternal power** and his **divine nature.** First, we are aware of our dependence upon a Power (*dynamis*) that presides over our existence. Through it we come into being, and in the face of it we know our nothingness. Moreover, when we consider the fleeting temporality of our own existence, this power we perceive to be **eternal.** It is not clear whether Paul thought of the experience of divine power in terms of what we call natural forces like wind, earthquakes, volcanoes, or of supernatural realities like miracles and other powerful spiritual manifestations, or both.

Second, we perceive the **divine nature** (*theiotēs*). The universe is not moved by blind power but by power that is divine in character—it is *God.* That is, what is **made plain** is that God is God and not a weak mortal. Observation of created life is sufficient to show that creation does not provide a key to its own existence.

We miss the point entirely if we take Paul as attempting to "prove" God's existence. In fact, the sins Paul castigates later in this chapter are not those of persons who do not believe in God but of those who *refuse to honor God as God.* This is why (*eis to,* **so that** as a result) sinners and unbelievers are **without excuse** (Rom 1:20; see 2:1). "God may rightly visit men with wrath because, though they may not have had the advantage of hearing the Gospel, they have rejected the rudimentary knowledge of God that was open to them" (Barrett 1957, 36).

■ **21** Sinful humanity suppresses the truth about God by silent ingratitude. Their sinful predicament consists in this: **although they knew God, they neither glorified him as God nor gave thanks to him** (v 21). As creatures, we owe our Creator praise and thanksgiving (see the sidebar "Glory" in connection with the commentary on 8:18-27). Glorifying God and giving him thanks "are comprehensive descriptions of human obligations toward God" (see 4:20; 15:6, 9; Jewett 2007, 156). To do so is not merely to acknowledge his existence but to recognize his lordship and to live in grateful obedience to him (see Isa 1:3; *2 Bar.* 48:40; 82:3-9).

Human pride refuses to acknowledge that God is God (and that we are not) and so fails to give him the grateful praise he is due. Preoccupied with ourselves, we turn away from God as the center of our being and source of our happiness—we turn from divine love to inordinate self-love. We are unwilling to recognize the Lord as the ground of our being; we choose instead to be lord ourselves and to glorify ourselves. This idolatrous setting up of self as the (false) end of life is humankind's original sin and the source of all our misery. Abraham is the father of all believers, because in contrast to what humanity as a whole refused to do, he "gave glory to God" (Rom 4:20; see also 15:9).

By suppressing the truth about God, humans made themselves victims of self-deception. Because they turned away from God, **their thinking** [*dialogismois, **reasonings***] **became futile and their foolish hearts were darkened** (v 21). *Dialogismos* is almost always used in both the LXX and NT in a bad sense as "perverse, self-willed reasonings and speculations" (Sanday and Headlam 1929, 44). Unlike earlier Jewish sources (see Ps 94:11; *1 En.* 99:7-8; *T. Levi* 14:4), Paul identifies suppressing the truth about God, rather than idolatry (see Rom 1:23), as the root sin.

Paul's Jewish background is obvious in his use of the word **heart** (*kardia*). It is used metaphorically as the organ of feeling (9:2), thought (10:6), and will (1 Cor 4:5; 7:37), the inward, hidden self (Rom 2:29; 8:27). Paul claims that the **darkened,** disabled, and distorted center of human affections, intellect, and volition due to universal rejection of God is a revelation of his wrath.

■ **22** Humans claim to be **wise** but become **fools** (v 22) by denying God his rightful place. Paul shares the view of the psalmists who consider fools those practical atheists who live as if there were no God (Pss 14:1; 53:1). Totally out of touch with reality, pretentious human speculations are actually senseless folly.

■ **23** Because they suppressed the truth about God, they invented human "religion." They **exchanged** [*ēllaxan;* see Rom 1:25-26] **the glory of the immortal God for images made to look like mortal man and birds and animals and reptiles** (v 23; see Ps 106:20; Jer 2:11). This illustrates the depths of folly to which reasoning sinks when humans reject God. "They got God down on two legs, then down on all fours, then down on the belly!" (Quimby 1950, 45-46). While they **claimed to be wise, they became fools** [*morons; emōranthēsan;* Rom 1:22]!

c. Humanity's Moral Depravity (1:24-32)

Paul now describes the shameful moral consequences of humankind's rebellion against God. If the *root* of human sin is religious perversity, the *fruit* is moral corruption. Cut off from the Source of life and happiness, humans seek satisfaction in the creature. Deprived of the life of God, humanity fell into depravity. In so doing, they became helpless slaves to the creature.

It is the curse of moral depravity that has befallen humankind—the curse theologians have for centuries called "the fall"—that Paul depicts in the remainder of this chapter. Three times he repeats the phrase **God gave them over** (vv 24, 26, 28), expressing with horrifying emphasis the devastating consequences of humanity's revolt. God has given the rebellious human race over to moral depravity expressed as sensuality (vv 24-25), sexual perversion (vv 26-27), and antisocial living (vv 28-32).

(1) Sensuality (1:24-25)

■ **24** The conjunction **therefore** (v 24) indicates that the retribution Paul describes is a just consequence of the antecedent sin of human rebellion (vv 18-23). Unbridled human sensuality, contrary to the notions of those who delight in it, is a disaster—the divine curse people suffer because they reject God. When humans reject God, God gives them what they want—the **desires of their hearts** (v 24). But their distortion of the truth about God and their twisted appetites result in self-destructive consequences. The first is moral **impurity** [*akatharsian*], which consists in the **dishonoring** [*atimazesthai*] **of their bodies with one another.** When humans refuse to honor God as God, they dehumanize and dishonor themselves.

■ **25** Inhumane humans have, to their own hurt, **totally** exchanged [*metēllaxan*; see vv 23, 26] **the truth of God** [see v 18] **for a lie** (*tōi pseudei, the lie;* v 25). The **truth** is that God alone is God; the **lie** is the exaltation of creature above **the Creator—who is forever praised. Amen.** While the immediate reference is to pagan immorality, Paul's ultimate reference is to the self-degrading desires of every human heart.

The **lie** is the creature's idolatrous usurpation of the divine glory. In the garden, the crafty serpent lied to the first pair, promising that if they should assert their independence of the Creator *they* would be "like God" (Gen 3:4-5) in power and wisdom. The unspeakable and irreparable conclusion of sin is the refusal to love **the truth** and to believe the **lie** (see 2 Thess 2:9-12). "In the light of the gospel, Paul has radicalized the story of the fall by emphasizing the element of willful distortion" (Jewett 2007, 170; see 190).

To refuse to reject the **lie** and not to believe **the truth** is to apostatize. Apostasy brings an end to the ability to make sound moral judgments, to do what is right. *Deprived* of a right relationship with God, humans become totally *depraved*. Such is the incurable religiousness of the human heart that, since they would not worship **the Creator,** they **worshiped** [*esebasthēsan*] **and served** [*elatreusan*] "the creature" (RSV) instead. In the Roman imperial religion the Greek title *Sebastos*, "the worshiped one," in its Latin form is "Augustus." Although we associate this title with the first Roman emperor, Octavian, it was used in the full names of all subsequent emperors. "Paul's audience could scarcely have missed this allusion to the most prominent form of 'venerating the creature' in Rome" (Jewett 2007, 170).

(2) Sexual Perversion (1:26-27)

■ **26 Because of this,** because godless humans gave themselves over to sensuality, **God gave them over to shameful** [*atimias,* ***dishonorable***] **lusts** (v 26; see v 24). Paul cites as examples of such enslaving and perverse passions same-sex intercourse—the **unnatural** [*para physin,* ***against nature***] practices of both lesbianism and homosexuality. Although the former was universally deplored, the latter was almost universally accepted in the Greco-Roman world of Paul's day. Consistent "with all other known branches of ancient Judaism and early Christianity" Paul presumed that "heterosexuality was part of the divinely created order for humankind" (Jewett 2007, 177).

Paul can only conceive of sexual relations with persons of the same gender as the perversion of a sacred gift (see 1 Cor 6:9-10). Despite the apostle's personal preference for celibacy, he considered sex God's gift for the procreation of the human race (Gen 1:27-28, 31) and personal fulfillment in a monogamous marriage (2:18-24; 1 Cor 7:1-7).

■ **27** To be **inflamed with lust for one another** (Rom 1:27) refers to the intense unnatural passion; it is not to be confused with the burning of 1 Cor 7:9, which finds its natural outlet in marriage. Here it is "the burning of an insatiable lust that has no natural or legitimate desire of which the lust is a perversion or distortion. It is lust directed to something that is essentially and under all circumstances illegitimate" (Murray 1959, 48). Perverted sexual passion as irrational, unsatisfying, and animalistic is a form of slavery (see Jewett 2007, 178-81).

Homosexual Behavior

The violation of the created order in human sexuality is, as Paul understood it, an outgrowth of the violation of the created order, a violation whose roots lie in self-deception and idolatry. For Paul, the kind of life he describes—**women** [*thēleiai, females*] **exchanged** [*metēllaxan;* see Rom 1:23, 25] **natural relations for unnatural ones.... Men** [*arsenes, males*] **committed indecent acts with other men** (vv 26-27)—cannot be understood as an alternate lifestyle, somehow also acceptable to God.

Homosexual behavior is, as Paul understands it, just one of the forms God's wrath takes when he allows sinful humanity free reign to abuse creation and one another. Such conduct may not be celebrated as another expression of God's grace. It is clearly portrayed here as a sign of God's wrath (Achtemeier 1985, 41). Despite the claims of some recent advocacy scholarship, Paul rejects all homosexual conduct, not just pederasty and homosexual rape. Furthermore, he would find wholly inconceivable "the modern concept of individual sexual orientation based on biological differences" (Jewett 2007, 176, 177, and n. 140).

Paul nowhere suggests that the sin of lesbian or homosexual practice is somehow more perverse than any other sin. In fact, many of the sins he mentions in his lurid exposé of humanity's downward spiral into depravity are often ignored by the same Christians who most loudly denounce homosexuality (see v 29).

Richard B. Hays' exposition of Paul's treatment of homosexuality in this passage is faithful but restrained:

> God's wrath takes the form of letting human idolatry run its own self-destructive course. Homosexual activity, then, is not a *provocation* of 'the wrath of God' (Rom. 1:18); rather, it is a *consequence* of God's decision to "give up" rebellious creatures to their own futile thinking and desires. The unrighteous behavior catalogued in Romans 1:26-31 is a list of *symptoms:* the underlying sickness of humanity as a whole, Jews and Greeks alike, is that they have turned away from God and fallen under the power of sin (see 3:9). . . .
>
> Paul singles out homosexual intercourse for special attention because he regards it as providing a particularly graphic image of the way in which human fallenness distorts God's created order [Gen. 1:27; 2:24]. God the Creator made man and woman for each other, to cleave together, to be fruitful and multiply. When human beings "exchange" these created roles for homosexual intercourse, they embody the spiritual condition of those who 'exchange the truth about God for a lie.' . . .
>
> Homosexual activity will not *incur* God's punishment: it is its own punishment, an "antireward." Paul here simply echoes a traditional Jewish idea. The Wisdom of Solomon, an intertestamental writing that has surely informed Paul's thinking in Romans 1, puts it like this: "Therefore those who lived unrighteously, in a life of folly, [God] tormented through their own abominations" (Wisdom of Solomon 12:23). . . .
>
> Repeated again and again in recent debate is the claim that Paul condemns only homosexual acts committed promiscuously by heterosexual persons—because they "*exchanged* natural intercourse for unnatural." Paul's negative judgment, so the argument goes, does *not* apply to persons who are "naturally" of homosexual orientation. This interpretation, however, is untenable. The "exchange" is not a matter of individual life decisions; rather, it is Paul's characterization of the fallen condition of the pagan world. In any case, neither Paul nor anyone else in antiquity had a concept of "sexual orientation." To introduce this concept into this passage (by suggesting that Paul disapproves only those who act contrary to their individual sexual orientations) is to lapse into anachronism. The fact is that Paul treats *all* homosexual activity as prima facie evidence of humanity's tragic confusion and alienation from God the Creator. (1996, 388-89)

The words **received in themselves the due penalty for their perversion** (Rom 1:27) refer to the thought expressed in vv 24-26; divine abandonment to immorality is the judicial consequence of human rebellion. The **penalty** for abandonment to sexual indulgence is probably "the growing unsatisfied lust itself, together with the dreadful physical consequences of debauchery" (Shedd quoted in Murray 1959, 48). Some interpreters speculate that Paul may have thought of these "dreadful physical consequences" as some kind of sexually transmitted disease. This description of the moral squalor of sinful humankind prepares us for the verse that follows.

(3) Antisocial Living (1:28-32)

Paul has selectively described the "ungodliness" of the world—its rebellion and idolatry. Its self-inflicted punishment is sensuality and sexual perversion. He now describes the other aspect of the world's sin—"unrighteousness"—and its punishment, "hardboiled and disruptive living" (Quimby 1950, 4).

■ **28** The apostle writes, **Since they did not think it worthwhile to retain the knowledge of God, he gave them over to a depraved mind** (v 28). The term **depraved** (*adokimon*) is literally "not standing the test." We find a play on words here: "As they did not *see fit* to take cognizance of God, God handed them over to an *unfit* mind" (Barrett 1957, 39). By rejecting God from their minds, they lost their minds, so to speak.

The evidence of this **depraved mind** is the practice of those things that **ought not to be done**. The phrase *ta mē kathēkonta* is a technical expression employed by Stoic writers, which may be rendered "things which are not proper" (NASB) or simply "improper conduct" (RSV). For Paul depravity is not expressed primarily in the character flaws of weak, perverse individuals, but in interpersonal relations and social systems gone amuck. The entire human race stands in depraved solidarity.

■ **29** The chaotic catalog of social vices in vv 29-31 apparently follows no rigorously systematic order, although Godet detects a grouping of associated ideas. The first four expressions of social pathology—**wickedness, evil, greed and depravity** (v 29*a*)—refer to injustices respecting the well-being and properties of others. The next five—**envy, murder, strife, deceit and malice** (v 29*b*)—are injustices harming the persons of our neighbors. The next six dispositions of the depraved mind center on pride—**gossips, slanderers, God-haters, insolent, arrogant and boastful** (vv 29*c*-30*a*). The last seven terms—**invent**ing **ways of doing evil, . . . disobeying parents**, being **senseless, faithless, heartless, ruthless** (vv 30*b*-31)—relate to the destruction of natural sentiments and affections (Godet 1883, 110-11).

This inventory of the evil deeds of humanity conforms to a widespread custom among both Jewish and pagan moralists of making lists of virtues and vices for pedagogical purposes (Leenhardt 1957, 70; see Jewett 2007, 183-90). Unlike most such moralists, Paul shows no interest in genetic tables of vices, showing how one vice leads to another. His point is that all vices "ultimately derive from the same primal lie" (Jewett 2007, 185). Although standard word-study resources should be consulted for detailed explanations, we summarize the "lowlights" here.

Every kind of wickedness (*adikia*; v 29*a*; see v 18) comprehends all the vices that follow. **Evil** (*ponēria*) conveys the idea of "active mischief" (Sanday and Headlam 1929, 47). **Greed** (*pleonexia*, **covetousness**)—the insatiable desire to have more—has a long history in Greek ethical writing.

> Its general connotation is that of ruthless, aggressive self-assertion. In Plato, for example, it is the characteristic vice of a tyrant; and all through Greek literature it describes the man who will pursue his own interests with complete disregard for the rights of others and for all consideration of humanity. (Dodd 1932, 27)

Such ruthless grasping may express itself in sexual relations but equally in other forms of conspicuous consumption. **Depravity** (*kakia*, **badness**) denotes a vicious inner disposition (Sanday and Headlam 1929, 47).

The next group of vices (v 29*b*) embrace social injustices injuring our neighbors. The adjective **filled with** (*mestous*) means literally "stuffed" (Godet 1883, 110). Classical writers frequently associated **envy** (*phthonou*) with **murder** (*phonou*) because they sounded alike; "besides, envy leads to murder, as is shown by the example of Cain" (Godet 1883, 110). If envy does not go so far as to destroy another, it always leads to **strife** (*eridos*; see Gal 5:26—6:5). Other ways to injure our neighbors include cheating them—**deceit** (*dolou*, **baiting**; see 1 Thess 2:3-8)—or making their lives miserable—**malice** (*kakoētheias*).

■ **30** **Gossips, slanderers, God-haters, insolent, arrogant and boastful** (Rom 1:29*c*-30*a*) describe sinners guilty of the vice of pride in one form or another. **Gossips** (*psithyristas*) poison their neighbors' listening ears privately; **slanderers** (*katalalous*) blacken their reputations publicly. **God-haters** (*theostygeis*) are "those who see that His justice stands in the way of their wickedness" (Calvin 1960, 38). **Insolent** (*hybristas*) is from *hybris*, the most cruel of all sins in the eyes of the Greeks. It is mingled pride and cruelty. "*Hybris* is the pride which makes a man defy God, and the arrogant contempt which makes him trample on the hearts of his fellow man" (Barclay 1957, 84-85). Jewett translates the term "bullies" (2007, 187). Such arrogant persons are inevitably **boastful** (*alazonas*), for they seek to attract admiration by claiming advantages they do not really possess.

■ **31** The last group of vices describes the deeds and dispositions of sinners: They **invent ways of doing evil, disobey their parents, are senseless, faithless, heartless, ruthless** (vv 30*b*-31). Sin's numbing effects include "the extinction of all the natural feelings of humanity, filial affection, loyalty, tenderness and pity" (Godet 1883, 111). Those who **invent ways of doing evil** spend their lives thinking up new ways of inflicting evil upon others. This is how the author of 2 Macc 7:31 characterizes the vicious tyrant Antiochus IV Epiphanes, who tried to destroy Judaism during the second century B.C. by making its practice a capital crime.

Both Jewish (Deut 21:18-21) and Roman law (see Jewett 2007, 188) called for the death penalty for those who **disobey their parents.** The next four vices all begin with an alpha-privative, characterizing evil persons in terms of what they lack. The **senseless** (*asynetous*) refuse to listen to counsel or heed advice from anyone (see Ps 32:8-9). In Greek the next word differs from the previous by the addition of a single letter—a theta (*th* in transliteration).

Those who are **faithless** (Rom 1:31) (*asynthetous*) are "covenantbreakers" (KJV) and "untrustworthy" (NASB). They are so self-centered they lack any sense of duty. The Greek word translated **heartless** (*astorgous*) is a negative form of one of the several Greek terms for "love" (*stergein*, **to have parent-child affection**)—cherish, foster, or caress. They are so narcissistic they lack all feelings of familial tenderness (see 2 Tim 3:3). To be **ruthless** (*aneleēmonas*) is to be "without . . . pity" (REB) or **unmerciful.** Such people not only lack natural affection but also applaud the flow of blood in gladiatorial contests and remain callously unmoved by the spectacle of human calamity or misery.

■ **32** Persons such as Paul has described, who **know God's righteous decree that those who do such things deserve death, . . . not only continue to do such things but also approve of those who practice them** (Rom 1:32). Because such antisocial behaviors were universally recognized as vicious, they were inexcusable. Paul had no doubt that his Roman audience would agree that such deeds **deserve death** "as God only can inflict it, the pains of Hades" (Godet 1883, 111).

The final clause of v 32 has been variously understood. It might suggest that encouraging others to commit such sins is worse than doing them oneself (Barrett 1957, 41). But Paul's point is rather that sinners eventually become so "deprived of discernment" that they abandon all sense of decency, "not only doing evil, but applauding those who do it!" (Godet 1883, 111).

As if it were not bad enough to do such evil, sinners find it entertaining and applaud the evil deeds of others in the shows and theater (Käsemann 1980, 52). Sin unchecked finally leads to a general breakdown of civility. "Not only are these terrible things done, but they are done with the tacit if not expressed approval of the whole society" (Knox 1951, 9:404). God has apparently withdrawn himself from such a society, leaving it not only in sin but in the darkness it has perversely chosen by suppressing the truth about God.

We miss Paul's point entirely if we assume the stance of the self-satisfied critic described in Rom 2:1-3. Even those who certainly do *not* approve of the disgusting assemblage of sinful vices the apostle collects in 1:28-32 will not be let off the hook. No one is morally superior simply because he or she is innocent of the more reprehensible sins of fallen humanity.

Paul's vice list is not an attempt to sketch a complete and exact portrait of humanity apart from God, left to its own devices (see 1 Cor 2:14). He knew that some Gentiles fulfilled many of the prescriptions of the Law (Rom 2:14), and that Greek and Roman moral philosophers condemned many of the forms of depravity he had described.

No sinner embodies all the depravity Paul describes. His concern is not just the faults of individuals, but social pathologies. We may find it easy to dismiss this indictment of sinful humanity, "I'm certainly not *that* bad." But we may not grade ourselves by comparison with other sinners; we must examine ourselves in light of the righteousness of God.

Self-examination is intended to bring us to the realization that each of us stands in solidarity with Adam and that every human social institution is ravaged to its depths by sin. We must confess, no matter what sin we see others committing, "But for the grace of God, there go I!" And as a part of fallen human society, I am complicit in its dysfunction. Paul writes not as a moralist but as a preacher of the gospel, in order to make us realize that apart from divine grace, we *all* stand under **the wrath of God** (v 18)!

FROM THE TEXT

Paul's essential point in Rom 1:18-32, as Hays correctly recognizes, is that human unrighteousness

> consists fundamentally in a refusal to honor God and render him thanks (1:21). . . . The genius of Paul's analysis lies in his refusal to posit a catalog of sins as the cause of human alienation from God. Instead, he delves to the root: all other depravities follow from the radical rebellion of the creature against the Creator (1:24-31). As Ernst Käsemann comments, "Paul paradoxically reverses the cause and consequence: moral perversion is the result of God's wrath, not the reason for it. . . ." The whole passage is "Paul's real story of the universal fall." (1996, 384, 385)

Theologically, Rom 1:18-32 supports a doctrine of original sin, but not necessarily its familiar Augustinian version.

According to Augustine, humankind was created holy. However, created out of nothing as he was, Adam tended to lapse back into nothingness and choose the lesser for the greater good. So Adam fell through *pride*, putting himself before God. As a consequence of his pride, humankind was cursed with *concupiscence*, expressed as idolatry and fleshly lust. Fallen in Adam, our moral will is now in bondage to sin. We still possess freedom of will in the ordinary sense of the term, in the sense that our acts are our own. But one thing we cannot do—we cannot choose God and live for him instead of self. The only way this is possible is by the infusion of divine grace, which liberates our will from sinful bondage, to serve God. This infused grace is irresistible and bestowed only on the elect. The rest of humankind is either left to die in their sins, or they are positively predestined to damnation. This came later to be called the doctrine of *double* predestination, an idea adopted and refined by Calvin.

According to Pelagius, the fall did not result in human depravity. Each of us is Adam of our own soul; original sin consists in the *imitation of Adam*. Even as sinners we possess free will—the power of choosing God and salvation. Each of us may of our own free will choose God and live, and carry through in complete obedience to perfection. In this choice God's grace assists us, but this grace is not essential to personal salvation. We initiate our salvation, God responds. Salvation is thus *synergistic,* a cooperative endeavor between us and God.

According to John Wesley, both Augustine and Pelagius are partly right. For Augustine, salvation is monergistic, wholly of God. For Pelagius, it is really a human work. Wesley avoids both extremes by his twin doctrines of original sin and prevenient grace. Wesley views humanity as *fallen in Adam.* Thus fallen, we are totally depraved, devoid of all good. The only freedom we have is the freedom to sin (following Augustine). Wesley also sees us as *recipients of prevenient grace through Christ.* This grace universally counteracts depravity. God's Spirit, who can be resisted, frees us sufficiently to enable us to choose Christ and live (following James Arminius). Wesley holds together human inability and personal responsibility. Because of original sin, we are unable of ourselves to turn and be saved. But because of prevenient grace, we have the God-given power to respond to his offer of salvation. For Wesley, the so-called natural man is an abstraction (1979, 6:512). No one, no matter how depraved, is totally devoid of grace.

2. God's Righteous Judgment (2:1-16)

BEHIND THE TEXT

A large part of the religion of some people seems to consist in their readiness to find fault with others. Such is the flaw of the interlocutor whom Paul addresses here in diatribe style. In contrast to the flood of pagan pollution Paul pictured in the preceding chapter, here is one who, like a judge, from his tribunal, sternly condemns the corrupt masses and the evil that pervades society, applauding God's wrath against it. Who is this self-appointed judge? Paul begins in 2:1 by addressing this person directly: *ho anthrōpe pas ho krinōn,* literally, "O human being who passes judgment!" (see v 3).

F. F. Bruce considers it possible that the hypothetical judge may have represented a Greek or Roman moralist like Paul's Stoic contemporary, Seneca. In contrast to the depraved pagan world characterized in ch 1, Seneca exalted moral virtues, exposed hypocrisy, and stressed the pervasive character of evil. "All vices," he wrote, "exist in all men, though all vices do not stand out predominantly in each man." He taught and practiced daily self-examination, ridiculed vulgar idolatry, and assumed the role of a moral guide. Yet he tolerated vices in himself not so different from those he condemned in others—the most flagrant being his complicity in Nero's murder of his mother Agrippina!" (Bruce 1963, 87).

Most modern commentators, however, agree that the critic represents a Jew who thinks himself morally superior to pagans. In 2:17 a hypothetical "Jew" is explicitly mentioned as Paul's dialogue partner. Verses 1-16 constitute an implicit indictment of Jews, which becomes overt only in v 17. Thus, Paul forces the Jewish judge to pass judgment on himself (Fitzmyer 1993, 297).

Regardless, the clear point of Rom 1:18—3:20 remains: Gentiles and Jews alike, moral and immoral alike—all humanity stands guilty before God as responsible sinners. To say they are "responsible sinners" is not to exonerate them, as if they sinned less offensively than most. It is to indicate that, from Paul's perspective, their sin is inexcusable—since they knew better, they are fully responsible for their sinful choices.

The evidence that the apostle is thinking primarily of Jews already in 2:1-16 is persuasive. Note his repetition of the phrase, **first for the Jew, then for the Gentile** (vv 9, 10). The propensity to judge Gentiles for their religious and moral perversity was characteristic of Jews, who were intensely conscious of their high privilege and prerogative as members of the chosen community of Israel.

Paul's account of pagan immorality in ch 1 is clearly indebted to the indictment of paganism preserved in the Hellenistic-Jewish apocryphal work known as the Wisdom of Solomon (chs 11—14). Paul addresses his interlocutor as one who enjoys in a special way **the riches of [God's] kindness, tolerance and patience** (2:4), as a covenant privilege. Paul's argument that special privilege or advantage does not exempt anyone from the judgment of God (vv 3, 6-11) seems particularly addressed to Jews (see Amos 3:2). Finally,

> the express address to the Jew in verse 17 would be rather abrupt if now for the first time the Jew is directly in view, whereas if the Jew is the person in view in the preceding verses then the more express identification in verse 17 is natural. (Murray 1959, 55-56)

Already in Rom 2:1-11, Paul insists that all human beings must stand before the tribunal of divine justice, to be judged according to their deeds. He contends that **doing good** (vv 7 and 10) is an essential requirement for a favorable judgment. This is no contradiction of his gospel of justification by faith, as some contend. Paul clearly expects good deeds as the fruit of justifying faith.

Jews are no exception to Paul's teaching; no one comes to salvation without God's grace; no one comes to justification on the basis of deeds only. Justification by faith must issue in a life of "true righteousness and holiness" (Eph 4:24; see 2:8-10).

IN THE TEXT

■ **I** Paul has so far emphasized the visible degradation of the world that has rejected the truth of God and stands under God's wrath for refusing to acknowledge God as God (Rom 1:18-32). But he knew there were those who joined in condemnation of such human wickedness, and he imagines one such critic objecting, "Yes, that's what the pagan world looks like. But surely you don't class me with such riffraff? They are lost, but as for us, we are neither lost, nor do we need the Savior you proclaim." In addressing this self-righteous critic, Paul spells out God's righteous judgment: **You, therefore, have no excuse, you who pass judgment on someone else, for at whatever point you judge the other, you are condemning yourself, because you who pass judgment do the same things** (2:1).

Paul addresses his readers in the ancient diatribe style. They are to imagine the apostle face-to-face with a heckler who interrupts his argument from time to time with objections. Paul anticipates potential objections based on more than two decades of missionary preaching. He heads off false conclusions with a "By no means!" (*mē genoito*—3:6; 6:1; 7:7; 9:14; see 4:1-12 and 8:31). Then he demolishes their perverse logic with reasonable answers. We may not reconstruct Romans Christianity based on such objections. But they probably do give us a glimpse of challenges Paul had faced elsewhere.

Therefore (*dio*) connects Paul's indictment of Gentile sinners to that of all Jews as equally sinful. Not until 2:17 does he specifically mention Jews. In vv 9-10 and 12-16, his condemnation is as applicable to morally discerning Gentiles as to Jews. But he seems to have primarily Jews in mind, although his argument is general enough to include other similar critics. Paul will apply the general principles of judgment in vv 1-16 explicitly to Jews in vv 17-29, with telling effect.

Therefore links 1:18-32 and 2:1-16 with repeated references to judgment (1:32; 2:1, 2, 3, 5), wicked practices (*prassō*, do/*practice*, in 1:32; 2:1, 2, 3; and *poieō*, do, in 1:28, 32; 2:3), and the expression **have no excuse** (harking back to 1:20). Just as those "who suppress the truth by their wickedness"

(1:18) are "without excuse" (v 20), so are those who **judge the other** [*ton heteron*; see 13:8] and yet **do the same things** (2:1 and 3). Judges are without excuse, because, although they know the Law, they condemn in others what they permit in themselves.

Paul could be certain that no one in his Roman audience approved of hypocritical bigots. Who would suspect that his rhetoric would be turned against them in ch 14? Jewett contends that this passage "provides the premises for an ethic of mutual tolerance between the competitive house and tenement churches in Rome, which could enable them to participate with integrity in the Spanish mission" (2007, 197).

The clue to ch 2 is the final clause of v 1. Self-appointed judges do the same things as those they condemn; that is, they refuse to honor God as God and to him give thanks, and yet they claim to be wise (see 1:21-22). Behind all sins in the catalog lies the sin of suppressing the truth about God and the human ambition to put self in the place of God. This is precisely what people do when they assume the right of condemning others. Spiritual pride and censoriousness cut them off from the love of God as surely as theft or adultery. God alone is qualified to judge (see 14:4, 10, 13; Matt 7:1-5; Luke 6:37; 1 Cor 4:5).

■ **2** Paul can be as certain that his audience rejects both pious frauds and pagan immorality. **Now we know that God's judgment against those who do such things is based on truth** (Rom 2:2). Those who "suppress the truth" (1:18) will find this "truth" used against them in the judgment. Paul elsewhere uses the expression **we know** to refer to generally accepted Christian assumptions (see 3:19; 7:14; 8:22, 28; 1 Cor 8:1; 2 Cor 5:1; Jewett 2007, 198). Here the assumption is that God's judgment is impartial (see Rom 2:11).

■ **3** Paul again addresses his imaginary critic: **So when you, a mere man, pass judgment on them and yet do the same things, do you think you will escape God's judgment?** (v 3). The second **you** is emphatic: Do you suppose that *you* of all people will escape? (Sanday and Headlam 1929, 55). The pretentious bigot undoubtedly did suppose this, imagining himself exempt from God's judgment, and instead "the object of God's kindness" (Barrett 1957, 43).

■ **4** Jews accepted their special relationship with God as a proof of divine partiality in their behalf. Paul considers such presumption concerning their exceptional status before God as no better than pagan ingratitude (see 1:21). **Or do you show contempt for** [*kataphroneis*, **despise**; see Hos 6:7] **the riches of his kindness, tolerance and patience, not realizing that God's kindness leads you toward repentance?** (Rom 2:4). These familiar attributes of God are deeply embedded in Jewish tradition and early Christianity.

Paul freely adopts the list of pagan vices found in the Wisdom of Solomon (ch 14). But he totally rejects Wisdom's assumption that Jews are not sinners like the Gentiles and are, therefore, exempt from God's judgment:

But you, our God, are kind and true,

patient, and ruling all things in mercy.

For even if we [Jews] sin we are yours, knowing your power;

but we will not sin, because we know that you acknowledge us as yours.

For to know you is complete righteousness,

and to know your power is the root of immortality.

For neither has the evil intent of human art misled us,

nor the fruitless toil of painters,

a figure stained with varied colors,

whose appearance arouses yearning in fools,

so that they desire the lifeless form of a dead image [idol]. (Wis 15:1-5 NRSV)

Paul rejects Wisdom's assumptions that Gentiles are incapable of coming to know God by way of so-called natural revelation (Wis 13:1). Wisdom may well reflect a widespread attitude of moral superiority among Jews (Barrett 1957, 44). But anti-Jewish pagan intellectuals counterclaimed that Jews had no "access to genuine knowledge of God," presuming "the educated have the possibility of knowing God, whereas fools and barbarians do not" (Jewett 2007, 154 and n. 59).

Paul considers such egocentric, elitist thinking, whether by Jewish or Greco-Roman, a fundamental misunderstanding of God's generosity and **patience.** Such spiritual complacency misses the whole point of divine forbearance. "God is kind, but he's not soft. In kindness he takes us firmly by the hand and leads us to a radical life-change" (Rom 2:4 TM). We have been given the power of moral judgment, not to censure our fellow creatures, but to judge ourselves and in **repentance** to turn back to God in obedience. "To know the good does not furnish us with a claim to divine indulgence. The fact that the hour of divine judgment has not yet struck does not by any means show that God judges us favorably" (Leenhardt 1957, 75).

■ **5** Jews know that God is kind and merciful. But in the face of divine mercy they exhibit **stubbornness** and an **unrepentant heart** (v 5). Their rebellion removes them from "the sphere of divine grace, as surely as does the sin of idolatry among the pagans" (Dodd 1932, 33). You presume upon God's favor, despising **the riches of his kindness** (v 4), only to store up **wrath against yourself for the day of God's wrath, when his righteous judgment will be revealed** (v 5).

Paul warns that God's wrath is coming upon this Jewish critic as surely as upon humanity in general (1:18). The phrase **the day of God's wrath** goes back to the OT prophets who warned of the fearful coming of the day of Yahweh: "That day will be a day of wrath, a day of distress and anguish, a day of trouble and ruin, a day of darkness and gloom, a day of clouds and blackness"

(Zeph 1:15; see Joel 2:2 and Amos 5:18). **Revealed** (*apokalypseōs*) implies that the **day of God's wrath** will manifest God's justice at the eschaton.

The revelation of wrath in 1:18 refers to a process already observable in human experience, whereas **the day of God's wrath** here is an end-time, future event. The difference is not great; these are two ways of looking at the same reality. As present salvation anticipates the final revelation of the righteousness of God (see the commentary on 1:16-17), so the present manifestation of God's wrath anticipates the final day of judgment (see the commentary on 1:18). "The main point that Paul wishes to urge is that, however the Wrath is revealed, there is no substantial difference between the Jew and the pagan when it is [finally] revealed" (Dodd 1932, 33).

There will be trouble and distress for every human being who does evil: first for the Jew, then for the Gentile. . . . For God does not show favoritism (vv 9, 11). At the judgment, ethnic descent and assumed moral superiority will be irrelevant. **God's judgment . . . is based on truth** (v 2). He has no favorites.

■ **6** God **will give to each person according to what he has done** (v 6). Although Paul makes no direct quotation from the OT, he assumes his readers will understand this statement as biblically based (see Ps 62:12; Prov 24:12; Jer 18:10; 32:18-23; Job 34:11; see Matt 16:27; 2 Cor 5:10; 2 Tim 4:14; 1 Pet 1:17; Rev 2:23; 20:12; 22:12). "Not hearing the law, being the proud and privileged possessor of it, but doing it is what matters" (Barrett 1957, 46).

Does this contradict Paul's doctrine of justification "by faith apart from observing the law" (Rom 3:28)? By no means. The faith that justifies is a "faith expressing itself through love" (Gal 5:6). Paul's teaching here parallels James: "Faith without works is dead" (see Jas 2:14-26). Unless faith is living and produces a harvest of "true righteousness and holiness" (Eph 4:24), it is not true faith (see Phil 1:9-21).

■ **7** Faith is not a one-time event; true believers are marked by their **persistence** [*hypomonēn*, **endurance**] **in doing good** (Rom 2:7; see Acts 9:36; 2 Cor 9:8; Eph 2:10; Col 1:10; 2 Thess 2:17; 1 Tim 2:10; 5:10; 2 Tim 2:21; Titus 1:16; 2:11-14; 3:1). Sustained faith does not receive the grace of God in vain (1 Cor 15:2; 2 Cor 6:1).

This understanding of the relationship between faith and works resembles what E. P. Sanders calls "covenantal nomism" in the Judaism of his time. Despite Reformed characterizations of Judaism as legalistic, Sanders demonstrates conclusively that most rabbis recognized grace as the sole basis for entering the covenant—"getting in." But obedience to the Law was expected as essential to "staying in" (Sanders 1985). This explains Paul's references to "the obedience of faith" (Rom 1:5 and 16:26 NRSV).

Verses 7 and 8 form a balanced couplet, which makes clear that only those who sustain a vital faith can hope for **eternal life** (see Dan 12:2; Rom

5:21; 6:21-22). This is the opposite of "death" (vv 20-23) and "destruction" (Gal 6:8). Here it "describes not the blessedness of the Christian life in this world but the greater blessedness of life beyond the judgment" (Barrett 1957, 46). It will be given those **who by persistence in doing good seek glory, honor and immortality** (Rom 2:7). "Both glory and honor are central motivations in the culture of the ancient Mediterranean world" (Jewett 2007, 205; see the sidebar "Further Reading on Honor and Shame in Mediterranean Society" in the Behind the Text section of the commentary on 6:1-23).

Persistence (*hypomonēn*) is "active perseverance." It is hope at work (see 8:24-25; 1 Cor 13:7; 1 Thess 1:3). Believers persevere in their faith-inspired and grace-empowered labors for God, hoping only to bring glory and honor to him (see Rom 14:6). The reward they receive is intrinsic, not extrinsic; and by association with **immortality,** it is not merely social recognition. **Glory, honor and immortality** are eschatological terms, and as such are God's gifts.

> The reward of eternal life, then, is promised to those who do not regard their good works as an end in themselves, but see them as marks not of human achievement but of hope in God. Their trust is not in their good works, but in God, the only source of glory, honour, and incorruption. (Barrett 1957, 46)

■ **8** The second half of this couplet concerns those whose recompense is **wrath** (*orgē*) and **anger** (*thymos*) (2:8). Who are these persons? They are the **self-seeking** (*eritheia*). *Eritheia* describes all too well the **partisanship** Paul will expose in the Roman Christian community in chs 14 and 15 (see 2 Cor 12:20; Gal 5:20; Phil 1:17; 2:3; Jewett 2007, 206). The reward they seek is extrinsic. It is not the glory of God but their own benefit. They "have no aim beyond self-interest" (Bruce 1963, 187).

Only divine **wrath** and **anger** await those who consider their good works as their own achievements, on the basis of which they expect to claim the favor of God. Such persons disobey the truth that God is the sovereign Lord. They follow **unrighteousness** as they live in rebellion against their Creator. Thus, selfishly motivated, judgmental bigots effectively **reject** [*apeithousi, disobey*] **the truth and follow** [*peithoumenois, obey*] **evil** [*adikiai, unrighteousness*]. They end up being just like *those who suppress the truth by their unrighteousness* (Rom 1:18).

■ **9** The fate of **every human being who does evil** [*to kakon*], regardless of their ethnicity, **will be trouble and distress** (2:9; see Isa 8:22; 30:6). The self-righteous will not **escape God's judgment,** despite their presumption (Rom 2:3). In fact, Paul insists that contrary to notions of Jewish exceptionalism, those who were the first beneficiaries of God's salvation will also be the first victims of his wrath—**first for the Jew, then for the Gentile** (*Hellēnos,* **Greek;** see 1:16). God shows no favorites in salvation or judgment.

■ **10** In 2:10 Paul describes the blessings of eschatological salvation as **glory, honor and peace** (see v 7; 14:17, 19; 15:13, 33; LXX Pss 8:5; 84:10-12; Jer 29:11; see the sidebars on "Peace" in the comments on Rom 5:1 and on "Glory" with those on Rom 8:18-27). These divine gifts will be bestowed on **everyone who does good: first for the Jew, then for the Gentile** (*Hellēni*, **Greek;** see 1:16).

■ **11** Romans 2:11 makes explicit the point Paul has been making all along: **God does not show favoritism** [*prosōpolēmpsia*; see Deut 10:17; Sir 35:15-16; Acts 10:34; 11:12; 15:9; Gal 2:6]. The Greek abstract noun *prosōpolēmpsia*, partiality, is a compound of the words *prosōpon* and *lambanō*. Thus, Paul communicates the same principle in Gal 2:6: God does not receive (*lambanei*) the face (*prosōpon*) of humans (see Luke 20:21; Barn. 19:4; Did. 4:3). Since by the figure of metonymy, the face represents the whole person, to receive one's face is to show preferences based on personal distinctions. God treats Jews and Gentiles alike.

■ **12** In Rom 2:12-16, Paul deals with an objection that might be raised to his conclusion that God does not make distinctions between Jews and Gentiles. They differ in more than race. Unlike Jews, they were not favored with the special revelation of the Law. Paul has already undermined this objection in 1:19-32, where he claims that Gentiles without the benefit of *special* revelation are guilty of responsible acts of rebellion against the Creator in view of God's *general* revelation in nature. The lack of a revealed law in no way excuses the Gentile from judgment. For **all who sin apart from the law will also perish** [*apolountai*, **will be destroyed**] **apart from the law** (2:12). Jews would agree with this. "Impartial judgment takes no account of cultural or religious background" (Jewett 2007, 210).

Paul maintains that God judges Jews as surely as he does Gentiles: **all who sin under the law will be judged by the law.** "The mere possession of the law gives the Jew no position of advantage; it only determines the standard by which he will be judged" (Dodd 1932, 34).

■ **13** **For it is not those who hear the law who are righteous in God's sight, but it is those who obey the law who will be declared righteous** ("justified" NRSV) (v 13; see v 7; 3:20-24; Matt 7:24, 26; 13:23; Luke 6:47, 49; 8:21; Jas 1:22, 23, 25). It is important to observe the sense in which Paul is thinking of being "justified" here. "The present passage refers only to the sentence, whether of condemnation or acquittal, pronounced at the last judgment" (Barrett 1957, 48). John Wesley calls this *final* justification, in distinction from *evangelical* justification, which is by faith alone (see Rom 3:24-28).

Justification by faith alone applies only to our *entrance* into salvation, not to the future time of judgment. When God graciously receives us as sinners, he asks nothing except faith. But from that moment on we enter into a new responsibility. God expects us, as the recipients of his gift, to bear the fruits of grace. Faith is not a license to sin. "It is, on the contrary, the means of overcoming sin, to live holy lives. If this fruit is not produced, faith is dead and in vain" (Godet 1883, 122).

■ **14** In 2:14 Paul returns to his opening statement in v 12, which, as it stands, appears open to objection. Paul must address the question: How can equitable judgment take place **apart from the law** (v 12)? Jewett (2007, 212) surveys the "wide variety of approaches" interpreters have taken to vv 14-16. Paul certainly does not deny grace as essential to salvation or suggest that some naturally do not need salvation. The expression **law for themselves** (v 14) does not mean that some **Gentiles** were "a law *unto* themselves," as this idiom is commonly used. It means just the opposite: By reason of what God has done, they are morally responsible. Their conscience took "the place of the revealed law possessed by the Jews" (Murray 1959, 73; following Meyer 1889).

Despite the NIV translation, Greek word order indicates that **by nature** (*physei;* v 14) does not clarify *what **some** Gentiles* (the plural noun *ethnē* has no article) ***do naturally.*** Instead it clarifies their identity—*who* they are. They are ***naturally* Gentiles, who** by definition **do not have the law.** Without the advantages of a Jewish background, these Gentiles came to know what God wills and forbids. Paul is aware that Gentile Christians make up the majority of the Roman church. This is evidence enough that some **Gentiles . . . do . . . things required by the law.** He essentially restates this same point in v 27, where he refers to **one who is not circumcised physically** [*ek physeōs, by nature*] **and yet obeys the law.** "This exegetical decision renders irrelevant the immense debate over natural law with regard to this verse" (Jewett 2007, 213 n. 207).

Natural Law

Some of what Paul says resembles the claims of certain Greek moralists. To the question, "Who shall govern the governor?" Plutarch replies, "Law, the king of all mortals and immortals, as Pindar called it; which is not written on papyrus rolls or wooden tablets, but in his own reason within his soul." Similarly, Aristotle writes, "The cultivated and free-minded man will so behave as being a law to himself" (*Nichomachean Ethics*, 1128A, both quoted in Dodd 1932, 36). Stoic philosophers spoke of this inner law as the "law of nature." Their teaching was that, as the universe is itself rational, each individual partakes of the universal *logos* or reason. Rational humans are capable of discerning the immanent law of human nature and of judging their actions by it.

■ **15** Morally renewed Gentiles have "internalized the law of God" so that "the gap between knowing and doing has been overcome" (see v 3; Jewett

2007, 214). **They show that the requirements of the law are written in their hearts** (v 15*a*). Despite their natural identity as Gentiles, their supernaturally transformed lives demonstrate that they are the eschatological people of God. That the Law is **written in their hearts** echoes the new covenant promise of Jer 31:33. Paul shares the early Christian conviction that the coming of the promised Holy Spirit enables the church actually to fulfill the Law (Rom 8:1-4; see 1 Cor 11:25; 2 Cor 3:2-6, 14). "The Jeremiah prophecy has been fulfilled in an unexpected manner as the gospel recruits Gentiles to become the heirs of the divine promise" (Jewett 2007, 215).

The **consciences** of believing Gentiles confirm their understanding of God's will, **also bearing witness, and their thoughts now accusing, now even defending them** (Rom 2:15*b*). The word **conscience** (*syneidēsis*) literally means "co-knowledge" or "knowing with." It is the "knowledge of reflective judgment which man has *by the side of* or *in conjunction with* the original consciousness of the act" (Sanday and Headlam 1929, 60). It is our ability as humans to rise above ourselves and view our actions and character more or less objectively. We are thus able to act or witness for or against ourselves. Our **accusing** or **defending . . . thoughts** denote the inner arguments that we have within ourselves as we struggle to determine the course of action we should take.

Believing Gentiles, after such inner debates of conscience, do instinctively what the Law requires. The apostle does not suggest that their obedience saves them. Such a conclusion is against the whole argument of this passage, which is intended to show the universal guilt of humanity and its need for God's righteousness. "There is no basis for deducing the power of the will from this passage," Calvin writes, "as if Paul had said that the keeping of the law is within our power" (1960, 49; see 7:14-24). Paul insists that the power to fulfill the Law comes only through the divine gift of the indwelling Spirit (see 8:1-17). The obedience of Gentile Christians demonstrates their status among the Spirit-filled people of God.

If vv 14-15 are taken as a parenthesis (as in NIV), Paul's parenthetical point is that no one—Jew or Gentile—is ultimately justified by merely possessing the Law without doing it (Godet 1883, 126). The apostle concludes his argument begun in v 13 in v 16: **Those who obey the law will be declared righteous . . . on the day when God will judge men's secrets through Jesus Christ** (vv 13, 16; see Sanday and Headlam 1929, 62; and Fitzmyer 1993, 311). "The final assessment of behavior, conscience, and reasoning belongs to God alone" (Jewett 2007, 217).

■ **16** On the day of judgment **God will judge men's secrets** (v 16; 1 Sam 16:7; Job 34:22; Ps 139:1-2; Jer 16:17; 17:10; 23:24; Dan 2:22; Sir 39:19; Matt 6:4, 6, 18; Mark 4:22; 1 Cor 14:25; Eph 5:12-13). God demands nothing less than holiness of heart and life; neither fine words nor merely outward displays of piety will do (Godet 1883, 126). He will judge the **secrets** of human hearts by **Jesus Christ.** Paul's words recall Jesus' claim that he would return as Judge of all (Matt 7:21-23; 25:31-36).

The meaning of the final phrase of Rom 2:16, **as my gospel declares** (see 16:25; 2 Tim 2:8), remains puzzling. Paul does not claim that his message is the criterion of divine judgment (Dunn 2002a, 38A:103). Nor is his expectation that Christ will be the final Judge (1 Cor 4:4; 2 Cor 5:10) unique to him. Perhaps, his point is particularly to emphasize the necessity of both present justification and future salvation. Those who are freely put right with God by faith in Christ will be finally judged on the basis of their ongoing faithfulness to God. Only those who remain in Christ will be ultimately saved.

> The Christian life is a process which begins in justification, is actualized in sanctification and is consummated with salvation. Critical for the final reception of salvation is . . . continued obedience and continued reception of God's freely offered gift of the Spirit who is at work in the believer as a part of the body of Christ. (See 2 Thess 2:13; Donfried 1976, 100)

FROM THE TEXT

Romans 2:1-16 sounds a warning against the intimately related sins of self-righteousness, religious bigotry, unconscious hypocrisy, and self-deception. Jeremiah's words come to mind: "The heart is deceitful above all things, and desperately wicked: who can know it?" (Jer 17:9 KJV; see Ps 139:23-24).

We must, of course, beware of the delusive dangers of both self-righteousness and presumption. But a still more insidious form of presumption upon God's mercy may be the claim that justified believers may be *simul justus et peccator,* "at one and the same time righteous and sinners." Prior theological commitments rather than exegetical evidence lead some interpreters effectively to dismiss the message of Rom 2.

Some Pauline interpreters have found it *"un*Pauline" and have attributed parts or the whole of ch 2 to an interpolator (see, e.g., O'Neill 1975, 46-49; and Fitzmyer 1993, 837). These scholars insist that Paul did not mean—and *could* not have actually meant—that only doers of the Law will be justified.

Stephen Westerholm counters such claims with compelling scriptural evidence:

> Throughout the Hebrew and Greek Scriptures, "righteous" and "wicked" are found side by side, in Israel and among all nations. The two are distinguished by their deeds. And whether one is "righteous" or "wicked" matters supremely when God judges the world and *all* its people in *righteousness* (LXX Ps. 9:98; 95:13; 97:9). . . . If the ordinary sense of

"righteousness" in the Scriptures is "what one ought to do," it would be extremely odd if Paul did not betray a similar usage. (2004, 256)

Westerholm offers further evidence that Paul did not use the word *righteousness* as only relational by appeal to Rom 6, particularly the apostle's vigorous argument in vv 15-19: "'Righteousness' . . . for Paul, as for the rest of Scripture, is 'what one ought to do.'" Paul believes God expects humans to do right. Human failure to do so explains Rom 1:18-32, where he characterizes this failure with "the charge of *un*righteousness (*adikia*) against all humanity" (v 18; Westerholm 2004, 256).

Westerholm recognizes "The (Ordinary) Righteousness of the Law" and "The (Extraordinary) Righteousness of Faith" as paradoxical but *not* contradictory. Those "declared" righteous by God are expected and enabled by the saving power of the gospel (v 16) actually to *be* righteous.

Those declared "righteous" in an extraordinary way are now to do what is "righteous" (in the ordinary sense, Romans 6). Paul is no less insistent than Matthew that his converts must actively serve "righteousness." Distinctively Pauline, however, is the conviction that such a life is possible as one is "led by the Spirit" (8:13-14; see v. 4), which has been given to all who belong to Christ (v. 9). The hostility toward God that is inherent in the "flesh" is no longer the mindset of those who "live according to the Spirit" (vv. 5-8). (Westerholm 2004, 264)

3. The Challenge to Jews (2:17-29)

BEHIND THE TEXT

Paul continues to use the rhetorical technique of diatribe—in which an imaginary dialogue partner poses challenging questions to which the apostle must respond. Only here does he identify his pretentious interlocutor, addressed as "you" (singular) in vv 17-27 (see vv 1-5), explicitly as a "Jew."

Here Paul reaches the point to which his argument has been building. Israel, resting on the Torah and their special calling as God's chosen people, has not fulfilled its vocation. The valid claims of the Torah have been invalidated by ethnic Israel through its misbehavior in the world. Israel must face the challenge of those non-Jews, who are now by the Spirit heirs of Israel's role in God's purposes.

In addressing the stereotypical Jew, Paul dramatizes and exaggerates what could be said of Jews generally. He does not suggest that all Jews are self-conscious hypocrites. His point is that ethnic Israel's boast of being God's chosen people is falsified by such sins as theft, adultery, idolatry, etc. Sinful behavior by Jews renders void Israel's boast and prevents it from fulfilling its calling to be a light to the Gentiles.

Within Rom 1:18—3:20, this passage demonstrates that Israel, along with the Gentile world, is sinful and in need of the gospel. But it does more. Within this overarching purpose, Paul insists that God chose Israel as a light to the nations and gave them the Torah to enable them to fulfill that mission. But the bearer of salvation has become his greatest problem. Called to be the light to the world, Israel has instead contributed to the world's darkness (Wright 2002, 445).

At the end of this dialogic confrontation, Paul seeks to forestall an objection, "Perhaps we Jews do not observe Torah as we ought, but we *are* circumcised. In this respect at least we have carried out God's command and bear the mark of the covenant?" Paul rejects this argument, because circumcision involves both God's promise and the Law's requirements. If the people do not observe the Law, the covenant is broken. The rite of circumcision was intended to symbolize a deeper reality. Real circumcision is not merely a mark in the flesh but a movement of the Spirit in human hearts, which manifests itself in faithful obedience to God. Therefore, it is useless for Jews to expect protection against God's wrath based on circumcision. It is not enough to agree with God's judgment on the Gentiles or to appeal to God's patience. To forestall God's wrath one must actually observe the requirements of the Law. Obedience is what it means to be a real Jew, a member of the covenant people of God.

Jeremiah 9:22-25 stands not far in the background of Paul's distinction between circumcision that is "only in the flesh" and that is "in the heart." The former situations are reversed: Gentiles, who do not possess the Torah and are uncircumcised, will stand with Jews at the judgment and condemn them by their obedience to God. Romans 2:26-27 reformulates 2:14-15. Uncircumcised Gentile Christians, who observe the requirements of the Law, are not only reckoned as if they were circumcised but also share in the destiny of Israel. Paul denies the name "Jews" to those who are Jews outwardly but not inwardly. He regards ethnic Jews as presently cut off from God's promises to Israel, which believing Gentiles inherit instead (chs 9—11).

Paul's argument offers three challenges to Jewish self-identity and claims to moral superiority (vv 17-18, 19-20, and 21-23). It concludes with a citation of Isa 52:5, accusing such Jews of blaspheming God by their disobedience (Rom 2:24), challenging the right of such Jews to bear the name (vv 25-29).

IN THE TEXT

As Paul addresses his hypothetical Jewish interlocutor, we must keep in mind that Paul himself is a Jew. He feels sincere personal grief that so many of his fellow Jews are in rebellion against the message of Jesus as the Jewish Messiah (9:1-5). This must be kept in mind as he challenges them to consider what it means to be a "Jew."

a. Privileges and Failures of Jews (2:17-24)

■ 17 Verses 17-20 are a single, incomplete sentence. **Now if** (*Ei de*) introduces a series of five conditions in vv 17-18b. The conditional particle *ei* (*if*) is not repeated, despite the NIV translation. Each condition involves a finite verb enumerating Jewish privileges. A second five-part series in vv 19-20a describes the alleged superiority of Jews in relation to non-Jews. Both vv 18c and 20b identify possession of the Law as the basis for Jewish self-confidence. An em dash punctuates this complicated conditional sentence, because it has no grammatical conclusion (no then-clause).

The *first* great privilege of Jewish identity is the name itself: **you call yourself a Jew** (v 17). Jews were those who identified with the "beliefs, rites, and customs of adherents of Israel's Mosaic and prophetic tradition" (Jewett 2007, 222). They bore the name as a badge of cultural and religious superiority. Possessing this name convinced them they were not sinners like the rest of humanity (see Gal 2:15).

Their *second* privilege was being able to **rely on the law.** They took considerable satisfaction in knowing the revealed will of God. God's gift of this unique revelation to them alone brought security and comfort (see *2 Bar.* 48:22-24).

Their *third* privilege is that they were able to ***boast in God.*** The verb *kauchasai* is used by Paul in both negative and positive ways. It can refer to self-serving braggadocio; but it can be used favorably to describe the honor one assigns God (see Jer 9:22-23; Rom 5:2, 11; 1 Cor 1:31; 2 Cor 10:17; Phil 3:3). Jews confessed faith in the one true God (Deut 6:4), who had chosen them as his "treasured possession" (Exod 19:5-6; Deut 7:6-8). He was *their* God, and they were *his* people; so they *boasted* in God. Although deeply felt pride in God may be entirely legitimate, the NIV translation properly conveys the audacious arrogance conveyed by the Jews' boast in the present context: **you . . . brag about your relationship to God.**

Boasting

Paul uses a form of *kauchaomai* in no less than 36 of its 37 NT occurrences. He uses the cognate term *kauchema* ten times out of its eleven occurrences; and, *kauchasis* also ten of its eleven NT occurrences. The word-group sometimes indicates a boasting that is laudable, such as boasting in God (5:11; 1 Cor 1:31), in Christ (15:17; Phil 3:3), or in the cross of

Christ (Gal 6:14). Christians can boast in their tribulations (Rom 5:3) and generally in things that show their weakness (2 Cor 11:30; 12:5, 9). They can also boast in their hope of future glory (Rom 5:2). But boasts in one's self or achievements is always considered reprehensible. (Morris 1988, 131)

■ **18** The *fourth* Jewish privilege is to **know God's will** (*to thelēma*, lit. *the will,* v 18). Baruch 4:4 reports the self-congratulation: "Happy are we, O Israel, for we know what is pleasing to God" (NRSV). Gratitude for this privilege can easily become presumption, as Wis 15:2 illustrates: "For even if we sin we are yours, knowing your power" (NRSV).

Their *fifth* privilege is being able to **approve** [*dokimazeis*; see Rom 12:2] **what is superior** [*ta diapheronta*, paraphrased "what really matters" in Phil 1:10 HCSB and NLT]. Paul adopts the language and the philosophical traditions Hellenistic Judaism used to describe issues of moral significance as opposed to the morally indifferent (*adiphora*). It seems unlikely that he accepted his imaginary interlocutor's claim to possess this as more than "transparent pretense" (Jewett 2007, 224). Nonetheless, Paul assures the Romans that their renewed Christian minds will enable them to "test and approve [*dokimazein*] what God's will is" (12:2). And he prays that the Philippians may be granted powers of ethical discrimination (*eis to dokimazein hymas diapheronta;* Phil 1:10).

The final clause in Rom 2:18c, **because you are instructed by the law,** translates an adverbial participle rather than a second person finite verb. Torah instruction is not a sixth privilege, but the basis for all five, or perhaps for the Jewish claim to possess superior powers of moral sensitivity. Jews were fundamentally defined by the role of the Law in their lives.

■ **19** The conditional sentence introduced in v 17 continues in vv 19-20 with a second series of five privileges Jews claim on the basis of their possession of the Law. It is introduced by a single verb joined with a complementary infinitive—**you trust yourself to be**—and four object complements (vv 19-20a).

Just as the name "Jew" defined the first privilege in the previous series, here Paul expresses Jewish self-confidence with the primary claim, **you trust yourself** [*pepoithas te seauton*]. Jewett cites a number of nonbiblical parallels in which this expression refers to "pretentious assurance," "naïve self-confidence," even "cocksuredness" (2007, 224). By way of contrast, Paul's description of Christian self-consciousness in Phil 3:3 denies that they trust themselves (*ouk en sarki pepoithotes*). Following **you trust yourself,** the infinitive **to be** has four object complements that define Jewish self-consciousness in relation to those who do not have the Law.

First, **you are a guide for the blind** (Rom 2:19a; see Matt 15:14; 23:16, 24; John 9:40-41). Both the terms *guide* and *blind* appear only here in Paul's letters. The stereotypical Jew regards all other people as blind. Given sight by the Torah, they, however, are commissioned to lead the clueless masses.

97

The *second* privilege of Jews—to be **a light for those who are in the dark** (Rom 2:19*b*; see 1:21; 13:12)—makes much the same point. In Israel's call to be the Servant of Yahweh, "light" and "darkness" symbolize ethical conduct (Isa 9:1; 45:7).

■ **20** The *third* and *fourth* privileges are also essentially synonymous. Paul's Jewish interlocutor claims to be **an instructor of the foolish** and **a teacher of infants** (Rom 2:20). To show how ludicrous the claims of his imaginary foe were, Paul humorously misuses the standard terminology in a way comparable to our referring to one as "a professor of kindergartners."

> A combination of ridiculous arrogance and audience resentment is . . . evoked by Paul's formulation, because this bigot who claims to be able to instruct everyone else does not appear to know the precise connotation of the titles he arrogates to himself, and he views his wards as fools and infants, which places the audience in a position of absolute, imputed inferiority. (Jewett 2007, 226)

God's revelation to Abraham and his descendants was to enlighten all nations about God. But Israel failed in its mission. Isaiah envisioned the Servant of Yahweh fulfilling this role, to be "a light for the Gentiles, to open eyes that are blind" (Isa 42:6-7; see 9:2; 49:6; 60:3). Israel's privilege was never meant to be the private treasure of one nation, which it could withhold from others. It was to share its revelation with the Gentiles who did not have it in a spirit of humility. Apart from God's light given them, Israel would have been as blind as any Gentile. Israel was not to exult in their privilege, but in what God had done, and to fulfill their responsibility (Morris 1988, 133).

The claim of Jesus to be "the light of the world" (John 8:12; 9:5) appears in a context in which "blind" Jewish leaders (vv 39-40) consider the Law, not Jesus, the definitive Revealer of God and God's truth (vv 16, 33; 1:16-18). In Matt 5:14, Jesus calls his followers to be "the light of the world." This implicit usurping of the role of the Law may explain his disclaimer in v 17, "Do not think that I have come to abolish the Law. . . ." The series of antitheses ("You have heard that . . . But I tell you that . . .") in vv 21-48, indicate that he expected his followers to incarnate the Law's provisions in lives of radical obedience.

Like Rom 2:18*c*, v 20*c* concludes with an adverbial participle, not a second person finite verb, despite the NIV interpretive translation: **because you have in the law the embodiment of knowledge and truth.** The word **embodiment** translates *morphōsen*, meaning **outward manifestation.** Jews held a remarkably high, hypostatic or incarnational, view of the Torah itself. In fact, many of the high christological claims of Christians affirmed as true of Jesus what Jews claimed for the Law (see, e.g., the commentary on the Prologue of John). Ordinary rabbis "in the Jewish tradition stood under the supreme authority of the law, and if anything, the law possessed" them. Only arrogant braggarts—or God's Messiah—could claim either to possess or embody the Law (Jewett 2007, 226-27).

The pagan world was indeed in moral and spiritual darkness. And, despite Paul's indictment of this presumptuous Jew, there is evidence that Jewish morality and monotheism often made a favorable impression on many in the Greco-Roman world. Almost every synagogue had attracted to itself a company of Gentile God-fearers and proselytes. "God-fearers" were Gentiles who embraced Jewish monotheistic faith and moral practice but who had not been circumcised and taken upon themselves the full "yoke" of the Law. Proselytes, on the other hand, had in effect *become* Jews by circumcision and submission to the Jewish Torah (see Acts 15:1-35).

As the Acts and Paul's letters make clear, such persons were the first to respond to Paul's gospel. Jewish synagogues were the bridge over which Christianity passed from Israel to the Gentile population of the Roman Empire. Synagogues remained a point of elitist attraction; they were not normally noted for the kind of evangelistic outreach (but see Matt 23:15) practiced by Christian missionaries.

■ **21** In Rom 2:21-23, five relative or adjectival participial clauses and matching verbs challenge the consistency of the Jews' claims and conduct. In view of the privileges Jews claimed, Paul asks his imaginary conversation partner, What have you done with them? We must remember that **you** in vv 21-24, as in vv 17-20, is *corporate*, addressed not to just one Jew, or every single Jew, but to *Israel as a whole*. Paul implies that Israel has squandered its inheritance.

> Paul is not engaged in "propagandistic denigration" of Jews, . . . but rather in the rhetorical demolition of claims of cultural superiority whose continuation would have sabotaged the mission to the so-called barbarians in Spain. (Jewett 2007, 227)

Paul's *first* challenging question is: **You, then, who teach others, do you not teach yourself?** (v 21*a*). Paul points to the inconsistency at the heart of the Jewish *practice* of the Law. He has already claimed self-righteous judges "do the same things" (v 1). Despite their boasting in God's supreme revelation—*the Law*, Israel has not kept it. To ignore God's supreme gift is to dishonor God. It is one thing to *know* the Law, it is another thing to *obey* it. Paul's accusation hits at the very heart of Jewish religious understanding. Whatever else they did or did not do, Jews claimed to give God the place of highest honor. Paul charges that Jewish practice denies its profession.

■ **22** Paul's *second* and *third* questions challenge Israel's obedience to the Decalogue. **You who preach against stealing, do you steal? You who say that people should not commit adultery, do you commit adultery?** (vv 21*b*-22*a*; see Exod 20:15, 14). Fairly or unfairly, Jews had acquired a reputation for injustice and deception in commercial affairs in their dealings with the Gentile populations among whom they lived. C. E. B. Cranfield reports that later rabbinic discussion acknowledges that "the conduct even of respected Rabbis often belied the strictness of their teaching" (1975, 1:168 n. 2).

Paul continues, **You who abhor idols, do you rob temples?** (Rom 2:22*b*; see Exod 20:4-5). This *fourth* charge of sacrilege has been understood in many ways. Desecrating pagan temples might seem consistent with Jewish revulsion for idolatry. But the evidence suggests that most Hellenistic Jews showed respect for non-Jewish religions and cult sites. The fanatical Jewish zealots who vandalized pagan temples only contributed to the widespread anti-Jewish feelings that culminated in the Jewish revolts of A.D. 66-73 and 132-133. Edgar Krentz "concludes that for Paul, 'Temple robbery means there is no respect for the concept, the name, the honor of God'" (Jewett 2007, 229).

F. F. Bruce suggests that Paul may have had in mind a specific scandalous incident involving four Roman Jews in A.D. 19 (see Josephus A.J. 18.81-84). When the matter came to the attention of Emperor Tiberius, he expelled all Jews from Rome (Bruce 1963, 93). Douglas Moo claims that Paul cited such failures of Jews to keep the Law as "exemplary of the contrast between words and works, possession of the law and obedience of it." His intention was to emphasize "the contradiction between claim and conduct" that pervaded Judaism (1996, 165). Jewett, however, insists, "Rather than decrying an alleged low state of Jewish morality," Paul's goal was "demolishing the premise of cultural exceptionalism" (2007, 228).

2:22-24   Whatever contradictions existed between theory and practice among non-Christian Jews, Paul's concern was that the Roman house and tenement churches should not effectively deny the truth of the Christian message by perpetuating the unbecoming rift between Jewish and Gentile believers (Rom 14—15) that would undermine the advance of the gospel in Rome and beyond.

■ **23** *Fifth*, the apostle concludes his series of questions challenging the consistency of his imaginary foil: **You who brag** [see 2:17 and the "Boasting" sidebar there] **about the law, do you dishonor** [*atimazeis*; see 1:21-27] **God by breaking** [*parabaseōs*, ***transgressing***] **the law?** (v 23; see 4:15; 5:14; Gal 3:19). Paul charges his self-righteous interlocutor with dishonoring God, just as surely as did pagans. By his self-idolatry, "the bigot who was intent on demonstrating his superiority over Gentiles ends up dishonoring the very God he claims to serve" (Jewett 2007, 230).

■ **24** As evidence supporting his indictment of Jewish complicity in dishonoring God, Paul cites the LXX translation of Isa 52:5: **As it is written: "God's name is blasphemed among the Gentiles because of you"** (Rom 2:24; see Ezek 36:20-23). Although Paul has referred to his imaginary opponent throughout using the second person singular "you," the quotation uses the plural, anticipating the point he will make in Rom 3:9, "confirming the universal sinfulness of all" (Jewett 2007, 231). Members of the Qumran community were warned to be careful in their dealing with Gentiles "lest they blaspheme" (Bruce 1963, 93). In 14:16, Paul will warn the weak and strong in Rome not to allow their intercommunity competition to cause the church to be blasphemed.

b. The Meaning of "Jew" (2:25-29)

■ **25** Paul is about to pursue his Jewish interlocutor "into his last retreat," to strip him of his final refuge, his illusive trust in the possession of circumcision. Paul insists: **Circumcision has value [***ōphelei***] if you observe the law, but if you break the law, you have become as though you had not been circumcised** (v 25). Although the NIV does not translate these argumentative features, Paul crafts his argument with formal precision. The conjunction *gar* (For) identifies vv 25-29 as substantiation of vv 17-24. His thesis is that *on the one hand* [*men*] *circumcision is beneficial . . . , but on the other hand* [*de*] *circumcision has become uncircumcision. . . .*

During the so-called intertestamental period, circumcision had become an essential boundary marker distinguishing Jews from Gentiles (see Jewett 2007, 231-32). It was unthinkable to Jews that one duly circumcised and admitted to the covenant should fail to achieve final salvation. "Rabbi Levi said, 'At the last Abraham will sit at the entrance to Gehenna and will not let any circumcised man go down there,'" and, "Circumcision will deliver Israel from Gehenna" (Cranfield 1975, 1:172 n. 1).

Against such presumption, Paul insists that circumcision *is beneficial* [*ōphelei*] *if you observe* [*prasseis*] *the Law* (see vv 14, 27). Initiation into the covenant is completely useless if one is *a transgressor of the Law* (see Gal 2:18, 15). The symbol does not match the spiritual state to which it points. Paul is not saying "that the Jew's circumcision has been annulled in God's sight" (see 3:1-2), "but that he has become uncircumcised in heart." He stands "outside that Israel within Israel, to which Paul refers" in Rom 9 (Cranfield 1975, 1:172).

Paul challenges the Jewish consensus, explicitly mentioning a category of people that will occupy him for much of Romans. These are those who, though uncircumcised, "keep the decrees of the Torah." His words have strong intertextual echoes with Ezek 36:26-27, as well as Deut 10:16; 30:6; and Jer 4:4; 9:25-26. "Circumcision had been given to Israel," Paul says, in effect, "as a consecration to circumcision *of heart*, an engagement to holiness, and not as a shelter from judgment in favor of disobedience and pollution" (Murray 1959, 85).

■ **26** Moreover, Paul says, **If those who are not circumcised keep the law's requirements, will they not be regarded as though they are circumcised?** (Rom 2:26). His rhetorical question expects an affirmative answer. Paul does not think of observing **the law's requirements** (*ta dikaiōmata tou nomou phylassei*) as only hypothetically possible (Barrett 1957, 58). In 8:4 he will insist that those who live according to the Spirit fulfill *the law's requirement* (*to dikaiōma to nomou plērōthēi*).

2:24-26

■ **27** In 2:27 Paul claims that "a remarkable role reversal" has occurred (Jewett 2007, 234). The would-be judge of others (v 1) is judged a transgressor by comparison to the uncircumcised Gentile who observes the Law (see Matt 12:41-42; Luke 11:31). **The one who is not circumcised physically and yet obeys the law will condemn you who, even though you have the written code and circumcision, are a lawbreaker** (Rom 2:27). Disobedience causes Jews to forfeit their advantages. This double transformation of disobedient Jews into Gentiles, and of obedient Gentiles into Jews, is unprecedented.

Paul insists that only those who are Jews **inwardly** by the **circumcision of the heart** (v 29) are truly Jews, regardless of their ethnic descent. Only obedient believers are members of the *true* Israel, the *Israel of God* (Gal 6:12-16). His claim "'that non-Jews could be counted as "circumcised" merely on the basis of "keeping the just requirements of the law" is an astonishing claim'" (Jewett 2007, 233; quoting John Barclay).

■ **28** In Rom 2:28 and 29 Paul explains and justifies his claims in vv 26 and 27. **A man is not a Jew if he is only one outwardly, nor is circumcision merely outward and physical. No, a man is a Jew who is one inwardly; and circumcision is circumcision of the heart, by the Spirit, not by the written code** [*en pneumati ou grammati*]. Paul's terminology contrasts the overt and covert Jew, the public and private Jew, the true and fraudulent Jew.

■ **29** True Jews are so **inwardly** (*en tōi kryptōi*, *in the secret*). That is, their Jewishness is hidden from external observation (see 2:16). "The hidden person of the heart" (*ho kryptos tēs kardias anthrōpos*; 1 Pet 3:4 NASB) is who one really is inwardly, as distinguished from external profession or pretense. Paul's concern is not to demonstrate the superiority of Christianity to Judaism but "to undercut every claim of cultural and religious superiority" (Jewett 2007, 236).

Circumcision of the heart echoes the language of the OT, particularly in Deut 30:6 and Ezek 36:25-27. The pseudepigraphal *Jub.* 1:23 looks forward to the circumcision of the heart as a purifying work that will be effected by the Holy Spirit in the last age. By internalizing his Law within his people, God would remove their inclination to stubbornness and rebellion and enable them to love and obey him fully. Paul claims that this future expectation has been fulfilled.

By referring to the secret/heart/Spirit people, Paul clearly means to designate those in whom the gospel has effectively done its transforming work. The OT promises of God have come true. God has done, in Jesus by the Spirit, what he had promised; the result is the creation of a people of the new covenant (see 2 Cor 3:1-6 and Wright 2002, 449).

Paul's concluding statement returns to the beginning of this section of the letter (Rom 2:17): **Such a man's praise is not from men, but from God** (v 29b). Whether Paul's readers were aware of the Hebrew etymology of the name **Jew** as "the praised one," they certainly grasped his central point: "God, who knows the heart" (Acts 15:8; see 1 Cor 14:25; Heb 4:12) is alone able to distinguish with certainty the true *Jew* from the fraud (see Matt 8:11). It is not a matter of human opinion; God knows with certainty who truly are his people (2 Tim 2:19). God's **praise** alone matters.

FROM THE TEXT

This passage raises one of the most important questions in Scripture: Who are the true people of God? Romans 2:17-29 suggests Paul's answer to that question—an answer that reflects the "mystery" of God's ways, which leads to doxology. It takes into account three important truths that are demanded by Scripture:

First, Israel's claim to be the chosen people of God descended from Abraham and called to be his servant to guide the Gentile world to a knowledge of the living God, is scriptural and legitimate (vv 17-20; see Gen 12:1-4; 15:5-6; 17:1-8; Isa 43:10-14; 49:6; etc.). *Second*, national Israel, since it rejected Jesus as its Messiah, is presently cut off from God. However, a new Israel of the Spirit (in continuity with obedient, circumcised Jews) has been created in Christ to fulfill ancient Israel's mission to the world (Rom 2:25-29; 9:6-8; see Mark 12:1-12; Gal 6:16; 4:24-31; Eph 2:11-22; 1 Pet 2:1-10; etc.). *Third*, God's love for Israel persists, and *"all Israel* will be saved" (emphasis added)— all believing Gentiles and Jews (see Rom 11:25-32). There are not *two* covenants, one for the Jew and another for the Gentile, but only *one* covenant for both Jews and Gentiles (3:29-30).

Meanwhile, in "the time between the times," God's promise to circumcise the hearts of his people so they may love him without reservation is being fulfilled through the gift of the Spirit. John Wesley's sermon "The Circumcision of the Heart" (1979, 5:202-12) describes it as

> that habitual disposition of the soul which, in the sacred writings, is termed holiness; and which directly implies the being cleansed from all sin, "from all filthiness both of flesh and spirit;" and by consequence, the being endued by those virtues which were in Christ Jesus; the being so "renewed in the image of our mind," as to be "perfect as our Father in heaven is perfect." (203)

4. The Advantage of the Jews (3:1-8)

BEHIND THE TEXT

Paul resumes the diatribe style and engages in further dialogue with his imaginary Jewish interlocutor. The passage abounds in rhetorical questions. Paul's exposé in 2:17-29 might be mistakenly taken to imply that Jews have no advantage over Gentiles. Does their acknowledged priority in salvation history—"to the Jew first" (1:16; 2:9-10; see chs 9—11)—mean nothing? Paul insists that, despite the divine oracles concerning salvation in their sacred books, despite the sign of the covenant God established in circumcision, the wrath of God will fall upon Jews as well as Gentiles. Nevertheless, Paul maintains that there is still room for Jews in God's new mode of salvation. All is not lost; their advantage remains.

Paul is unwilling to deny the Jews this advantage, although Jews and Gentiles alike stand under God's wrath. The Jews' advantage does not rest on anything they have done or are but entirely on what God has promised and done. He chose Israel to be his own people and made irrevocable promises to them (11:28). Through his covenant with their forefathers, God established a favored status for Israel, a status that gives Jews a unique place in salvation history. In the light of God's promises to Israel, Paul reinterprets circumcision as "the sign of the covenant," a mark of God's promises to Israel. Israel's failure to maintain its part of the agreement in no way undermines God's faithfulness to his covenant promises.

The present passage forms an integral part of Paul's argument. It employs dialogue to clarify why the apostle rejects the assumptions of his Jewish interlocutor. Verses 1-4 identify the advantage of the Jews as God's faithfulness to his covenant, his promises, and his oracles. Verse 3 raises the leading question of the entire passage: Will Jewish faithlessness **nullify God's faithfulness**? In vv 5-8 Paul does not mention Jews; his language is general enough to embrace everyone. He argues that, if there had been no sin, there would have been no necessity for the gospel, and we would never have known the meaning of God's righteousness. He raises and dismisses the possible implication of this truth: If human sin advances God's purposes and reveals his righteousness, how can he punish sinners for doing him a favor? Paul will show the error of such antinomian logic in ch 6; here, he simply comments: People who think this way justly deserve to be condemned.

The discussion in these verses prepares the way for the conclusions Paul reaches in 3:21-33 and chs 9—11. It is a key to the thought and structure of the rest of the letter. Israel failed to carry out its divine commission, to be the means of the world's salvation. But God continues to be faithful to his covenant plan, despite Israel's failure. In 3:1-8 Paul clears the ground for the point that Jews have joined Gentiles in the dock, guilty as charged (Wright 2002, 453).

IN THE TEXT

■ **I** The discussion begins with the question: **What advantage** [*perisson;* see v 7]**, then, is there in being a Jew?** (v 1). That is, what inferences (*ti oun,* **What**

. . . **then**) may be drawn from Paul's argument in 2:17-29? What benefit do ethnic Jews have over Gentiles in regard to salvation? **Or what value is there in circumcision?** (3:1). Does "the sign of the covenant" really have any use to Jews—as Jews?

■ **2** Paul's unexpected answer is Yes. **Much in every way!** He explains: *Primarily,* **they have been entrusted with the very words of God** [*ta logia tou theou*, v 2]. Four times in vv 2 and 3 Paul plays with words derived from *pist-*, harking back to "faith," which is central to the letter's theme (see 1:16-17).

God had **entrusted** (*episteuthēsan*) the Scriptures to the Jews. What we call the OT was the revelation of God's will. Acts 7:38 refers to the Law as "living words" (*logia zōnta*) that God communicated to Moses on Mount Sinai. Elsewhere in the NT (Heb 5:12; 1 Pet 4:11) the phrase refers to the OT in general or to the divine message of salvation. Whether conceived as words spoken by God or about God, these words include the promised Messiah (Sanday and Headlam 1929, 170), the blessings promised to the children of Abraham, and more. God's words express his faith in Israel—a clear advantage of Jews (see Deut 4:7-8).

■ **3** **What if some did not have faith** [*ēpistēsan*]? (Rom 3:3). An interlocutor's reference to **some** as unfaithful must be taken as an example of meiosis—deliberate literary understatement, in view of the frequent OT examples of Israel's infidelity to God. Paul's question may have had in mind of the faithful "remnant" in Israel (9:27; 11:5) who, despite the "unbelief" of the majority, accepted Jesus as the Messiah. The question does not excuse unbelievers, but **some** stresses God's graciousness toward all Israel. Paul does not say, "What if some did not believe in Christ?" or "What if some did not believe in God?" By leaving it vague, it can be taken either way.

The rhetorical question continues, **Will their lack of faith** [*apistia*] **nullify God's faithfulness** [*pistin*]? Israel's infidelity does not undo **God's** fidelity to Israel. The negative *mē*, which introduces the question, would lead readers to expect a negative answer. But to be certain they do not misunderstand his rhetoric, Paul deploys the first of ten such strong denials of perverse logic in Romans: **Not at all!** (*mē genoito*; v 4; see also 3:6, 31; 6:2, 15; 7:7, 13; 9:14; 11:1, 11; elsewhere only in 1 Cor 6:15; Gal 2:17; 3:21; and 6:14). This is a standard fixture of diatribe style.

■ **4** God's fidelity is not measured by human infidelity: this idea is basic to Paul's teaching on the righteousness of God (Rom 3:30; 11:25-32). **Let God be true, and every man a liar** (v 4). Even if every human proves to be a liar (see Pss 58:3; 116:11), God will vindicate his truthfulness. The apostle does not encourage dishonesty. Human unfaithfulness only calls attention to the remarkable character of divine faithfulness.

Paul contends that Israel has been unfaithful to its divine trust. It rejected its prophets and its Messiah. But God kept his promises nonetheless. Israel's stumbling over the crucified Messiah only became the occasion for a fresh display of God's faithfulness (see Rom 9—11). God would not be without a people, so he grafted into Israel's stock believing Jews and Gentiles, who now constitute the *new* Israel of God, the Christian church (see 9:22-33; 11:11-21; 15:6-13).

Paul appeals to Scripture to clinch his argument: **As it is written: "So that you may be proved right** [*hopōs an dikaiōtheis*, "so that you may be justified" NRSV] **when you speak and prevail** [*nikēseis; conquer*] **when you judge"** (3:4). The word "justified," quoting Ps 51:4, anticipates what Paul will say about justification later in this chapter (Rom 3:21-26). In the death of Jesus God justifies himself as God (vv 25-30), making justification available to all, both Jews and Gentiles, who believe the gospel. Human unfaithfulness, far from nullifying God's faithfulness, has *manifested* it (1:17; 3:21)! The word **prevail,** which departs from the LXX quotation, emphasizes God's apocalyptic victory (Jewett 2007, 246).

In the thematic introduction to Romans (1:16-17), the faithfulness and righteousness of God are inextricable. The quotation from Ps 51:4 allows Paul to shift his emphasis from the former (Rom 3:1-3) to the latter (3:4-8). Divine faithfulness, righteousness, and wrath belong together in his thinking (see 1:16-18). Paul has his imaginary opponent pose a pair of questions, which seek to preserve some measure of Jewish exceptionalism, despite Paul's claim that *everyone is a liar.*

■ **5** Paul poses the questions of his Jewish interlocutor only to show his flawed logic: **But if our unrighteousness** [*adikia*] **brings out God's righteousness** [*dikaiosynēn*] **more clearly, what shall we say? That God is unjust** [*adikos*] **in bringing his wrath** [*orgēn*] **on us?** (3:5). For the sake of the discussion, the questioner accepts Paul's claim that Jewish (**our**) sins magnify God's righteousness, only to argue: Is it not then unjust for God to pronounce judgment on them (**us**)? That is, if the alleged unrighteousness of the Jews gave God an occasion to display his righteousness in Christ, surely it would not be right for him to punish Jewish wrongdoing. The framing of the second question expects a negative answer: *Surely you are not* [*mē*] *saying that God is unjust to bring his wrath, are you?*

Paul, of course, does not agree that his gospel has such implications, as his parenthetical qualification makes clear enough: (**I am using a human argument**) (v 5). It is blasphemous even to suggest the possibility of such infidelity in God. Paul rejects this suggestion because it attributes to God an all-too-human way of speaking, thinking, and behaving (see 6:19; 1 Cor 9:8; Gal 3:15). His rejection of the perverse logic of his imaginary opponent becomes explicit with another emphatic denial: **Certainly not!** (Rom 3:6; see v 3), which has the force of a negative oath: *May it never be!*

■ **6** If that were so (*epei, for otherwise,* v 6) refers back to the rejected implications of preceding questions. Paul insists that for God to encourage Jewish sinfulness to highlight his holiness or to fail to hold them responsible for their actions would disqualify God from being who he is, the righteous Judge of all. **If that were so, how could God judge the world?** Paul emphatically rejects both the possibility that God might be a dispenser of cheap grace to Jewish favorites (see 2:9-11) and that he might be guilty of injustice. If God cannot judge Jews, he cannot judge Gentiles. He is, after all, the Judge of all **the world** (see Gen 18:25; 1 Sam 2:10; 1 Cor 6:2; 11:32)!

■ **7** The opening words of Rom 3:7 in the NIV—**Someone might argue**—have no basis in Greek, mistakenly suggesting that only at this point does Paul cite the words of an imaginary challenger: "If [*ei de*] **my falsehood enhances God's truthfulness and so increases his glory, why am I still condemned as a sinner?"**

By referring to **my falsehood,** the interlocutor accepts Paul's argument in vv 4-6, which dismisses his logic as "evasive rationalization. . . . Nevertheless, he claims that the lie really serves an ameliorating purpose" (Jewett 2007, 249). *My lie only shows how truthful God is, greatly advantaging* [*eperisseusen;* see *perisson* in v 1] *his honor. So why am I of all people* [*kagō*] *still condemned as a sinner?* Clearly, the concern of the interlocutor is "to evade the classification of himself . . . as a sinner" (Jewett 2007, 249). By definition, only Gentiles are sinners, not Jews like he (see Gal 2:15; Luke 18:11). Paul dismisses such reasoning as not only blasphemous but also worthy of condemnation as such (Rom 3:8).

■ **8** Paul concedes that some Jewish detractors of the gospel distort its logic in precisely this way: **Let us do evil that good may result** (v 8). The first person plural (**us**) suggests that such defaming of the gospel as antinomian is not just an attack on Paul but upon Law-free Gentile Christianity as a whole (Jewett 2007, 250). Paul rejects this charge as not only slanderous also but self-condemned, a contradiction of terms.

God's truth is always within a hair's breadth of error, but the gospel of justification "by faith apart from observing the law" (v 28) *can never mean antinomianism,* as Paul shows conclusively in ch 6. There he demonstrates that the justified person has *died* to sin! At this point he is content to retort that such reasoning can come only from a twisted moral nature, which would make light equivalent to darkness.

Paul indignantly concludes this part of his debate with his hypothetical Jewish opponent with: **Their condemnation is deserved** (*hōn to krima endikon estin,* lit. "Of whom the judgment is just," v 8*b*). Paul not only rejects such reasoning as perverse but also insists that those who put it into practice are more than worthy of the destruction of judgment they will receive for espousing such views. Paul has demonstrated to his satisfaction that he has shown the Jewish assumption that they are exempt from divine wrath as patently false (2:1—3:8).

All Have Sinned

Robert Jewett considers Rom 3:1-8 "a brilliant tour de force" (2007, 252). In it Paul has demonstrated to a Christian audience that in light of
> the righteousness of God as revealed in the cross and resurrection of Christ, even the most brilliant and legally loyal interlocutor responds with evasions and lies, ultimately showing himself to be a hypocrite who wishes to avoid accountability by claiming to advance his understanding of divine glory while smearing others with falsehoods. This diatribe achieves the most difficult part of Paul's proof that "all have sinned and fallen short of the glory of God" [3:23] ...What 1:18-32 did in showing Gentile suppression of the truth, 3:1-8 accomplishes in showing that Jews also participate in falsehood and lies. (Jewett 2007, 252)

FROM THE TEXT

3:1-8 Paul has nearly achieved what he set out to do in 1:18—to demonstrate the universal scope of human sinfulness and the inescapability of divine wrath. Even Jews are not exempt, despite their favored status in the history of salvation. But the bad news should not blind us to the good; God does not operate on the basis of reciprocity. His ability to remain faithful, to be truthful, to be righteous does not depend on us.

Professing Christians would do well to consider how to avoid falling victim to the same presumption that was the undoing of Paul's hypothetical Jewish interlocutor. Let us not imagine that baptism, whether as infants or believers, or church membership, or a one-time conversion experience, or some overwhelming spiritual experience irrevocably marks us as members of the new covenant community. With privilege comes responsibility. Grace can be received in vain (see 2 Cor 6:1). The Scriptures reveal the will of God, but merely possessing them is no guarantee that we will do it. This explains Paul's concern for "the obedience that comes from faith" (Rom 1:5; see 15:18).

Central NT theological assumptions about God underlie Paul's reasoning in this passage. Although the history of salvation preserved in the OT is marred repeatedly by Israel's dismal failure to fulfill its calling to be a source of blessing for all nations, God remains faithful (see 1 Cor 1:9; 10:13; 2 Cor 1:18; 1 Thess 5:24; 2 Thess 3:3; 2 Tim 2:13; 1 John 1:9; Rev 3:14; 19:11). His saving purposes are not easily thwarted by the unfaithfulness or rebellion of those who profess to be his people. The impartial justice/righteousness of God (see e.g., Rom 3:26; 2 Thess 1:6; 2 Tim 4:8; 1 John 1:9) is essential to his role as Judge (see, e.g., Acts 17:31; Rom 2:16; 14:4, 10; 2 Tim 4:1, 8; Heb 10:30; 12:23; Jas 5:9; 1 Pet 4:5). Christians no more than Jews should imagine that we will be exempt from divine judgment.

5. No One Is Righteous (3:9-20)

BEHIND THE TEXT

Paul's claim in Rom 3:19—whatever the law says, it says to those who are under the law—that follows a string of supporting scriptural proof texts, is the clue to the present section. Having already argued for the universality of Gentile sin and guilt, Paul appeals to the Law to clinch his argument that Jews, alongside the Gentiles, not only are accountable to God but also stand guilty before him. This is where his argument has been leading all along, despite his acknowledgment of the advantages Israel enjoys as God's special people (2:17-29; 3:1-8). Israel's bungled privileges, in fact, have made it more deserving of judgment than it would have been otherwise. This is consistent with Jesus' principle: "From everyone who has been given much, much will be demanded; and from the one who has been entrusted with much, much more will be asked" (Luke 12:48).

This section of the letter begins with a climactic dialogue between Paul and his imaginary Jewish interlocutor in diatribe style in Rom 3:9. It continues with a carefully selected catena of biblical quotations in vv 10-18. Paul's application of the list of passages in vv 19-20 inescapably demonstrates the universal scope of human sin.

Because these citations come from Israel's own Scriptures, they indict not Gentiles, but Jews. Scripture itself, in other words, bears witness against those to whom it was entrusted, leaving the entire world accountable to God. Paul reasons: Those who were privileged to know God's will have certainly not obeyed it. So, if the favored few who knew God's demand also failed to obey, all are disobedient and lost.

Paul insists that it is impossible for *anyone* to be justified by the Law, since all Law can do is make humans conscious of sin (v 20). The indictment he levels against all human beings stems from their condition without the good news of what Christ Jesus has done to transform human history. Left to their own devices, all human beings are nothing but sinners in God's sight. This opens the way for Paul to demonstrate how the revelation of God's righteousness in the gospel deals precisely with the problem of the world's sin.

IN THE TEXT

a. All Humanity Under the Power of Sin (3:9)

■ **9** In the opening words of v 9, Paul's imaginary interlocutor raises two questions. The first consists of two words in Greek: *Ti oun*—*What . . . then?* The second consists of a single word, whose meaning is disputed: *proechometha*. It could mean **Are we any better?** or, **Are we any worse?** (NIV margin).

Within the diatribe style, **What . . . then?** serves a transitional function—to introduce a question prompted by the preceding discussion. Precisely what Paul meant by this question is debated. Douglas Moo suggests four possibilities: (1) "Am I [Paul] making an excuse for the Jews?" (2) "Are we Jews trying to excuse ourselves?" (3) "Are we Jews surpassed [by the Gentiles], so as to be disadvantaged?" (4) "Do we Jews have an advantage?" (1996, 200).

Paul's answer to the question is equally brief: *ou pantōs*, **Not at all!** Whether his questioner asks if Jews are at an advantage or disadvantage, his answer is negative. Jews have an unassailable advantage as far as salvation history is concerned (3:1-2; see 11:29). Despite their head start, Jews have no advantage when it comes to God's impartial judgment of all people without exception according to their works (2:17-29). Both Jews and Gentiles have falsified the truth about God (1:18-32; 3:1-8). Thus, all humanity is in the same boat; and it's sinking!

This is the issue Paul addresses in v 9, as his negative response indicates: **We have already made the charge that Jews and Gentiles** [*Hellēnas*, lit. **Greeks,** as in 1:14, 16; 2:9, 10; and 10:12] **alike are all under sin.** This summarizes the apostle's comprehensive indictment of sinful humanity in 1:18—2:29. He has hailed, first, Gentiles (1:19*b*-32) and then the Jews (2:1-29) before the judgment bar of God. And he has offered irrefutable evidence of the guilt of both. Both deserve the penalty of death.

Romans 3:9 is Paul's own comment on the purpose of 1:18—3:20. All who have not experienced the power of God's righteousness in the gospel are *hyph' hamartian,* **under sin.** This personification of Sin as an oppressive power is "unparalleled in Paul's other letters or in other early Christian literature" (Jewett 2007, 258). He insists that all of humanity is held captive to Sin's power. Paul's understanding of all people, Jews as well as pagans, is that they are not just sinners. It is not merely that they have transgressed the Law; they are helpless pawns under Sin's power. Sinners are enslaved, as it were, to "Sin," personified as a cruel and irresistible taskmaster, forcing all of its subjects to do its evil and self-destructive bidding.

ROMANS

3:9

Sin as a Ruling Power

Walter Bauer (1979, 43) summarizes the evidence for Paul's use of "sin" in almost personal terms "as a ruling power." Like a tyrant, Sin entered the world (5:12) and reigns there (v 21; 6:14). It lives in humanity (7:17, 20; 8:3; see 6:6). It has its own law (7:23; 8:2). Everything was subjected to it (Gal 3:22). People are sold into slavery to it (Rom 7:14), are its slaves (6:17, 20), and serve it (v 6). People may be set free from it (v 22). It may die (7:8) and revive (v 9). And it pays wages—death (6:23; see 5:12). It is noteworthy that *hamartia* appears with the definite article *hē* (lit. "the sin") no less than twenty-eight times between 5:12 and 8:10, identifying sin as a ruling power and principle, which Christ alone can dethrone by the greater power of the indwelling Holy Spirit. Only in 4:7; 7:5; and 11:27 does the plural form "sins" appear in Romans.

Paul allows no exception to this rule; and nothing more clearly shows the desperate need of the gospel. What humans need is more than forgiveness. They need a superior power to break in and set people free from sin. Paul insists that this new power exists, and that its liberating effects may be experienced only in the gospel of Jesus Christ (Moo 1996, 201). Like Sin, "Gospel" is personified. Paul's point is not that either Sin or Gospel is actually a person. It is that sinning makes victims of its willing participants. And, that those who trust the proclaimed good news about Jesus Christ are set free from their addiction to sinning. But it is not so much the message that liberates as it is the reality to which the message bears witness—the true sovereign of the universe, Jesus Christ.

For all of the foregoing reasons, **under sin** is better translated "under the power of sin" (NRSV). Up to this point in Romans Paul has not employed the noun *hamartia* ("sin"). He has used the verb *hamartanō* ("I sin") to describe the failure to obey of both Gentiles and Jews (in 2:12) and the noun *hamartōlos* ("sinner") to describe liars (in 3:7). It is often said that *hamartanō* ("I miss the mark") defines the *act* of sinning. But we "miss the mark," says Wesley, not because we are poor marksmen but because we choose the wrong mark and hit it squarely—sin is turning from God, our "last end," to self, our false end (Wesley 1979, 9:456). And Bauer notes that in the NT, *hamartia* refers not only to the action of departing from the right way but also to its result, its characteristic quality, its principle, and personal power (1979, 43).

Clearly, Paul's charge that all humanity lives "under the power of sin" (v 9 NRSV) accurately summarizes all he has said so far. The noun *hamartia* introduces the next major theme of the letter—"Sin" as a personified force that took possession of the human race with Adam's disobedience, and which rules our human existence until we appropriate God's liberating grace offered *all* through "Jesus Christ our Lord" (5:21, see 5:12-21).

b. Scriptural Demonstration (3:10-18)

■ **10** **As it is written** (v 10) is a formula Paul typically reserves for introductions to quotations from the OT (see 1:17). But nowhere else in his letters does he collect a list of quotations so long or drawn from so many sources. The rabbis called such a catena of thematically linked verses "pearl-stringing." Paul's purpose in citing these verses is clearly to substantiate his claim that Sin's rule is both universal and comprehensive. His carefully arranged list consists of biblical quotations held together thematically by their references to various parts of the body: throat, tongues, lips, mouth, feet, and eyes. The clear implication is that human beings are totally enslaved to Sin, that every part of the human person has participated in evil. The Jews' own scriptures are cited to demonstrate that they as fully as the Gentiles are **under sin**'s domination.

Paul opens his indictment with the broad charge that **no one** is **righteous,** anticipating the conclusion of 3:20. Sin is so universal as to admit *not a solitary exception.* The series of OT quotations clinch a case already established by various arguments.

(1) Sin in Human Character (3:10-12)

The quotations in these verses are taken from Ps 14:1-3 (= Ps 53:1-3). Paul departs from the Psalms text, which reads, "There is no one who does *good*" (Ps 14:1 = 53:1, emphasis added), to insist instead, **There is no one right-eous** (v 10, emphasis added). Given the importance of *righteousness* language in this part of Romans (see 3:4-5, 8, 19-20), Paul has evidently drawn from Eccl 7:20 ("There is not a righteous man on earth who does what is right and never sins") to "theologize" the Psalms quotation. "Paul also deletes the reference to the 'fool' in Ps 13:1, thus eliminating the traditional distinction between the wise, righteous person and the foolish, wicked one" (Jewett 2007, 259).

■ **11** Apart from divine grace, **there is no one who understands** or **seeks God** (Rom 3:11; see 1:21-25). The OT parallels suggest that such persons place themselves "among God's sworn enemies [who] participate in betraying the faith" (Jewett 2007, 260).

■ **12** **All have turned away** (3:12*a*) from God rather than toward him; i.e., they are unrepentant rebels. **They have together become worthless** (v 12*b*), i.e., made "useless" and "depraved" (Bauer 1979, 128). And thus, **there is no one who does good** (v 12*c*). Again Paul's modifications of the LXX text eliminate the distinction between the righteous and unrighteous and the presumption of the favored status of some (see 1:23, 26-31). "The final line of 3:12 claims that 'not a single person' performs a proper act, which is an awful indication of the universal corruption of the human race" (Jewett 2007, 261).

Apart from God's grace (see Phil 2:13), and deprived of a right relationship with God, all human beings without exception are blind, helpless, and corrupt. They embody what theologians call "total depravity." Their character is marked by a steady disposition to rebel against God.

(2) Sin in Human Speech (3:13-14)

■ **13-14** As in the citations in vv 10-12, Paul omits all distinctions between the righteous and wicked found in the three psalms he excerpts here (Jewett 2007, 261). **"Their throats are open graves; their tongues practice deceit"** (v 13*a* from Ps 5:9). **"The poison of vipers is on their lips"** (Rom 3:13*b* from Ps 140:3). **"Their mouths are full of cursing and bitterness"** (Rom 3:14 from Ps 10:7).

Jesus warned his disciples that since "out of the overflow of the heart the mouth speaks. . . . on the day of judgment . . . by your words you will be acquitted, and by your words you will be condemned" (Matt 12:34, 36-37; see Jas 3:6-12). Whereas Jesus uses direct speech, all of the Psalms quotations are examples of the figure of speech known as synecdoche (a subvariety of metonymy), in which a human body part represents the whole. Each of the parts involved in speaking is used to refer to human speech as a whole. In Rom 3:15-17, the same figure is used to refer to human behavior in general. Similarly, in v 18 "eyes" and in v 19 "mouth" represent human beings as a whole (see Bullinger 1898, 640-49).

The order of the Psalms quotations may intentionally follow the successive mechanisms of speech: throat, tongue, lips, and mouth. Describing **throats** as **open graves** underscores both the inner corruption of the speakers and the lethal effects of their speech. Deceitful **tongues** use flattery with evil intent—all that is said are lies (see 1:29; 3:7). Poisonous **lips** use speech to inflict injury and destruction on others. Mouths **full of cursing and bitterness** create the community chaos expressed in 1:29-30.

(3) Sin in Human Conduct (3:15-17)

■ **15-17** **"Their feet are swift to shed blood; ruin and misery mark their ways, and the way of peace they do not know"** (vv 15-17, from Isa 59:7-8 and Prov 1:16). In these quoted verses the prophet indicts the nation of Israel for its corruption and the social disaster its sins have caused. The **feet,** as the means of walking, symbolize the nation's lifestyle of sinful corruption. Paul charges Israel *as a whole* with the same violent unrighteousness marking Gentile sinners (see Rom 1:29-32).

(4) The Cause of All Sin (3:18)

■ **18** Quoting Ps 36:1, Paul says, **"There is no fear of God before their eyes."** The OT frequently describes pious obedience as either the "fear of God" or the "fear of the LORD." "The fear of the LORD is the beginning of wisdom" (Ps 111:10; Prov 9:10). "The fear of the LORD is the beginning of knowledge" (1:7). Paul has come full circle to his point of departure in Rom 1:21-32. Disrespect for God—irreverence—is the root error that gives rise to all the various sins of humanity. "Since Gentile sympathizers drawn to the moral and spiritual legacy of Judaism were called 'God-fearers,' to be entirely lacking in fear places the Jewish person below the worst of Gentiles" (Jewett 2007, 263).

The OT metaphor of turning one's eyes to the Lord (see Ps 25:15) refers to living in prayerful dependence on God. Sinners refuse to glorify God as God, preferring to live on their own (Rom 1:21).

"With Paul's elimination of the distinction between the righteous and fools, the catena relegates all Jews along with all Gentiles to the category of sinners and traitors, . . . enemies of God" (Jewett 2007, 263). In the pictures of sinful humanity reflected in the catena, drawn from scattered lines of psalmists and prophets, Paul does not imply that each of those base characteristics is found equally developed in every human being. Some, even most, of these sins remain latent in many persons; but they *all* exist *in germ* in the selfishness and pride of all of us. No one can predict what circumstance may trigger them to become active so long as the **fear of God** does not govern the heart. Such is the *cause* of the divine condemnation that is suspended over the human race (Brunner 1959, 26).

c. The Application: Universal Guilt (3:19-20)

■ **19** Paul now draws the implications of his long list of quotations for the position of human beings before God. **We know** (v 19) introduces shared convictions upon which Paul and his hearers agree (see 2:2). In this case, it is the applicability of **whatever** [*hosos, **everything***] **the law says** to those under its jurisdiction—those who are **in the realm of Law** (*en tōi nomōi*).

Paul's first use of **law** (*nomos*) in 3:19 refers to the series of scriptural quotations in vv 10-18, not to the Torah, as it does in its second instance (and often in his letters; see 1 Cor 9:8, 9; 14:21, 34; Gal 4:21). The difference is not great, since both the Scriptures and the Law were peculiar to the Jews, who live within the sphere of the OT revelation of God and under the authority of the Mosaic law.

The Jewish law obviously addresses Jews. Thus, the litany of scriptural quotations covering the full gamut of human evil refers to Jewish sinners. Paul apparently employs a fortiori reasoning—reaching an inescapable conclusion that necessarily follows from generally accepted facts: If Jews, favored with the revelation of God's will embodied in the Law, are enslaved to Sin—from head to toe, surely no one is exempt from Sin's oppressive rule.

Paul insists that the OT passages quoted in Rom 3:10-18, while not equally applicable to every Jew, do speak to Jews generally. They cannot be excluded from the judgment of God. Law demonstrates that the Jews are sinners like the Gentiles, condemned with them before God at the judgment (see 1:16). Their transgressions of the Law show that Jews, like Gentiles, are "under the power of sin" (3:9 NRSV; see 7:14-25).

Paul concludes that Law exists for this purpose: **so that** [*hina*] **every mouth may be silenced** before God and **the whole world held accountable to God** (3:19). Here **mouth** is an example of synecdoche, in which the part represents the whole. God brings unrighteous and deceptive words and deeds to an end. Universal lying must stop so that praise may begin (see 15:5-6). **World** is an example of synecdoche in reverse, in which the whole represents the part. The point is that no one can say anything in self-defense; all human beings are guilty as charged. There are no excuses.

The purpose for which God's law addresses the Jews is **that every mouth may be silenced and the whole world held accountable to God.** The Greek word translated **accountable** (*hypodikos*) is found nowhere else in the NT or LXX, but it is a technical legal term used in extrabiblical Greek to mean "answerable to," "liable to prosecution," or "under indictment" (see Bauer 1979, 844). Paul pictures God as both the injured party—the plaintiff—and the judge who weighs the evidence and pronounces the verdict. All humanity stands guilty before God, in the divine law court, accountable to God for willful and inexcusable violations of his will, awaiting the final condemnation their sins deserve. Israel's own Scriptures place them "firmly 'in the dock' along with everyone else" (Dunn 2002a, 38A:152).

Paul's accusations against the Jews become the basis for his claim that all people are guilty before God. If God's chosen people cannot be excluded from the judgment of God, then surely Gentiles, who have no claim on God's favor, are also guilty. But Paul's purpose in 1:18—3:20 is *not* to demonstrate that the Gentiles are guilty sinners in need of God's righteousness. This he assumes (see 1:18-32). His purpose is to demonstrate that Jews bear the same burden and the same need for deliverance from the tyranny of sin as do Gentiles. While all humans are included in the scope of vv 19-20, the particular reference is to Jews.

■ **20** If Jews as well as Gentiles are responsible sinners—self-conscious rebels against God, guilty, and awaiting judgment, what does this imply about the Jewish law? Paul concludes, echoing Ps 143:2: **Therefore** [*dioti*] **no one will be declared righteous in his sight by observing the law; rather, through the law we become conscious of sin** (Rom 3:20). The KJV more literally translates Paul's Greek: "Therefore by the deeds of the law there shall no flesh be justified in his sight: for by the law is the knowledge of sin." "Flesh" here is used as a synecdoche for a human person as a whole.

The "deeds of the law" cannot be limited to the ritual and ceremonial aspects of the Mosaic law. It must include even the Decalogue and conscience—the Law written on the hearts of Gentiles (see 2:14-16). It must embrace the moral deeds of both Gentiles and Jews (see vv 17-29). Nothing humans attempt to do as a means of self-justification will succeed.

Paul's citation of Ps 143:2 substitutes "no flesh" for "no man living" (perhaps influenced by *1 En.* 81:5—"no flesh is righteous in the sight of the Lord" *APOT*). "Flesh" (*sarx*) refers most basically to the muscle and skin that covers the bones of humans and animals. But Paul uses it in a wide variety of ways (see the sidebar "Flesh" in Rom 7). The NIV, e.g., translates *sarx* more than a dozen different ways in Romans alone. Here Paul seems to use "flesh" (NRSV) as a synecdoche for human persons as a whole. Thus, "no flesh" means **no one** (see Gal 2:16).

But Paul characteristically thinks of Flesh in contrast to Spirit—weak human beings as compared to the powerful presence of God (see Rom 8:3). Thus, what the apostle says about *sarx* here may also anticipate his later elaboration on "flesh" in 7:5, 14, 18 NRSV. Fallen humans in their own strength cannot possibly please God (8:8). They have no righteousness of their own. Only those suffering under the delusion of legalism or moralism imagine they can extricate themselves from their sinful predicament by simply treating God's commands seriously. Circumcision of the flesh alone is insufficient (2:28).

Paul does not mean that God's law is irrelevant for salvation. The Law cannot make us righteous, but it can reveal to us what is wrong with us. "For by the law is the knowledge of sin" (3:20 KJV). Law can diagnose the human problem, but it cannot cure it. Law effects, not salvation, but wrath (4:15). This is no insignificant matter.

> The Law, taken seriously, breaks the arrogance of man; yes, it breaks man himself. But only as someone who is broken, as a person who is thoroughly shaken, as someone who has come to the end of his tether, can he understand what has to be said to him as being the one and only Gospel message. (Brunner 1959, 27)

According to Paul, the final purpose of Law is to bring us to a ***real knowledge*** (*epignōsis*) of Sin. Law unmasks Sin's character as a powerfully enslaving force of evil and self-destruction in our lives from which *Christ* alone can deliver us.

Before Law was promulgated, human beings did evil in blissful ignorance. They were unable to recognize their wrongs as transgressions (4:15; 5:13), i.e., as acts of rebellion against the expressed will of God. If Law declares all people sinners and makes them conscious of their condition, then it all the more follows that Jews, to whom the Law is addressed, are just as much an object of God's wrath as the pagans, whose moral perversion and degradation reveal their condition. Paul anticipates here the discussion about the Law he will undertake in 7:7—8:4 (Fitzmyer 1993, 339).

Paul has made his case. Apart from the grace of God, the entire world stands guilty in the sight of the holy God. The way is now open for Paul's pronouncement of the message with which this first major section of Romans opens: the way of *God's righteousness* revealed in the gospel (1:16-17).

FROM THE TEXT

Before we turn to Paul's teaching of justification by faith (3:21—4:25), we need to be apprised that Luther's influential interpretation of this doctrine has come under serious scrutiny in NT scholarship in recent years.

The leading figure in questioning the classical canons of the doctrine as developed by Luther and most of the Reformation tradition has been E. P. Sanders. His *Paul and Palestinian Judaism* placed Paul's relation to Judaism and the OT in a new light. The debate continues, and not all have been persuaded by Sanders' alternative. But there is no way to talk about justification and its relation to Judaism and the OT today without critical interaction with this "new perspective" on Paul and its outlook in biblical studies. James D. G. Dunn, one of the participants in the debate, has put the issues in proper perspective in light of biblical scholarship.

Luther's conversion experience and the insight it gave him began a tradition of biblical interpretation, which resulted in the neglect of other crucial biblical insights related to the theme of divine justice. Luther's misunderstanding of "justification by faith" involved a significant misunderstanding of Paul.

Dunn is not saying that Luther was "wrong" as much as that the Lutheran expression of the doctrine of justification has been misguided by some questionable assumptions that call for critical examination. Luther overlooked and neglected some other dimensions of the biblical doctrine of God's justice and of Paul's teaching on justification.

One of Dunn's main concerns is that we recover Paul's focus on the *relational* nature of justification—not only relationship to God but also relationship between the Jews as God's elect people and the Gentiles as the outsiders of the covenant. We must remind ourselves that Paul based his doctrine of justification solidly on Judaism and the OT.

Luther and his Protestant followers set Paul's gospel in opposition to Judaism, which he viewed as a degenerate, legalistic religion. Sanders and other biblical scholars espousing the "new perspective" paint a different picture of Judaism contemporary with Paul as a religion of grace, with human obedience understood always as a response to that grace. The covenant was given by divine initiative, with the Law providing instruction as to the means of *remaining within* the covenant, not the means of *entering* it. To express the balance between grace revealed in God's election of Israel and the obedience God expected of Israel, Sanders christened the expression "covenantal nomism." (See the summary on p 30 of the Introduction above.)

What Sanders calls "covenantal nomism" seems to be precisely what Paul has been arguing in Rom 2:1—3:20. In accord with what we find elsewhere in the apostle's letters, grace is always prior; human effort is always the response to divine initiative (Phil 2:12-13). Good works are the fruit and not the root of salvation (Gal 5:6, 13-15, 22-25; Eph 2:8-10). To win the crown of final acceptance we must continue in faith and obedience (Col 1:21-23). And salvation is through-and-through covenantal (vv 12-14). Thus, Paul should not be read as an opponent of contemporary Judaism but as one intent on taking it seriously in light of his conviction that Jesus is the Jewish Messiah.

The Reformed theologians who in the past maligned Wesleyan theology as Pelagian, or semi-Pelagian at best, failed to understand both Paul and John Wesley. Wesley understood and taught the Pauline doctrine of salvation. For Wesley, grace is always prior; human effort is always in response to the divine initiative; good works are the fruit and not the root of salvation; justification is inseparable from regeneration and sanctification; justification is not earned, initially or finally; final salvation is "by works as condition, not works as merit."

However, we are getting ahead of Paul. To this point in the letter, he has not given a full exposition of his soteriology, but only the hamartiology that underlies it. This he will begin to do in the next section of the letter (Rom 3:21-26).

B. God's Righteousness Provided (3:21—8:39)

1. The Gospel of Justification (3:21—4:25)

The good news of 3:21—5:21 stands out all the more brightly as we move from the shadows of 1:18—3:20. God has acted to spare sinful humanity from the results of its rebellion, but at what a cost to God! He could not forever ignore evil, like an indulgent parent blind to the truth about his children. To let sinners "get by" on their way to self-destruction would besmirch his character as well. In Christ, God at once revealed the seriousness of sin *and* his willingness to give humanity a fresh start.

Paul now begins to take up the theme he so boldly set forth in 1:16-17. He has demonstrated the utter failure of humankind—both Jews and Gentiles—to achieve righteousness before God by means of the Law. "But now" the righteousness of the new covenant—the eschatological righteousness witnessed to by the Law and the Prophets—has broken into history. [The word "eschatological," from the Greek *eschata* ("last things"), refers to the period between the two Advents (see Acts 2:16-21).] God has himself resolved the dilemma created by the coming of the Law and now through the gospel is providing a righteousness "apart from law," through the redemption won by his Son Christ Jesus and given freely to all who will receive it by faith. This end-time righteousness effects justification, sanctification, and glorification.

a. The Meaning of Justification (3:21-26)

BEHIND THE TEXT

"This pericope sums up, advances, and eloquently climaxes the preceding argument of the letter" (Jewett 2007, 271). Here the imagery of the courtroom, the slave market, and the sacrificial altar provide the cultural backdrop for Paul's account of the good news of salvation. As sinners we stand guilty be-

118

fore the Judge of the universe, but we find that he also stands beside us as our Advocate, intent on finding a way to do justice while extending mercy. We stand as hopeless slaves under Sin's dominion, but we find that the Sovereign God has already acted to emancipate us. We stand before the altar of God with nothing to offer, but there we meet the God who in Jesus Christ has acted as both our Priest and Sacrifice to provide deliverance from Sin's tyrannical rule. The cross, the violent instrument of Jesus' death, became the sacrificial altar of the universe. There, God himself made atonement for the whole sinful human race (see Oord and Lodahl 2005, 91-141).

The gospel reveals God's righteousness in two ways: first as wrath and second as salvation. The wrath of God is a present reality (1:18). Thankfully, God's faithfulness to his creation is also a present reality, in spite of human unfaithfulness (v 17; 3:21, 26). God's righteousness is his power to reestablish his lordship over his creation and so restore it to a positive relation to himself. He does so by breaking the power of Sin, cleansing sinners of their depravity, and reconciling them to himself.

Law pointed out, but was powerless to remedy, the problem of Sin (vv 19-20). The seriousness of Sin became apparent in its awful aftermath. Sin occasioned God's judgment of sinners, but it also occasioned his extraordinary measures to redeem. God's unprecedented measures to save were not unexpected. The Scriptures anticipated the reckless self-abandon of God. Many popular notions of the OT are simply wrong. It is not a book of *law* in contrast to the NT as a book of *grace*. God did not get converted between the Testaments. God has always been gracious. The cross shows how far he was willing to go to save. Jesus Christ demonstrates God's faithfulness to his fallen creation. He has done what the Law was powerless to do (see 8:3-4).

Implicit in the words **But now,** which open this section (v 21), is the stark contrast between what was once true and the new reality. Something remarkable has happened **at the present time** (v 26), says Paul, something that has won a foothold in the darkened scene of human history and changed the face of the world forever. **But now**—at a critical moment in human history around A.D. 30—two "poles" in the nature of God—holiness and love—met in Jesus of Nazareth, through whose death, resurrection, and exaltation the Triune God accomplished the world's redemption.

The passage is loaded with key theological terms, notably the phrase *dikaiosynē theou.* In vv 21 and 22 the phrase means **a righteousness from God**—that is, "righteousness only God can provide." In vv 25 and 26 the equivalent phrase is *tēs dikaiosynēs autou*—**his justice** or "his righteousness." In vv 24 and 26, the verb root *dikaioō* ("I justify") appears twice, and the adjective **just** (*dikaios*) once. In v 25, **righteousness** is the gracious provision of Christ's **sacrifice of atonement. Justice** (= "righteousness" NRSV) is at once

God's "saving righteousness" in Christ and his "integrity" as God. He acts in complete conformity to his character as the holy, loving God. Through the death of Christ God reveals "that he himself is righteous and that he justifies the one who has faith in Jesus" (v 26 NRSV). In the cross, God justifies *himself* as God, while at the same time he justifies *sinners* who put their trust in the crucified and risen Lord (see Acts 2:36-39; 1 Cor 1:20—2:5).

The concentration in Rom 3:21-26 of so many rare words and concepts that are not typical of Paul's exposition of the gospel in his other letters suggests to many scholars that Paul is quoting early Christian tradition (for the evidence, see Jewett 2007, 270-71). Among these terms in v 24 are *dikaiosynē* used with the rare meaning **justice;** and *apolytrōsis,* **redemption,** used to refer to a past event. Four rare terms figure significantly in v 25: *protithemi* with the meaning **presented;** *hilastērion,* **sacrifice of atonement;** *haimati,* **blood;** and *paresis,* **unpunished.** Furthermore, the notion here of God passing over *previously committed sins* finds expression nowhere else in Paul's letters.

The anacoluthon [break in the Greek construction] at the end of v 25 also supports the supposition that this is a "pre-Pauline formula, a confession of faith, which was perhaps employed liturgically in Hellenistic-Jewish Christianity" (Reumann 1966, 432). A similar interpretation of the saving work of Christ is found in the anonymous Hellenistic-Jewish homily we call Hebrews. There, chs 7—10 view Jesus' death as fulfilling the sacrifices of the Mosaic law, particularly the Day of Atonement ritual. Perhaps Paul drew on such tradition because it not only supported his argument but also created another point of contact with his Roman audience.

IN THE TEXT

■ **21** Paul grandly announces, **But now a righteousness from God, apart from law, has been made known, to which the Law and the Prophets testify** (v 21). The opening words **But now** (*nyni de*) might signify a logical contrast and be translated, "But as it is." But it seems best here to take the words as announcing a temporal contrast, a shift from the way things were in the past to the way they are in the present, **But now** (see 7:6; 15:23, 25; 16:25-26; 1 Cor 15:20; 2 Cor 8:22; Eph 2:12-13; Col 1:26-27; 2 Tim 1:9-10; Phlm 9, 11; and Heb 9:26). The NT consistently contrasts pre-Christian and Christian dispensations as time periods (see Acts 17:30; Gal 3:23, 25; 4:3; Heb 1:1).

Elsewhere in the NT *pephanerōtai,* **has been made known,** is always used with expressions denoting time (see Gal 4:4-7; Titus 1:3; 1 Pet 1:20; Sanday and Headlam 1929, 82). God has made his righteousness publicly and histori-

ROMANS

3:21

cally visible in the Christ event, and the gospel announces this as good news (see Rom 1:16-17).

The new order predicted by the ancient prophets has appeared. *The old order has gone; a new order has already begun* (2 Cor 5:17*b*). "All this has been the work of God" (2 Cor 5:18*a* REB). This new situation is not a human achievement; it has been brought about by God's intervention. **Now,** because of the coming of Jesus Christ, the miracle has happened. This miracle is the end-time fulfillment of the promise of justification, sanctification, and glorification.

Paul's message is that now, in the new age Christ inaugurated, **a righteousness from God** (see Rom 3:5) "has been manifested" (v 21 NASB) in the gospel. Here *dikaiosynē* refers to God's own righteousness—the quality of *being* just or righteous. Of course, it also refers to the justifying *activity* of God and the righteousness the Church enjoys as a consequence of God's saving activity in Christ (Godet 1883, 146).

Ernst Käsemann properly cautions against limiting the concern of divine righteousness to personal human salvation to the neglect of cosmic restoration.

> *Dikaiosynē Theou* is for Paul God's sovereignty over the world revealing itself eschatologically in Jesus. . . . It is the rightful power with which God makes his cause to triumph in the world which has fallen away from him, and which yet, as creation, is his inviolable possession. (Käsemann 1969b, 180)

Cosmic and human salvation are inseparable because "the subject of divine righteousness remains God himself" (Jewett 2007, 272). In Rom 3:21-26, as in Ps 98, the Creator intervenes in history "to restore the order of creation and of human society that has been corrupted by sinful human activity." God demonstrates his righteousness by making right the world and its inhabitants (Rom 3:26; Jewett 2007, 272-73).

God's righteousness, **made known** in the gospel, is **apart from law** (*chōris nomou*; see 3:28; 4:6; 7:8-9), i.e., it is manifested "quite independently of law" (REB). Thus, doing what Law requires cannot effect the right relation with God Sin destroyed (3:20). It is impossible to be made righteous **from law,** as in "by observing the law." Here Paul universalizes "without the law" to mean beyond the national and religious boundaries of Israel (Dunn 2002a, 38A:165).

However, he quickly adds a disclaimer. Although the gospel is not confined to the normal Jewish parameters, **the Law and the Prophets testify** to its truth (see 1:2). Here **the Law** coupled with **the Prophets** refers to the first division of the Hebrew canon. Since the final division, the Writings ("the Psalms" in Luke 24:44) was not yet settled, the pair refers to the entire OT Scriptures (see Matt 5:17; 7:12; Luke 16:16; Acts 13:15; 24:14). The testimony of **the Law and the Prophets** indicates that "the new order of things is in no way contrary to the old, but rather a development which was duly foreseen and provided for" (Rom 1:2; 3:31; 4:1-25; 9:25-33; 10:16-21; 11:1-10, 16-29; 15:8-12; 16:26; Sanday and Headlam 1929, 83).

Since Paul does not indicate which specific biblical passages he has in mind, we would do well not to speculate. He takes for granted that "the divine righteousness in Christ is affirmed by Scripture as a whole" (Jewett 2007, 275). The apostle has spoken of the source of this **righteousness** both positively and negatively—**from God** and not **from law**. Now he expands his exposition, identifying the means by which it was **made known** (*pephanerōtai*, "manifested" NASB = *apokalyptetai*, "revealed" in 1:16-17) in the gospel.

■ **22** The gift of **righteousness from God comes through faith** [*pisteōs*] **in Jesus Christ to all who** *have faith* [*pisteuontas*; 3:22]. The phrase **to all who believe** has the same force as "by faith from first to last" in 1:17. For the first time, however, Paul makes it clear that the faith that justifies (see 3:24, 26) is specifically **faith in Jesus Christ**—*pistis Iēsou Christou*, literally *the faith of Jesus Christ* (emphasis added).

Protestants have traditionally taken this as an objective genitive, referring to "the faith Christians place in Jesus Christ," but this makes the conclusion of the verse, referring to the benefit of this faith **to all who** *have faith* seem an unnecessary repetition (tautology). Thus, some interpreters of the "new perspective" take the phrase as a subjective genitive, referring to "the faithfulness shown by Jesus Christ," as in the parallel, *the faithfulness of Abraham* in 4:16.

Jesus demonstrated his faithfulness to God by choosing to die for the sinful world. Thus, *pistis Iēsou Christou* would refer to "the faithfulness shown by Jesus Christ" specifically on the cross. Advocates of this position argue that it makes more sense linguistically (Moo 1996, 224 nn. 24, 25) to avoid the tautology of asserting the importance of human faith twice. Furthermore, the translation *through the faithfulness of Jesus Christ to all who have faith* results in a natural Pauline combination of divine initiative and human response.

Despite these arguments, the traditional Protestant reading has much to commend it. Certainly, the Greek word *pistis* can mean "faithfulness" (see 3:3), and Paul can trace human justification to the obedience of Christ (5:19). However, throughout 3:21—4:25, *pistis* normally refers to the faith exercised by people in God/Christ, as the sole means of justification.

However, the question remains: If Paul refers to human faith in the first phrase, why does he repeat the phrase **to all who believe** in v 22? Traditional Protestant interpreters answer: to highlight the universal availability of God's righteousness. Jewett claims that Paul uses **faith** "twice in this sentence to indicate that participation in righteousness is available to all groups regardless of their status or ethnicity" (2007, 276). Righteousness is accessible only through faith in Christ—but it is offered freely to *anyone* who has faith in Christ.

Jewett explains the popularity of the subjective genitive reading—"faithfulness of Jesus Christ" (see his bibliography of its advocates; 2007, 277 n. 75)—as an effort to overcome the shortcomings of overly individualized, intellectualized, and dogmatized conceptions of faith. He charges that this reading fails to appreciate adequately "the social dimension" of **faith** in early Christianity as "jargon for participation in the community of the converted" (Jewett 2007, 277) or "entrance into the 'spiritual fellowship of believers'" (276). Moreover, he correctly cautions against erecting "a theology on the interpretation of a case ending" (277).

Paul's central concern in v 22 is not the christological basis for justification (as in v 24), but the universal availability of justification. **There is no difference** [*diastolē*] any longer between Israel and other nations (a reversal of Exod 8:23). The one God of both Jews and Gentiles (Rom 3:29-30) "does not show favoritism" (2:11). Paul is persuaded that he has satisfactorily demonstrated in 1:18—3:20 that in the final analysis **there is no difference** between Gentiles and Jews, **because** [*gar*] **all have sinned** (v 23; see 3:9). The universal scope of sin makes obvious the universal need for **righteousness from God** (v 21).

Paul closely associates "godlessness and wickedness" (1:18) with the human refusal to glorify God as God (v 21) and to exchange God's glory for idols (v 23). Therefore, not surprisingly, here he places collective sinning in parallel with continuous falling **short of the glory of God**. Their sin disqualified Adam and Eve from participating in the honor God intended for them, thwarting God's creation-purposes for humanity (*Apoc. Mos.* 20:2; Jewett 2007, 279).

Apart from divine intervention, all people are hopelessly entrapped by their addiction to sinning. But the scope of sin, all-encompassing as it is, is more than outmatched by the reach of God's grace (5:20). In fact, Paul somewhat incautiously claims that **all . . . are justified freely by his grace through the redemption that came by Jesus Christ** (3:23-24). This might mistakenly be taken to imply that human **redemption** is as extensive and all-inclusive as human sinfulness. This is true in potential, but God's free gift of **redemption** is not unconditional, nor is salvation universal.

Paul's qualification remains in place: Justification is for believers in Christ only (v 22); and the **sacrifice of atonement** is **through faith in his blood** (v 25). Of course, we should not minimize Paul's conviction that God has already done all that is necessary to salvage lost humanity. Nor should we gloss over the necessity of an obedient response to God's offer of universal salvation. God respects human choices too much to force anyone to be saved against his or her will.

The gift of being made right with God is available to all. The universality of salvation by faith, affirmed in 1:17, is explained in 3:22-23. Just as sin knows no ethnic boundaries, so it is with salvation. Salvation is as extensive as sin. But only in the sphere of Christ's lordship—within the Church—is there universal salvation. Paul's negative proof that "Jews and Gentiles alike are all under sin" (v 9) is the basis for his positive claim. All whom God puts right with himself are righteous, but this righteousness is not a status people possess. As a relationship between persons, it is preserved intact only as God's gracious lordship, restored in Christ, is sustained through obedience. A right relationship with God is neither static nor private.

All who have faith are transformed by the Spirit into Christ's "likeness with ever-increasing glory" (2 Cor 3:18). "In being honored by God through Christ who died for all, the formerly shamed are integrated into the community of the saints in which this transformation process occurs, under the lordship of Christ" (Jewett 2007, 281). Only believers will enjoy final salvation and participate in the eschatological **glory of God** intended for all (see Rom 5:2; 8:30).

■ **23** The universality of sin is affirmed, but not explained. **All have sinned** (3:23). As a result, **All . . . fall short of the glory of God**. God's glory is the reality of his presence. To be in God's presence is the greatest honor imaginable. Sinful human beings are deprived of God's favor and presence. The right relation between creature and Creator has been lost. Though God has been wronged, he has taken the initiative to make things right. He offered his Son as **a sacrifice of atonement** (v 25)—to reconcile the previously alienated parties, to restore the forfeited honor.

That **righteousness from God comes . . . to all** in v 22 stands in striking contrast to 1:18, which refers to "the wrath of God . . . revealed from heaven against all the godlessness and wickedness of men." All these genitive constructions are clearly subjective. "The wrath of God" is not human anger directed toward God, but God's judgment directed toward sinners. The "godlessness and wickedness of men" are not injustices inflicted upon people, but obviously the sins people commit. Just so, *the righteousness of God* is his saving activity of bringing sinners who will trust him into a right relationship with himself.

God's righteousness that justifies all who believe comes totally undeserved—**by his grace**. Although God extends his grace **freely** (*dōrean, as a gift*) to helpless sinners, it cost him dearly. "The gift of righteousness" (5:17) is entirely unilateral. Nothing humans did compelled him to act graciously.

■ **24** God's **gift** is made available to sinners **through** [*dia*] **the redemption that came by Christ Jesus** (3:24). Sanday and Headlam note that the Greek word *apolytrōseōs*, **redemption,** in economic transactions denoted "a deliverance obtained by purchase (*lytron*)." In numerous NT passages (Matt 20:28; Mark 10:45; Acts 20:28; 1 Cor 6:20; 7:23; Gal 3:13; 1 Pet 1:18; 2 Pet 2:1; Rev 5:9) "Christians are said to be 'bought,' or 'bought with a price'" paid entirely by God, but "the emphasis is on the cost of man's redemption. We need not press the metaphor yet a step further by asking (as the ancients did) to whom the ransom or price was paid" (Sanday and Headlam 1929, 85-86).

Paul's point is not the purchase but its result: Christ's death sets sinners free, liberates, releases, and delivers them from slavery to sin. The Greek root of *apolytrōsis* is *lyō*, which means "loose, set free." The freedom Christ freely gives, not the means by which he achieved it, whether imaged as military struggle or economic price, is Paul's concern. In **Jesus Christ** the sway of the powers that oppose God is broken once for all, and those who are in Christ are set free from those forces that formerly held them captive. And **the glory of God** (Rom 3:23), which was forfeited by Adam's rebellion, is now being progressively restored to believers by "the Lord, who is the Spirit" (2 Cor 3:18; see 1 Cor 15:45).

As hopeless slaves to Sin, humans can change lords only by first being set free from their bondage—that is, by **redemption** (Rom 3:24). But **redemption** has already been won once-and-for-all **by Christ Jesus.** God gives his costly freedom **freely** to all who will take it. It remains for sinners only to accept the gift—this is **faith** (vv 22, 25, 26). Sinners must admit they are slaves to sin and helpless to free themselves. They must turn from their rebellion to trust the God who is, abandoning the gods of their own creation to surrender to the lordship of their Creator. God **justifies those who have faith in Jesus,** restoring them to the relationship intended between humans and their Creator (v 26). That is, God actually makes sinners righteous.

■ **25** That the figurative language should not be pressed too far is clear in Paul's shift from economic imagery in v 24 to sacrificial imagery in v 25, as he again attempts to explain how God manifested his **righteousness.** The apostle now pictures the death of Christ in terms of priest and sacrifice. **God presented him as a sacrifice of atonement** (v 25). Although *proetheto,* **presented,** may refer to plans and purposes, as in its other NT instances (Rom 1:13; Eph 1:9), here it means "offer" (Bauer 1979, 722).

Theologians debate whether this atoning sacrifice is an "expiation" or "propitiation." They agree that what sinful humanity needed was a right relationship with God, only God himself was able to provide. This sacrifice reconciles to God only those sinners who have **faith in his blood** (Rom 3:25), i.e., who trust Christ's death as the sole means of salvation. The word *hilastērion,* **sacrifice of atonement,** has been at the center of the unresolved theological debate for nearly two millennia (see Jewett 2007, 284 n. 149 and 285 nn. 165 and 168 for recent studies). Despite agreement *that* the death of Christ is the means of atonement, Christians have never reached consensus as to *how* it accomplishes this.

The noun *hilastērion,* used only here and in Heb 9:5 in the NT, is a compound of *hilas-* and the suffix *-tērion,* which refers to a "place." Whether "pro-

3:24-25

pitiation" or "expiation," this is where it happens. The LXX uses the term to designate the "place of the sin offering." This is better translated "purification offering," indicating its function in relation to the holy place and altar (Dwight Swanson e-mail 2/16/07). In the LXX *hilastērion* identifies the *kapporet*, the "cover" in Hebrew, on the ark of the covenant, which was behind the veil in the holy of holies.

English translations traditionally render *hilastērion/kapporet* "mercy seat," but the word *hesed*, "mercy," has no Hebrew basis. The ark's golden lid covered the historical reminders of God's interventions in Israel's history, including the oracles of God (Exod 25:17-22). Above it God manifested his presence (1 Sam 4:4; 2 Sam 6:2; Ps 80:1-2) and spoke to Moses (Exod 25:22; Num 7:89). Preeminently, it was the place where, on the Day of Atonement, the Temple was cleansed by the sprinkling of sacrificial blood, making it a fit place for people to be reconciled to God (Lev 16:11-22).

The Jerusalem Bible, which translates *hilastērion* "a sacrifice for reconciliation," goes to the heart of biblical "propitiation." The death of Christ demonstrates that God has no hostility toward the alienated human race and invites his enemies to be reconciled to God (Rom 5:10). God always takes the initiative in dealing with the problem of human sin. So here Paul writes, **God presented** [Jesus] **as a sacrifice of atonement** (3:25). In 2 Cor 5:17-21 the apostle makes it explicit that the atonement is the work of God himself: "God, who reconciled us to himself through Christ . . . was reconciling the world to himself in Christ" (vv 18-19).

The **sacrifice of atonement** (Rom 3:25) is qualified by two parallel and complementary phrases. First, God's propitiating/expiating work becomes effective **through faith**—the human response to God's offer is its subjective condition. Second, atonement is **in his blood** (a dative of metaphorical space) or "by his blood" (an instrumental dative)—the death of Christ is the historical or objective condition of the atonement.

Of course, **blood** does not refer to the fluid flowing in Jesus' veins and arteries. By metonomy, here as often in both OT and NT, it refers to the offering up of life in death. Atonement is provided by the Savior's death on the cross; but it must be received through faith to be effective (see Godet 1883, 153). Although 4 Macc 6:29 and 17:22 similarly claim atoning benefits for the blood of pious martyrs, 4 Maccabees limits this atonement to the people of Israel. Paul insists that the blood of Christ atones for all who have faith, overcoming ethnic and religious boundaries. Thus, we may paraphrase Rom 3:25a: **In the death of Jesus Christ, God publicly offered himself as the means of salvation for all who will receive it by faith.**

The implications of the phrase **through faith in his blood** have been debated. The English word order in the NIV and KJV seems to imply that the object of faith is the **blood.** But for Paul, faith is always in a person. Christ's sacrificial death came as he shed his blood, as he poured out his life to save sinners from death. The death of Christ, which Paul more often associates with the cross than with the **blood** Jesus shed there, was the dramatic and conclusive condemnation of the world's sin, the final proof that God is holy and just.

For Christ to be the **sacrifice of atonement** specifically **through faith** requires believers to accept God's objective condemnation of their sins. The Gospels and Acts refer to repentance and forgiveness of sins. Paul normally refers to faith as the appropriate human response to God's gracious offer of salvation. In all Paul's letters, only 4:5-8 equates justification and forgiveness. In Eph 1:7 and Col 1:14, "forgiveness of sins" and "redemption" (*apolytrōsis;* see Rom 3:24) are equated. However, the terminology of "forgiveness" (*aphesis/aphiēmi*) never appears in vv 21-26. **Through faith** sinners identify with Christ's death, accepting God's judgment upon their sins—dying to them, in order to receive God's life and salvation (see Gal 2:19-21).

Faith as Identification with the Crucified Jesus

In Israel's ritual practice, the slaughter of sacrificial animals and the sprinkling of their blood (as in Lev 4:33-34) symbolized the process by which sinners, whom the animals represent, surrender their previous life conditions and allow themselves "to be abandoned to God in self-consecration and self-offering." Sinners identify with their sacrificial victims by placing their hands on the heads of the animals, affirming and effecting their identification with the dying victims. By participating in the ritual, sinners recognize that their sins made the sacrifice necessary; i.e., they confess their sins, and they recognize that they, not the innocent victim, deserved to die. The identification of believers and the sacrificial victim realized in the ritual gives them "access to the renewing and revitalizing forces released by contact with the altar, that is, with God, through this vicarious sacrifice." This vicarious identification with the atoning sacrifice is what Paul means by faith in the blood of Christ (Leenhardt 1957, 103).

3:25

In the death of Christ, God was able **to demonstrate** [*endeixin,* **proof**] his justice [*dikaiosynēs;* **righteousness**], because in his forbearance [*anochēi,* **delay**] he had left the sins committed beforehand unpunished (Rom 3:25*b*). Paul's claim challenges the popular misconception that the OT presents God as demanding and inflexible in contrast to the NT presentation of God as loving and forgiving. Paul assumes that God passed over human sin in the time before the coming of Christ. It is not that God generously forgave these sins, or that he overlooked or disregarded them. Rather, he merely let them go unpunished. However, God could no longer "wink" at human ignorance and sin (see Acts 17:30-31; 2 Macc 6:12-17). The OT sacrificial system merely provisionally postponed the final solution for the problem of sin and sinning—the death and resurrection of Christ (Dunn 2002a, 38A:173). "Christ's death . . . replaced the temple as a means of reconciliation with God" (Jewett 2007, 290), a means open **to all who have faith** (Rom 3:22), not just Israel.

■ **26** Verse 26 concludes Paul's long sentence begun at v 21. In Christ's death God acted **to demonstrate** [*endeixin*] **his justice** [*dikaiosynēs*, **righteousness**] at the present time [see v 21], so as [*eis to*] to be just [*dikaion*, **righteous**] and the one who justifies [*dikaiounta*, **makes righteous**] **the one who has** faith in Jesus. The purpose (*eis to*) of this remarkable proof of the seriousness with which God takes Sin was at once to vindicate God's own **righteousness** and to **make righteous** all who have faith in Christ. Christ's death is in this present age the sign of judging righteousness, as well as forgiving love. It publicly displayed at once God's wrath against every kind of human unrighteousness and his incomprehensible mercy on everyone **who has** faith in Jesus (Brunner 1959, 30). At the cross, in one final, great redemptive act of God, "love and faithfulness meet together; righteousness and peace kiss each other" (Ps 85:10), but the righteousness of God is not on display only at the cross. As Jewett observes:

> The righteousness of God manifests itself in the restoration of the fallen world in the small communities of faith whom Paul wishes to enlist in the project to carry this gospel of the crucified Lord to the end of the known world. (2007, 293)

FROM THE TEXT

The term *hilastērion* cannot resolve the debate as to which of the debated English terms—"propitiation" or "expiation"—best explains how Christ's death on the cross effects atonement. It clearly affirms that this is *where* God deals with the problem of human sin, but not *how*. Paul hints that the death of Jesus was the great Day of Atonement. God made the death of Jesus "the new place of atonement, epiphany, and divine presence," the new means of access to God open to all (Jewett 2007, 287). If Roman Christianity originated in the synagogue, Paul's use of this ancient Christian hymn put him on common ground with his Jewish audience.

Should *hilastērion* be translated "propitiation" (KJV, NASB) or "expiation" (RSV; REB: "expiating") in Rom 3:25? Was the death of Christ "a propitiatory sacrifice," a softening of God's wrath and manifesting his justice? Or was it "an expiatory sacrifice," covering or cleansing away the guilt of human sin? The choice between the two will be determined by the interpreter's understanding of the atonement. Avoiding the hermeneutical dichotomy, a number of recent translations, like the NIV and NRSV, translate the term neutrally, as **a sacrifice of atonement.**

Although the more extreme understandings of both expiation and propitiation must be rejected, in reality, aspects of both are inherent in *hilastērion* and seem to some interpreters necessary to a balanced biblical doctrine. "Propitiation" has a *Godward* reference: through the death of Christ the justice of God as Judge is revealed. "Expiation" has a *human* reference: Christ's sacrifice wipes away the guilt of human sin.

Extreme views of *propitiation* effectively make God subject to some higher law to which he must answer—when justice demands, even God must comply. It evokes images of a vindictive deity prepared to throw a temper tantrum, placated by a display of sacrifice that melts his hard heart, satisfies his craving to punish someone, and renders him incapable of doing what justice otherwise demands. And it makes the death of Christ akin to divine child abuse. Such an understanding is obviously unworthy of God. Christ is not God's naive and helpless victim. Trinitarian faith insists that on the cross God offers himself, accepting the awful consequences of human rebellion. If we speak of Christ's sacrifice as propitiation, we must do so against the background of Romans. It nowhere suggests that "the wrath of God" (1:18) had to be appeased or that the death of Jesus satisfied God's offended honor.

Extreme views of *expiation* also have serious objections. Some understand it as hiding sin rather than cleansing it away. They imagine a god who tricks himself, hiding continuing human sinfulness behind the righteousness of Christ, which he pretends belongs to sinners. Such notions of imputed righteousness make salvation a ruse and God a party to self-deception. Both extreme approaches fail to do justice to Paul's meaning in 3:25.

What Paul says the death of Christ accomplishes, not theologically biased assumptions about propitiation and expiation, must nuance definitions of both terms. If the terms are to be salvaged, both extreme views must be rejected. Unless excesses and folk misunderstandings of atonement perpetuated in unfortunate sermon illustrations are discarded, both terms may need to be eliminated from our theological vocabulary. There has never been a universally accepted doctrine of the atonement, and probably with good reason. The NT uniformly agrees *that* Christ's death on the cross provides the means of salvation, but its various witnesses use a variety of images to explain *how*.

Biblical "propitiation" means that God has found a way **to demonstrate his justice** (vv 25 and 26) while extending mercy to **those who have faith in Jesus** (v 26). Within the community of faith, God offers sinners—those who made themselves his enemies—a place to be reconciled to God and restored to righteousness.

Biblical "expiation" correctly emphasizes the affect of the atonement on humans. In Christ guilty rebels are freed from their slavery to Sin and cleansed from its defilement. "God made him who had no sin to be a sin offering for us, so that in him we might become the righteousness of God" (2 Cor 5:21 margin). Jewett correctly stresses:

> In contrast to expiation, which functions regardless of the behavior or attitude of recipients, atonement in the Pauline sense of reconciliation of those who declared war against God is effective only for those who respond to the good news in faith. (Rom 3:25-26; 2007, 288)

b. Three Conclusions from God's Justifying Act (3:27-31)

BEHIND THE TEXT

In the history of interpretation this brief passage has been overshadowed by preoccupation with the previous passage (vv 21-26) as it affects theories of the atonement. For Paul, however, the main purpose of that passage was not to reflect as a "systematic theologian" on the meaning of Christ's sacrifice. It was to show how God's righteousness became the source of human righteousness through faith in Christ.

Paul returns to the diatribe style of discourse, allowing his audience to "overhear" his dialogue with an imaginary Jewish objector. The conclusion is significant: If all hope of righteousness based on human efforts to keep the Law is illusory (vv 10-20); and, if God has provided a new possibility of righteousness, universal in scope and based on faith (vv 21-26); no grounds whatsoever remain for pursuing righteousness by observing the Law. Faith is the only appropriate response to God, whose "oneness" reflects his singular desire to save the entire human race. In vv 27-31 Paul draws this necessary conclusion, while warding off any suggestion that faith somehow nullifies the Jewish law. Faith does not overthrow Law, it upholds it (Byrne 1996, 135)!

IN THE TEXT

■ **27** Paul draws three inferences (*oun*, **therefore**, v 27) based on the preceding passage. These inferences are supported by three underlying assumptions: Righteousness is by faith alone. There is just one God. And, law and faith are not antithetical but complementary.

(1) Righteousness by Faith Excludes Boasting (3:27-28)

Paul's interlocutor asks, **Where, then, is boasting?** (v 27*a*). If all humanity, including Jews, are helpless victims of Sin's power (v 9) and fall short of God's glory (v 23), can Jews no longer claim a special standing before God (2:17, 23)?

Paul insists that all such bragging rights no longer exist. **It is excluded** (*exekleisthē,* **It has been eliminated**) for all once-and-for-all. "If Jewish boasting is illegitimate, so is Gentile boasting. By its very nature, honor granted through grace eliminates the basis of all human boasting" (Jewett 2007, 296). God's new way of freely reconciling humanity to himself through Christ has barred the door to all competitive claims.

The imaginary questioner asks, **On what principle? On that of observing the law?** To which Paul responds, **No, but** [*ouchi, alla*] **on that of faith** (v 27*b*). **On what principle?** is literally, *Through what law* [*dia poiou nomou*]? Here *nomos* seems to refer to "a system of law" or a "constituted order of things." Thus, the questioner asks, "Under what kind of system is this result obtained?" (Sanday and Headlam 1929, 95). Paul's formulation of the dialogue presumes a clear distinction between true and false uses of the Law (see 2:17-24; 3:21). He opposes exclusion of boasting *through a law of works* [*dia . . . nomou . . . tōn ergōn,* **of observing the law**] vs. *through a law of faith* [*dia nomou pisteōs,* **on that of faith**] (see 4:6; 7:8, 9). Paul's point is not to undermine the Jewish Torah. It is to maintain the underlying antithesis between human achievement and divine gift.

Law in Romans

The word **law** (*nomos*) is used by Paul in various ways in Romans. *(a)* In 3:21, that God's way of righteousness through faith is witnessed to by "the Law and the Prophets" clearly uses Law to refer to the Pentateuch, the first five books of the OT. *(b)* The statement in v 19—"Now we know that whatever the law says, it says to those who are under the law," uses law in the first instance referring to a catena of scriptures from Psalms, Ecclesiastes, and Isaiah (see vv 10-12). Thus, in both instances law must mean the Hebrew Scriptures, our OT. *(c)* In v 27 "law" means what we would express by some expression such as "religious system" (see 7:21, 23). *(d)* Often it refers to the moral law, the commandments of God known at least to some degree even by Gentiles (2:14-15), but disclosed to Israel in the Decalogue and elsewhere in Torah. This is the form in which Paul had come to know Law in his own experience (7:7-13). It is the sense in which he thinks of Law in 3:20; 4:15; 5:13; 7:14, 22, 25*b*; 8:3; 9:31-32; and 13:8-10. However, Sin perverts this Law into self-righteousness—moralism and legalism, delusive beliefs that flawed humans can fulfill God's law by their own efforts. *(e)* By this means, God's

131

law becomes "the law of sin and death" in contrast to "the law of the Spirit of life" (8:2). Here law refers to an operative principle, an observable truth about the nature of reality, something comparable to our reference to the law of gravity. It was not literally "the law of the Spirit of life" that freed him from "the law of sin and death." The life-giving Holy Spirit set him free from sin and death.

Paul distinguishes "between the law as a power that demands righteousness that humans cannot achieve and law as Scripture that affirms righteousness through faith." In 2:1—3:20 Paul demolished the arrogant and demonstrably false presumption of Jews who imagined that salvation was a matter of **observing the law.** Such a law "demands good works but produces only the awareness of sin" (Jewett 2007, 297). In ch 4 he will demonstrate from the Law (as Scripture) that righteousness is not a human achievement but is received as a gift from God based solely **on . . . faith.** "This is a distinction between an interpretation of law that enhances boasting and an interpretation of law that excludes boasting" (Jewett 2007, 297). Paul clarifies his understanding of the terms *law, works,* and **faith** to prepare the way for his first inference.

■ **28** Therefore, **we maintain that** [*logizometha,* **we reckon that**] **people** [*anthrōpon,* **a human being**] **are** justified [*dikaousthai*] **by faith apart from observing the law** (3:28, summarizing vv 21-26). Righteousness before God is "by faith alone." Yet faith has no power apart from its Object. Faith is but "the hand of the heart" that receives the gift of God's righteousness through Christ (see 1 Cor 1:30-31).

Faith here may refer to both "the faithfulness of Christ" and "the human response of faith." If Law as the system of salvation by human achievement is rejected as the means of being made righteousness, faith as the system of trusting the crucified Christ alone for salvation includes both aspects of **faith** as used in Romans. The traditional Protestant way of reading the passage does not imply that faith is something humans can do to earn salvation, despite the failure of law-keeping as a means. Romans 3:21-26 explicates what the faithfulness of Christ required and made possible; vv 27-31 explicate what it excludes and implies. Because righteousness is by faith, it is a gift pure and simple; thus **boasting . . . is excluded.**

(2) Righteousness by Faith Is for All (3:29-30)

■ **29** If it were otherwise (*ē, Or* introduces v 29 in Greek) the theological implications would be catastrophic. Paul's dialogue-partner asks rhetorically, **Is God the God of Jews only? Is he not** [*ouchi kai*] **the God of Gentiles** [*ethnōn, nations*] **too?** The formulation of the question presumes an affirmative answer, which Paul provides, **Yes,** God is the God **of Gentiles too** (v 29).

Paul no longer contrasts Jews and *Greeks* as earlier (1:16; 2:9-10), adopting here the impolite Jewish language distinguishing **Jews** and **Gentiles, circum-**

cised and **uncircumcised** (3:29-30; see 2:25-27; see Jewett 2007, 301 for the ancient force of these epithets) to refer to humanity in its entirety. Both Paul and his Jewish interlocutor can now agree that ethnocentric thinking challenges the central monotheistic credo of Israel (Deut 6:4). There are not two gods (see also 1 Cor 8:4, 6; Gal 3:20; Eph 4:6; 1 Tim 2:5). There is no room for the Jewish particularism that insists that, although God is the Creator and Lord of all nations, he is the God of Israel only (Dunn 2002a, 38A:188).

Jewish Particularism

One of the more blatant examples of Jewish particularism may be found in the pseudepigraphal book of Jubilees, which seems to date from the mid-second century B.C.

... [God] chose Israel to be His people. And He sanctified it, and gathered it from amongst all the children of men; for there are many nations and many peoples, and all are His, and over all hath He placed spirits in authority to lead them astray from Him. But over Israel He did not appoint any angel or spirit, for He alone is their ruler, and He will preserve them and require them at the hand of His angels and His spirits, and at the hand of all His powers in order that He may preserve them and bless them, and that they may be His and He may be theirs from henceforth for ever. (*Jub.* 15:30-32 *APOT*)

■ **30** However, Paul and his questioner seem to part company on the implications of monotheism. (See Jewett 2007, 300 nn. 57-62 for the literature surveying the monotheistic consensus of many religious traditions in the first century A.D.) Paul reasons, **Since** [*eiper*] **God is one** (Rom 3:30), it is impossible for him to have two different methods of saving humankind (Thomas 1947, 122). **God will make righteous** the circumcised by faith [*ek pisteōs*] **and the uncircumcised through that same faith** [*dia tēs pisteōs*]. God's one method is **faith** (see 11:30-32). The difference in the prepositions—**by** vs. **through**—"is probably merely stylistic"—"it is the faith which counts, not the preposition'" (see 3:22, 26, and 27; Dunn 2002a, 38A:189, citing A. Maillot).

"In the light of 1:18ff. faith must be another word for that responsive dependence on God as Creator which man has failed to give; and this indeed is how Paul goes on to define it in 4:18-21" (Dunn 2002a, 38A:189). The death of Christ marked the end of the old age and the dawning of the new in which former distinctions were obliterated.

(3) Righteousness by Faith Upholds the Law (3:31)

■ **31** Paul answers his interlocutor's accusing question, **Do we, then, nullify** [*katargoumen*, *are we abolishing*] **the law by this faith?** (see 3:8) with his usual strong denial, **Not at all** [*mē genoito*]! **Rather, we uphold** [*histanomen*, *we are confirming*] **the law.**

When Paul declares that **through faith . . . we uphold the law,** he means in the immediate context that there is no contradiction between the gospel and the OT, as the example of Abraham will demonstrate in ch 4. Justifying faith does not make the Law void. On the contrary, it harmonizes with the true meaning of the Law (Godet 1883, 166). The Law itself teaches justification by faith (see 4:3-8). This underscores the fact that the old covenant is a covenant of grace (see comments on 2:25-29). Paul will say more about the relationship between Law and faith in chs 7—8. God's sanctifying grace in Christ allows the law of God to be fulfilled in believers according to its original intent through the power of the indwelling Holy Spirit (see 5:3-5; 8:3-4; 13:8-10; see Barth 1959, 88-92). Thus, far from nullifying the Law, the gospel validates it (see Heb 10:4-22).

FROM THE TEXT

Until 1999 and the Lutheran-Catholic *Joint Declaration on the Doctrine of Justification*, nothing divided the major Christian traditions more than their different understandings and appropriation of Paul's doctrine of justification. The *Joint Declaration* reflects marked changes in both classic Protestant and Catholic positions. The statement steers a middle course on justification—between the one-sided Reformed forensic language of imputed righteousness and the Catholic language of imparted righteousness. It maintains a distinction between justification as righteousness and sanctification as the inward work of the Holy Spirit.

Since the eighteenth century, Wesleyan theology has offered its own "synthesis of the Protestant ethic of grace and the Catholic ethic of holiness" (Cell 1935, 347). It maintains that the *relative* change effected by justification—a new relationship with God—provides the necessary foundation for the *real* change of sanctification—renewal in the image of God, which is the ultimate goal of salvation.

c. Scriptural Witness to Righteousness by Faith (4:1-25)

BEHIND THE TEXT

God took sin so seriously that he gave his own Son, not only assuming the consequences of sin himself, but also demonstrating beyond all doubt his love for sinful humanity. The death of Jesus Christ is the means by which God has made redemption available to all who will receive it. Since all people are sinners, all who are put right with God receive this justification as a gift—it is grace, pure and simple.

The implications of this are mind-boggling, as Paul emphasizes in Rom 3:27-31. Since people are put right with God by trusting in what Christ has done in their behalf, not by doing what the Law requires, Christians can take no satisfaction in their own achievements. Because we are put right with God and enabled to live right in God's sight on the basis of what Christ has done, "boasting . . . is excluded" (v 27).

Paul is insistent that the new thing God has done in Christ is not the un- doing of all he has done in the past. On the contrary, Paul affirms that scrip- tures are upheld, established, fulfilled in Christ (v 31). And in Rom 4, the scriptural story of Abraham is presented as the parade example to prove the point that God has always put people right with himself on the basis of faith, not works.

In the course of the dialogue with his Jewish interlocutor in the early chapters of the letter, Paul maintained that, although God's righteousness is made known to believers "apart from law," the "Law and the Prophets" testify to it. Here he allows his predominantly Gentile audience to listen in on the conversation as he demonstrates that the Jewish Scriptures support his claims that the gospel is for the entire world.

Paul's scriptural exposition focuses on Abraham as presented in Gen 15—17. The force of Paul's claims depends very much on the position occu- pied by Abraham in the Jewish tradition, which provides the framework of discussion. Within this symbolic universe, Abraham is not simply one biblical figure among many, or even a notably suitable figure. He is the prototypical Jew. As in his challenge to the circumcisers in Galatians (3:6-29; 4:21-31), Paul *must* conduct his argument in terms of Abraham, since around the figure of Abraham the key issues of Jewish identity and hope revolve. The choices Abraham made and the promises he received were representative of the fu- ture of the *nation*. It was not possible to "define" Israel, in particular the glori- ous Israel of the messianic age, without "defining" Abraham and what it means to be his "offspring" (Rom 4:13). This explains the necessity for Paul to claim Abraham for faith, to show that it is *believers*, not observers of the Law, that constitute the "seed" of Abraham, the heirs of the promise he received (see Gen 12:1-3).

Paul must achieve two things in his scriptural recasting of Abraham. First, he must show that Scripture presents Abraham primarily as a person of faith, as one who became "right with God" on the basis of *faith alone*; and, sec- ond, that it was upon the basis of this righteousness with God brought about by faith, that Abraham received for himself and all his descendants the bless- ings of salvation contained in the promise (Rom 4:13-17a).

Based on these proofs, Paul redefines Abraham as not merely the father of Jews, but as the father of a great multitude of both Jews and Gentiles. Believing in God's power to call "things that are not as though they were" (v 17c), Abraham becomes the father of this multitude of descendants, who will receive the promise on the basis of their faith alone (see 9:6-8).

The sequence of events in Gen 15 and 17 is central to Paul's argument. In response to Abraham's complaint about his childlessness (15:3-4), God makes two promises to Abraham: progeny and land. Although the terminology of "promise" is not explicit in the biblical text, Paul and his contemporaries understood God's words to Abraham in these terms.

Progeny: God promises Abraham that he will have a son and progeny as numerous as the stars of heaven (vv 4-5). To this specific promise he responds in faith (v 6a); and Scripture comments: God "credited it to him as righteousness" (v 6b).

Land: After a lengthy covenant-making ceremony (vv 7-20), God promises Abraham that his descendants will inherit the land of Canaan on which he stands (12:7; 13:15; 17:8; 24:7). Notably, the "land" promise *follows* upon the righteousness ascribed to Abraham on the basis of his faith in the "progeny" promise. Paul considers it particularly significant that all this occurred *before* any mention of circumcision (17:9-14). In postbiblical Jewish tradition, the "land promise" was equated with the promise that Abraham would bless "all peoples on earth" (12:3). The promise of the land of Canaan came to include the entire world (see the apocryphal Sir 44:21; *Jub.* 17:3; 22:14; 32:19; *1 En.* 5:7; *4 Ezra* 6:59) and, in the eschatological and transcendent sense, even "the world to come," with its blessings of salvation (see Matt 5:5; Heb 1:2).

What is at stake, then, in this discussion concerning Abraham is nothing less than the definition of God's eschatological people: Who are the "progeny of Abraham" (see Rom 9:6-8)? And, thus, who are promised a share in the world to come, and upon what terms? Paul appeals to Scripture to establish a place for uncircumcised believers within the community of salvation, which the "one God" of all (3:29-30) has purposed to create for the entire human family (Byrne 1996, 143).

Within then contemporary Judaism (see Jas 2:18-24), Abraham "was characteristically understood . . . as the archetype of the devout Jew who demonstrated faithfulness to the covenant by keeping the law and who thus was reckoned righteous" (Dunn 2002a, 38A:196). Jewish apocryphal writings claim that Abraham did not need grace, because he perfectly observed the as yet unwritten law of God (e.g., *Jub.* 16:28; 17:15-18; 18:16; 19:8—24:11; *2 Bar.* 57:1-2). Romans 4 makes a case for a 180-degree opposite understanding of Abraham from the claims found in Sir 44:19-21:

Abraham was the great father of a multitude of nations, and no one has been found like him in glory. He kept the law of the Most High, and entered into a covenant with him; he certified the covenant in his flesh, and when he was tested he proved faithful. Therefore the Lord assured him with an oath that the nations would be blessed through his offspring; that he would make him as numerous as the dust of the earth, and exalt his offspring like the stars, and give them an inheritance from sea to sea and from the Euphrates to the ends of the earth. (Sir 44:19-21 NRSV)

The diatribe style continues in Rom 4:1, 3, 9, and 10, where questions posed by Paul's interlocutor advance his scriptural exposition. Paul skillfully blends the diatribe with the interpretive techniques of rabbinic midrash, which would have been persuasive to his imaginary Jewish dialogue partner. Rabbinic midrash was a commentary-like exposition of thematic key words in a biblical passage, explained by appeal to parallel passages. Paul's midrash on Gen 15:6 (appealing to Ps 32:1-2 and Gen 17:5), far from presenting Abraham as a model of virtue validated by God, depicts the patriarch as a sinner justified on the basis of his trust in God's promise alone.

IN THE TEXT

Because Abraham was justified by faith, Paul contends that the OT revelation "contains within it a conception of religion as personal trust in God, more fundamental than the legal strain in it which received one-sided emphasis in Pharisaic Judaism" (Barth 1959, 88-92). From this point of view Abraham, recognized by the strictest Pharisee as the ideal religious man, was justified by faith rather than by works of the Law. In proving this point Paul makes the strongest possible scriptural defense for his doctrine.

(1) Abraham Justified by Faith, Not Works (4:1-8)

■ 1 Paul's imaginary dialogue partner sets the agenda with the opening question: **What then shall we say that Abraham, our forefather, discovered according to the flesh?** [*kata sarka*—see the sidebar "The Translation of *Sarx*" with the comments on ch 7] (v 1). The NIV omits the final phrase, apparently subsuming it with **forefather,** as a reference to physical lineage. But this is contrary to Paul's claim about Abraham subsequently in the chapter. In light of the context, the point of the question seems to be: *Did Abraham find justification before God on the basis of some achievement of his flesh?* That is, could he boast of some human accomplishment that led God to consider him righteous (see 3:27-31; Jewett 2007, 308)?

■ 2 Within contemporary Judaism, Abraham was, in fact, believed to have been **justified by works** (4:2; see 3:28; Sir 44:19-21; 1 Macc 2:52). He did what the Law required, even before it was written (Barrett 1963, 25-26). Such thinking fundamentally undermines Paul's argument to this point in the letter, because the merits of righteous Abraham were thought to accrue to his physical descendants. Israel's claim to the land depended on God's promises to Abraham. Thus, Paul accepts the challenge to prove the opposite. He argues: **If, in fact, Abraham was justified by works, he had something to boast about—but not before God** (Rom 4:2; see 3:27).

■ **3** In 4:3, responding to the interlocutor's question, Paul cites the biblical evidence that will serve as the basis for his counterargument: **What does the Scripture say?** Paul answers, referring to Gen 15:6 (LXX): **"Abraham believed God, and it was credited to him as righteousness."** Abraham believed the promise of God: "He took him outside and said, 'Look up at the heavens and count the stars—if indeed you can count them.' Then he said to him, 'So shall your offspring be'" (Gen 15:5). Faith does not operate in a void; it is always based on God's promise (see Rom 10:17).

Abraham's trust in God's promise was **credited to him as righteousness** (4:3). God considered Abraham acceptable because he believed God's promise. God justified Abraham simply because he trusted God's word (see vv 17-22). True to midrash style, Paul fastens on a key word—the verb **credited** (*elogisthē*), "counted" (KJV), or "reckoned" (NRSV). This accounting term means "to set down on the credit side." Used metaphorically here as in Mal 3:16, it refers to God's record book in which the good or evil deeds of humans are kept (see Ps 56:8; Isa 34:16; Dan 7:10; Rev 3:5; 13:8; 17:8; 20:12-15; 21:27; Sanday and Headlam 1929, 100).

Evidently, if faith is **credited as righteousness,** it is not itself identical with, but distinguishable from, righteousness. Faith is not a refined kind of righteousness that God accepts instead of legal obedience. Paul's point is that faith and righteousness operate in two different spheres. The faith by which Abraham was justified derived its power from God. Faith is not relying on human trust; it is *relying upon God* (see Rom 4:20-21). Faith is not an optimistic outlook on life, in contrast to the dismal attitudes of doubt and despair.

Believing is not something people do instead of obeying the Law as a means of winning God's approval. The point Paul makes is that faith is not a work, not something people do at all. "For Paul, righteousness is the gift of a new relationship with God that comes when humans stop competing for honor and accept the grace that they could never earn" (Jewett 2007, 312). People are not justified by the virtue of their faith, but *by God.* Otherwise they would have **something to boast about—but not before God** (v 2).

■ **4** Paul refuses to consider faith a human work of any kind (vv 4-5). Quite the contrary, faith trusts in God's word and work so completely that it despairs of human work as a means of gaining God's favor. In a sense, faith is nothing more than grateful receptivity to God's gift. Justification by grace through faith is wholly apart from any trace of human merit.

Paul explains: **Now when a man works, his wages are not credited** [*logizetai*] **to him as a gift** [*charin, grace*]**, but as an obligation** [*opheilēma, debt*]**. However, to the man who does not work but trusts** [*pisteuonti*] **God who justifies the wicked, his faith is credited** [*logizetai*] **as righteousness** (vv 4-5). The contrast between **a gift** and **an obligation** is instructive. **Wages** are earned by working; an employer must pay this debt for services rendered. **Works** and **obligation** belong together. But gifts are given freely; they are graciously **credited** to one's account solely on the basis of the giver's generosity. *Pistis*—believing, trusting, or faith—prompts God's gift of righteousness, because it relies on the divine benefactor, not human achievement. Thus, **faith** and ***grace*** similarly correspond, and it is to this latter pair that "crediting" belongs.

Contrasts

works ↔ faith
debt ↔ gift
wages ↔ credited

■ **5** It follows that since Abraham had righteousness **credited** to him, he was the recipient of grace. To be justified by grace through faith is to be *given* a righteousness that one does not deserve. Despite the NIV translation, Paul does not identify the object of Abraham's faith as **God,** but as ***the one*** who justifies the wicked (v 5)—Abraham had no right to be made righteous.

That God should accept ***the ungodly*** (*asebē*, see 1:18; 5:6) as righteous seems to fly in the face of Scripture (Exod 23:7; Prov 17:15; Isa 5:23). It scandalizes those who feel that the sinners must *do* certain things to *make themselves worthy* of justification. When we read that God **justifies the wicked,** we are to understand that God acquits the guilty sinner for reasons of his own mercy, apart from any human worthiness or merit. Justification is an act of sheer grace on the part of God, but this is no slight-of-hand deception. "God makes the ungodly person a new creature; he really makes him righteous" (Käsemann 1980, 112-13). "God in Christ restores a right relationship with those who have not earned it" (Jewett 2007, 314).

In examining the doctrine of the atonement in Rom 3:21-26, we saw that to be justified sinners must "submit to the divine sentence upon sin." Accepting God's verdict of guilty as charged, or acknowledging their lost condition, in other biblical witnesses is called confession or repentance. Paul, however, prefers the language of **faith**. Whatever it is called, submission to God's judgment is not a meritorious work; it is merely openness to his saving grace, accepting his invitation of shameful sinners to participate in the community of the righteous people of God. Since people are "justified by faith apart from observing the law" (v 28), justification is "by faith alone" because it is "by grace alone."

■ **6** The focus of Paul's OT evidence for the doctrine of justification by faith is clearly Abraham, but he is certainly not the only example. Paul turns next to the case of **David,** quoting Ps 32:1. In joyful relief at the assurance of divine pardon, the psalmist exclaims: **Blessed are they whose transgressions are forgiven, whose sins are covered. Blessed is the man whose sin the Lord will never count against** [*logisētai*] **him** (Rom 4:7-8).

■ **7-8** The connection between Gen 15:6 and Ps 32:1-2 is the repeated verb root *logizomai* (Rom 4:3-8), translated "credited" in vv 3, 4, 5, and 6; but "count against" in v 8. The principle of *gezerah shawah'* ("equal category") in rabbinic exegesis encouraged the interpretation of one passage by comparison with another based on the association suggested by their common terminology (Bruce 1963, 115).

Paul concludes, contrary to standard rabbinic assumptions, that Abraham was justified as a sinner. Thus, his justification is not a divine stamp of approval on his life of flawless obedience. After all, God justifies only the wicked (v 5). The conclusion to be deduced from this comparison of biblical passages is that the "crediting of righteousness" is equivalent to the "not counting of sin." What other biblical witnesses call forgiveness, Paul prefers to call justification. He emphasizes not remorse, repentance, and restitution but righteousness.

Abraham's justification ("crediting as righteous") is not God's recognition of his human virtue, which Jews supposed he had; it is **blessing** of having his past sins canceled. The synonymous parallelism of the passage equates the forgiveness of transgressions, the covering of sins, and God not counting our sins against us. However, Paul's point is not to offer theological equations. It is to emphasize the **blessing** of being one credited with righteousness by God. Note that a form of the root *makar-*, **bless-,** appears four times in vv 6-9.

If "the faith of Abraham" is not a demonstration that he was a religious man—if God does not simply acknowledge Abraham's existing piety, is it perhaps something else he did that was the basis for his justification? Was Abraham counted as right with God because he obediently accepted the sign of circumcision? In 4:9-12, Paul's answer is an emphatic, NO!

(2) Abraham Justified by Faith, Not by Circumcision (4:9-12)

■ **9** Thus far Paul has used general rabbinic exegetical methods to interpret Gen 15:6. He now applies the conclusions of his *gezerah shawah'* (see the comments on vv 7-8 above) in reverse, using Gen 15:6 to illuminate Ps 32:1-2 (Barrett 1957, 89-90). In Rom 4:9*a*, he returns to the diatribe style, allowing his imaginary questioner to advance the argument: **Is this blessedness** [of being forgiven of which David speaks] **only for the circumcised, or also for the uncircumcised?**

Nothing in this psalm answers the question. Since David was a member of the chosen people, Paul's contemporaries supposed that this **blessedness** was uniquely a Jewish privilege (see the evidence in Jewett 2007, 317 nn. 126-29). However, Paul's application of the *gezerah shawah'* approach yields a different answer. It is **also for the uncircumcised,** since **we have been saying that Abraham's faith was credited to him as righteousness** (v 9*b*).

■ **10** The apostle now reaches his clinching argument. He has the interlocutor ask, **Under what circumstances** [*pōs oun, **How then**] **was it credited? Was it after he was circumcised, or before?** (v 10*ab*). Paul knew his OT and assumed his Roman audience did as well. The account of Abraham's justification is reported in Gen 15 and his circumcision in ch 17, many years later. Therefore, Paul answers without hesitation, **It was not after, but before!** (Rom 4:10*c*). *Abraham was a Gentile when God credited righteousness to him.* He believed as a Gentile and continued to walk in that same faith as a Jew. Thus, he is the forefather of all believers—but first of Gentiles, then of Jews.

■ **11** In v 11*a*, Paul answers an unspoken but obvious question: If Abraham was already justified by faith, and if circumcision cannot justify, why then was he circumcised? Paul's answer is that Abraham **received the sign of circumcision** (see Gen 17:11) as **a seal of the righteousness that he had by faith while he was still uncircumcised** (see Rom 2:25-29; Gen 17:11, 13). The expression **sign of circumcision** means simply "a sign consisting of circumcision." This sign marked him as a Jew. As a **seal,** circumcision merely confirmed God's previous justification of Abraham; it did not confer this status (see 1 Cor 9:2). His circumcision only validated the existing reality that he had already been made righteous by faith; it did not effect it.

In Rom 4:11*b* the apostle draws two inescapable inferences from the fact that Abraham was circumcised after he was justified. **So then** [*eis to, **for the purpose that**], **he is the father of all who believe but have not been circumcised, in order that** [*eis to*] **righteousness might be credited to them.** Paul radically reverses the assumptions of contemporary Judaism.

(a) Abraham is first of all the father of believing Gentiles. "Abraham's example legitimates the acceptability of Gentiles who have responded to the message of unconditional grace in Christ" (Jewett 2007, 319).

■ **12** *(b)* Abraham is the father of the Jews, not because of their circumcision, but on the grounds of their faith. Recall that true circumcision is a matter of the heart, "by the Spirit, not by the written code" (2:29). Thus, for Jews and Gentiles alike, there is but one way to righteousness—the way of faith alone. In 4:12 Paul adds that only those Jews who are not only Abraham's natural descendants but **who also walk in the footsteps of the faith that our father Abraham had before he was circumcised** are his true children (see 2:25-29). Paul treats **the footprints** [*ichnesin*] **of the uncircumcised faith of our father Abraham,** not his circumcision (*peritomēs*), as exemplary.

(3) Abraham Justified by Faith, Not by Law (4:13-17a)

■ **13** If circumcision had nothing to do with Abraham's justification, the Law had even less to do with it. **It was not through law that Abraham and his offspring received the promise that he would be heir of the world, but through the righteousness that comes by faith** (v 13). Some years earlier, Paul had pointed out to the Galatians that the Law was given some 430 years after God gave his promise to Abraham (Gal 3:17).

■ **14** The word **promise** (*epangelia*) appears for the first time in Romans (see vv 14, 16, 20; 9:4, 8, 9; 15:8). Although it does not appear in the OT, "the fact that God had made such a commitment was a basic element in Israel's faith (see, e.g., Exod 32:13; 1 Chron 16:14-18; Neh 9:7-8; Ps 105:6-11; Sir 44:21; Wisd. Solomon 12:21)" (Dunn 2002a, 38A:212). The term first appears within the biblical tradition in Hellenistic Judaism (see 3 Macc 2:10-11; *Ps. Sol.* 12:6; *T. Jos.* 20:1).

Paul does not insist that Abraham's **offspring** primarily refers to Christ here, as he does in Gal 3:16-19. However, he does presume here as there (v 29) that Abraham's **offspring** (a collective noun in Rom 4:16 and 18; as also in 9:7-8, 29; 11:1; 2 Cor 11:22) include all who by faith participate in Christ, not just Jews. Paul understands the "land" promise to Abraham (see Behind the Text above) like most of his Jewish contemporaries as assurance that **he would be heir of the world** (Rom 4:13). But unlike them, Paul does not understand this in terms of Israel gaining worldwide political dominance. Instead, he looks forward to the inclusion of all nations sharing in the **promise** of **the righteousness that comes by faith.**

God did not give his law to invalidate his earlier promises or to restrict their scope (see Gal 3:17). **For if those who live by law are heirs, faith has no value and the promise is worthless** (Rom 4:14). Here, **those who live by law** (*hoi ek nomou*) is merely another designation for Jews ("the circumcised" in vv 9, 12). When the promise was made, Abraham was a Gentile. So how could Jews be his only legitimate **heirs?** "If the promise were restricted to those who conform to the Torah, it would no longer be valid for 'the ungodly' (4:5)" (Jewett 2007, 327). If long after **the promise** was given, it had been made conditional on obedience to the **law,** which had not been mentioned at the time of the original promise, the whole basis of the promise as promise would have been rendered meaningless—of **no value . . . worthless.**

■ **15** God's **promise** assured blessings that are received in the gospel's revelation of the saving righteousness of God. The Law does not promise blessings on those who observe it; rather it invokes a curse on those who violate it. In view of the universal sway of sin, the curse is more prominent than the blessing. **Law brings** [*katergazetai,* **produces;** see 7:8, 13, 15, 17, 18, 20] **wrath** (v 15*a;* see 1:18; 2:5, 8; 3:5).

Paul adds parenthetically: **And where there is no law there is no transgression** (*parabasis;* v 15*b*). This argument interrupts the connection between vv 14 and 16, but it fits into Paul's logic. The opening word of v 15, **because** (*gar,* "for"), looks back to v 13, which begins with the same Greek word. Thus, v 15 offers further grounds for Paul's claim in v 13 that God's promise to Abraham and his offspring came through faith, not through the Law.

The term **transgression** (see 2:23) refers to a conscious or willful disobedience, the crossing of a forbidden boundary. A sinful tendency may be present in the absence of law, but it takes a specific commandment to crystallize that tendency into a positive transgression or violation of a law (see 5:13, 20; 7:7-13, and comments there). The purpose of Law is to show how "utterly sinful" (see 7:13) sin is. The Law reveals wicked behavior for what it is, as a **transgression** of God's law, which is, of course, naturally and rightly visited with God's wrath. Law, although good in itself (see vv 12, 14), is closely bound up with sin (see v 5) and **wrath** (4:15*a*). So, it is unthinkable to consider law a basis of promise. The gracious promise God made to Abraham belongs to an entirely different order of reality than law.

■ **16** Abraham's justification and its attendant blessings were not founded in law; they were based on his faith in God. They were not earned by effort or merit on his part, but were bestowed by God's grace. Paul draws the logical conclusion (*Dia touto,* **Therefore**) of his argument to this point: **the promise comes by faith** (v 16). The word **promise** does not appear in the Greek of v 16. The subject of Paul's verbless sentence—*ek pisteōs,* **by faith**—must be inferred from the preceding context.

God's gifts to Abraham and his heirs are based on faith for two purposes: **so that** [*hina*] **it may be by grace** and **in order that** [*eis to*] **it may be guaranteed to all Abraham's offspring** [= all humanity]—**not only to those who are of the law** [= the Jews] **but also to those who are of the faith of Abraham** [= all believers]. **He is the father of us all** (v 16; see 1:16; 4:11).

The principle on which God dealt with Abraham applies also to **all** his descendants—**not only** to his natural descendants, the Jews, "the circumcised" who are subject to the obligations of the Law (v 12). Here as in chs 9—11, Paul does not seem prepared to exclude "law observant Jews [from] the realm of Abraham's promise even if they do not . . . yet . . . share his faith" (Jewett 2007, 331). Perhaps the apostle anticipates here the problem he addresses in chs 14—15 concerning Gentile Christians in Rome who have marginalized law-observant Jewish believers as "weak in faith."

The **promise** is **not only** to Jews **but also** extends to Abraham's spiritual descendants—those "who also walk in the footsteps of the faith our father Abraham had" (4:12). Here, the reference is not merely to Gentile Christians but to both Gentile and Jewish believers. "Only a system of salvation by grace alone can provide such" an all-inclusive guarantee, because it depends on the reliability of God's "commitments and promises" and not on "human frailties" (Jewett 2007, 330).

■ **17** Paul claims that the inclusion of both Jews and Gentiles among **Abraham's offspring** is what God meant when he gave Abram the name **Abraham** in Gen 17:5. God said there, **"I have made you a father of many nations"** (Rom 4:17a). The Greek word translated nations (*ethnē*) is normally translated "Gentiles" and refers to the nations other than the Jews, but here Paul takes **many nations** to include all who are justified by faith—Jews and Gentiles alike. *Abraham is the father of all believers* (v 16). As in v 13, his heritage includes the whole world. It is not just ethnic descent but faith that makes one a child of Abraham. In vv 16 and 17 Paul seems to refer to a spiritual Israel (see 2:28-29) alongside of, not merely in contrast to, physical Israel (see the commentary on chs 9—11).

Paul apparently finds the perfect tense of the verb **I have made** [*tetheika*] **you** in his LXX quotation of Gen 17:5 (see also Gen 12:3; 28:14) theologically significant. The perfect tense in Greek characteristically refers to a present state resulting from a past event, but when these words were spoken, Abraham remained without an heir. These words were spoken before Isaac had even been conceived. Yet, God does not say, "I *will* make you," but treats his as-yet-unfulfilled promise as good as done. This explains Paul's description of God as the one who **calls things that are not as though they were** (Rom 4:17b).

The early sections of ch 4 answer the question, What is the faith of Abraham? primarily in a negative fashion. It is not a good work of any kind; it is not the reward for performing a ritual act; it is not adherence to a book of rules that God counts as righteousness; it is faith alone. In the final section of the chapter, Paul answers the question positively and explains why the faith of Abraham resulted in his justification.

(4) Abraham's Faith Anticipates Christian Faith (4:17b-25)

Abraham is the **father** of Jewish and Gentile Christians, not by virtue of any human relationship with them, but **in the sight of God, in whom he believed—the God who gives life to the dead and calls things that are not as though they were** (v 17b). In vv 17 and 18 the apostle reflects on the Genesis account of the birth of Isaac, the child of promise (see 9:7-9), and intended sacrifice (see Heb 11:19).

The God in whom Abraham had faith **gives life to the dead**. This expression "appears to be drawn from the second benediction in the Eighteen

Benedictions used by many Jews on a daily basis, 'Blessed be you, Lord, who gives life to the dead'" (Jewett 2007, 333). Although there is no unambiguous reference to resurrection hope in Jewish tradition before the postexilic period (see Dan 12:2), later Jews take for granted that Abraham's was a *resurrection faith* (see Heb 11:17-19; see Dunn 2002a, 38A:218).

Abraham's God is also the Creator, who "calls into existence the things that do not exist" (Rom 4:17 RSV, NRSV). Jewish belief in creation *ex nihilo* is first attested in the postexilic period (*2 Bar.* 21:4; 48:8). Abraham's *creation faith* is presumed on the basis of his reliance on God's power to do the impossible (see Rom 4:19). He did not consider the chronological challenge of being 100 years old and his wife in menopause, or even the potential sacrifice of an only son, problems too hard for the God who provides (see Gen 18:14; 22:8, 14).

■ **18** It was on this basis that **Against all hope, Abraham in hope** [*par' elpida ep' elpidi*, **Beyond hope in hope**] **believed and so became the father of many nations, just as it had been said to him, "So shall your offspring be"** (Rom 4:18, citing Gen 15:5). What happened in the birth of Isaac was beyond anything Abraham could have reasonably expected. "That Abraham's descendants would become a vast multitude from many nations rested solely on the power of God's word" (Jewett 2007, 336).

Believers persist **in hope** (see Rom 5:2; 8:20) at the very point where there is, in the earthly sense, nothing more to hope for. They do not bypass realities but are aware of them and hold their ground just the same. They do not escape into illusion. They dare to trust the divine promise, contrary to every earthly reality (Käsemann 1980, 124).

The **hope** of believers is unquenchable, not because of an optimistic outlook on life but because they rely on the God who raises the dead, who creates out of nothing, who justifies the ungodly, and who says to a childless man, "I have made you a father of many nations" (4:17). When this God makes a promise, even before it enters into human experience, it is as good as done. "Abraham's faith was exercised in the confident hope which the promise of God engendered" (Murray 1959, 148).

■ **19** According to v 19 Abraham **faced the fact that his body was as good as dead . . . and that Sarah's womb was also dead**. The late Byzantine manuscripts, followed by the KJV, however, say exactly the opposite: Abraham "considered *not* his own body now dead, . . . *neither* yet the deadness of Sara's womb" (emphasis added). Modern translations follow the better and more ancient Greek manuscripts, which recognize that faith does not close its eyes to human realities, nor retreat into a world of illusion. Abraham faces squarely the physical challenges that made conceiving the heir God had promised him and Sarah impossible. He is, after all, **a hundred years old** and Sarah is in menopause. However, these realities do not cause **weakening in his faith.** Why

145

not? Because Abraham trusts in a reality beyond the ability of eyes to see, in the God who allows a barren old couple to conceive a child of promise.

■ **20** Abraham's faith did *not* weaken when he considered the human impossibility of God's promise. **He did not waver through unbelief regarding the promise of God** (v 20). On the contrary, "he grew strong in his faith" (RSV, NRSV) under these circumstances. What does Paul mean when he makes this claim? And what in the Genesis story permitted Paul to make it?

When Paul writes that Abraham grew strong in faith, he cannot "mean that on account of his faith Abraham became a strong man, a forceful 'personality'" (Barrett 1957, 91). His bungling attempts to secure the promise through human schemes confirm that. Recall his attempts to pass off Sarah as his sister, his proposal to adopt his servant Eliezer as his heir, his unfortunate union with Hagar and the birth of Ishmael. These hardly suggest the pilgrimage of a man growing in faith. Paul does not seem to mean that Abraham was possessed by a greater quantity of faith—that he believed more intensely, that the promise became increasingly more reasonable, that his attitude became progressively more positive.

On the contrary, the demonstration that Abraham's faith had grown apparently came precisely at the point when he realized that he could not secure the promise through human striving. His laughter in the face of the promise that his wife would bear him a child demonstrates that he recognized God's promise as totally unreasonable on human terms (Gen 17:17). If a full-grown faith relies exclusively on God alone, the evidence of Abraham's strengthening faith was demonstrated best when in the posture of worship, he could no longer choke back the laughter that he and Sarah would have a child. Only then did he realize that his efforts to secure the promise were of no avail.

Abraham **did not waver** [*diakrithē*] **through unbelief regarding the promise of God** (Rom 4:20). Of course, Abraham had doubts; but his doubts did not cause him to waver in that area where faith in God is mixed with a trust in the possibilities of human achievement. "Wavering" [*diakrinomenos, doubting*] is the word Paul uses to describe the "weak in faith" in 14:23. Rather than wavering, Abraham **gave glory to God.**

By his unwavering confidence that God could and would fulfill his promise, Abraham gave glory to God; that is, he did precisely what the unbelievers of i.21 did not do. He recognized God as God; the Creator, as such altogether different from creation. . . . Only faith can so give glory to God; to perform 'works of law' with a view to establishing a claim upon him, or to throw off all sense of obligation to him is to dishonor God. . . . Faith (in Paul's sense) grows stronger as it is unmixed with confidence in any thing or any one other than God himself. (Barrett 1957, 92)

■ **21** Paul offers another explanation of what he means by the faith of Abraham in v 21: Abraham was **fully persuaded** [*plērophorētheis*] **that God had the power to do what he had promised.** Paul uses the same Greek verb (*plērophoreisthō*, "should be fully convinced") to describe what he means by strong faith in 14:5.

■ **22** The apostle concludes his midrash on Gen 15:6, where he began (Rom 4:3) by quoting the passage again in v 22: **This is why** [*dio*, **Therefore;** see 1:24; 2:1] **"it was credited to him as righteousness."** He has explained why God justified Abraham on the basis of his faith.

■ **23** Before Paul can move on, he must apply the results of his midrash to his readers: **The words "it was credited to him" were written not for him alone, but also for us, to whom God will credit righteousness** (4:23-24a). The future dimension—**he is going to credit** [*mellei logizesthai*] **righteousness**—is from the perspective of the Genesis account, but the present experience of believers (Jewett 2007, 341). Paul makes similar claims about the contemporary implications of the Scriptures as he applies his midrash on Israel's negative example in 1 Cor 10:1-13: "Now these things occurred as examples to keep us from setting our hearts on evil things as they did" (v 6). Paul was convinced of the continuing relevance of the OT: "For everything that was written in the past was written to teach us, so that through endurance and the encouragement of the Scriptures we might have hope" (Rom 15:4).

■ **24** **God will credit righteousness . . . for us who believe in him who raised Jesus our Lord from the dead** (4:24; see 8:11; Acts 3:15; 4:10; 13:30). There is a precise correspondence between Abraham's faith in God and the faith of Christians. Abraham believed in "the God who gives life to the dead" (Rom 4:17); Christians believe in the God who raised Jesus from the dead.

■ **25** Here, Paul holds, is where Abraham's faith is the example and type of all who believe in Christ. When we believe in Jesus as **delivered over to death for our sins, and . . . raised to life for our justification** (v 25), we believe in the "God who gives life to the dead" (v 17). Here Paul summarizes his exposition of gospel in 3:21-26, which occasioned his appeal to Abraham. His point was to demonstrate that the OT upholds his claim that faith has always been the means by which humans participate in the righteousness of God.

In 3:21-26, Paul quotes from and elaborates on the creedal formulations of Jewish Christianity. Similarly, his words here: **He was delivered over to death for our sins** [*paraptōmata*, **transgressions;** see 5:15-20], seem to echo "one of the earliest theological reflections about Jesus' death" (see 8:32; Gal 1:4; 2:20; Eph 5:2, 25) based on Isa 53 (esp. vv 6 and 12; Dunn 2002a, 38A:224). *Paredothē,* **was delivered,** was used by early Christians "to embrace the double thought of Jesus' betrayal by man (Judas) and his being handed over by God" (see Mark 9:31; 10:33, 45; 14:1-2, 10, 21, 41; 15:1; Matt 10:4 and Acts 2:23; 3:13; Rom 8:32; 1 Cor 11:23; Dunn 2002a, 38A:224).

Whether He . . . was raised to life for our justification quotes an established creed (Rom 4:25; see 6:4, 9; 7:4; 8:34; 1 Cor 15:12; 2 Cor 5:15) or originated with Paul is debated. Regardless, "It would be a mistake to read theological significance into distinctions (between the effect of Jesus' death and the effect of his resurrection) which are purely rhetorical" (Dunn 2002a, 38A:225). This is ruled out by what Paul will say in Rom 5:9. Christ's death and resurrection are two aspects of one divine event. Without the resurrection, the death of Jesus would not avail for **our justification** (see 1 Cor 15:17).

Faith in Christ is at the same time, and even more deeply, faith in **him who raised Jesus our Lord** (Rom 4:24). Faith of this kind justifies "not because of its strength, quality and beauty, but only because of its object, because of Jesus Christ, because of the omnipotence, fidelity, and constancy of God, continued, revealed and active in Him" (Barth 1959, 54).

FROM THE TEXT

The faith of Abraham is the prototype of Christian faith. Christian faith is in the God of Abraham and must be of the same character as Abraham's faith if we are to be justified. Righteousness before God demands Abraham-like faith.

Christian faith is not a work we do instead of the OT law. On the contrary, it is surrender, abandonment of schemes of self-salvation, which really are self-destructive. Jesus insists that those who would save their lives will lose them. Christian faith is a trusting response in God's gracious offer of redemption in Jesus Christ, who died for our sins and was raised for our justification. Christian faith is the realization that if we are ever to be saved, God will have to do it; we cannot save ourselves. That this is Paul's point becomes perfectly clear in Rom 5—8, in which he develops the consequences of justification.

What is the faith of Abraham? It is not a work, not a sign, not an achievement. It is trust in God alone. Why does the faith of Abraham result in his justification? Because it is faith in God unmixed with faith in human achievements. And why does this matter? Because this same faith is necessary for us, if we are to experience the righteousness of God.

Martin Luther felt "reborn altogether" when he saw the scriptural truth of justification while lecturing on Romans at the University of Wittenberg. Two hundred years later, while listening to the reading of Luther's Preface to his commentary on Romans, describing the change God works in the heart through faith in Christ, John Wesley felt he did "trust in Christ, Christ alone for salvation."

There are significant differences between the two Reformers' doctrines of justification, but both agreed on what constitutes the basis of the life-changing experience of justification—faith in God alone. Luther's concern, to challenge the Roman Catholic doctrine of merit, led to his emphasis upon justification as an act of sheer grace on the part of God, the imputation of an entirely "alien righteousness," so that believers remain at once justified and sinners. Wesley's concern, to challenge the Roman Catholic confusion of justification and sanctification in the *ordo salutis*, led him to emphasize that justification marked the beginning of the Spirit's sanctifying and genuinely life-changing work in the lives of believers.

Luther on "Alien Righteousness"

Everything . . . is outside us and in Christ. . . . For God does not want to save us by our own but by an extraneous righteousness which does not originate in ourselves but comes to us from beyond ourselves, which does not arise on our earth but comes from heaven. Therefore, we must come to know this righteousness which is utterly external and foreign to us. That is why our own personal righteousness must be uprooted. . . . Virtues are often the greater and worse faults, since they cause us to trust in ourselves rather than in Christ. . . . But now Christ wants all our feeling to be so bare that, on the one hand, we are not afraid to be cast into confusion on account of our faults, nor delight in praise and vain joy on account of our virtue, yet, on the other hand, we do not glory before men in that external righteousness which, coming from Christ, is in us, not suffer defeat of those sufferings and evils which befall us for his sake. (Luther 1961, 15:4, 5)

ROMANS

4:1-25

Wesley on Justification and Sanctification

We see plainly how groundless that opinion is, that holiness or sanctification is previous to our justification. For the sinner, being first convinced of his sin and danger by the Spirit of God, stands trembling before the awful tribunal of divine justice; and has nothing to plead, but his own guilt, and the merits of a Mediator. Christ here interposes; justice is satisfied; the sin is remitted, and pardon is applied to the soul, by a divine faith wrought by the Holy Ghost, who then begins the great work of inward sanctification. Thus God justifies the ungodly, and remains just, and true to all His attributes! . . . If a man could possibly be made holy before he is justified, it would entirely set his justification aside; seeing he could not, in the very nature of the thing, be justified if he were not, at that very time, ungodly. (Wesley 1950, 532; on Rom 4:5)

2. The Hope of the Gospel (5:1—8:39)

a. Justification (5:1-21)

The opening statements of Rom 5 mark a major transition in the Epistle. Up to this point Paul's exposition of the gospel has focused on faith. If Gentiles are to be included as equal citizens within the household of faith, then faith, not the "works" of the Jewish law, must be the way of entrance into the righteousness that leads to final salvation. Paul has locked in the principle of justification by faith by demonstrating the Scripture's witness to it in the case of Abraham and of David. Now the focus shifts from faith to hope. Paul expounds and celebrates the hope of salvation—justification leading to sanctification, sanctification leading to glorification—as God's ongoing gift of salvation for every believer—"first for the Jew, then for the Gentile" (1:16).

Nonetheless, 5:1-11

> are intimately bound up with 4:23-25. Unless that is realized, the opening verses of chapter 5 appear as a somewhat disconnected series of reflections on various themes appropriate to the Christian faith and life but somehow unrelated to their immediate context. (Achtemeier 1985, 90)

Toward the end of ch 4 the apostle prepared the way for this transition from faith to hope, by stressing the perseverance of Abraham's faith (4:18-21). His faith was in "the God who gives life to the dead and calls things that are not as though they were" (v 17).

The affirmation of faith in the work of God alone, which forms the heart of 3:21—4:25, becomes the main theme of the new major section that now begins (5:1—8:39). Recall that ch 4 concludes with the affirmation that we have been set right with God through the death and resurrection of Jesus Christ (4:24-25). We are challenged to hear this good news in such a way that the hope of full salvation and final redemption stays alive and accomplishes God's intended purpose in our lives.

Romans 5—8 is bound together by two "bookends": 5:1-11 and 8:14-39. The two passages are bound together by *hope*—a hope that rests upon the peace with God resulting from justification (5:9; 8:31-34) and effected by the Spirit of promise (5:5; 8:14-15, 23-27; Byrne 1996, 163). It is a hope, moreover, that confronts and endures the sufferings of the present (5:3-4; 8:17-18, 35-39) and guarantees final salvation in Christ—"if indeed we share in his sufferings in order that we may share in his glory" (v 17).

If the hope does, in fact, rest upon the righteousness brought about through faith in Christ, the challenge for believers is to *live out* that righteousness to the end—to the final judgment. This is why Paul continues his skirmish with the Law. Key to his argument that the power of the Spirit is the source of the necessary righteousness required for final salvation is his assumption that the Law is powerless to save (7:14—8:16).

The hope of salvation is there *because*—not despite—the fact that "the Spirit of life in Christ Jesus has set you free from the law of sin and death" (8:2 [NRSV]). This concern to establish the superiority of the Spirit explains the long "ethical section" [sanctification] that enters in between 6:1 and 8:13, before the argument of hope in the face of suffering resumes for the remainder of chapter 8. (Byrne 1996, 164)

Romans 5—8 depicts the "overlap" of the two ages, the life of the Church in "the time between the times," i.e., between the two Advents. We are "no longer" what we once were, but "not yet" what we shall be. "As to the spirit, we are in the *age to come;* as to the body, in the *present age*" (Godet 1883, 313; see Gal 1:3-5). Our hope is the return of Christ, who shall redeem creation and glorify the bodies of the faithful (Rom 8:17-25)!

(1) The Sure Hope of Full and Final Salvation Springing from Justification (5:1-11)

BEHIND THE TEXT

Romans 5:1-11 is *not* about *how* we are put right with God. It is about the consequences of justification. When we are right with God, there are tangible consequences. Here Paul mentions three: peace, grace, and hope. But these three gifts, described as abstract nouns, express concrete realities.

The claim in v 5*b* that "God has poured out his love into our hearts by the Holy Spirit, whom he has given us," prepares the way for Rom 5:6—8:39. Paul's focus on God's already proven love for fallen humanity (5:8) and the redemptive work of the Holy Spirit (v 5; see 8:1-30) in human experience set the agenda for the next several chapters. In much the same way, 12:9, which refers to **genuine** human **love,** will be the focus of 12:9—13:10. *Agapē* love is not just grand concept; it does something.

Eschatological hope is the overarching theme of 5:1-11. But the eagerly awaited future resurrection from the dead does not exhaust Paul's eschatology (i.e., his beliefs about the last days). He is convinced that the resurrected and reigning Christ has already inaugurated the age of the Spirit, and with the gracious gift of the Spirit, the OT promise of heart holiness, closely associated with peace in both OT and NT, has become a present possibility. Peter Stuhlmacher proposes that

> in being filled with the Spirit, the promise of Ezek. 36:26ff. is realized for those who believe, so that they become capable of returning the love of God bestowed upon them (v. 8), that is, to love God as their creator in accordance with his will. In this active love, supported by the Spirit, Christians complete the state of grace into which they were transferred by Christ. (1994, 80)

The new covenant prophecies of Ezek 36:22-32 and Jer 31:31-34 hold out the promise of a new obedience. With their fulfillment, God's Spirit-filled people are empowered by grace to fulfill the Great Commandment of the Law—to love God completely and to love their neighbors as themselves (Matt 22:34-40; Rom 8:1-4; 13:8-10). The hoped-for age of peace (5:1) and reconciliation (vv 10-11) has already begun through the gift of grace—God's presence in the person of the Holy Spirit (v 5), which is God's poured out love, demonstrated in the death of Christ (vv 6-11). "The *Shema* is at last fulfilled, in Christ and by the Spirit the creator/covenant God has created a people that, in return, for redemption, will love him from the heart" (cf. 8:28; 1 Cor 8:3; Wright 1999, 45). In light of what God has already done, the present experience of suffering (Rom 5:3-4), far from destroying us, only inspires hope for the final consummation, when we will **be saved through his life** (v 10), **saved from God's wrath** (v 9).

IN THE TEXT

■ **1** The inferential particle *oun* (**Therefore;** v 1) and the adverbial participle *dikaiōthentes* ("having been justified" NASB) introduce 5:1—8:39 as the consequences of Paul's discussion of justification by grace through faith in 3:31—4:21. The participle makes it clear that his concern is not so much with theological implications of the doctrine, but with the practical results of the Christian experience of being justified—**since we have been justified through faith.** Paul will mention three: **peace** (5:1), **grace,** and **hope** (v 2).

A small but significant textual variant in v 1 has puzzled interpreters for centuries. The earliest and best MSS read *echōmen* (hortatory subjunctive, "let us have") rather than *echomen* (indicative, **we have**). Jewett defends the subjunctive reading, which "produces an admonition about the concrete embodiment of faith in the life of the congregation" (Jewett 2007, 348). Despite the external evidence favoring the hortatory reading, most modern commentators agree that the internal evidence overwhelmingly supports the indicative reading: **We have peace with God** (Sanday and Headlam 1929, 120; Nygren 1949, 194; Barrett 1957, 102; Cranfield 1975, 257 n. 1; Metzger 1994, 452; Byrne 1996, 165; Dunn 2002a, 38A:245). This is not an invitation for Paul's readers to join him in the experience of being justified. He clearly assumes his Roman audience is already Christian (see 1:6, 7, 8, 12, etc.). He is about to spell out the experiential consequences of justification by faith.

The first consequence of justification Paul mentions is **peace** (5:1). **Peace** is not something so easily deceived and deceptive as human emotions. Simply because we become Christians is no guarantee of perpetual inner tranquillity. We may not feel cool, calm, and collected at all times, but the fact remains, **we**

have peace with God. We are no longer his enemies. By faith, we have accepted the terms of peace and are no longer at odds with God.

Peace

The Hebrew word most commonly translated "peace" in the OT is šālôm. It is not simply a negative concept—the absence of conflict. It conveys the positive notion of wholeness, health, and well-being. Completeness is at the heart of the meaning of šālôm—"peace." Debts that are paid are šālôm; vows that are fulfilled are šālôm. Conflicts that are resolved result in šālôm.

In ancient (as in modern) Israel, šālôm is the common daily greeting we would translate, "Hello." Like the old English root meaning of "hello," it really expresses a wish for good health—"may you be well." The greeting of "peace" is an implied prayer: "May you have the physical and spiritual resources you need. May you enjoy the blessings of the age to come."

The Greek word eirēnē appears in every NT book (except 1 John), a total of about 100 times. However, it is the Hebrew concept of šālôm that undergirds the Christian view of peace. Peace is a state of well-being that is God's gift to people who live faithfully under his covenant.

Jesus told those he restored to wholeness: "Go in peace"—whether his gift to them was healing (Mark 5:34; Luke 8:48) or forgiveness (7:50). Jesus' parting gift to his disciples was peace (John 14:27; 20:19, 21, 26).

In Rom 16:20 Paul predicts that "the God of peace will soon crush Satan under your feet." Peace may already be experienced to a limited extent (see 12:18), but he presumes that peace in its fullest sense requires the final defeat of evil.

Peace with God is not about subjective feelings, but about an objective reality: We are no longer God's enemies, but his friends. This is the point of Paul's discussion of "reconciliation" in 5:9-11. Reconciliation is about restored relationships. It is **peace with God.** We have been reconciled to our Creator. We have no reason to fear death. We can approach God with confidence. Because **peace with God** is the first consequence of justification, justification and reconciliation are indistinguishable in Christian experience.

Our reconciled relationship with God is the basis for renewed relationships on the human level. The root cause of it all is sin and a broken relationship with God. Although human sin occasioned the problem, God took the initiative to resolve the problem—**through our Lord Jesus Christ** (see 3:21-26). At incalculable personal expense, God sought to reconcile his rebellious creation to himself and to one another. God's dying love makes it possible for humans truly to love one another.

Both peace and reconciliation presume wholesome personal relationships—<u>we</u> have peace (emphasis added). Both must be experienced within the context of a community. Peace and reconciliation are not just for me, but for *us*. Because perfect peace awaits the age to come, present peace cannot be taken for granted. We must continually pursue what makes for peace (see 12:18; 14:19; 16:17-20; Eph 4:3; Heb 12:14). Thus, the hortatory reading, **Let us have peace with God** (margin), is not entirely inappropriate.

■ **2** The second consequence of our justification is **grace. Through** our Lord Jesus Christ **we have gained access by faith into this grace in which we now stand** (Rom 5:2*a*). Like ambassadors to the court of a previously hostile but now friendly power, we **have gained access** (*prosagōgēn;* only here and Eph 2:18; 3:12) into the **grace** (*charis*) **in which we now stand.** "The rendering 'access' is inadequate, as it leaves out of sight the fact that we do not come in our own strength but need an 'introducer,' Christ" (Sanday and Headlam 1929, 121). "The LXX employs the verbal form of this term with reference to approaching the altar with an offering. . . . Only those qualified and unblemished can approach God in this way." That the Christian's access to **grace** is by faith in Christ reverses "the cultural expectation that approaching either God or the emperor requires a high level of purity and clout" (Jewett 2007, 349 and 350).

Both verbs, **we have gained access** and **we stand,** are in the perfect tense, referring to a present state resulting from a past action. **We stand** translates *estekamen* and literally signifies "we stand fast or firm." The LXX uses the term to refer to the ministry of priests and Levites who "stood before the LORD" (Lev 9:5; 2 Chr 29:11). Elsewhere Paul refers to standing in faith (1 Cor 15:1; 16:13; 2 Cor 1:24), in the Lord (Phil 4:1), or in the Spirit (1:27). It seems to refer to a provisional status, freely and impartially given (see Rom 14:4).

The notion of "standing grace" is eloquently expanded in 8:31-39. But it is not evidence for a doctrine of unconditional Christian assurance. Grace is not so irresistible (2 Cor 6:1) that it guarantees our salvation is eternally secure. Grace is not, as some misguided theologians would have us think, such that when we are converted, God forgives all our sins—past, present, and future. This perverts grace into a license to sin.

God's **grace** is not to be confused with divine indulgence. God does not simply overlook our shortcomings and dote over us like a permissive, cosmic Grandpa. True, God loves us enough to accept us just as we are—sin and all, but he loves us too much to leave us as we are—wallowing in and enslaved to our sin. Grace sets us free to enjoy *a new quality of life* (Rom 6:4), which may be characterized as obedience or the life of holiness (see vv 15-22).

Standing **grace** is not simply about God's free gift of righteousness, which ignores our rebellious past. It is about our new life of obedience that necessarily *follows* justification. It is the ongoing experience of grace that enables us to live so as to please and honor God. Grace is not only the doorway into the Christian life but also the invigorating air of the Spirit in which we live and breathe and thrive.

The **grace** Paul has in mind is the God-given ability to be and do what we could never be or do on our own. Grace brings us into the realm of God's rule. As we choose to live under his sovereignty, we find ourselves empowered to obey him. We are not left as God found us. We increasingly become new creations. "The old has gone; the new has come!" (2 Cor 5:17; see Rom 6:1-7, 19).

Living in **grace** does not release us *from* obedience; it empowers us *for* obedience. We must not surrender any part of ourselves to sin. Instead, we must "give [ourselves] to God, as those who have been brought from death to life, and surrender [our] whole being to him to be used for righteous purposes. Sin must not be [our] master; for [we] do not live under law but under God's grace" (6:13-14 TEV).

The third consequence of justification Paul mentions is **hope** (5:2*b*). In view of all that God has already done for us, Paul continues, **we rejoice** [*kauchōmetha*, **boast**] **in the hope of the glory of God.** The real focus is on what lies ahead. Our confident expectation for a future share in the reality of God is not based on our status or human achievement, but solely on the grace and power of God.

In this **hope** we **rejoice** or "exult" (NASB, REB, JB). Given Paul's critique of boasting in 2:17, 23; 3:27; and 4:2, his report or recommendation (the verb could be construed as either indicative or imperative) of it here seems unexpected. However, this boast is not about our present status or past achievements. It is paradoxically in our present **sufferings** (5:3) and our future **hope** (v 2). "Neither was a suitable basis for boasting in the honor-shame systems of the first century" (Jewett 2007, 351). It is not the honor of our contemporaries we seek, but that of God alone—**the glory of God.** (See the sidebar "Further Reading on Honor and Shame in Mediterranean Society" with 6:1-23.)

Before we were put right with God, we *all sinned and continually fell short of God's glory* (3:23). Justification not only frees us from the chains of our sinful past and the ongoing needs of the present but also opens up possibilities that did not exist before: A right relationship with God that gives us hope for the future. We no longer have to compete for honor from others. God's favorable assessment alone matters (see 2:9-10).

Paul rejected prevailing societal notions about honor. "It was held that the winning of glory was the only adequate reward for merit in public life, and that, given the doubt as to the state of man after death, it was the effective assurance of immortality" (Jewett 2007, 351). Christians do not simply pursue the same goal as others—self-centered **glory,** but with a willingness to accept delayed satisfaction in the interests of receiving it from a superior source— **God.** Paul's point is that *we boast* in our **hope** that in the future **God** will be appropriately honored as God. Of course, as God's children and heirs, we share in his glorious future (8:17, 21, 30).

Popular notions about **hope** are also quite different from Paul's understanding. Hope is not merely optimism about the future. The fact is, as Paul admits, Christians will have troubles (5:3-5). As followers of the Crucified One, we should not expect to be exempt from suffering in the present age. In fact, if we are "God's children" and "co-heirs with Christ," Paul insists that "we share in his sufferings in order that we may also share in his glory" (8:16, 17) But "our present sufferings are not worth comparing with the glory that will be revealed in us" (8:18). We are not in heaven yet, but we can rest assured that *we will be saved from the wrath of God* (5:9).

Christian **hope** is not about wishful thinking. It is "faith oriented to the future" (Rudolf Bultmann), and like faith, hope is no more reliable than the one whose promises we trust. The hope God inspires in us for a bright future "does not disappoint us, for God has poured out his love into our hearts by means of the Holy Spirit, who is God's gift to us" (v 5 TEV).

Christian **hope** for the future is based on God's already proven love for us in the past. Christ died to save us and poured out the Holy Spirit so that we could live obediently until then. We can trust God's promises because he has already delivered on his OT promises. "For when we were still helpless, Christ died for the wicked . . . It is a difficult thing for someone to die for a righteous person," much less a sinner (vv 6-7 TEV). "But God proves his love for us in that while we still were sinners Christ died for us" (v 8 NRSV). "What then shall we say to this? If God is for us, who is against us? He who did not spare his own Son but gave him up for us all, will he not also give us all things with him?" (8:31-32 RSV).

The glory of God in which we rejoice refers to a future that reflects the language of Gen 1:26-28 (see especially in Ps 8:5-8). Here **glory** denotes the "likeness to God" based on bearing God's "image." The process of salvation will be complete when we arrive at the fullness of **glory,** the Creator's intent for his children (see Rom 8:29). As "the last Adam" (1 Cor 15:45) Christ both facilitates and "models" this glory (1 Cor 15:42-49; 2 Cor 3:18; 4:4-6; Phil 3:20-21). (See the sidebar "Glory" with Rom 8:18-27.)

■ **3-4 Not only** do we rejoice in our future hope, **but** [*ou monon de, alla kai*, *Not only, but also;* see 5:11; 8:23; 9:10; 2 Cor 8:19] **we also rejoice in our sufferings** (Rom 5:3). Even **in our sufferings** (*en tais thlipsesin;* see 2 Cor 12:9), we have reason to **hope,** because they set in motion a chain reaction that **produces** in turn **perseverance** (*hypomonēn*, **endurance**), **character** (*dokimē*), and **hope** (Rom 5:3-4). *Dokimē* (only here in Romans; but with cognates in 1:28; 2:18; 12:2; 14:18, 22; 16:10; see 2 Cor 2:9; 8:2; 9:13; 13:3-7) refers to the *approval* that comes from passing a test. That **suffering** produces constructive results lies deep in the Jewish tradition, reflected here.

As Paul uses it, *thlipsis* might include physical afflictions, "hardships, persecutions, eschatological troubles, or daily trials." Jewett speculates that Paul may have thought of the difficulties the Roman congregation had faced due to Claudius's expulsion of Jews from the city and their subsequent return (2007, 353).

■ **5** Believers are united to Christ; as his sufferings led, through God's power, to his glory (Rom 8:17), so we may hope the same pattern will prevail in us. But the **hope** God produces by way of chain reaction **does not disappoint** [*kataischynei;* present tense] **us** (5:5). Thus, we boast in a hope that *does not put us to shame* (see Pss 22:5; 25:20). We triumph over the shame of our sufferings already in the present (see 1 Cor 1:27-30), through the confidence we have that God loves us.

The Greek of Rom 5:5*b* literally says that *the love of God has been poured out.* This almost certainly refers to what God has done to demonstrate his love for us, not to our being enabled by the gift of the Spirit to love God (see v 8; 2 Cor 13:14; Gal 2:20). Thus the translation, **God has poured** [*enkechytai*] **his love into our hearts by the Holy Spirit** (Rom 5:5), is appropriate.

Elsewhere the verb *encheō* is used literally of the shedding of blood (see 3:15; Gen 9:6; Matt 26:28) and metaphorically of the giving of the Holy Spirit (see Acts 2:16-17; 10:45; echoing Joel 2:28). The perfect tense of the verb here describes a present state resulting from our first experience of God's **love.** Unlike Western notions, Paul thought of **hearts** not as physiological organs or human emotions but as "the seat of understanding, knowledge, and will" (Jewett 2007, 356).

God's love becomes known to us **by** (*dia*) the gift (*tou dothentos;* an aorist passive participle) of **the Holy Spirit.** Does the Spirit communicate this as information, "God loves you"? Or, is the resulting presence of the Spirit himself in our lives evidence enough? The liquid imagery and association with the gift of the Spirit suggest some association of the experience of God's love with the event of baptism (see Rom 6:1-4).

As a result, **we,** the eschatological people of God, are cleansed from sin and given the new life of the Spirit (see Ezek 36—37). The presence of the Holy Spirit in the Christian community is the sure proof that we are already living in the new age, already enjoying our filial relationship with God, and already enabled to cry out "Abba, Father" (Rom 8:15; Gal 4:6-7). The old age lingers for now, and so does our **suffering,** but the assurance that God loves us saves us from disgrace.

■ **6** The **hope** that springs up from God's **love** in us comes in two "waves," which Paul identifies in Rom 5:6-10 (Byrne 1996, 167). In the first "wave" Paul dwells on the death of Christ as the proof of God's *agapē* (**love,** see 1

John 4:10): **Christ died for the ungodly** (*asebōn*, Rom 5:6; see 4:5). And we were among impious humanity, subject to God's wrath (see 1:18). *While we were still* [*eti*] *weak* [*asthenōn*, powerless; see 14:1, 2, 21], *still* [*eti*] *at that time* Christ's death proved God loved us.

■ **7** To stress the enormity of the sacrifice involved, Paul invites us to consider on what terms most humans might be prepared to die for another. Even if it is for the sake of a **righteous man** (*dikaios*; but see 1:18—3:23), giving up one's life is very difficult; it is conceivable that for a really **good** (*agathos*) person **someone might possibly dare to die** (5:7). **But God demonstrates his own love for us in this: While we were still sinners, Christ died for us** (v 8; see 14:15; 1 Cor 8:11; 15:3; 2 Cor 5:14; 1 Thess 5:9-10).

■ **8** The source of the Christian's confidence for the future is the unprecedented, unparalleled demonstration of God's love for us objectively revealed in the death of Christ—he died for us as a vicarious sacrifice when we were **powerless, ungodly** (Rom 5:6), no **good**, not **righteous** (v 7), **sinners** (v 8). "The widely used formula of Christ dying in behalf of others should be understood 'in terms of representation and not in terms of substitution'" (Jewett 2007, 362, quoting Daniel Powers). He died the shameful death we deserved to die. Christ's self-gift reveals and demonstrates the eternal love of God to the undeserving (see 8:31-32, 39). This is grace expressed.

■ **9** Paul is persuaded that God's love for us, proven in the past at the cross, and still presently experienced in the Lord's Supper (see 1 Cor 11:23-26; note the present tense of the verb **demonstrates**), has even greater implications for the future. **Since we have now been justified by his blood, how much more** [*pollo malon;* see Rom 5:10, 15, and 17] **shall we be saved from God's wrath** [see 1:18; 3:5-6; see 1 Thess 1:10; 5:9] **through him!** (Rom 5:9). Here Paul returns to the theme of justification, repeating *dikaiōthentes*, the participle with which he began this section of the letter in v 1. He rehearses and clarifies the implications of *having been made righteous* by faith in the death of Christ (see the comments on 3:25), the new means of atonement **now** available to all (see 3:26).

The completion of the salvation proclaimed in the gospel (see 1:16-17) is still in the future. Nonetheless, presently "justified" believers can confidently expect that God's love will usher them safely through the final barrier of the judgment. Jewett notes that

> the theme of forgiveness is conspicuously absent here, where the context is defined by God's love. Despite the weight of the Augustinian tradition that construes salvation primarily as individual forgiveness, Paul's concern is with overcoming the shameful status of "sinner" through divine love that accepts each person and group without qualification as demonstrated on the cross of Christ. (2007, 361)

That God's love for us expresses itself in such indiscriminate acceptance of all explains why Paul expects this same kind of mutual acceptance among Christians (see chs 14—16).

■ **10** The second "wave" of God's love in 5:10 offers a more concise statement of the same argument, but with a different metaphor. **For if, when we were God's enemies, we were reconciled to him through the death of his Son, how much more, having been reconciled, shall we be saved through his** [risen] **life!** Clearly, *we* made **enemies** of ourselves, treating God as our enemy by our disrespect for him. That he did not treat us as *his* enemies is proved at the cross. He was the wronged party, but he took the initiative to remedy the alienation. The gift of righteousness makes present reconciliation possible; former enemies may become friends. Of course, apart from God's initiative (2 Cor 5:19), we could not "be reconciled to God" by our own volition (v 20).

As the future tense makes clear, **saved through his life** denotes salvation in the full and final sense (Godet 1883, 313). Paul normally reserves explicit "salvation" language to refer to final salvation (see Rom 8:18-25). For the present, Christians "are being saved" and their future salvation is contingent on ongoing faithfulness to God (1 Cor 15:2; see 2 Cor 2:14). The new **life** in Christ anticipates what Paul will say in the remainder of Rom 5—8 (see 5:15, 17, 18, 21; 6:2, 4, 10, 11, 13, 22, 23; 7:1, 2, 3, 9, 10; 8:2, 6, 10, 12, 13, 38; Jewett 2007, 366).

■ **11** In 5:11 Paul concludes this section of the letter on a note of triumph. **Not only** do we have hope for the future prospect of salvation, **but right now** [*nyn*] **we also rejoice in God through our Lord Jesus Christ.** Paul repeats the "not only, but also" construction from v 3. Here, as in v 2, **Rejoice** may be better translated ***boast*** (*kauchōmenoi*).

Paul's argument has come full circle. The Jewish claim to "rely on the law and brag about [their special] relationship to God" (2:17) has been completely excluded (3:27) in the light of God's work in Christ, corroborated by Scripture (4:3). Yes, we do "boast in God" (see 1 Cor 1:29-31); no longer in ourselves. We ***boast*** while still suffering in this present age. But we are already the eschatological people of God composed of all those, Jews *and* Gentiles, who **through our Lord Jesus Christ . . . have now received reconciliation** (Rom 5:11). In the Elizabethan English of the KJV, "reconciliation" is "at-one-ment." Reconciliation is **peace with God** (v 1) and offers the potential for peace with all those for whom Christ died.

FROM THE TEXT

To be God's people of the last days (i.e., eschatological) is a precarious calling. Because we have been justified by faith, we already enjoy some of the blessings of salvation expected only in the age to come—especially, the gift of the Spirit and all he brings. However, we are not yet saved in the fullest sense of the word. We suffer and die. Our future hope of participating in the glory of God is not yet realized. For now, we await the hope of this glory. "By faith we eagerly await through the Spirit the righteousness [*final justification*] for which we hope." For the present, "The only thing that counts is faith expressing itself through love" (Gal 5:5-6). John Wesley insisted that "'faith working by love' is the length and breadth and depth and height of Christian perfection" (1870, 1:xxiii).

Because of the love of God demonstrated definitively in Jesus Christ, even our suffering gives us reason to hope. Our past may be defined by our solidarity with Adam and all of the rest of fallen humanity. And, in a sense, because we are subject to bodily death, we continue to live in Adam. But since we have been justified by faith, our present is defined by our solidarity with Christ and his cross, and our future will be determined by his resurrection.

With this introduction to Rom 5:1—8:39, we are now prepared to turn to the two racial heads, Adam and Christ, in 5:12-21, a passage that may better be titled "Christ and Adam," since the weight of Paul's argument is not upon the first Adam's sin, and the death that followed, but upon the "much more" grace that is in the last Adam, reversing the fall and ushering in eternal life for all who believe in Jesus Christ our Lord.

In the dark days of World War I, a young Swiss pastor, schooled in the optimism of nineteenth-century liberal Protestantism, found himself with nothing to say to his congregation. Turning to Paul's letter to the Romans, Karl Barth found renewed hope in the challenging word of God. His writings sparked a revival of orthodox Christian faith that had languished in the heyday of liberalism. His commentaries and massive, multivolume systematic theology won him international acclaim.

On a visit to the United States in the 1960s, Barth was invited to speak to a large gathering of scholars and students at Richmond Theological Seminary. One of those present asked him, "Dr. Barth, after all you've read and written, what is the most profound thought you have ever had?"

With hardly a moment's hesitation, Barth replied: "Jesus loves me, this I know, for the Bible tells me so."

(2) The Two Ages: Adam and Christ (5:12-21)

BEHIND THE TEXT

While Paul refers to Adam first and then to Christ in his reflections on "the Fall" and our restoration, this section should properly be called "Christ and Adam." Adam is only "a type [*typos*] of the one who was to come" (v 14 NRSV). Adam is the shadow; Christ is the substance. The emphasis throughout this passage is placed upon the "much more" grace that comes through Christ. The fall in Adam is but a foil for the redemption that is in Christ Jesus our Lord.

Paul has no interest in developing a consistent doctrine of sin or even of Adam's fall; his main concern is to show the all-encompassing and surpassingly glorious effect of Christ on those who belong to him. (Jewett 2007, 380)

This, for Paul, was life's deepest certainty: "For anyone united to Christ, there is a new creation: the old order has gone; a new order has already begun" in Christ (see 2 Cor 5:17 REB). The new age has dawned in Christ Jesus our Lord, and all who are in him have been taken out of the old order of Adam, where sin reigns in death, and transferred to the new order of Christ, where grace reigns in righteousness to eternal life. That is the theme of the passage.

For Paul, "Adam" is who he is in Genesis—not only the first man "Adam" (Gen 4:25) but also '*adam, humanity* "in the image and likeness of God" (1:26-27). Following the tragic events reported in 3:1-7, for Paul in Rom 5:12-21 (as in Gen 5:1-3), "Adam" is *humanity* in the likeness of <u>*fallen Adam*</u> (see Greathouse 1998, ch 3). For Paul, Christ and Adam are more than two individuals; they are the heads of two contrasting yet overlapping orders of existence. "The comparison between the realms of Adam and Christ . . . expressed in various ways no less than eight times" (Jewett 2007, 370) is the key to the entire passage.

In contrast to Enlightenment rationalism, which views humanity as an aggregate of separate "individuals," Israelites and their Mediterranean neighbors thought of humanity "collectively"—in terms of family, clan, nation, or race. Thus, "Israel" could identify either their great ancestor or the nation. On this view Paul can think of "Adam" as either the first man (see Gen 4:25) or as "humankind" (see 5:1-3 NRSV). Adam is both the progenitor of the race and "our old selves" (Adam—and ourselves in him). Christ, on the other hand, is both the Redeemer and "the new humanity" (Christ—and ourselves in him). Adam and those in him are the old, fallen humanity; Christ and those in him are the new, redeemed humanity—his body, the church.

Some interpreters prefer to think in terms of "representation." When the head of a nation, for example, declares war, that person does so as its representative. In this way, Adam in his disobedience involved us all in his sin. Similarly, Christ's obedience involves us all in his righteousness; in Christ we all are redeemed. "We are convinced that one died for all, and therefore all died," Paul writes in 2 Cor 5:14-15, "And he died for all, that those who live should no longer live for themselves but for him who died for them and was raised." In Adam we *potentially* died <u>in</u> sin; in Christ we *provisionally* died <u>to</u> sin. Adam and Christ, in each case, acted as our representative, affecting our destiny. Thinking this way, some expositors speak of Adam and Christ as "fields of force." From each radiates forces that touch us profoundly.

Paul would have us know that the crucifixion of Jesus was the nailing to the cross of "our old self" (*palaios hēmōn anthrōpos*, Rom 6:6) and that his resurrection was the raising of "the new self [*ton kaoinon anthrōpon*] . . . in true righteousness and holiness" (Eph 4:24). "Christ on the cross concludes the old Adam," "and his resurrection commences the new" (Chilton and Neusner 1995, 93). In the purpose and provision of God the crucifixion and death of Jesus was the "conclusion" of the old Adam (Adam—and ourselves in Adam) and the resurrection of Jesus the "commencement" of the new humanity (Christ—and ourselves in him).

Such an understanding of Christ's work is key, not only to Rom 5—8, but also to Paul's gospel, which may be summarized in the words:

> God . . . the Father . . . has qualified [us] to share in the inheritance of the saints in the kingdom of light. For he has rescued us from the dominion of darkness and brought us into the kingdom of the Son he loves, in whom we have redemption, the forgiveness of sins. (Col 1:10, 12-14)

This is the pith and marrow of the NT gospel, a truth that Paul in Rom 5:12-21 couches in terms of Adam (the age of sin and darkness) and Christ (the age of grace and light). (See Charles Wesley's sermon on Eph 5:14, "Awake, Thou That Sleepest," in Wesley 1979, 5:25-36.)

IN THE TEXT

(a) The Likeness Between Adam and Christ (5:12-14)

■ **12-14** The opening words of v 12, *Dia touto*, **Therefore,** suggest that vv 12-21 offer a conclusion arising from the preceding argument (5:1-11 or 1:17—5:11). The conjunction *hōsper*, **just as,** prepares the way for the comparison between Christ and Adam, heads of two contrasting, overlapping ages, two orders of human existence.

Paul boldly presents Adam as instrumental in the invasion of **sin** and **death through sin** into **the world** (see Wis 2:24) and its epidemic impact on the entire human race (see 1 Cor 15:22). In a way that is characteristic of this part of the letter (5:12—8:10; see 3:9), Paul personifies **sin** (*hē hamartia*) and **death** (*ho thanatos*) as tyrannical powers (in chs 5—8, the singular noun "sin" appears 41 times; "death," 22 times).

Both death and sin appear to function here as cosmic forces under which all humans are in bondage. The language of "personification" does not do justice to the apocalyptic worldview within which Paul is operating. To speak of sin as "entering" the world and death as "reaching" all persons clearly implies that neither was present prior to Adam's act. However one explains the background of this thought, it remains clear that Paul depicts Adam's act as decisively determining the behavior of his descendants. A social theory of sin appears to be implied here in which the actions of forebears determine those of their descendants. (Jewett 2007, 374-75)

The death that follows Adam's sin is primarily *spiritual death*. As a result of Adam's fall from divine grace, humans are cursed with an infinite craving, a void the world cannot fill. They are *depraved* because they are born *deprived* of the sanctifying grace of the Holy Spirit. As a consequence of Adam's sin, every member of the human race has been afflicted with the situation of **death**— conceived as moral bankruptcy, weakness, and corruption (as the body is physically corrupted when one dies). Paul conceives, therefore, of a human solidarity in sin, which he will set in contrast to a much more powerful solidarity in grace (see 1 Cor 15:45).

The Consequences of Adam's Sin

Augustine's doctrine of original sin depends, in part, on the Latin Vulgate's mistranslation of the Greek expression *eph' hō* in Rom 5:12 as *in quo*, as "in whom." This understands Paul to say, "All sinned implicitly in Adam" (as Levi paid tithes "in the loins of" Abraham [Heb 7:5, 9 NRSV]). But there are no grounds for treating the idiom *eph' hō* so woodenly as to mean "in whom." Elsewhere in the NT it means **because,** or **so that,** or **with the result that** (Fitzmyer 1993, 332-38).

5:12-14

To understand the phrase **because all sinned** to mean that individuals die *merely* **because** they *personally* sin would seem to contradict the aim of the entire passage: Adam is ultimately responsible for the death of all people, even as the life of all depends on Christ. Thus, Paul must mean that all of Adam's descendants share in the adverse *consequences* of his sin, which extend to the entire human race.

This same paradox between Adam's role and the role of all humanity in the endemic problem of sin and death may be found earlier than Paul in the pseudepigraphal *2 Bar.* 54:15, 19:

> For though Adam first sinned
> And brought untimely death upon all,
> Yet of those who were born from him
> Each one of them has prepared for his own soul torment to come....
> Adam is therefore not the cause, save only of his own soul,
> But each of us has been the Adam of his own soul. *(APOT)*

Paul portrays salvation in a divine drama in which believers are rescued from the tyranny of Sin and Death, so as to come, through Christ, under the sway of Grace and Righteousness. Freedom from Sin is our sanctification; freedom from Death is our glorification. As justification leads to sanctification (Rom 6:1-22; 7:6; 8:1-17), so sanctification climaxes in glorification (6:23; 8:18-25).

In personifying Sin, Paul does not mean to suggest that humans are the helpless pawns of a literal cosmic power separate from themselves. Sin, for Paul, is like a deadly virus in humanity, a fundamental revolt against the Creator that places self and its perceived needs in the place that should be only occupied by the sovereign God.

Without denying personal responsibility, Paul views sin as "collective" in that the sins of individuals are all manifestations of a radical selfishness that tyrannizes our human existence. It is also collective in the sense that its origin can be traced back to the disobedience of **one man** to the command of God (Gen 3:1-7), from which it spread in such a way that it came to dominate human existence. Thus, humans enter the "solidarity" of sinfulness, which both precedes each one's personal history and works destructively on it (Byrne 1996, 175).

Paul appeals to the **one man,** Adam, as a foil for what he says about **the one man, Jesus Christ** (Rom 5:15). Christ establishes a *new* solidarity of **the grace of** that **one man,** which may now overflow **to the many** (= *all people*, v 18). By the **death** that followed the sin of the **one man,** Paul means more than physical death, which was not part of the Creator's original plan (8:10-11). **Righteousness** removes the "sting" of death sin caused—the sting that turns physical death into the eternal "death" of separation from God (1 Cor 15:56). It is death in this final sense that Paul has in mind as the counterpart to the **eternal life** that is the gift of God **through Jesus Christ our Lord** (Rom 5:21; see vv 17*b*, 18*b*).

Paul qualifies his doctrine of human racial solidarity in Sin and Death in vv 13-14. Neither the presence nor absence of Law affected the universal reign of Death as a punishment for Sin (but see 4:15). **Death reigned from the time of Adam to the time of Moses, even over those** whose sinning was not like Adam's, in defiance of a specific law (see Gen 2:15-17). Death became a reality for all human beings, based on their repetition of the sin of Adam. This was true even if sinning was not the same for those who sinned before **the time of Moses** and the giving of the Law. Paul obviously does not share the view of some Jews that the Law was eternal (Bar 4:1; *Jub.* 24:11). He refused to limit sin to a violation of Jewish law (Jewett 2007, 377).

Before Moses, **sin** [*hamartia*] **was in the world,** but it was **not taken into account** (Rom 5:13). That is, it was not "reckoned" (*ellogeitai,* ***charged to one's account***). Although God did not hold wrongdoers accountable (see 3:25), their "sin" was still their undoing. It was simply not recognized that sin was re-

164

sponsible for the misfortunes of the human condition. **Sin was in the world, but it was not like the trespass** (*paraptōma*) of Adam (5:15).

Although the heirs of Adam were not in the same situation as Adam (who sinned by disobeying a direct command), they were still subject to **death** (v 14). That is, people continued to die; but in the absence of law, no one knew why. **Death reigned** [*ebasileusen;* vv 14 and 17] like a cruel tyrant because all humans sinned against the light of creation (1:20-21) and conscience (2:14-15), if not Jewish law. For those who had no objective law, responsibility was diminished, and the penalty of their sin was mitigated.

Although the expression **from the time of Adam to the time of Moses** (5:14) is primarily chronological, it is not strictly so. It has a logical sense also, applicable to the category of persons in a similar situation. Paul is thinking theologically rather than historically; he is explaining humans to themselves. He is not describing merely humanity's past. What he says may apply equally to those who have never been privileged to know the will of God as revealed in the Law and the gospel. The passage, therefore, has a present application in the world outside the reach of Christianity and Judaism.

We have no choice as to whether or not we enter the human race, and we have no choice as to whether we reign or are reigned over. Our choice is restricted to which humanity we will belong, Adam's or Christ's. That choice determines everything else. Adam's disobedience brought the reality of sin into the world. Adam is our common ancestor. He represented the whole of humanity; and he represented us poorly. Because Adam sinned, sin was in the world from the beginning. With sin came death. Death became a part of the experience of the entire human race, not just because Adam sinned, but **because all sinned** (v 12). All humans repeat the sin of their ancestor Adam. Paul will shortly emphasize that heredity need not decide our destiny. There is a way out; but it is not the way of law.

Law is not a solution to the problem of sin. Law serves the function of making people conscious of sin (3:20). What Adam did is not counteracted by law, but by Jesus Christ. Law identifies sin as sin, but it is powerless to set people free from its deadly grip. Only Christ, God's gracious gift to fallen humanity, sets people free from the power of sin and the curse of death.

But if law is not the solution of the sin problem, neither is it its cause. Sin was a reality even before the coming of the Law. Apart from the Law it operated like an invisible, poisonous gas. The evidence of sin's pervasive presence in the world before the coming of the Law was that people died. They died even though they had not sinned in the same way Adam did. He disobeyed a specific command, "You must not eat from the tree of the knowledge of good and evil" (Gen 2:17). Apart from law, sin did not exist as trespass, but it obviously did exist as a death-dealing power. Law makes sin visible, but it does not give life (Rom 7:7-12).

Though opposite in the consequences of their acts, Adam and Christ are also alike (5:14). <u>Each is the head of a human family.</u> Adam is the founder of a family doomed to death; <u>Christ, of a family destined to life.</u> Because Adam sinned, death became our ruler. However, grace overflows the boundaries drawn by sin (v 16). In Adam we live under the curse of divine condemnation, but the free gift of God, despite the many sins of Adam's children, is justification. In Christ we are acquitted. We are freed from death's oppressive reign, to share in the "reign in life" through Christ (v 17). Our lord, not our heredity, determines our destiny.

(b) The Contrastive Analogy of Adam and Christ (5:15-17)

■ **15** At the end of the previous section Adam is seen as a **pattern** [*typos*, *type*] **of the one to come** (v 14). Adam is the type of the Coming One in the sense that he is a figure of universal significance for the race. His one sin breathed an influence that affected the destiny of **the many** (v 15). In this one respect we can speak of the *likeness* between Adam and Christ.

Despite their similarities, Paul emphasizes the contrast between Adam and Christ in v 15: **But the gift is not like the trespass** [*to paraptōma*]. **For if the many** [*hoi polloi*] **died by the trespass of the one man, how much more did God's grace and the gift** [*to charisma*] **that came by the grace** [*hē charis*] **of the one man, Jesus Christ, overflow to the many!** Most interpreters agree that **the many** (*hoi polloi*) in v 15 is to be equated with *all people* (*pantas anthrō-pous*) in vv 12 and 18 (see Jewett 2007, 380).

Paul contrasts Adam's **trespass** (*to paraptōma;* see 4:25) with the free **gift** (*to charisma*). The term *charisma* describes the result (the force of the *-ma* ending) of the enabling gift of **God's** grace (5:14-15). The coming of Christ concretely embodied God's grace. That in both cases the act of **one man** affected **many** underscores the *likeness* between Adam and Christ.

However, v 15 underscores the *contrast* between the two. With reference to Adam Paul makes a simple statement: **Many died by the trespass of the one man.** But with reference to the gracious act of Christ Paul formulates an extravagant statement of **God's** free gift of grace (*hē charis*) that overflowed (*eperisseusen;* see v 17) **much more** (*pollō mallon*) to the many. Adam was simply a tragic human being, but the self-sacrificing death of Jesus made Christ "a life-giving spirit" (1 Cor 15:45; see Rom 8:2). **The gift is not like the trespass:** "God's act of grace is out of all proportion to Adam's wrongdoing" (REB). Whereas the first wave of God's overflowing grace emphasizes what lay "behind" Christ's act embodying **God's grace,** the second focuses on what it brought as **the gift** (*to dōrēma*) for the benefit of **the many** (5:15).

■ **16-17** Paul now introduces a somewhat intrusive explanation: **The judgment** (*to . . . krima*) **that followed one sin . . . brought** God's **condemnation** (*katakrima*) for all (v 16). This paves the way for Paul to magnify the wide-ranging **justification** (*dikaiōma*, v 16) now offered through **God's abundant provision** [*perisseian*] **of grace and of the gift of righteousness . . . through the one man, Jesus Christ** (v 17). By these definitions, Paul effectively equates God's acquittal of sinful humanity with grace and the gift of righteousness.

Paul conceived of God's grace as always "superabundant," "more than enough" (note the *periss-* root in vv 15, 17, and 21). In this he shared the prophetic conviction that in the future messianic age God "would reinstate the plenitude of paradise" (Isa 25:6-8; 27:6; 65:17-25; Ezek 47:9-12; Amos 9:13; *4 Ezra* 8:52; 2 Cor 8:2; 9:14; 10:15; Jewett 2007, 381).

Dikaiōma (with its cognates) is one of the great words of Romans. Its use in Rom 5:16 to mean **justification** ("verdict of acquittal" REB) is rhetorically motivated, to provide a fitting contrast to the word *katakrima*, **condemnation**. In 2:26 it refers to the obedient, inwardly Spirit-circumcised Gentile believers who "keep the requirements of the law" (NRSV). In 8:2 the singular *dikaiōma* is used to proclaim "the law of the Spirit of life" in Christ Jesus that fulfills "the just requirement of the law" (v 4 RSV) by pouring God's "love into our hearts by the Holy Spirit" (5:5; see 13:8-10).

Paul describes the results of Adam's **trespass** with the imagery of universal sovereignty: the fall inaugurated a reign of terror over all of Adam's descendants—**death reigned** [*ebasileusen;* see v 14] **through that one man** (v 17*a*). "King Death" ruled as a vicious tyrant who destroyed his unwilling subjects. But the good news is that **those who receive God's . . . grace** and **gift of righteousness** will **reign** [*basileusousin*] **in life through . . . Jesus Christ** (v 17*b*).

If the contrastive parallelism in v 17 were perfectly balanced, we might have expected Paul to have continued the personification and said something like "life will reign through Christ," comparable to what he writes in v 21 of the contrasting reigns of sin and grace. But here Paul claims that believers *will reign.* Jewett argues that

> this detail confirms that Paul's interest is not in developing a doctrine of Adam's sin but rather to employ the Adamic material as a foil to explain the abundant life in Christ that overturns the legacy of sin and death. (2007, 383)

The future tense of the verb **will . . . reign** may point to another of the eschatological tensions found throughout ch 5 (vv 2, 5, 9, 10). Justified believers are already receiving grace (progressive present tense), but they are not yet reigning. This must await their still future final vindication at the Last Judgment (v 16). Perhaps the close association of end-time events with the future resurrection of the dead explains the expression **reign in life.** Although as justified believers we already enjoy a new quality of life through our participation in Christ (see the comments on 6:4), we still eagerly await the future "redemption of our bodies" (8:23; see the comments on 8:18-25). It was a characteristic feature of Jewish and early Christian eschatological expectation that the righteous would rule in the coming age (Dan 7:22, 26-27; Wis 3:8; 5:15-16; Matt 19:28; 1 Cor 4:8; 2 Tim 2:12; Rev 1:6; 5:10; 20:4, 6; 22:5). Yet, since the risen Christ is already Lord, in one sense, believers already **reign in life through the one man, Jesus Christ** (Rom 5:17; see Dunn 2002a, 38A:282).

The overflowing gift of righteousness (v 17) leads to life (see 8:10*c*) and paves the way for full human entrance into the lordship of the universe according to the original design of the Creator (Gen 1:26-28; Ps 8:5-8). Physical death remains as the abiding legacy of Adam, but the gift of righteousness ensures, "Death has been swallowed up in victory . . . through our Lord Jesus Christ" (see 1 Cor 15:54-56).

(c) Adam and Christ: Like and Unlike (5:18-19)

■ **18** With the overwhelming superiority of Christ established, Paul is now in a position to allow the full expression of the comparative contrast between Adam and Christ, broken off at v 12, to move ahead in vv 18 and 19. Paul characterizes Adam's **trespass** (*paraptōmatos*, v 18) as an act of **disobedience** (*parakoēs*, v 19). He sets it in a contrastive parallel (apparently) to Christ's death on the cross, which he characterizes as an **act of righteousness** (*dikaiōmatos*, v 18) or **obedience** (*hypakoēs*, v 19). This parallelism also suggests that the expression **the many** (*hoi polloi*, v 19; see v 15) refers to all people (*pantas anthrōpous*, **all men**).

■ **19** Paul does not explain *how* it is that **through** (*dia*, "because of") Adam's sin all people **were made** [*katestathēsan*] **sinners** (v 19). He merely claims *that* all humans are sinners in solidarity with Adam. In its only other occurrence in the Pauline corpus outside the present passage, the Greek word here translated **made** (from *kathistēmi*) means "appointed" (see Titus 1:5). This suggests that everyone came to be considered sinners by divine decree. Because of Adam's sin, God condemned all humanity to the judgment of death—**condemnation** (*katakrima*, Rom 5:18; see v 16). Personal choice must have something to do with it, since v 12 claims that "death came to all men, because all sinned."

Because of (*dia*, **through**) Christ's death, God provides **justification** [*dikaiōsin*] **that brings life for all men** (v 18), so that all people **will be made** [*katastathēsontai* from *kathistēmi*] **righteous.** As with Adam and universal sinfulness, Paul says nothing here about humanity's part in God's universal justification, but this is no reason to imagine that the claims he has previously made about the necessity of faith sharing in God's righteousness are forgotten.

God's guilty verdict decreed because of the first Adam's disobedience is overturned by the obedience of the last Adam (see 1 Cor 15:45). Paul seems to say that because the first human did wrong, consequently all human beings are sentenced to death. However, he also insists that because the last human did right, all human beings are put right with God and given the gift of life (Rom 5:18).

Is the life-giving work of Christ really as all-inclusive as the death-dealing work of Adam? Is salvation in Christ actually as universal as condemnation in Adam? Paul seems to say yes. Does this then imply that since the time of Christ all people are "saved" without respect to their response of faith in God's offer? Paul's answer, explicit throughout his letters, is clearly no.

The Influence of Isaiah 53

The idea of one person's obedience making "many righteous" appears to echo the Hebrew text of Isa 53:11, "the righteous one, my servant, shall make many to be accounted righteous." In Shum's words, "what Paul draws on from the Suffering Servant song is not simply (Second) Isaiah's language, but the prophet's concept of a *one-many-solidarity-relationship*" [Shiu-Lun Shum, *Paul's Use of Isaiah in Romans*, 2002]....The context denies "the limited nationalism of the normal Jewish hope" that restricts the number of the "righteous" to those following the Torah. The *polloi* ("many") in this context as in [Rom] 5:15 includes all those who have accepted the gospel, . . . both "weak" and "strong," without regard to their adherence to the law. (Jewett 2007, 387)

Both Christ and Adam have representative significance for Paul. They are the heads of two very different humanities. Christ is "the one whose action (like Adam's) determines the character and condition of those who belong to the age he inaugurated" by his obedience to God, just as surely as Adam's disobedience did the same (Dunn 2002a, 38A:285). How do people enter into solidarity with one or the other head?

If faith is essential for justification, is there anything comparable to it that is essential for condemnation? Are all human beings made sinners solely by the disobedience of Adam without respect to their own choice to rebel against God? Paul's final answer again seems to be no. All humans are sinners and subject to death **because all sinned** (v 12). Because of Christ, heredity need not be our destiny. We may choose to continue to live in Adam and die. Or, through grace we may choose to live in Christ and truly live. The freedom to choose the part of the human family to which we will belong is not natural. It is a benefit of God's overflowing grace. Only grace can dethrone the tyrant "King Death" to install a new Sovereign in its place, Jesus Christ.

(d) Sin and Grace, Death and Life (5:20-21)

■ **20** Up to this point Paul has spoken of Adam and Christ as though there was no intervening stage in salvation history. But this is to overlook a most significant event—the giving of the Law and the period from Moses to Christ (see v 14). How does the Jewish law fit into the divine scheme of salvation? Paul challenges widely cherished Jewish assumptions about the saving role of the Law. He insists, on the contrary, that **Law sneaked in** (*pereisēlthen;* see Gal 2:4), **so that the trespass might increase** (Rom 5:20; see 7:5; Gal 3:21-25). Moffatt translates, "Law slipped in to aggravate the trespass." God interposed the Law alongside the sin that was already in place, not as a solution, but as a stopgap measure. Consequently, the giving of Law is far less significant than the epoch-making events with which Paul has been dealing, the fall of Adam and the redeeming death of Christ.

Yet the Law's intrusion has a divine purpose. God gave the Law "in order to" (*hina;* **so that**) increase Israel's consciousness of wrongdoing (see Rom 3:20; 4:15; see Gal 3:19). Contrary to traditional Jewish assumptions, the Law was not given to distinguish between righteous Jews and Gentile sinners (see Gal 2:15), but, as J. D. G. Dunn recognizes,

> to make Israel more conscious of its solidarity in sin with the rest of Adam's offspring. This is not to say that Paul would thus confine the law's trespass-increasing effect to Israel: Paul was at one with his fellow Jews in his belief that the law increased the Gentiles' sins. (Dunn 2002a, 38A:286)

Humans will never see their need of a Savior until their sin becomes transgression (Rom 4:15). The Law is, therefore, a precursor to grace. The accentuation of the **trespass** is answered by overflowing grace. That Paul can replace **trespass** with **sin,** as he does here, suggests that the two should not be so sharply distinguished as interpreters sometimes do.

Whatever we may call it, sin is no match for grace. For **where sin increased, grace increased all the more, so that, just as sin reigned in death, so also grace might reign through righteousness to bring eternal life through Jesus Christ our Lord** (5:20-21). Superabounding grace means

> not only the remission of that sin which Adam brought on us, but of all our own; not only the remission of sins, but the infusion of holiness; not only in deliverance from death, but admission to everlasting life, a far more noble and excellent life than that which we lost in Adam's fall . . . divine life, leading to glory. (Wesley 1950, 539; on 5:21)

■ **21** In v 17 Paul personified Death as a reigning tyrant. In v 21 he personifies Sin in the same sinister role—**sin reigned** [*ebasileusen*] **in death** (see 1:18-32; 4:15; 6:16, 21, 23; 1 Cor 15:56). God's grace super-overflowed (*hypereperisseusen,* see Rom 5:15 and 17) **through Jesus Christ our Lord** (v 21; see 14:4-12). If the aorist tense of the verb points to a single past moment when this extraordinary display of grace occurred, the cross must be that event. Jesus died for one purpose: **so that** [*hina*] the tyrant Sin-Death might be overthrown and that **grace might reign through righteousness to bring eternal life**

(5:21) instead. The cross of Christ was the instrument of Death that decisively broke the power of Sin. **Sin reigned in death, so** that . . . **grace might reign.** "The climactic human sin of the crucifixion of the Messiah and the death of that Messiah . . . reveal the superabundance of grace" (Jewett 2007, 389). The coming of Grace to **reign through righteousness** (see 4:13) through the faithfulness and obedience of Christ is shown supremely on the cross.

The new age was formally inaugurated as Death was defeated in the resurrection of Christ. But, for the time being, only Christ is raised, and Death remains an enemy yet to be defeated in connection with the second coming of Christ (1 Cor 15:20-28). Justification (**righteousness**) may be a present reality for believers; but **eternal life** (see Rom 5:10, 17, 18; John 4:14, 36; 6:27; 12:25) in its fullness awaits the eschaton. Sin and death characterized the old humanity in Adam, but grace characterizes the new humanity that has come to be in Christ.

Law did not solve the lethal problem of sin. God in Christ did. Law only made sins more evident. Because law defines the will of God, wrongs that had once been done in blissful ignorance were now seen for what they had been all along—offences against a holy God. **Sin increased** (Rom 5:20). The introduction of law resulted in an overflowing abundance of sin, but God's superabundance of grace far surpassed the damage caused by sin. Grace dethroned the sinister monarch Death to reign in its stead (see the comments on v 17). The benefits of this revolutionary event are freely ours, although it cost God dearly. All we need do is enter into the life of grace through faith in Christ.

FROM THE TEXT

It should now be obvious that any pessimistic reading of Rom 5:12-21, which leaves the human race hopelessly mired in the sin that entered with Adam's disobedience, misunderstands completely what Paul is saying. Justification and life are for every member of Adam's race. Christ completely reverses the effects of the fall, making it possible for humans to live a righteous and holy life. There is no basis for a deterministic reading of these verses that would limit the atonement to a select few—overlooking the fact that for Paul "the many" in this passage refers to "all people." Some sort of "optimistic" view of Christ's redemptive work, which views salvation to be "by grace through faith—for all," is demanded by this definitive passage. "Whereas much Christian theology in the West, especially after Augustine, has concentrated on verses 12-14 as the basis for the doctrine of 'original sin,' Paul was more interested in verses 15-21" (Keck 2005, 151).

If our exegesis of the passage is correct, reviewing and developing Paul's thesis, we may conclude:

(i) Adam and Christ are the heads of two humanities or aeons—two contrasting, overlapping ages, realms, or orders of human existence. The old—initiated by Adam's disobedience—is an order in which sin reigns in death (see ch 7). The new—initiated by Christ's obedience—is an order where grace reigns through righteousness to eternal life (see chs 6 and 8).

(ii) Apart from the grace of God, all humanity exists as sinners in solidarity with Adam. Sin is a racial fact before it becomes an individual act. Sin exists as a social reality before it is embraced as a personal choice. We are *guilty* sinners, not because we are descendants of Adam, but because, like Adam, we all sin. The universal assertion of self-sovereignty in defiance of God's sovereign right to rule is the essence of original sin—Adam's and ours. In our vaunted attempt to rule ourselves, to be like God, we find ourselves victimized instead by the rule of the tyrants Sin and Death. Spiritual death is not our inevitable destiny as children of Adam. It takes effect, however, when we embrace it by asserting our propensity to self-sovereignty and choose personal transgression (see 7:9 and 4:15). We are like Adam, but worse off than he, because our choice to sin is made while we are deprived of a right relationship with God.

(iii) By grace we are in Christ, through whom we have received "the gift" of "justification that brings life for all" people (5:17, 18). This gift of God's grace is twofold: *(a)* Wesley held out the hope of universal, unconditional justification for infants and the intellectually deficient, along with *(b)* prevenient grace counteracting original sin, making saving faith possible. Every human being born on earth is covered by the atonement, until we choose to sin, to assert our self-sovereignty, and to become our own Adam. We receive free grace from Christ in sufficient measure to respond to the gospel and be saved.

(iv) When as sinners we appropriate God's grace by a personal act of faith in Christ, we are re-created and transferred to the order of Christ in which grace reigns in righteousness. "For if, by the trespass of the one man, death reigned through that one man, how much more will those who receive God's abundant provision of grace and of the gift of righteousness reign in life through the one man, Jesus Christ" (v 17). This overflowing grace is ours "not only in the remission of that sin that Adam brought on us," Wesley notes, but also in an "infusion of holiness" (1950, n. on Rom 5:20).

(v) The grand announcement of this passage is, therefore, vv 20-21. Paul's pessimism of nature is more than matched by his optimism of grace. "Law came in, to increase the trespass; but where sin increased, grace abounded all the more, so that, as sin reigned in death, grace also might reign through righteousness to eternal life through Jesus Christ our Lord" (RSV).

b. Sanctification and Glory (6:1—8:39)

How does Christ create the new humanity that is freed from sin? How is the universality of sin and death in Adam replaced by the new race in Christ leading to righteousness and eternal life? If the Law was not given to promote righteousness, then what is its role? What is God's method of setting humanity free from "the law of sin and death"?

Paul's underlying position is that those who are *righteous* before God are those who are *sanctified* by God (Barth). To be justified by faith is to have *a new existence in Christ,* to be actualized by death to sin and union with Christ. Freed from the dominion of sin through union with the risen crucified Savior, we may rise to walk in holiness through faith and total surrender of ourselves to God (6:1-14). This new existence *demands and enables obedience.* As former slaves of wickedness, we are now to offer ourselves as slaves to righteousness for sanctification (*hagiasmos*) now and for eternal life in the future (v 19; see vv 15-23).

Death to sin has its counterpart in death to the Law, since under the Law we are united to sin. Humans enslaved to Law are those living on their own, apart from Christ (7:1-6). This bondage to sin under Law, however, must not be construed to mean that the Law is sinful *per se*. The Law points up our human obligation to God, but Law is totally powerless to save us from sin. And we are powerless to save ourselves. Due to this compounded weakness, *sin* has perverted God's holy law into **the law of sin and death** (8:2).

When the command of the holy God confronts our conscience, sin springs to life, and we die spiritually. The Law is God's agent to show us how **utterly sinful** (7:13; see vv 7-13) sin really is. The Law claims my total devotion, **but I am unspiritual, sold as a slave to sin** (v 14). Because of **sin living in me** (v 17), I am morally and spiritually impotent. **I have the desire to do what is good, but I cannot carry it out** (v 18). The more heroically I struggle, the more pathetic my existence becomes (vv 14-25).

However, what we humans cannot do for ourselves God has done for us, through **the law of the Spirit of life** in Christ Jesus. **For what the law was powerless to do in that it was weakened** through *sarx* (the "flesh" in formal equivalence translations like the KJV, NASB, RSV, NRSV) **God did** for us. **By sending his own Son in the likeness of sinful** flesh, and *for sin* (*peri hamartias*), God **condemned sin in the flesh, in order that the righteous requirements of the law might be fully met in us, who do not live according** to the flesh, **but according to the Spirit** (8:1-4). In the outpoured Spirit (5:5) believers have deliverance, guidance, assurance, help, and restoration to the image of God.

In this section of Romans Paul explicates the vital connection between justification and sanctification: "Justification by faith is the means, and sanctification the end. The more precisely we distinguish between these two divine gifts, the better we apprehend the bond that unites them" (Godet 1883, 233). God justifies us in order that he may sanctify us, and he sanctifies us that we might serve him as his instruments in this world, share fully in the likeness of Christ, and participate in his glory in the world to come.

As justification issues in sanctification, so sanctification issues in glorification, and glorification occurs along with the final renewal of the created order. Meanwhile, we humans have the gracious ministry of the Spirit to help us in our weaknesses, along with our confident expectation that nothing in all creation will be able to separate us from the love of God that is in Christ Jesus our Lord (8:1-39).

(1) Sanctification Through Death to Sin (6:1-23)

BEHIND THE TEXT

The closing part of ch 5 places sin, law, and grace in juxtaposition. This raises acutely a question to which Paul alluded in 3:8: "Why not say—as we are being slanderously reported as saying and as some claim that we say—'Let us do evil that good may result'?" That is, if justification is based wholly on faith, not on human obedience to the Law, why obey? If the Law's commands to live a holy life serve only to encourage sin, why resist? If grace increases all the more wherever sin increases, why not instead sin wholeheartedly, that grace may increase? That Paul deals at length with such questions shows how seriously he takes his doctrine of free grace.

In 3:5-8 Paul dealt with the question from Jewish premises: God is Judge, and the Judge of all the earth will do right (Gen 18:25). Now he gives a thoroughly Christian answer, once again resorting to the diatribe style (see comments on Rom 2:1). His interlocutors are imaginary and hypothetical. But the necessity of responding to such flawed thinking may arise from Paul's experiences with actual scofflaws in his churches. Thus, he anticipates and heads off the antinomian inference that sin should be indulged in to the full, in order to experience even more of God's grace. He rejects such implications as a wholly mistaken, not a logical or necessary implication of his gospel of grace.

Christians cannot continue their former careers as sinners. In our baptism we "died" with Christ to sin and were "raised" with Christ to a new kind of life. Paul claims that so far as sin is concerned, we are dead. The person we once were was "crucified" with Christ. But what does this mean? Obviously, we have not been physically crucified nor are we literally dead. Apparently, Paul's language is figurative, but even metaphorical language is not meaningless. It points beyond itself to a reality that cannot be adequately expressed using merely literal language. What is this reality?

Because of what Christ has done for us, we are no longer helpless slaves to sin. In fact, the enslaving power of sin in our lives is broken. Sin no longer reigns as our master. Through the liberating power of Christ's saving death we are free not to sin. For the first time in our lives we can say no to sin. We no longer live in Adam but in Christ. Thus, our past does not determine our present or future. Thoroughly changed, the person we once were is "dead." It is as if we enjoy a new life that is not our own.

Water baptism does not effect this reality, but it is a visible demonstration of our faith in the saving benefits of Christ's death. Christ is the Liberator. Faith accepts the freedom he offers. Baptism is only the tangible expression of that faith. But it is more. With our "burial" beneath the baptismal waters, a bond of unity is created with Christ. Our baptism reenacts the burial and resurrection of Christ, and we participate in the drama of salvation with him.

Our present participation in the benefits of Christ's saving death provides the basis for our confidence that we will be resurrected in the future. Resurrection life will not be fully ours until the Parousia. We will die, whereas Christ has already been raised, never to die again. Nevertheless, the power of Christ's resurrection already enables us to live a new kind of life. Bodily resurrection remains future (6:5, 8; see 1 Cor 15:23, 53). Until then, the new life we live by faith is not ours, but Christ's (see Rom 6:11; see Gal 2:20).

How are we to understand this new life of ours? Does Christ literally take up residence within us? Does his personality invade our minds? Are we like zombies totally under the control of an alien force? Do we have no mind or will of our own? It does the apostle an injustice to take his clearly metaphorical language literally. But Paul nowhere explains precisely *how* we participate in Christ; i.e., in what sense we live in Christ and Christ in us. Are we to understand this in terms of metaphorical space? Do we somehow spiritually reside in heaven and heaven in us? Do we enjoy the benefits of the life of the future already? Do we live in a historical situation fundamentally altered by the events of the life, death, and resurrection of Jesus Christ? Do we live in Christlike ways, doing what he would do? Figurative explanations of Paul's participation-language seem more plausible than literal readings.

Paul insists that because Christ has been raised from the dead, **death no longer has mastery over him** (Rom 6:9). Thus, to be alive or dead is to be under the lordship of the personified powers of Life or Death. To be alive to something is to exist within its sphere of influence. To be dead to something is to be out of its sphere of influence. Christians are dead to sin because sin no longer reigns as our master. Jesus Christ is our new Lord.

Our new life in Christ is lived in a new sphere of influence that is invisible to the naked eye. But the new quality of life we have in Christ visibly shapes and influences our present lives as surely as relationships of love mutually bind us to our loved ones. We thrive in an atmosphere charged with the power of the mutual commitments we enjoy with parents, spouses, children, siblings, and friends. Love lives only where it is mutual—both given and received. Love requires love in response (see 2 Cor 5:14-15). Because Christ is who he is, our mutual relations with him are characterized by holy love. This explains Paul's preoccupation with sanctification—the implications of the life of holiness—in Rom 6.

Alternative Modes of Existence

Paul can envision only two alternative modes of human existence: In Adam vs. In Christ. His understanding of these contrasting spheres in which humans live may be graphically represented in the table of contrasts below:

Alternative Spheres of Existence

In Adam	↔	In Christ
disobedience	↔	obedience
death←shame←condemnation←sin←Adam	↔	Christ→right→justification→sanctification→life
impurity/lawlessness	↔	righteousness
humans	↔	God
slavery	↔	freedom
law	↔	grace
doing/works	↔	trusting/faith
flesh	↔	Spirit

From 5:12 to 8:39 the apostle fleshes out his basic anthropological insight. Western thinkers may find themselves perplexed by Paul's prominent placement of "shame" as the polar opposite of "sanctification." People within the ancient Mediterranean world, unlike those in the modern West, operated within an honor-shame society (see Jewett 2007, 46-59). The experience of shame, contempt, disrespect, disgrace, or public humiliation was considered a fate worse than death. The antitheses clearly imply that the life of holiness (sanctification) brings not only appropriate honor to God but also the life intended by God to command the respect of even unbelievers (see 1 Thess 4:1-12). Within Paul's cultural and theological framework, the gospel of sanctification and glory, as honor bestowed by God, belong inextricably together.

Further Reading on Honor and Shame in Mediterranean Society

Carter, T. L. 2002. *Paul and the Power of Sin: Redefining "Beyond the Pale."* Cambridge: Cambridge University Press.

deSilva, David A. 2000a. "Honor and Shame." In the *Dictionary of New Testament Background*. Downers Grove, Ill.: InterVarsity Press.

deSilva, David A. 2000b. *Honor, Patronage, Kinship and Purity: Unlocking New Testament Culture*. Downers Grove, Ill.: InterVarsity Press.

Gilmore, D. D., ed. 1985. *Honor and Shame and the Unity of the Mediterranean.* Washington, D.C.: American Anthropological Society.

Malina, Bruce. 1981. *The New Testament World: Insights from Cultural Anthropology.* Atlanta: John Knox.

Moxnes, Halvor. 1988a. "Honor, Shame, and the Outside World in Paul's Letter to the Romans." Pages 207-18 in *The Social World of Formative Christianity and Judaism.* Edited by Jacob Neusner, Peder Borgen, Ernest S. Frerichs, and Richard Horsley. Philadelphia: Fortress.

Moxnes, Halvor. 1988b. "Honor and Righteousness in Romans." *Journal for the Study of the New Testament* 32:61-77.

Moxnes, Halvor. 1996. "Honor and Shame." Pages 29-40 in *The Social Sciences and New Testament Interpretation.* Edited by Richard L. Rohrbaugh. Peabody, Mass.: Hendrickson.

IN THE TEXT

Romans 6 is divided by two questions: **Shall we go on sinning** so that **grace may increase?** (v 1), and, **Shall we sin because** we are not under law but under grace? (v 15) The answer to each is a resounding **By no means!** Accordingly, the chapter divides as follows: A New Life Under the Sovereignty of Grace (vv 1-14); and Sanctification: A New Kind of Slavery (vv 15-23).

(a) A New Life Under the Sovereignty of Grace (6:1-14)

■ **1** Paul looks backward to ask: What conclusions shall we draw from my preceding position that as sin increases, grace increases all the more (5:20-21)? **What shall we say then? Shall we go on sinning so that grace may increase?** (6:1; see 5:20). Paul's object is not to draw logical consequences from his teaching about surpassing grace but to reject the false inference that grace makes continuing sin inconsequential. The second question must be that of the imaginary interlocutor, since its subjunctive mood makes its force hortatory, "Let us remain in sin, so that grace might abound?" (Jewett 2007, 390, 394; but see Keck 2005, 157).

The threat of sin is not imaginary, but Paul presents the prospect of Christians voluntarily submitting to their former slave master, personified Sin, as unthinkable, even laughable. Why would we allow Sin to continue to rule our lives? Should we who have been justified live on in the same relationship with Sin that we had before we came to Christ? Should we sustain an attitude of cordiality with our mortal enemy Sin in order that we may receive all the more of Sin's antidote from our more powerful friend, Grace? Of course not.

As with Sin, the personified abstract noun **Grace** is not a thing or a person. It is clearly a way of referring to God's activity of freely forgiving and making sinners right with himself in Christ. However, it also refers to his empowering presence that enables forgiven sinners to live in obedience and honor God with their transformed lives.

■ **2** Paul's forceful rejoinder is: **By no means** [*mē genoito*]! **We** [*hoitines*] **died to sin; how can we live in it any longer?** (6:2). The indefinite relative pronoun associated with the first person plural verb is used qualitatively to refer to persons of a certain type—"people such as we" (Bauer 1979, 586, s.v. *hostis* 2.b). How can we *as Christians* go on living in sin, since we *as Christians* have died to sin? If we have been *liberated* by Christ, how can such people as we even *think* of sinning? It is "unthinkable," in view of our having died and been buried with Christ in baptism, that we should *intentionally* **go on sinning**, in order **that grace may increase** (v 1; see vv 15-19).

This passage emphasizes the foundation of Christian morality. Those who have appropriated the death of Christ for themselves can no longer live as they did before. The aorist tense of the verb **died** points to a particular moment at which Christians may be said figuratively to have experienced this death.

■ **3** In v 3 Paul associates this moment with their baptism. But baptism merely dramatizes the spiritual reality of appropriating the life-giving benefits of Christ's atoning death (see 3:21-26; 2 Cor 5:14; Gal 2:20). Life and death cannot be reconciled. There is only one possible interpretation of Paul's words: Justified believers have been **justified from Sin** (Rom 6:7). Because Christians have been freed from sin, they are no longer tyrannized by the spirit of revolt that has plagued the race since Adam's defection. "Dying to the realm of sin means living in the realm of Christ; the two realms are as incommensurate as the antithesis between 'life' and 'death'" (Jewett 2007, 396).

Paul provided the basis for his present argument in 5:12-21. Adam was the head of the old humanity over which Sin had established its control; Christ is the head of the new humanity from which Sin has been excluded in shameful defeat. "For Paul dying with Christ means a change of lordship" (Tannehill 1967, 18). To be "in Christ"—the new man—is to participate in the new humanity whose Lord is Christ. Therefore, "those who receive God's abundant provision of grace and the gift of righteousness reign in life by that one man, Jesus Christ" (v 17).

In 6:3-5 Paul presents additional support for his argument. Up to now his argument has hinged on the place of faith in justification; now he relates faith to baptism. **Or don't you know** ["Have you forgotten?" v 3*a* REB; see 7:1] **that all of us who were baptized into Christ Jesus were baptized into his death?** (6:3; see 1 Cor 10:1-2).

Christ *recapitulates*—i.e., takes up fully into himself in a representative

178

way—the new humanity God wishes to raise up. In the plan of God, he gathers into his own person all those who will be united with him and so share in the benefits of his saving work. In this way Christ initiates the new humanity—"the church, his body, of which he is the Savior" (Eph 5:23; see Leenhardt 1957, 153). Bonhoeffer insists:

> It is impossible to become a new man as a solitary individual. The new man means more than the individual believer after he has been justified and sanctified. It means the Church, the Body of Christ, in fact it means Christ himself. (1995, 11)

Thus, our sanctification is in Christ, in both his person (1 Cor 1:30) and in his body (12:13; Col 2:9-12).

It follows that to be **baptized into Jesus Christ** is to be **baptized into his death** (Rom 6:3). We participate in the saving benefits he provides only to the extent that we share metaphorically in the means by which he won our salvation. The best commentary on the phrase **baptized into his death** may be v 10*a*: When Christ died, he died to sin, forever. His death completely and finally severed him from contact with sin. Just so, our baptism is a sign and seal of our death to sin, *our* severance from sin. "To be baptized into Christ's shameful death is to quit the life of sin. The divisive competition for honor is exposed and laid to rest by the cross" (Jewett 2007, 398).

We must be careful here not to drag into Paul's teaching notions of magical or automatic sacramental grace, which he has already repudiated in principle in his treatment of circumcision (see 4:9-11). In fact, Paul safeguards his position against sacramentarianism by distinguishing believers' deaths from their resurrection with Christ. The latter he handles cautiously and incompletely, referring to it in the subjunctive mood or future tense (6:4-5, 8). "There is no sacramental *opus operatum* by means of which believers can assure themselves, independently of faith and moral seriousness, that they have risen from death to enjoy the life of the Age to Come" (Barrett 1957, 123).

Paul could take for granted that his Roman readers were baptized believers (v 3). Such was every NT congregation; there were no unbaptized Christians, except for catechumens who were still preparing for church membership (see v 17*b*). Neither Paul nor any other early Christian hypothetically considered the question whether an unbaptized believer might become a member of Christ's body or whether a baptized unbeliever could participate in the body of Christ. Nevertheless, a doctrine of justification by faith necessitates a distinction between the act of saving faith and the confession of that faith that is made in baptism (as 10:6-13 implies).

■ **4** This distinction is demanded by the next sentence: **We were therefore buried [***synetaphēmen, co-buried***] with him through baptism into death** (6:4; see Col 2:12). Paul's letters employ dozens of *syn-* compound words, some freshly coined, to emphasize Christian "communality in Christ" (Jewett 2007, 398; see Dunn 2002a, 38A:313). *Burial presupposes death through identification with Christ* (see Gal 2:20). Paul understands baptism as "a ritual reenactment of incorporation . . . into Christ's death" (Jewett 2007, 398). What Jesus' burial was to him, baptism is to us. It follows our prior death to sin, publicly demonstrating its finality.

Christ's Death and Our Baptism

Paul probably assumes baptism by immersion (*baptō* means "dip"), a ritualized "burial." Accordingly, Paul sees an analogy between Christ's being raised from the realm of the dead and the immersed being raised from the water. What actually matters here, of course, is not the analogy itself but what being baptized signifies for one being baptized—*a radically transformed life*. (Keck 2005, 160; emphasis added)

The **death** into which we are baptized is at once *his* and *ours* included in his. **Baptism into death** is **in order that** (*hina*) we may be raised with him to **live a new life** (*hēmeis en kainotēti zōēs peripatēsōmen*, "we also should walk in newness of life" v 4 KJV; see 2 Cor 5:17; Gal 6:15). "The verb *peripateō* is Paul's characteristic term for ethical behavior, . . . and the aorist subjunctive implies 'a decisive transition to a new lifestyle'" (Jewett 2007, 399; citing Dunn 2002a, 38A:316). Believers' *new quality of life* follows their burial with Christ, as his rising followed his burial. Both are mighty acts of God. In reality it is only one act, since believers are indissolubly linked with Christ.

This mighty act is **through the glory of the Father** (v 4). **Glory** is an eschatological term (2:7, 10; 5:2; 8:17, 21; see the sidebar "Glory" associated with the commentary on 8:18-27). God brings the power of the future resurrection to bear on this present age as he gives believers a quality of life that anticipates that of the last age—the eschaton. Jesus' resurrection ushered in the time of fulfillment, the new age, which begins for us as we are raised to "newness of life." "For Paul, *baptism does not end mortality; it begins a new morality,* one that must be actualized" (Keck 2005, 161). The Christian ethic displays the glory of God, honoring him.

■ **5** **If we have been united with** Christ **in his death, we will certainly also be united with him in his resurrection** (6:5). If we have "died" figuratively to sin as Christ literally died for our sins, we will also be raised to life as he was literally resurrected. This future bodily resurrection, of course, awaits his Parousia, but this "not yet" realized hope is not Paul's immediate concern (see 8:17-23). Already, in this present age, Christ conveys to us his risen life, so that we may enjoy a **new quality of life** even now (6:4). What is true "already" in this life is not freedom from physical death but freedom from the power of Sin. Paul is fully cognizant that this morally new kind of life is lived in dying bodies in a world that is still under the power of Sin. As in Gal 2:20, the consequences of our co-crucifixion linger (perfect tense)—i.e., we no longer live. And yet, we do live, but our life for the time being is his, and ours only as we share by anticipation his risen life.

Already and Not Yet

In Rom. 6:4, the new life embodies both "the already" and the "not yet" of Christian existence. Because its moral import is anticipatory, it leans toward the future for its fulfillment, formulated in verse 5: "For if we have been united with him in a death like his, we *will* certainly be united with him in a resurrection like his" (RSV). At this point, and not before, the liberation from sin and death will be complete. But it will be! Being united with Christ in baptism guarantees it, for thereby one is united with the *whole* Christ event. (Keck 2005, 161)

"Baptism is not the subject of this pericope" (6:1-14), since "the rest of the pericope reverts to the basic theme of dying and rising with Christ without any further, explicit references to baptism" (Jewett 2007, 400). Clearly, Paul does not consider Christian baptism a mere optional add-on to justifying faith; it is how faith first expresses itself. In baptism we confess our faith that "Jesus is Lord" (10:9), ritually reenacting a death to our illusions of self-sovereignty that has already occurred. By submitting to baptism we publicly acknowledge the sovereignty of the living Lord. Symbols cannot be detached from the realities they convey. They are the dramatic *means of entering into that reality*. Through baptism we *participate* by faith in the Christ event, so that we *are* no longer the persons we once were (v 5). We do not literally die, but we do embark on a new kind of moral life (1 Cor 6:11).

The **If** (*ei*) that begins Rom 6:5 might be better translated **Since**. Our being **grown together** (Bauer 1979, 780 s.v. *symphytos;* only here in the NT) with Christ is not merely hypothetical. The perfect tense of the verb **we have been** (*gegonamen*) implies that we "share an indivisible, organic unity with Christ. . . . a new relationship inaugurated in the past, but whose effects continue through the present" (Jewett 2007, 400). But, for the present, our conformity to Christ's **likeness** (*homoiōmati;* see 1:23; 5:14) is limited to **his death.** By identifying with Christ, Christians sign a death warrant to the opinions of this world (see Gal 6:14), "sever old relationships and become part of the new, persecuted community of faith" (Jewett 2007, 401).

It is necessary to fill in the ellipsis to translate the conclusion of Rom 6:5: *then [alla, but] we will also be joined together in the likeness of Christ's resurrection* (see 1:4). The future tense is not merely logical; it is eschatological, referring to the final resurrection (Dunn 2002a, 38A:318). Our full appropriation of the gift of life remains contingent on our sustained surrender to Christ's sovereignty, as we walk in new quality of life that is already ours (see 6:8).

■ **6** In vv 6 and 7 Paul elaborates on the implications of "the freedom from sin enjoyed by believers" (Jewett 2007, 402): *We know that the old person we once were [ho palaios hēmōn anthrōpos] was co-crucified [synestaurōthē; see Gal 2:19-20] with Christ, in order that [hina] our career as sinners [to sōma tēs hamartias, the body of sin] might end completely [katargēthē, see the commentary on Rom 7:6], in order that we might no longer owe any allegiance to Sin [tē hamartia]. For the dead have been set free from Sin [dedikaiōtai apo tēs hamaritias, lit. justified from Sin].*

The traditional KJV translation, "our old man is crucified with him," is problematic on several counts. If the convictions Paul expressed in Gal 2:20 are presumed here, the "old man" cannot refer to some "thing" or "nature" within us that must be extracted. It is not an alien, cancerous tumor living metaphorically within us that dies—*we* die in some real, yet figurative, sense. We cannot identify "the old man" with "carnality" or "the sinful nature," as some nineteenth-century Holiness interpreters did. "Our old man" must be the sinful persons we once were, our former pre-Christian selves, the old Adam that once defined our existence as humans (see the commentary on Rom 5:12-21).

The expressions **our old self** and **the body of sin** (6:6) refer to our corporate existence in Adam—*the old humanity*—that comes to an end as we participate in Christ—the new humanity (see 5:12-21). The old attachments and allegiances of our pre-Christian lives come to a decisive end for this purpose (*hina*): to destroy, abolish, completely do away with (Bauer 1979, 417 s.v. *katargeō*) *our career as sinners.*

By **body of sin** (6:6) Paul does not mean to suggest that human bodily existence itself is sinful. He is not responsible for the Platonic imposition on the gospel, which equates the physical and material with the sinful. His point is that the persons we once were have been metaphorically crucified with Christ so that we ourselves might no longer live hopelessly enslaved to sin. The purpose of our "death" is not to escape the body-prison, but that we might be released from Sin's lordship. Through justification, the compulsive power of sin in our lives is decisively broken, and we die, not to escape this world, but to live morally within it (v 7).

Although the conjunction *hina* is not repeated in v 6c, the repetition of *in order that* in our interpretive translation clarifies the purpose of our co-crucifixion with Christ. The destruction of **the body of sin** liberates us from its enslaving power, so that *we might no longer owe any allegiance to* [*douleuein*, to be enslaved to] *Sin.*

> This clarifies that the human plight is caused not by bodily existence itself but by sin, which exercises its dominion over the entire human race outside of Christ. . . . The burden of [Paul's] argument throughout this pericope is that persisting in sin is a logical and relational contradiction for those in Christ. Freed from bondage to the cosmic power of sin, Paul is contending that believers "cannot sin" because they are under the lordship of Christ. (Jewett 2007, 404)

■ **7** Verse 7 draws an obvious generalization from v 6: Dead people cannot sin. To be *justified from Sin* (see 1 Cor 5:7-8; 2 Cor 3:6, 14; Gal 6:15; Col 3:9) is to be *set free from* its claims.

■ **8** Verse 8 builds on the conclusions of the preceding verses. *And since we died with* [*syn*] *Christ, we believe that we also will live with* [*syzēsomen*] *him* (see 2 Cor 4:14; 13:4; Phil 1:23; Col 2:13, 20; 3:3-4; 1 Thess 4:14, 17; 5:10). All believers "recognize that their former life has now died with him, which enables a new life under his grace and lordship to emerge" (Jewett 2007, 405). Here, for the first time in Romans (see 10:9) the verb *pisteō* refers to intellectual assent that something is true, common elsewhere in the NT (Luke 1:45; John 4:21; Acts 27:25; Heb 11:6; Jas 2:18-26; 1 John 5:1, 5).

Here as in Rom 6:5, the future tense should be taken seriously. The life of Christ has present implications for our corporate lives as believers (v 11; see 2 Cor 4:10-11; 6:17; Gal 2:20); but it also has an eschatological dimension. Paul's point here is that "believers cannot simultaneously live in sin" and enjoy the life of Christ (see Rom 5:10, 17, 21; Jewett 2007, 406). However, "the parallel between believers and Christ is not complete, inasmuch as they must still face their own physical deaths" (Jewett 2007, 407).

■ **9-10** *We know that since Christ has been raised from the dead, he dies no more. Death has no control over* [*kyrieuei*, lords it over] *him now. Because Christ died, he died to sin* [*tē hamartia*] *once and for all. But because he lives, he lives to God* (6:9-10).

> While Christ's crucifixion was an unrepeatable moment of being subjected to the power of sin, his current life . . . is in relation to God. The two forms of existence are diametrically opposed, both in time and effect. Again, what is claimed for Christ . . . pertains in equal measure for believers. . . . He died to sin "once for all" and so do believers; their life "to God" eliminates the possibility of living on under the power and lure of sin. (Jewett 2007, 407-8)

"Dying and living with Christ eliminate the possibility of living in the ongoing death that is sin" (Jewett 2007, 406), but not the prospect of physical death. Nevertheless, the lordship of Death has been broken (5:14 and 17), so that believers are no longer subject to it. We need not fear its power, for death cannot separate us from "the love of God that is in Christ Jesus our Lord" (8:39; see vv 37-39).

■ 11 In 6:11, Paul draws out the logical implications of his negative answer to the rhetorical question in v 1 that set in motion the argument in vv 1-10. *So [oun, **Therefore**] you also must consider yourselves to be truly dead to Sin [tēi hamartia], but just as truly alive to God in Christ.* What is potentially true must become an experiential reality in the daily lives of believers. Our existence can only be described paradoxically.

We must *consider* ourselves **dead to sin** and **alive to God in Christ Jesus,** because we *are.* The verb *logizesthe,* **consider** or **count,** is the same accounting term used of God's crediting righteousness to Abraham's account in 4:3, 5, 6, and 8 (see commentary). To **count** ourselves **dead to sin but alive to God** is "not a pretending ('as if'), nor a mere ideal, but a deliberate and sober judgment on the basis of the gospel, in that it accepts as its norm what God has done in Christ . . . by faith" (Cranfield 1975, 1:315).

■ 12 Paul expects his readers to take the truth of the gospel as a fact, the indicative basis for the gospel imperative: **Do not let sin reign** [basileuetō; see 5:21] **in your mortal body so that you may obey** [hyakouein] **its . . . desires** [epithymias; 6:12]. The word **evil** is ellipsed from the translation, since it has no basis in the Greek text and lends itself to a Platonic body-mind dualism entirely alien to the thought of the NT. Paul does not assume that "physicality or sensuality [is] the source of sin" (Jewett 2007, 409).

Christian freedom from sin, which is stated as a fact in vv 1-10, is treated as a command in vv 11-14. Our death and new life in Christ depend on a sustained union with him. These new realities cannot be taken for granted; they exist for us only as we participate in them. They are possibilities of grace, not personal entitlements. If we are "dead" to Sin, we cannot allow it to control our lives. In Christ, we may be "dead" to sin; but Sin is not dead. It will assert its oppressive rule wherever a power vacuum exists. Where Christ does not reign, sin will.

The power of Sin in our lives is decisively broken when we become Christians. Freed from the slavery to Sin, the justified person stands between two powers calling for submission. In ch 8 Paul describes these powers as Flesh and Spirit. In ch 6, they are Sin and God, Law and Grace. We must choose sides. Thus, Paul urges, **Do not let sin reign** (v 12). Deliverance from Sin is not magical or automatic; Christians must resist its sham claims to sovereignty.

Obviously, Paul's strong language in vv 5-11 does not mean that Christians are *incapable* of sinning. By the grace of God and the power of the Spirit, however, we are enabled *not* to sin. But we must say no to its overtures to

obey its . . . desires. Sin seeks a foothold for its illegitimate reign in our **mortal body.** This language reminds us that until the final resurrection our **body** is still subject to the inevitability of death, along with vulnerability to the power of bodily desires. We may still sin if we choose, because we continue to be descendants of Adam and a part of this present age. However, our once helpless victimization to Sin has come to an end, because in the risen Christ we already participate in the powers of the age to come.

Anyone who has died is **freed from sin** (v 7), but not yet freed from physical death. Until Christ's return, when our bodies will be transformed (1 Cor 15:50-57), resisting sin's reign occurs in our not-yet redeemed body (see the commentary on Rom 8:18-25), because of its **desires.** What matters is *not yielding to* desire (see in Jas 1:14-15). Christians are still human beings in "the Adamic condition," which will not be healed until their bodies are glorified at Christ's return (Rom 8:23). Consequently, Christians, like all other humans, must cope with what theologians since Thomas Aquinas have called "natural concupiscence." Even the sinless Jesus was not exempt from such desires, as his wilderness temptation surely demonstrates (see Matt 4:1-11; Mark 1:12-13; Luke 4:1-13). Although the natural human desire for the necessities of life—food, shelter, self-preservation, etc.—are not sinful in themselves, they leave us susceptible to sin and make self-discipline an ongoing necessity (see 1 Cor 9:27).

■ **13** The power to refuse to **offer** ourselves again as slaves to sin comes from offering ourselves, and the **parts of** our **body** [*melē*] to God **as instruments of righteousness** (Rom 6:13). The Greek *hopla* (**instruments**) is a military term ("armor" in 13:12; "weapons" in 2 Cor 6:7 and 10:4). We must make our bodily parts available as "weapons for righteousness" (2 Cor 6:7 NASB) to advance the purposes of God in this world. When we yield to our selfish **desires,** we allow our human "faculties" (Dunn 2002a, 38A:337) or "capabilities" (Moo 1996, 384) to be used as "weapons for wickedness" (NASB).

In Rom 6:13, Paul repeats his negative admonition from v 12 before making his positive appeal. The negative imperatives are both in the present tense; the positive, in the aorist. If the tense shift has any significance (which Moo [1996, 385] denies), the point may be that the audience is no longer to continue their previous lifestyle but to begin a new way of life marked by entirely new commitments (Dunn 2002a, 38A:338).

Paul's twofold imperative—**Do not offer** [yourselves] . . . **to sin, . . . but rather offer yourselves to God** (v 13; see vv 16 and 19)—employs the Greek verb *paristēmi*. **To offer** oneself may mean to put oneself at another's disposal to be used as the other sees fit. This involves serving the purposes of the other, becoming "a willing instrument in its system of domination" (Jewett 2007, 409). In 12:1 the verb has the added force of a technical term "in the language of sacrifice *offer, bring, present*" (Bauer 1979, 627, 628 quote). We put ourselves fully at the disposal of God or Sin—there are no other alternatives. We are not given the option of autonomy or neutrality.

To place oneself "at the disposal" of sin would be to participate willingly in the war against God and to deny the redemption experienced in Christ. In the "eschatological struggle for power" over the control of the world, believers are called to make a choice between serving sin and serving God. (Jewett 2007, 410)

As Christians, we have been delivered from slavery to freedom (6:6-8). However, we are not simply free to be free. We **have been brought from death to life** (v 13; see vv 8-12). The question remains: For whom or for what will we live? As embodied creatures, we cannot refuse to take sides. Our bodies will be used as tools of either **wickedness** or **righteousness.**

■ **14** The difference depends on our choice of **master** (v 14). That is, it depends on whether we **let sin reign** or let Christ reign, whether we **obey** our bodily **desires** or God (v 12), whether we **offer** ourselves **to sin** or **to God** (v 13).

Paul calls for a moral showdown—a personal crisis. His aorist imperative and the logic of his sacrificial imagery (see 12:1-2) imply the need for decisive action: "Once and for all present yourselves to God." Emancipated from the old life of sin, we face a new possibility. We may return to the old life, or we may put our redeemed selves at the disposal of God. Absolute freedom is an illusion, and neutrality is impossible.

We are free only to choose our **master** (v 14). God gives us life. It is ours to decide what we will do with it. Paul urges us to **offer** ourselves to God as *weapons of righteousness* (v 13; see 12:1, 2) in his battle with evil. However, God's "new, nonviolent campaign to restore righteousness in a corrupted world" (Jewett 2007, 411) is a dangerous undertaking that calls for a totally committed people.

The future tense of the verb *kyrieusei* (see 6:9) might have an imperatival force: **sin shall not be your master** (v 14)! But the opening conjunction *gar,* **For,** suggests that it is a logical future. As you offer yourselves unreservedly to God, *Sin will not lord it over you.* This is "thoroughly reassuring" news for believers: "the reign of sin is surely at an end" (Jewett 2007, 411). Victory over **Sin** is possible **because** (*gar*) of **grace.**

Thus, Paul concludes his argument in v 14 where he began in v 1, with the gospel-logic of **grace.** *Grace* is not implicit permission to sin with reckless abandon; it is the power of God that liberates sinners from sin's mastery. However, it is also the power of God that invites freed former sinners to submit their redeemed selves to God in order to live the new kind of lives grace enables, under the rule of God, in the service of righteousness. *Grace,* recall, is not a thing. The term personifies an abstract noun, encapsulating within it the entire gospel story of God's free gift of salvation through the crucified and risen Lord and his gift of the Holy Spirit.

Grace is God's total commitment of himself and his inexhaustible re- 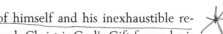 sources to fallen humanity in Christ. Although Christ is God's Gift for us, he is no less our Lord. Grace is God's power that enables obedience; and so it demands it. We must live as people who have died to sin. Because of grace, we may. Grace challenges us to exploit the privileges that are ours, not in self-indulgence, but in surrender to the sovereign love of God. God did not set us free for nothing; it cost him everything, and it demands nothing less of those who would keep it. Freedom makes claims on those who want to remain free (see Gal 5:1, 13). We must resist the powers of sin and self ("the flesh") that would enslave us to unworthy lords. We can serve only one sovereign.

Romans 6:14 not only concludes vv 1-13 but also anticipates 6:15—7:25. Paul has not mentioned Law since 5:20, focusing instead on the "reign" of sin vs. the "reign" of grace in 6:1-14. With vv 14 and 15, he picks up again the subject of Law with the reminder: **You are not under law, but under grace** (v 14). "In all of Greek literature, not counting later patristic sources, this expression *hypo charin* ('under grace') appears only in Rom 6:14, 15" (Jewett 2007, 412 n. 231).

To be **under** (*hypo*) a power, of course, is to be its subject, to be reigned by it, to be under its mastery. Thus, Christians must not only refuse the would-be sovereignty of the dethroned power **Sin** but also reject life under the mastery of Sin's presumed opposite—**Law**. The sovereignty of **Grace** tolerates no rivals, whether license or legalism.

(b) Sanctification: A New Kind of Slavery (6:15-23)

Even after the issue of sovereignty has been settled, victory over Sin is not inevitable. For this reason, it is a mistake to speak of a "state" of holiness; it is always a maintained "condition." Since it exists only by virtue of a sustained relationship of loving obedience to the holy God, it can never be conceived of as a human possession. This explains what motivates vv 15-19.

Paul begins in v 15 with a rhetorical question very similar to the one he raised in v 1. But the differences between the two questions are equally noteworthy (for a contrary view, see McCant 1981). Regardless, both questions are strongly denied: **By no means** should Christians imagine that grace is an implicit license to sin.

Paul's diatribe style question challenges the potentially antinomian implications of life under the sovereignty of **grace** vs. the sovereignty of **law** that could be drawn from v 14. However, he does not actually resume a direct discussion of "Law" until ch 7. Instead, in 6:16-23 he develops the imagery of slavery already mentioned explicitly in v 6 and implicitly in v 14 with the mention of its antithesis—mastery or lordship (*kyrieysei*). In v 19a Paul seems to apologize for the necessity of the extended illustration: **I put this in human terms because you are weak in your natural selves.**

Within a culture in which the institution of slavery was as taken for granted as appliances and electronic gadgets are in ours, Paul's imagery is not surprising. His use of it should certainly not be taken as an endorsement of the practice, as if he had no misgivings about the justice of humans being treated as chattel (see 1 Cor 7:21-24).

Voluntary Slavery

Studies of slavery in the ancient world indicate that somewhere between one- and two-thirds of the population were either slaves or former slaves, and that among the significant avenues of replenishing the supply of slaves, who were often manumitted after reaching the age of thirty or forty, [was] . . . voluntary selling of oneself as a slave. . . . This social reality is the basis of the comparison Paul draws with service to sin. . . . Once the step into slavery was made, there was legally no escape except for death or manumission at the discretion of the owner. The owner literally had the power of life and death over his slaves. . . . They were simply his property, and whatever rights they may previously have enjoyed were eradicated. (Jewett 2007, 416)

Paul certainly did not hold modern notions idealizing human autonomy. He was convinced that human beings enjoy freedom only within the confines of some lordship (Käsemann 1980, 179). We will be slaves of some master—worthy or unworthy. We will serve some end—good or bad. Before we became Christians we were hopeless slaves to sin. As Christians we are free to choose our lord—whether sin or God. But we are never free to choose the consequences of our choice of masters.

Further Reading on First-Century Slavery

Bartchy, S. Scott. 1992. "Slavery (New Testament)." Pages 65-73 in Vol. 6 of *The Anchor Bible Dictionary*. Edited by David Noel Freedman. New York: Doubleday.

Harrill, J. A. 2000. "Slavery." In the *Dictionary of New Testament Background*. Edited by Craig A. Evans and Stanley E. Porter. Downers Grove, Ill.: InterVarsity.

Harris, J. Murray. 2001. *Slave of Christ: A New Testament Metaphor for Total Devotion to Christ*. New Studies in Biblical Theology, 8. Downers Grove, Ill.: InterVarsity.

Lyall, Francis. 1984. *Slaves, Citizens, Sons: Legal Metaphors in the Epistles*. Grand Rapids: Academie Books.

Martin, Dale B. 1990. *Slavery as Salvation*. New Haven, Conn.: Yale University Press.

Tsang, Sam. 2005. *From Slaves to Sons: A New Rhetoric Analysis on Paul's Slave Metaphors*. Studies in Biblical Literature, 81. New York: Peter Lang Publishing.

If we choose to offer ourselves once again in servitude to Sin, the inevitable result will be increasing lawlessness, shame, and ultimately death (Rom 6:16, 19, 21, 23). If we choose to offer ourselves in the service of God, the result will be sanctification, lives of holiness, and ultimately eternal life (vv 13, 19, 22, 23). Here, the Christian's choice is not between competing lords but between two contrasting kinds of slavery.

Slavery to God expresses itself in obedience (v 16) and righteousness (vv 13, 20). These qualities involve more than an inner disposition. Sanctification takes physical expression. When we offer ourselves to God, our bodies are put at his disposal. We are not made holy simply to be saintly, but to serve. We are not immediately transported to heaven. We are enlisted in the cause of right in this world. Lives of obedience, righteousness, and holiness made possible through sanctification are expressions of worship to God (12:1-2).

■ **15** This section emphasizes that those who are **not under law but under grace** (6:15) live in a relationship of servitude to God that involves wholehearted obedience (v 17). In v 19 Paul refers to his illustration as a **human** way of speaking, a concession to his readers' natural weakness. He introduces this discussion to make himself absolutely clear, just in case what he has said in vv 1-14 is not sufficiently understandable. At the same time, Paul insists that his words are not to be understood legalistically but heard and understood in light of, and as an application of, what he has just said about our death with Christ to sin.

In v 15 Paul picks up again the hypothetical question that has occupied him since v 1—**Shall we sin . . . ?** Does grace give Christians a license to sin? His answer continues to be a resounding denial of the perverse logic of antinomianism. However, his rationale changes, due to his shift from the metaphors of death/life and competing sovereignties to that of slavery and freedom.

Paul's restatement of the question—***Are we to sin*** [*hamartēsōmen*], because we are not under law but under grace? (v 15)—is not merely a repetition of v 1. The present subjunctive formulation of the first question challenges the notion that a career of habitual sinning might be consistent with a graced life: ***Shall we continue in Sin . . . ?*** (v 1). Jewett notes that the expression **under grace** (*hypo charin*) in vv 14 and 15 "appears nowhere else in Greek literature" (2007, 415). But **grace** is merely an abstract noun characterizing the freely given dying-love of Christ, which constrains an appropriate response (see 2 Cor 5:14-15).

The question in Rom 6:15 is formulated in the aorist subjunctive: **Shall we sin . . . ?** The first question: "Are we to continue to allow Sin to rule our lives?" becomes, "Shall we excuse any known sin, because are not under law but under grace?" Verse 1 deals with unbroken slavery to Sin; v 15 with individual acts of disobedience.

189

In vv 1-14 Paul argues for the fundamental incompatibility between Grace and Sin that had existed before we were justified. By faith in Christ we have been transferred from the old order of Adam into the new order of Christ. This new existence is free from the rule of Sin. Paul rejects any hint of antinomianism with his emphatic denial: **By no means!** (vv 2 and 15). His rhetorical questions implicitly state the ideal: the notion of sinning Christians is an oxymoron.

■ **16** In v 16, to drive home his point, Paul asks, **Don't you know that** [see 11:2] **when you offer** [*paristanete*; see v 13] **yourselves to someone to obey** [*eis hypokoēs, for obedience;* see 1:5; 15:18; 16:26; 1 Pet 1:2] **him as slaves, you are the slaves to the one whom you obey—whether you are slaves to sin, which leads to death, or of obedience, which leads to righteousness?** Now that God's grace has given us a choice, to place ourselves voluntarily at the disposal of Sin is incomprehensible. What we serve matters, because of the dramatically different consequences of the competing kinds of slavery. "Man has a lord, one way or the other. He is either a servant of sin, or a servant of obedience. Sin and obedience are therefore not in the first place our actions, but powers which have dominion over us" (Barth 1959, 72).

By putting the two powers of *Sin* and **Obedience** in juxtaposition, Paul demonstrates that Sin, as he understands it, is no mere unintended "missing of the mark"; it is rebellion against God. It is such a serious affair that believers who willfully disobey God find themselves enslaved once again to Sin. Jesus' strong warning comes to mind: "Everyone who sins is a slave to sin" (John 8:34). But, for those who have been justified, slavery to Sin is not an unfortunate, involuntary condition; it involves willingly putting themselves at Sin's disposal (see the commentary on Rom 6:13).

As moral creatures we humans make choices that lead us finally to eternal life or death. Godet cautions: "A single affirmative answer to the question, 'Shall I commit an act of sin, since I am under grace?' might have the effect of placing the believer again on the inclined plane which leads to the abyss" (1883, 202). Such is the force of Paul's conclusion: **For the wages of sin is death, but the gift of God is eternal life in Christ Jesus our Lord** (v 23). Thanks to grace, we are free to choose. Eternal issues are at stake in our probationary period of grace.

■ **17** Paul again takes for granted the universal scope of sin, as he reminds his readers: **You used to be slaves to sin** (v 17), and, **You have been set free from** [*eleutherōthentes . . . apo*] **sin** (v 18; see v 7). This is the first appearance in Romans of a word from the *eleuther*-cognate group (see also 6:20, 22; 7:3; 8:2, 21), "freedom," the precise opposite of "slavery." In previous settings terms such as *apolytrōsis* ("redemption" in 3:24) and *dikaioō* ("freed," lit. "justified" in 6:7) communicate a similar semantic force. In Galatians, a letter one-third the size of Romans, the *eleuther-* word family appears nine times (Gal 2:4; 3:28; 4:22, 23, 26, 30, 31; 5:1, 13), apparently because of the greater prominence of the imagery of slavery there.

Paul presumes that the Romans were justified believers: Slavery to Sin defines their past, not their present lives. And for this change, he gives **thanks . . . to God** (see 2 Cor 2:14; 9:15). But here he does *not* describe the transition from their old to their new lives using his familiar language of justification by faith. Instead, he refers to catechetical instruction as the basis for their Christian standing. A significant minority of Romans scholars propose to solve this discrepancy by removing 6:17*b* as a non-Pauline gloss (consistent with 16:17-20; Jewett 2007, 417-19 and 417 n. 30).

Here Paul refers to his Jewish audience's "conversion" as: **You wholeheartedly obeyed the form of teaching to which you were entrusted** (v 17*b*; see 1 Tim 1:5; 1 Pet 1:22). That they obeyed "from the heart" (*ek kardias*) implies an obedience that was a "deeply felt and deeply motivated action from the innermost being, but also as implying a contrast with an obedience which was less deeply rooted, whether coerced (sin's unwilling slave) or superficial" (see Rom 2:15, 29; 5:5; 10:9-10; Dunn 2002a, 38A:343).

■ **18** Such "conversions" by assimilation through catechesis were then (as now) less dramatic than the stereotypical darkness-to-light conversions. But, are they any less real? They were just as truly former slaves of Sin, now **enslaved to Righteousness** (6:18). That the personification of their new slave master subtly changes from "Obedience" (v 16) to "Righteousness" reminds us again that this is all imagery. Christ, of course, is the real Lord of all Christians.

The form [*typos*, "pattern" or "example"] **of teaching to which** they had been **entrusted** (*paradothēte*, "delivered") seems to refer to a succinct baptismal summary of faith to which they freely committed themselves when they became believers. The Christian pattern of teaching would include not only the faithful account of God's saving work in Christ Jesus but also the exemplary conduct they had seen modeled before them (see Phil 3:17; 2 Thess 3:9) by the anonymous Jewish preachers who brought them the gospel, which they in turn had received from others.

The Greek word *paradothēte* used here may refer to the passing on of tradition (1 Cor 11:2, 23; 15:3), but the NT also uses the term to refer to the handing over of persons from one authority to another (see Rom 1:24, 26, 28; 1 Cor 5:5; 13:3; 15:24; 2 Cor 4:11; Dunn 2002a, 38A:343). Thus, a slave owned by Sin is transferred to its new owner Obedience.

Regardless of Paul's precise nuance, both Jewish and Gentile Roman Christians knew that in their baptisms they had **been set free** [*eleutherōthentes*; see the comments on this word in Rom 6:7] **from** their former involuntary slavery to **sin** to **become** obedient **slaves to righteousness** (v 18; see Fitzmyer

1993, 449). Obedience and Righteousness serve only to personify the benevolent divine counterpart to the sinister slave master Sin. Obedience, in reality, is the right things people do, by the grace of God, in acknowledgment of his rightful claim to sovereignty in their lives.

■ **19** Paul blames the necessity for his homely analogy on the difficulty of explaining divine truth in language accommodated to human weakness: **I put this in human terms** [*anthrōpinon*] **because you are weak in your natural selves** [*sarkos,* "flesh"] (v 19*a*). *Anthrōpinon* refers to the colloquial language of everyday life (Bauer 1979, 67). "Paul was no doubt well aware that the metaphor of slavery, so antithetical to Greek ideals, is an inadequate one for talk of their relation with God" (see 8:15; Dunn 2002a, 38A:345). But the limitations of their mortality (*astheneian,* "weakness") demanded some means of communicating their absolute and ongoing obligation to God.

Paul expands the analogy of slavery, introducing still other personified powers into the cast of characters in the "formerly-now" description of his Roman readers: **Just as you used to offer the parts of your body in slavery to impurity and to ever-increasing wickedness, so now offer them in slavery to righteousness leading to holiness** (6:19*b*). Paul uses the words **impurity** (*akatharsia,* **uncleanness;** see 1:24; 2 Cor 6:14—7:1) and **wickedness** (*anomian,* **lawlessness;** see Acts 2:23; 1 Cor 9:21) consistent with contemporary Jewish descriptions of the immoral ethical behavior typically characterized Greco-Roman paganism's alienation from and rebellion against God (Jewett 2007, 420).

In his application of the comparison between the two slaveries, Paul turns from factual statements using verbs in the indicative mood. These facts characterized the former existence of his Gentile audience. He now turns to commands in the imperative mood, behaviors that should characterize their existence now. He has not used imperatives since Rom 6:13. Thus, his illustration becomes the basis for exhortation, urging his acknowledged Christian readers to move beyond their present location to a new destination, namely *sanctification* (*hagiasmon,* **holiness**).

In v 19 Paul refers to the necessity of believers voluntary offering ourselves as slaves (as in vv 13 [see the comments there] and 16). As believers, we apparently are free only to choose whether to put ourselves at the disposal of one or the other competing would-be masters: Sin *or* God (v 13), Sin *or* Obedience (v 16), and now **Impurity** and **Wickedness** *or* **Righteousness** (v 19).

An ethic of genuine love, spelled out later in 12:9-21, provides the guideline for this new type of righteousness. The consequence of such righteous slavery is *hagiasmos* ("sanctification"), which appears here for the first time in Romans. Although it is ordinarily interpreted as an individual virtue, the second person plural imperatives throughout this pericope point to a new form of social life as the primary embodiment of holiness. (Jewett 2007, 421; see 5:5; 12:1; 14:17; 15:13; 1 Cor 3:16-17; 2 Cor 13:14; 1 Thess 4:3)

Our choice of masters determines the community within which we serve and the character and outcome of our service. The community of the Crucified One is distinguished by a quality of life consistent with his. Thus, Christian holiness is distinguished by a new people that embody mutual service (Rom 15:25, 31) and love (12:9-21; Eph 1:15).

Slavery to Sin makes us "instruments of wickedness" (*adikias*, "unrighteousness"). Slavery to God makes us "instruments of righteousness" (Rom 6:13). Slavery to Sin "leads to death"; whereas, slavery to Obedience "leads to righteousness" (v 16). Slavery to **_Uncleanness_** and **_Lawlessness_** leads only to more **_lawlessness_** (*tē anomia eis tēn anomian*, **to ever-increasing wickedness**), but slavery to **Righteousness** leads to **holiness**, or better to **_sanctification_** (*eis hagiasmon;* v 19).

> Whereas the English word "sanctification" can refer to either the process or the result, . . . Greek vocabulary allowed one to indicate one thing or the other. To express result, Paul probably would have used *hagiosynē* [holiness] as in 2 Cor 7:1 and 1 Thess 3:13. Here, however, he uses *hagiasmos*, [i.e., sanctification,] the process of making holy. (Keck 2005, 171)

The Roman Christians, already God's property by right of redemption and, therefore "holy" in an initial sense, are called upon to become slaves by virtue of their own free choice, so God may begin within them the process of sanctification.

What Is Holiness/Sanctification?

To define the terms "holiness" and "sanctification" as they are used in the Bible calls for attention to the origins and meanings of both the English terms and the underlying Hebrew and Greek terms they translate. We begin with words, but this is only the beginning. To understand the precise meanings of words, we must study them within their various biblical contexts.

The English words "holiness" and "holy" come from the Germanic (Anglo-Saxon) roots of our language. In old English "holiness" referred to the state of being "whole" or "healthy." "Sanctify" and "sanctification" come from the Romance (Norman-Latin) origins of English. The Latin verb *sanctifico* meant "to make sacred," that is, "to set apart for the service of the gods." The underlying Hebrew and Greek words both English word groups translate are from the same word families (Purkiser 1983, 13-14).

In the Hebrew OT, the abstract noun *qodesh* is usually translated "holiness." Its use in contrast to the "profane" or "common" (*hol* in Lev 10:10; Ezek 22:26) suggests that its essential nature is "that which belongs to the sphere of the sacred" (McComiskey 1980, 2:787). Thus, to speak of the "Holy One" (using the adjective *qadosh* as a noun) is to refer to God. The Hebrew verb *qadash* means "to make holy" or "to sanctify." The Temple is called *miqdash,* the "holy place" or "sanctuary."

Strangely enough, the Hebrew word *qadesh,* from this same word group, refers to male and female temple prostitutes (in Gen 38:21-22; Deut 23:17; 1 Kgs 14:24; 15:12; 22:46; 2 Kgs 23:7; Job 36:14; Hos 4:14). From the Canaanite perspective, these were priests and priestesses set apart for the worship of the god Baal and his mother-consort Asherah, whom they called "Holiness." From Israel's perspective such so-called holy men and women in Canaan's idolatrous fertility religions were far from morally upright. Their "holiness" consisted solely in their total devotion to their perverse gods. Their corrupt morality matched that of the deities they served. Given the very different literary contexts of these Hebrew terms, it would be inappropriate to translate them, despite their common origin, with the same English words.

In the New Testament, "holiness" usually translates the Greek words *hagiasmos* or *hagiōsynē,* but in 2 Cor 1:12 it translates *hagiotēs.* It is derived from the adjective *hagios,* which means "holy." Thus, holiness is the quality or state of being holy. To be holy is to be "set apart," "unique." "Sanctification" may translate the Greek word *hagiasmos.* The noun, also derived from *hagios,* refers to the act or process by which one is made to be or recognized as holy. The plural form of the adjective *hagios* becomes the noun *hagioi,* which we customarily translate "saints." It obviously refers to "holy people." Thus, we might translate the verb *hagiazō*—"I *saintify" or "I *holify," but standard practice calls for "I sanctify" or "I make holy." A sanctuary is a *hagiasma.*

Scripture refers to God as "holy" for two reasons. The first derives from what theologians identify as divine transcendence. That is, God is utterly distinct from his creation. He alone is the Creator; all else that exists is his creation. He is unique; there is only one God. Second, God is uniquely just and loving in his dealings with his creatures. That is, he is holy in his being and behavior. God alone is holy in this underived sense.

Communities may be holy in the derived sense that they belong to God, the uniquely Holy One. "I am the LORD, who makes you holy" (Exod 31:13; Lev 22:32). "I am the LORD your God; consecrate yourselves and be holy, because I am holy. ... I am the LORD who brought you up out of Egypt to be your God; therefore be holy, because I am holy" (Lev 11:44-45; see 19:2). "Consecrate yourselves and be holy, because I am the LORD your God" (20:7). "You are to be holy to me because I, the LORD, am holy, and I have set you apart from the nations to be my own" (20:26). It is expected that God's people will behave in a manner consistent with their special calling to know him and make him known. "Just as he who called you is holy, so be holy in all you do; for it is written: 'Be holy, because I am holy'" (1 Pet 1:15-16).

"Holiness" defines the community identity of the people of God—the boundaries separating the holy community from outsiders. Within the OT context, holiness explains the vitality of the wholeness, well-being, ethical sensibilities, wholesome mutual relationships, and fruitfulness of God's people. As individual "members contribute to the community's common life . . . , the fruit of their labor is holiness," which cannot be reduced "to moralistic strictures" (Jewett 2007, 425).

Paul has acknowledged that much of his discussion of slavery is of necessity couched in figurative language—analogy and personification. Our choice, in fact, is not between slave masters. It is whether or not we will put ourselves fully and unconditionally at God's disposal. Will we volunteer to be used as he sees fit in the cause of right?

Apparently, only volunteers will do. In justification God sets us free from our involuntary slavery to Sin, but he leaves it to justified believers to decide how we will use our freedom. Only as we submit to slavery to God do we find real freedom. To serve anyone or anything other than God is to rejoin the rebellion against him. It is to be victimized by the illusory dream of autonomy. It is to become hopelessly addicted to a lifestyle opposed to all that is just, right, and holy. It is to waste our lives in pursuit of a hollow dream that is doomed to defeat and death.

Christians are not justified merely to be proudly displayed as trophies on the wall of God's heavenly den. God has an earthly mission for the former sinners he has salvaged from their headlong plummet to certain death. He has things he wants done in this world, and he wants the church to do it. Paul's imperatives imply that God will not coerce us to serve him; we must choose to cooperate in his cause.

Please, indulge me as **I put this in human terms because you are weak in your natural selves** (Rom 6:19a). To change the analogy again, justified believers are not merely airlifted out of a war zone and placed in a holding pattern awaiting permission to land in the Celestial City. There's a war to be fought to recover the sovereignty of this rebellious planet to its one rightful Master, and we are enlisted to serve as God's weapons (v 13) against the insurgency. If we make ourselves fully and exclusively available to God, he will not only set us apart for his purposes but also set us within a holy community that will equip us with the holy character we need to accomplish these purposes. Under these circumstances, neutrality is impossible.

■ **20** In vv 20-22 Paul develops further the very different consequences (*gar, For,* introduces v 20) of slavery to Sin vs. slavery to God. When the Romans **were slaves to sin** they **were free from the control of righteousness** (v 20). If the apostle were writing today, he would almost certainly have enclosed the word **free** within quotation marks to distinguish what is actually licentiousness from true freedom. His language of liberation in v 20 is both ironic and metaphoric.

195

To be liberated "with respect to righteousness" is to be free for anything but life itself; to live under the bondage of sin is to experience an abstract kind of freedom that disallows a relationship with the only thing that matters, the righteousness of God. This verse therefore posits two contrary forms of freedom, freedom from sin, which is at the same time a life under the constraint of righteousness, and freedom from righteousness itself, which is inevitably caught in the bondage to sin and destined for death. (Jewett 2007, 421-22)

■ **21** As evidence for the sham character of such so-called freedom, Paul challenges his readers to think pragmatically: **What benefit** [*karpon*, "fruit"] **did you reap at that time . . . ?** (v 21). From its biological origins, the imagery of "fruit" in the mental and spiritual realm refers to results, outcomes, consequences, or advantages (Bauer 1979, 405). What gain accrued to them as a result of their service to Sin? **Things they are now ashamed of! Things that result** [*telos*, *end*] **in death!** As with the ironic use of **free,** the word **benefit** should certainly be enclosed in mock quotation marks. All of the consequences were shameful—negative, counterproductive, embarrassing, and self-destructive. The gospel, far from being the occasion for shame (see 1:16), has the power to free believers from the rule of Shame, Futility, and Death (see 5:14, 17, 21; 6:16).

■ **22** Verse 22 describes the twofold antithesis (*nyni de*, **But now;** see 3:21) to Christians' former lives as **slaves to sin** (6:20) and victims of shame (v 21): **you have been set free** [*eleutherōthentes*] **from sin and have become slaves** [*doulōthentes*] **to God** (v 22). The passive voice of both participles implies that God is the source of their liberation. Of course, their newfound freedom is not to be confused with autonomy; nor is their slavery to God merely a change of tyrants (see v 19). "To be a slave of God is to be bound to divine righteousness or, in the metaphor developed in 6:13, to become a 'weapon of righteousness'" (Jewett 2007, 424).

The consequences of their new lives are also exactly opposite to those of their old lives (see v 21). The present (*echete*, **you have** in v 22 vs. *eichete*, *you were having* in v 21) **benefit** (*karpon*, *fruit*) that comes with this exchange of lordship **leads to holiness** (*eis hagiasmon*). Sanctification is the work of God's Spirit within the life of the Christian community. However, Paul refers to it as *your fruit*, because believers remain accountable for what they allow God to do within them. The end **result** [*telos*] of sanctification **is external life.** As in the Johannine literature, eternal life refers to the "fullness of existence for the saints in the present that continues" into unending life after death (Jewett 2007, 425).

■ **23** From the biological world, in v 23 Paul's metaphor shifts to the economic, as he continues to elaborate on the contrasting consequences of slavery to Sin vs. slavery to God: **For the wages** [*opsōnia*] **of sin is death.** Like **"free"** and **"benefit"** (v 22), **"wages"** should be enclosed within mock quotes. The deadly compensation for sinning can only ironically be called **wages**—"punishment" might be more accurate.

In Paul's day the word **wages** was the designation for ration money paid to soldiers for their service (see Luke 3:14; Bauer 1979, 602). This may have prompted Paul's use here, since **death** is the "pay" received by those who volunteer to serve "as weapons of unrighteousness" (v 13, HCSB). "Since wages are paid in increments as well as at the end of a task, the death that Paul has in mind is a present reality that will extend into the future" (Jewett 2007, 426). "Sin's (final) payoff . . . [is] not just natural death, but death as the forfeiture of eternal life" (Dunn 2002a, 38A:349).

The apostle refuses to call the reward for a life of faithful service to God **wages** (see 4:4-5). Because the Christian's new life of obedience is possible only on the basis of God's grace, its reward—**eternal life** [see 2:7; 5:21] **in Christ Jesus our Lord** (6:23)—can only be called **the gift** [*charisma*; see 1:22; 5:15-16] **of God** (6:23; see 5:21).

FROM THE TEXT

Wesley demonstrated that we need not diminish the importance of justification to make more room and necessity for the further work of sanctification. He properly stressed that the state of justified persons is inexpressibly great and glorious. We are born again. We are children of God. We enjoy the peace of God. Our bodies are temples of the Holy Spirit. We are new creatures in Christ Jesus. We are washed and sanctified. Our hearts are purified by faith. From the moment we are justified, we have power over both inward and outward sin. Believers have been set free from the power of sin, yet sin remains, although it does not reign. And Christ cannot reign where sin remains. Sin remains as self-centeredness, self-will, and self-trust. That sin remains is shown by our obsession with the illusion that we can maintain our new life and freedom on our own, in our own power. (This paraphrases Wesley's sermon "Sin in Believers"; 1979, 5:149-51.)

Paul insists that the fruit of justification can be sustained only by total self-abandonment to **righteousness.** Wesley calls this "entire sanctification," appropriating the language of "through and through" sanctification found in 1 Thess 5:23. That justified believers still cherish the illusion of self-sovereignty demonstrates their need for heart purity and inward conformity to the character of the holy God. The power of Sin that is broken in justification must be removed by the ongoing work of sanctification, so that God may reign without rival. And to give ourselves to anything other than God is to continue in the realm of Sin.

The free grace of God has repeatedly been replaced by a deceptive surrogate, the sinister product of antinomianism. Wesley rejected this product of misguided gospel preaching. But so did Martin Luther and others in the Reformed tradition. At its best, all truly Christian theology has insisted that grace is not a license to sin. Grace is not divine permission to rebel, but God's gift of moral power to which we may submit. Only by submission to obedience may holiness be realized.

Dietrich Bonhoeffer called grace's antinomian substitutes "cheap grace." This perverted doctrine threatens the evangelical message when Paul's cautions in Rom 6 are forgotten. The antinomian says, "Since I am covered by the righteousness of Christ, all my sins, past, present, and future, are 'under the Blood.'" Such perverted teaching, says Bonhoeffer (1995, 43; see 11), turns the justification of *sinners* into the justification of *sinning!* Wesleyans by no means hold a monopoly on "holiness," in either theory or practice.

Romans 6 provides what may be Scripture's clearest treatment of the already-but-not-yet of justification. Wesley learned from Paul that justification is the gracious work of God in Christ for us. It is rescue from the compulsive, enslaving power of sin. Freed from their former slavery to sin, Christians must refuse to yield to its claims any longer. And they must present themselves unreservedly to God, so that he can sanctify them as surely as sin shamed them. Justification is incomplete apart from sanctification, the gracious work of God through his Spirit in us—a subject Paul will take up again in Rom 8. Christians must accept responsibility for the freedom God has given. **Christ died and returned to life so that he might be the Lord** (14:9). Lutheran NT scholar Karl P. Donfried emphasizes that there can be no glorification unless justification is followed by sanctification (1976).

Wesley insists that justification and entire sanctification begin in Christian experience in distinct transforming moments. However, he is insistent that both works of grace must be sustained and renewed "from moment to moment." It is only as the power of Christ continually rules our lives that we are able to be all that his grace makes possible. He alone enables us "to continue in spiritual life, and without [him], notwithstanding all our present holiness, we should be devils the next moment" (Wesley 1979, 5:167; "The Repentance of Believers"). The present life of **holiness,** like its future **result—eternal life—** forever remains **the gift of God . . . in Christ Jesus our Lord** (v 23).

(2) Sanctification Through Death to the Law (7:1-25)

(a) Freedom from the Law (7:1-6)

BEHIND THE TEXT

Romans 7 returns to and develops further Paul's claim in 6:14 that Christians are "not under law, but under grace." In 6:15-23 Paul rejects a potentially antinomian misunderstanding of the gospel of grace as a license to sin. Paul's refutation of this specious notion employs the analogy of slavery. It is unthinkable that Christians should sin, for their lives are lived in the new order of Obedience. Living under the rule of Grace, Christians are now *slaves to Obedience, which leads to Righteousness,* just as formerly they were *slaves to Sin, which leads to Death* (6:16). Indeed, only as believers are set free from Sin *can* they serve God in Obedience.

Believers who live in subjection to the righteousness of God (not their own) can serve God fruitfully and see sanctification and eternal life result from their service. Having described the dethroning of Sin, one would-be rival to the sovereign rule of God, Paul is prepared to challenge its weak companion, Law, in ch 7. To do so, Paul introduces a new analogy, that of marriage, to make substantially the same point about the inadequacy of Law he had made about Sin. Christians are not only free from slavery to Sin but also released from a slavish relationship to Law. Obviously, this new analogy needs explication.

Throughout the long development of Paul's theological reasoning up to this point in the letter, Law has never faded totally out of sight. It has hovered in the background, a dark shadow at which Paul has from time to time thrown wounding shafts, linking it ever more explicitly with the onslaught of Sin: "through the law we become conscious of sin" (3:20); "law brings wrath" (4:15); "The law was added so that the trespass might increase" (5:20).

Paul insists that the Law was given, not to resolve the Sin problem, but to show up Sin as a disease that only God can heal through Christ and the Spirit (8:1-17). Law serves as a negative foil against which to show off the freedom and promise of lived-out holiness contained in the gospel.

The background of ch 7 is found in 5:12-21, in which Paul gives his view of salvation history. It is an account in three stages: from Adam to Moses, from Moses to Christ, and finally from Christ to the End. From Adam to Moses "death reigned . . . even over those who did not sin by breaking a command, as did Adam, who was a pattern of the one to come" (5:14). In the second period, when "law was added," people's evil deeds became violations (5:20). At that point Law became "the power of sin" (1 Cor 15:56) in human life. In the third period, in which "sin increased, grace increased all the more, so that, just as sin reigned in death, so also grace might reign through righteousness to bring eternal life through Jesus Christ our Lord" (Rom 5:21).

Since God's plan of salvation *from the beginning* was to send his Son to liberate his people from sin (8:3), the Law's purpose was to prepare the way for the grace that God would, in the fullness of time, provide through Christ (see Gal 4:4-7). In the divine drama of salvation, Sin took possession of the Law and perverted it into "the law of sin and death." It is from this "perverted" form of the Law (Käsemann 1980, 198) that Christ came to deliver us.

IN THE TEXT

■ **1** Paul continues his use of the diatribe style, opening this section with another rhetorical question (see Rom 6:3). He addresses his readers directly, as **brothers** and sisters **who know the law** (7:1)—a community of experts in the "the legal order" (Käsemann 1980, 187). Of course, as Romans, they knew Roman law, but undoubtedly, as mostly Gentile Christians, they were well acquainted with the law of Moses. In fact, it was probably the Jewish moral code that attracted them to become converts to Judaism, or at least "God-fearers," before they became Christians. Paul repeats this kinship language again in v 4 and frequently thereafter (8:12; 10:1; 11:25; 12:1; 15:14), probably for the same reason—to improve the likelihood they will share his conclusions.

Paul calls attention to his readers' knowledge of Law, however, not to discuss its content, but only to limit the duration of its **authority** (*kyrieuei*)—as long as a person is alive. The word *kyrieuei*, "exercises lordship," suggests that Paul understands Law as another personified power that, like Sin and Death, "lords it over" those under its authority (6:14-15).

■ **2** He illustrates Law's enduring authority by appealing to **the law of marriage: By law a married woman is bound to her husband as long as he is alive, but if her husband dies, she is released from the law of marriage** (7:2; see 1 Cor 7:39). The Law's authority for the **married woman** endures only during the lifetime of her husband. The rare word for "married woman," *hypandros* (*one under a man*), is found only here in the NT (but see the LXX of Prov 6:24, 29). It defines a wife solely in terms of her husband, as his property, powerless, and without rights or duties under Jewish law (see Deut 24:1-4; Jewett 2007, 431). Such a woman is **bound to her husband as long as he is alive. But if her husband dies,** "she is discharged [*katērgētai*; see the commentary on Rom 7:6] from the law concerning her husband" (v 2 NRSV).

■ **3** In v 3, Paul concludes, ***Therefore*** (*ara oun*; see 5:18; 7:25; 8:12; 9:16, 18; 14:12, 19) the former husband's death creates an opportunity for her to marry **another man.** Within Paul's analogy, the violation of **the law of marriage** makes the wife an **adulteress.** This, of course, represents unfaithfulness to the exclusive claims of God, which defines sin. We can have just one lord.

The parallels to Paul's language describing release from Sin's rule in 6:6, 9, and 14 imply that the Law is another power from which believers are freed (Jewett 2007, 430). The key to understanding this analogy is in 6:6: When we became Christians "our old self was crucified" with Christ—we died to Sin and were freed from its slavery. To die to the Law is at the same time to die to Sin (Gal 2:19-21). In both instances, death of the *old* self is followed by a "resurrection" of the *new* self. "The 'self' is double; there is an 'old self' and a 'new self'; or rather the 'self' remains the same throughout, but it passes through different states, or phases" (Sanday and Headlam 1929, 172).

The living **husband** of Rom 7:2*a*, who is also subject to **the law**, exists *in the flesh* (v 5) as "the old self" (6:6), bound under "the law of sin and death" (8:2)—the only law Paul is concerned with in chs 7 and 8. This law, according to 7:5, is **at work in our bodies . . . for death.** So long as we (= the husband) live in the flesh as that "old self," we (= the wife) are governed by the law, which binds him and therefore ourselves (Barth 1959, 77).

■ **4** So [*hōste,* ***consequently***; see vv 6, 13; 13:2; 15:19], **my brothers** and sisters, **you also died to the law through the body of Christ** offered on the cross, **that you might belong to another, to him who was raised from the dead, in order that we might bear fruit to God** (7:4). The Greek verb translated **you . . . died** (*ethanatōthēte*) actually means ***you were put to death*** or ***you were killed.*** The passive voice of the verb may suggest that God is responsible for bringing an end to our old lives (see the active voice of the same verb in v 6 and 6:2, 7, 8).

The aorist tense points to a past event. Christ's crucifixion brought an end to the old humanity and the old age (see vv 1-6). Paul's point is the same one he makes in vv 2-6 and Gal 2:19-21: Our old lives have come to an end through the saving work of God. The agent of death—**through the body of Christ** (Rom 7:4)—is the crucified Christ (see Heb 10:5, 10; 1 Pet 2:24), not the church (see Rom 12:5; 1 Cor 10:16; 12:27; Eph 4:12). Through faith in the Crucified, we have died to the Law's condemnation (Rom 8:1) and jurisdiction (6:6).

But the conversion or subsequent baptism of believers was the decisive moment in which believers voluntarily accept Christ's death as their own. "Participation in the body of Christ" in 1 Cor 10:16 refers to the ongoing experience of believers in this decisive event through the Eucharist. "The body of Christ" (see Rom 12:5) is the new community in which believers find, not only freedom from Sin and Law, but also a new and sustained relationship with Christ and other believers.

The metaphorical death of believers is no natural death, nor is it a suicide; this is a crucifixion (see *synestaurōthē* in 6:6, also in the passive voice). That **you also** (*kai hymeis*) were put to death moves behind the analogy of the passing on of a husband in 7:2-3 to the point where Paul began in v 1: The Law rules only the living, and you, too, are dead, thank God! (Dunn 2002a, 38A:361).

Our death was specifically **to the law.** This signals no antinomian end of morality, as if anything goes for Christians. Paul's point is that Christ's death brought an end to the old age. With it, the distinction between Jews and Gentiles imposed by the Mosaic law also came to an end. All humanity stands on level ground at the foot of the cross: All are sinners; therefore, all must be justified by faith (3:21-26).

The termination of our old lives sets us free to commit ourselves fully to **another;** but not just *any* other—we are free for only one person—**him who was raised from the dead,** that is, the risen, glorified Christ. Paul conceives of "the relationship between believers and Christ . . . as totally encompassing as the relationship between a husband and wife" (Jewett 2007, 434). And we are free for only one purpose—**in order that** [*hina*] **we might bear fruit** [*karpophorēsomen*] **to God** (7:4; see 2 Cor 11:2).

The word **fruit** suggests childbearing with the metaphorical force of the moral outcome of liberation from Sin for the undivided service of God. As in Rom 6:21-22, the "fruit" (*karpon*, "benefit") of wholehearted service to God is the life of "sanctification." The repetition of **bore fruit** in 7:5 makes this quite clear (see Gal 5:22-23). Paul will describe in greater detail the fruit of this new union in Rom 8 under the rubric of life in the Spirit. But, first, he must overthrow the hollow claims of the feeble tyrant Law, which is only a helpless vassal of the real scoundrel, Sin.

The point of Paul's analogy of the husband and wife emerges more clearly if we put his conclusion as a question: Apart from divorce, under what circumstances is a married woman free to marry someone else? Answer: At the death of her husband. Thereafter she is free to belong to another man and be "fruitful" (Keck 2005, 177). Admittedly, Paul seems to mix the metaphor, since in his application it is not the first husband (= Law) that dies, but the wife (= the Christian).

■ **5 For when we were controlled by [the flesh (margin)], the . . . passions aroused by the law were at work in our bodies** [*melesin;* lit. "members" or "body parts"], **so that we bore fruit for death** (7:5). The unfortunate translation of the word **flesh** as **sinful nature** reflects the Reformed Evangelical bias of the NIV translation and is unjustified by the evidence.

There is nothing wrong with being creatures of **flesh**—we are weak human beings, just creatures. Problems arise when humans live as if we were not weak, as if we were autonomous, as if we could please God without his empowering presence (see 8:1-11). This is what it means to be *in the flesh* (*en tē sarki*) here: to orient our lives around the created order rather than to acknowledge our ongoing dependence on the Creator. Christians "are not in the flesh" (8:9 NRSV), although we continue to live as creatures of flesh (see Gal 2:20).

To be *in the flesh* is to allow Flesh to become another in the parade of the personified would-be sovereigns—like Sin, Death, Uncleanness, Lawlessness, and Law. These tyrants can only enslave us and prevent us from serving our one rightful Lord. To serve them is to trust in the creature instead of the Creator and so to be **controlled by** [the flesh] instead of God.

To be *in the flesh* for law-abiding Jews expressed itself in boastful confidence in membership in the covenant community, their circumcision, and their unique standing with God (Gal 6:13; Phil 3:3-4). To be *in the flesh* for "wise Greeks" may have involved overconfidence in their cultural sophistication and superiority compared to the "foolish" barbarians (see Rom 1:14). The gospel undermines all vaunted human claims to autonomy (see 1 Cor 1:18—4:7) and self-aggrandizement. Dominated by self-seeking, fleshly interests, we pervert the Law. Obeying it was intended to bring honor to God. But instead, we turn it into a means of achieving honor for ourselves at the expense of others.

The word **sinful** is deliberately ellipsed in the above quotation of Rom 7:5, because human **passions** (*pathēmata*), like "desires" (*epithymia*) in 6:12 (see the comments there), are *not* evil per se. In fact, this is one of the few NT instances of the word that does not refer to "suffering" (Bauer 1979, 602). It is the sinful ends of human passions that pervert them (see Gal 5:24). Cranfield quotes Calvin's comment on Rom 7:5: "The work of the law, in the absence of the Spirit . . . is to inflame our hearts still more, so that they burst forth into such lustful desires" (see vv 7-8). "Challenged by the law," Cranfield adds, human "self-centeredness—the sinful ego—recognizes that it is being called into question and attacked, and so seeks all the more furiously to defend itself" (1975, 1:337).

The **fruit for death** (v 5) refers to the inevitable consequences of allowing Law to assume the rightful throne of God. Whether we approach Law as antinomians or legalists, the results are the same. Enlisting Law as a competitive means of achieving honor results in death for all who engage in the struggle (Jewett 2007, 437). Likewise, sin and rebellion against God bring inevitable shame and death. Such is the outcome of refusing to submit to the sovereignty of God and the righteousness that leads to sanctification (see 6:20-23). We will **bear fruit to God** or **fruit for death** (7:4, 5). We cannot choose to be childless.

■ **6** Anticipating what he will say in 8:1-17, Paul concludes this section in 7:6 by explaining what it means ethically to be freed from the Law. The death-resurrection of Christ is an eschatological (= end-time) event precisely because it marks a transition from the old age to the new. The point of Paul's **now** (*nyni*) is that, by participating in Christ by faith, we find ourselves ushered into this age of fulfillment (see 3:21; 6:22).

With the coming of Christ—historically *and* existentially (= in our personal experience)—the age of Law (see the comments on 5:12-14) comes to an end to make way for the age of the Spirit (see Gal 3:10-29). What became a potential reality in the historical event of A.D. 30 does not become effective for us until we share in Christ's death.

It is **the law** that **once bound** [*kateichometha;* see Rom 1:18; 6:6] **us** (7:6). Even God's "holy, righteous and good" Law (v 12) can enslave and kill when it is victimized by Sin (vv 7-12). But our death to Law set us free so that we might live to God (Gal 2:19; see 3:23-26; 4:1-3).

The Greek verb translated **released,** *katērgēthēmen,* in Rom 7:2 and 6 has a wide range of application. In 3:3 Paul uses it to challenge the prospect that human unfaithfulness might "nullify God's faithfulness" and in v 31 that justification by faith might "nullify the law"; in 4:14, that law might make God's promise "worthless." In 6:6 we are crucified with Christ so that "sin might be done away with." Paul's point here seems to be that our metaphorical death to Law renders Law's illegitimate claim to rule our lives powerless and ineffective. Its enslaving influence is abolished, freeing us from its dominion (see Bauer 1979, 417). We are inducted into the promised new age.

We must abandon allegiance to the enslaving powers of the old age to experience the powers of the new age of freedom. But, our newfound freedom is not to be confused with autonomy or antinomianism, as if we are free to do whatever we please. We are freed from slavery to the Law for one purpose (*hōste,* **so that** + the infinitive): *to serve as slaves in the newness* [*kainotēti,* see 6:4] *of the Spirit.*

Although the infinitive *douleuein,* **to serve,** is from the same Greek cognate group as slave (*doulos*), we are not "slaves to the Spirit," for the Spirit brings freedom "from the law of sin and death" (8:2). "Those who are led by the Spirit of God . . . [do] not receive a spirit that makes [us] a slave again" (vv 14-15).

This new kind of "slavery" is, in fact, perfect freedom by comparison to **the old way of the written code** (*grammatos,* **letter**) of the Law (7:6). Paul anticipated the contrast between **letter** and **Spirit** in 2:28-29. There he described the true Jew as one whose "circumcision" is not merely "outward and physical," but inward, "by the Spirit," that is, whose circumcision is "of the heart." The OT expected the gift of the Spirit to enable God's new covenant people to love him without reserve (Deut 30:6) by changing their stubborn hearts to obedience (Ezek 36:26-27) and writing the law on their hearts (Jer 31:31-34; see 2 Cor 3:1-6; Phil 3:3). The **old way** involved external coercion; the **new way** involves internal motivation to obey.

The point of Rom 7:6 is resumed in 8:1. Both passages insist that freedom from Sin involves freedom from Law as well. But before Paul can expand on "the new life of the Spirit" (v 6 NRSV) in ch 8, he must first prevent the mistaken conclusion that might arise from 7:1-6 that the Law is Sin (v 7). The thesis of vv 7-25 is that it is legalism, not law, that is the path to death (see v

5). Merely human efforts to observe the Law end in death because of the enslaving power of Sin. Where Sin rules, it perverts Law into legalism and human effort into moralism—both idols that must be broken. This bad news prepares us for the good news of ch 8. Christ succeeds where Law and good intentions fail. The life of holiness is possible only where Christ rules as Lord through the power of the Holy Spirit.

FROM THE TEXT

Some interpreters see Paul's illustration of marriage in this passage to be "confused and misleading." Others find Paul's analogy consistent: (i) The **woman** is the true "self" capable of passing through different states or stages. It may live either under law (bound to Adam) or under grace (united to Christ). (ii) The **law of marriage** is the Mosaic law, specifically the Decalogue (see 7:7-12). (iii) The first **husband** is our status in Adam, to whom we are bound under Law. (iv) The new husband is the risen Christ, to whom we are united by faith (see Eph 5:31-32).

Under Law we were "married" to Adam. That is, ***we were in the flesh*** (*ēmen en tei sarki*)—we lived for self-centered, merely human ends. **The sinful passions aroused by the law were at work in our bodies, so that we bore fruit** [*karpos*] **for death** (Rom 7:5). The consequences of self-centered living are **fruit for death.** That is because those who do "the works of the flesh . . . will not inherit the kingdom of God" (Gal 5:19, 21 NRSV).

Under Grace (see Rom 6:14-18) we are "married" to Christ. This is the "new life of the Spirit" (7:6 NRSV). Deliverance from the Law does not mean license, but just the opposite. It is the power to serve God in love and fulfill the Law's requirement (see 8:3; Gal 5:22-23). Those who live out of the Spirit's resources do God's will spontaneously in love, not because of Law's demands.

The antithetical language of "oldness" vs. "newness" or "the letter" vs. "the Spirit" is similar to that used in Paul's sustained argument in 2 Cor 3:4-18 for the superiority of the "new covenant" as compared to the "old." The old covenant, being one of "letter," involved a ministry of death (see Rom 7:5). The new covenant, characterized by the Spirit, gives life (*zōopoiei*, 2 Cor 3:6*b*).

"Letter" refers to the Law as simply external code. It "kills" because, as Paul will explain in Rom 7:7-25, it imposes obligation and specifies sanction without giving the power necessary to resist the selfish impulse of "the flesh" to rebel. It thus leads, through actual sin, to eternal death.

"The Spirit," on the other hand, is the power of the new age, which is released effectively into the human heart to create the righteousness that leads to eternal life (6:23; 8:10-11). This rich complex of intertextual motifs, seen as the fulfillment of Ezek 36:24-27 and Jer 31:31-34, lies behind Rom 7:6. The power of the new age is **the new way of the Spirit** that will illuminate Paul's exposition of the gospel in 8:1-16. The Spirit is the agent of sanctification.

Furthermore, in 7:5-6 Paul sets the contrast between the past "under the law" and the present "life in the Spirit." Verse 5 anticipates Paul's characterization of life "under the law" in vv 7-25, while v 6 anticipates life "in the Spirit" in 8:1-13. These two passages—the negative (7:7-25, especially vv 14-25) and positive (8:1-16)—each illuminate the other by way of contrast.

(b) The Function of the Law (7:7-13)

BEHIND THE TEXT

With this passage Paul begins the description of life under the Law, which he intends as a foil to highlight life in the Spirit (8:1-16). The description comes in two parts, each with its own perspective. Whereas the present passage (7:7-13) tells of the encounter with the Law in the form of a narrative relating past experience, vv 14-25 explore the same encounter from the vivid perspective of present experience. Both sections begin with the first person plural (we): **What shall we say, then?** (v 7) and "We know" (v 14). But the first person singular (I) dominates both vv 7-13 and 14-25.

Verses 7-25 are among the most notoriously controversial passages in all of Paul's letters. Three issues have dominated the modern interpretation of the passage. The *first* concerns the identity of the "I" who speaks throughout the passage. The *second* has to do with the stage of religious experience out of which the "I" speaks. Does the anguished struggle depicted in vv 14-25 describe present Christian experience, or religious experience prior to and/or apart from life in Christ? The *third* involves the nature of the divided state described in these verses. Is the problem a weak, divided human will in the face of the Law's demand that is too hard? Or, is it a discrepancy between noble intentions and dismal achievements? Although these issues are closely intertwined, we postpone consideration of the second to From the Text and the third to In the Text comments below.

As to the identity of the "I" in vv 7-25, the most obvious interpretation is to assume that it is autobiographical: This is Paul's account of his own experience under the Law. If this is so, we apparently have in vv 7-13 Paul's rehearsal of how he had once been **alive** in the innocence of youth (v 9), but when he reached adolescence and became *bar mitzvah*, that is, "a son of the commandment," his innocence **died** (v 9). Verses 14-25 would then seem to be an account of Paul's futile attempts to keep the Law. Driven to despair, he was finally delivered by his conversion to Christ.

For all its apparent naturalness, this view must confront serious problems. Elsewhere Paul suggests that his attempts to observe the Law were not failures but "faultless" (Phil 3:6). A pessimistic interpretation of his life under the Law is at odds with his own testimony in Gal 1:13-14. And it is also difficult to see how one born as a Jew and circumcised on the eighth day (Phil 3:4-6) could describe himself as once **alive apart from law** (Rom 7:9).

If ch 7 is autobiographical—relating the personal experience of Paul, it must be understood as a retrospective reassessment of his pre-Christian Jewish experience from his later Christian perspective. This is *not* how Saul the Pharisee saw himself *then* but how Paul the Christian came to see his former life *later.* This is not a diagnosis from plight to solution, but from solution to plight. That is, Paul was not aware of any problem with Law until after he found Christ its solution. Paul did not come to Christ as a self-conscious rebel against God, plagued by guilt, deeply conscious of his own sin, and desperately seeking salvation. On the contrary, it was the revelation of the crucified Jesus as the Christ of God that caused a self-righteous zealot for the Law (Gal 1:13-14) to understand himself and Jesus (2 Cor 5:16-21) in an entirely new light.

The difficulty with the autobiographical approach has led many interpreters to see the "I" as a literary device referring to humanity in general. First Corinthians 13:1-3 obviously uses "I" in this typical sense. It is not simply Paul who would be nothing should he exercise the various spiritual gifts without love. This is true of anyone and everyone. This typical view of Rom 7 usually sees it as pointing back to ch 5 and the experience of Adam as the representative human, who yields to the temptation to take the forbidden fruit (see Gen 2:17 and ch 3).

7:7-13

If the "I" of Rom 7 is used in this sense, the "I" represents the experience of "Every Jew" or "Everyman" or "Everywoman" under the Law—whether the Mosaic law or the law of conscience (2:15). Numerous parallels exist of this universal "I" in Greco-Roman literature, in the Psalms, and elsewhere in Paul's own letters (see e.g., 1 Cor 8:13; 10:29-30; 13:1-3, 11-12; Gal 2:18-21). The Greco-Roman rhetorical convention of *prosōpopeia* used a "speech-in-character." This argumentative technique allowed "an imaginary person or type . . . to speak in the first person in order to make an emotionally effective argument" (Jewett 2007, 443; see 441-45). That this "I" was typical does not resolve the debate as to who it represented. A great variety of candidates have been proposed, far more than can be discussed here.

There seem to be unmistakable allusions to the narrative of Gen 2—3 (esp. 3:11) that lend the "I" an Adamic significance. But Adam did not live "under the law" of Moses. He did, however, live under the command of God in 2:16-17 (see Rom 5:14). If Paul shares the sentiment of the pseudepigraphal *2 Bar.* 54:19, he may have understood that each of us is his or her own Adam. Thus, the "I" is representative of every person.

However, Paul's language in Rom 5:20 also tells the story of Israel's confrontation with the "law" in the form of the Decalogue (particularly, Exod 20:17; Deut 5:21). Could the "I" speak for Israel and reflect its experience of receiving the Law at Sinai? This would make the "I" represent a typical Jew.

Perhaps Paul wanted his audience to hear the "I" in tones evocative of *both* Adam in Eden *and* of Israel at Mount Sinai. However, Israel's experience of the Law is told in terms of the effect of God's command on Adam. When the Law "was added" at Sinai, it had the same effect on Israel as it had on Adam (Wright 1991, 197), with the result that Israel "recapitulated" Adam's sin. Rather than setting Israel apart as a "holy nation," the Law brought it down to the level where Jews and Gentiles were alike "under sin" (Rom 3:9). In fact, the Law actually *concentrated* sin in Israel, so that where "sin increased" (in Israel), grace through Christ might increase "all the more" (5:20*b*; Wright 2002, 530). Paul makes this painful story a foil to the rescue, equally universal in scope, by the grace of "the last Adam, a life-giving spirit" (1 Cor 15:45).

To dismiss any autobiographical reference in Rom 7:7-25 seems questionable, but there can be little doubt that the "I" in this text is not simply Paul's unique story. It is also typical of other persons in this situation "under" the domination of Law. For all the ambiguity that remains, his contextual point in chs 5—8 is clear enough: What God has done in Christ by the power of the Spirit has succeeded where the Law failed.

IN THE TEXT

■ **7** Paul continues to exploit the diatribe mode: **What shall we say, then** [*oun*]? (7:7). What are the implications of the foregoing—that is, of the mysterious link between Sin, Law, and Death? Paul demonstrated to his satisfaction that to be free from one is also simultaneously a deliverance from the others and that, equally, liberation from one can occur only if there is also deliverance from the others.

This raises the question, **Is the law sin?** (v 7). Since under Law "sinful passions" are aroused (v 5), and their "fruit" is death, is **the law** itself a power opposed to God? **Certainly not!** (see 3:4, 6, 31; 6:2, 15). **Indeed I would not have known** [*egnōn*] **what sin was except through the law** (7:7). The Greek verb *ginōskō* "refers to knowledge gained through experience, thus implying that without the presence of a law, [people] would not have been aware of sin" (Jewett 2007, 446).

Biblical Knowledge

Biblical "knowledge" is not intellectual; it is intimate and personal, as in marital intercourse (Gen 4:25 KJV, NRSV; see JB). This is preeminently true of "the knowledge of God" (Hos 6:6 KJV, NRSV). This generally agreed scholarly view of biblical "knowledge" governs Rom 7:4 (as well as in Gen 4:25 and Hos 6:6 KJV, NRSV, JB).

This seems to reiterate Paul's claim in Rom 3:20 that "through the law we *become conscious* of sin" (emphasis added). Through acquaintance with the Law we learn that specific violations of it bring divine judgment, but we do not know an act or attitude is wrong until Law forbids it. In 7:7 "knowing" **sin** is not simply about acquiring information; it is about the personal *experience of sin itself.*

Thus, Paul continues with an explanation, **For** [*te gar*] **I would not have known what coveting really was if the law had not said, "Do not covet."** I coveted precisely because the Law said, "You shall not covet" (Exod 20:17; Deut 5:21). The prohibition triggered my existing proclivity to rebel. Inward rebellion against the Creator is the self's attempt to usurp the place of God as the end of human existence. It exists everywhere; and everywhere there exits enough light to make such rebellion responsible and blameworthy (see Rom 1:19-20; 2:14-15). But only where **the law**—the explicit command of the living God—exists can sin emerge in perceptible and measurable form. **The law** turns transparent sin into visible transgression (4:15; 5:13).

This, however, does not exhaust Paul's meaning here. "The law is not simply a reagent by which the presence of sin may be detected; it is a catalyst which aids and initiates the action of sin" (Barrett 1957, 141). The Law stirs up illicit desire (7:5). This desire is precisely the exaltation of the ego, which is the essence of sin (1:19-23). Our craving for autonomy is an unexpressed desire not only to have the forbidden but also to be god, when God's law says, "Do not covet."

■ **8 But sin, seizing the opportunity afforded by the commandment, produced in me every kind of covetous desire** (v 8*a*). An *aphormē*, **opportunity** (see also v 11), is literally "the starting-point or base of operations for an expedition." But it is used metaphorically in the NT to refer to "the resources needed to carry through an undertaking . . . , *occasion, pretext, opportunity*" (Bauer 1979, 127). Personified Sin slips in, in the guise of the serpent in the garden, to take advantage of existing human desire to experience the unknown, which was not wrong in itself. In Gal 1:14 Paul characterizes his preconversion experience as marked by competitive zeal to surpass his contemporaries in Law observance. Even the pursuit of religious ends can produce perverse results.

Sin deceived me (see Rom 7:11) and **produced** (*kateirgasato*) from something neutral something evil. The root verb *katergazomai*, used throughout ch 7 (vv 8, 13, 15, 17, 18, and 20), refers to the results, achievements, or accomplishments of an activity. Paul's point is not that the commandment forbidding coveting created desire, but that it had this result, nonetheless: perverted desire became selfish and grasping (Dunn 2002a, 38A:380). The serpent's lying claim, "You will not surely die . . . you will be like God" (Gen 3:4-5) resulted in sparking the perverse desire to imitate God in his power, to be independent and autonomous, and the even more perverse desire to be my own god.

Covetous desire translates *epithymian* (see Rom 7:7). Of course, *epithymia* applies to all **desire** and is not necessarily always *covetous* or wrong (see Ps 119:20; Isa 58:2; Phil 1:23; 1 Tim 3:1), but its clear association here with the tenth **commandment** (see Rom 13:10) suggests that its specific reference is to forbidden desires to have what belongs to others (Exod 20:17). It is certainly not limited to sexual desire. Stoic philosophers considered *epithymia* one of the four beastly human passions to be subdued (Jewett 2007, 448).

By Paul's day most Jews considered covetousness the root sin and the sin of Adam and Eve in the garden (see 4 Macc 2:6; 2 Esd/4 *Ezra* 3:20-26; 4:30-31; *Apoc. Mos.* 17:1-2; 19:3; *Apoc. Ab.* 24:10; Jas 1:15). Within Romans, **covetous desire** (Rom 7:8) would apply to the overweening human drive for self-assertion, self-exaltation, and self-rule (see 8:6-7; Isa 14:12-14). It would include the perverse human aspiration to dethrone the Creator and enthrone the creature (see Rom 1:18-25).

For apart from law, sin is dead (7:8*b*). Paul is not referring to a return to an idyllic time before the giving of the Mosaic law, when sin was merely not recognized for what it truly was. He makes clear in 4:15 and 5:13 that there is nothing to be said for such blissful ignorance. In Paul's metaphor here to be **dead** is to be "ineffective, powerless" (Dunn 2002a, 38A:380), "incapable of achieving its object" (Jewett 2007, 450). Apparently, depriving one member of the trinity of Law-Sin-Death off its throne brings an end to the oppressive rule of the others as well (see 1 Cor 15:56).

■ **9** Once I [*egō*] was alive apart from law; but when the commandment came, sin sprang to life [*anezēsen, came to life again*] and I died (Rom 7:9). This is the first time in the letter that the pronoun *egō*, "I," appears (see also vv 10, 14, 17, 20, 24, and 25). The "I" seems to refer typically to universal human experience, including Paul's (see the Behind the Text discussion). This should not be taken to suggest that Paul was nostalgic for blissful, youthful ignorance of the Law. In fact, it is impossible to identify any known moment in Paul's life when the opening statement seems particularly apropos to his experience. But this difficulty has not prevented commentators from speculating.

Paul never idealizes human existence—his own or humanity's—prior to or apart from the Law; humans need to know what causes spiritual death. But he is convinced that Law is no Savior. On the contrary, Law gives Sin the opportunity it wants. Does this lend support to the conventional wisdom that forbidden fruit is always the sweetest? Prohibition provokes the protest, Why not?

Dunn proposes that Paul's **once** refers to the "once upon a time" childhood of the human race, before God's **commandment came,** forbidding the fruit of one tree in the garden (2002a, 38A:382). However, Jewett insists that no ancient Jew presumed a period of idyllic innocence prior to Gen 2:16, when Adam and Eve first received the commandment. Jews considered the Law eternal (Jewett 2007, 451).

Before the **commandment** came, Sin was already there. **Law** only gives **sin** the opportunity it needs. Sin springs **to life** (*anezēsen*, "came to life again") in Gen 3:1-2 with the appearance on the scene of the crafty serpent, misquoting God's commandment (see 2 Cor 11:3). As Paul says in Rom 5:12-21, the resulting sin and death arising from the rebellion of Adam became the experience of all humankind. I died describes the separation from God that befell the original pair in the garden, entailing estrangement, shame, and loneliness (Gen 3:7-10), even before God had spoken a word of judgment. Understood autobiographically, Paul describes his first awareness of Law's ability to determine his relation to God and his fellow humans (Jewett 2007, 451).

■ **10** Paul summarizes the process in Rom 7:10: I [*egō*] found [*eurethē*, *I discovered*] that the very commandment that was intended to bring life [*eis zōēn*] actually brought death. This could be an allusion to the command received by Adam (Gen 2:16-17). It was **to preserve life**—to safeguard humans from the death disobedience would bring (Rom 5:12, 15, 17, 21; 6:23), not to restrict their freedom. If the first pair had obeyed God, they would have enjoyed free access to the tree of life (Gen 3:22). Instead, this **very commandment** (Rom 7:10) brought them death. Paul does not blame God for the commandment's failure, which is discovered in human experience, but not explained.

In Gal 3:21 Paul insists that law was never able "to make alive" (*zōopoiēsai*). Law can only diagnose sin as such; it is incapable of curing the problem. It can point us to the Physician, but Law is not the prescription for the sinister disease. Thus, if the **commandment** here refers to the Mosaic law, Paul challenges the standard Jewish assumption that it could ever achieve the life it promised (based on Lev 18:5 [quoted in Rom 10:5 and Gal 3:12]; Deut 6:24; 30:15-20; Prov 6:23; Sir 17:11; 45:5; Bar 3:9; 2 Esd/4 Ezra 14:30). The illusory ideal state in which Law might promote life did not exist, because of the more powerful influence of Sin. Sin perverts God's law into "the law of sin and death" (Rom 8:2).

■ **11** Other than a change in the Greek word order and a shift from the conjunction *de* (**But**) to *gar* (**For**), 7:8 and 11 begin identically: **Sin** took advantage of the situation created by the **commandment.** Verse 11, however, moves beyond the illicit desire that made Sin attractive (see the comments on v 8) to mention Sin's deception (see Gen 3:13; 2 Cor 11:3; Eph 4:22; 1 Tim 2:14; Heb 3:13) and the result of disobedience—**death** (see Gen 2:17; Rom 5:12). In its autobiographical application, Paul's success at law-keeping, not his failure, led to deadly results.

■ **12** Having said this, Paul immediately absolves the Law of any responsibility for human sin (see 2 Esd/*4 Ezra* 9:36-37). **So then, the law is holy, and the commandment is holy, righteous and good** (Rom 7:12). The Law is **holy** because "it springs from, and partakes of, the holy nature of God" (Wesley 1950, 544; on 7:12). Paul may speak separately of **the law** and **the commandment** to indicate that not only the Law as a whole but also each commandment is **holy.** Or, **the commandment** may refer specifically to the tenth commandment cited in v 7. Or, this may simply reflect Hebrew synonymous parallelism, in which case no distinction between the two terms was intended. The Law is **righteous** because it defines right relationships—among humans and between humans and God (see Deut 4:8). It is **good,** in that it not only flows from the goodness of God but also is perfectly adapted to human need (see Prov 4:2).

■ **13** **Did that which is good, then, become death to me? By no means! But in order that sin might be recognized** [*phanē*, "revealed"] **as sin, it produced death in me through what was good, so that through the commandment sin might become utterly sinful** (Rom 7:13). Paul heightens the paradox of Law as life-promising yet death-dealing with rhetorical flourish. Despite Law's good intentions, through Sin it became an instrument of Death (summarizing vv 8-11; see 6:12-14). What Paul vehemently denies here is the *equation* of Law with Sin and Death (see the comment on **not at all!** in 3:4), despite their nexus. Law did not **become death to me,** *but Sin did* (*alla hē hamartia*).

Graciously, even this served God's purpose: in order that (*hina*) through Law Sin's true character might be exposed (see 3:20; 4:15; and 5:13) as **utterly sinful.** To admit that Law **produced** [from *katergazomai;* see 7:8] **death in me** (v 13) is only to acknowledge what happened, not to explain it. The Law is not responsible for how Sin manipulated it.

Sin shows how **utterly sinful** it is by its ability to pervert even the best of intentions into disastrous results. Even those who succeed through rigorous self-discipline to maintain their resolve not to rebel find themselves victimized by sin's deceit. Although they may comply with God's demand in their own strength (or imagine that they do), their very success at law-keeping proves to be their undoing. Legalistic self-righteousness cannot bring about a right relationship with God. Sin "perverts the finest dimension of religion into a system of dominating others and demonstrating the superior virtue of one's own group, whatever that might be" (Jewett 2007, 460).

FROM THE TEXT

In the Sermon on the Mount Jesus reminded his disciples that he came not "to abolish the Law or the Prophets; . . . but to fulfill them" (Matt 5:17). Precisely what he meant is open to widely varying interpretations. The challenge in preaching the Law, whether in the NT or OT, is how to avoid the pitfall of legalism or moralism.

We live in an age in which opposition to Law is popular even among church folk. Christian freedom is widely seen as irreconcilable with external constraints of any kind. The apostle Paul is often presented as the patron saint of this view. After all, didn't he write that no one is put right with God by obeying the Law (Rom 3:20, 28; 9:30—10:4)? Far from saving us, the Law only makes us conscious of sin or even increases sinning (3:20; 5:13, 20; see also 1 Cor 15:56; Gal 2:16; 3:10, 13; 5:4; Phil 3:2-11).

Romans 7:7-13 begins and ends with rhetorical questions, answered emphatically, **Certainly not!** (v 7) and **By no means!** (v 13). In view of the close relation Paul saw between Law and Sin, the question that introduces vv 7-13 is not surprising: **Is the law sin?** (v 7). What is surprising is the apostle's strong no and his conclusion in v 12 that the Law is **holy, righteous and good.** But is it surprising? In 2:13 Paul insists that it is only "those who obey the law who will be declared righteous." In 8:4 he adds that Christ's redemptive work was intended to enable the Law to be fulfilled in us. Does Paul contradict himself?

In 7:7-13 Paul insists that far from being an ally of Sin, Law is its bitter enemy. Law exposes sin as sin wherever it is. Paul found that he **would not have known what sin was except through the law** (v 7). Law drags sin into the light of day to expose its sinister character—**that sin might be recognized as sin** (v 13). As John Wesley observed in his sermon "The Original, Nature, Property, and Use of the Law," Law tears away sin's disguises and shows it for what it really is (1979, 439).

Paul consistently insists that the Law is not evil; Sin is. The Law, **which is good** (v 13), is not the source of death; Sin is. The Law's problem is its weakness. It was never intended to be the means of salvation (Gal 3:21). On the contrary, the Law is God's instrument of convicting the fallen world of its sinfulness and need of a Savior.

Paul was convinced that the path of Law-observance, even when it seems to succeed, leads in the wrong direction—to self-righteousness. It was not Paul's failure to keep the Law but his (imagined) success that made him unacceptable to God. He had misunderstood the Law's purpose and perverted it. License is clearly not the answer, but neither can legalism rescue me from sin. Sin's perversion of the holy law of God points out how **utterly sinful** sin is (Rom 7:13).

(c) The Futility of the Law (7:14-25)

BEHIND THE TEXT

The preceding passage (vv 7-13) described the encounter with the Law as a quasi-narrative of the past. It contrasted life before or apart from the Law with what happened when the "commandment" arrived on the scene and sin sprang to life in its full power and virulence, bringing spiritual death. Now, changing to the present tense, the "I" describes from experience the consequences of that fatal encounter: the servitude to sin under the Law.

The question concerning the identity of the "I" continues in the second half of ch 7 (vv 14-15). On the one hand, the gripping account of a personal struggle appears to suggest that Paul is speaking out of personal experience. On the other hand, the desperate struggle to fulfill the Law appears to contradict what is undeniably an autobiographical account of the apostle's prior life as a Pharisee found in Phil 3:5-6 ("as for legalistic righteousness, faultless" v 6b). Paul's concern here is not to communicate his own experience under the Law to the Romans but to convey powerfully the *impossibility* of living in loving obedience apart from God's grace in Christ and to apply it to themselves. The "I" remains, therefore, the typical "I" of the preceding section.

Related to this issue is the time reference of Paul's struggle with Sin. Does the continued use of the present tense in such a vivid way, as well as the undeniably "Christian" appeal of Rom 7:25a, argue that Paul is referring to normal, *present* Christian experience? Or, do we have here an "I" looking *back* to a stage of his experience *prior* to his encounter with Christ?

Whatever difficulties arise from the present tense in this section, from a Christian perspective three things must be said: (1) Paul clearly insists that Christians have "died to the law through the body of Christ" to be united with him so that we "might bear fruit for God" (v 4). (2) Furthermore, there is a notable absence in vv 14-25 of any reference to the Spirit, for Paul the determining factor of the Christian life. (3) Finally, the "pre-Christian" reference of vv 14-25 preserves, across 7:14—8:16, the contrast prepared for in 7:5-6 between "life in the flesh" where law is at work (v 5) and service "in the new way of the Spirit" in Christ (v 6). The rhetorical effect of this "new way," the breakthrough into the freedom of the Spirit proclaimed in 8:1-2, is completely lost if 7:14-15 is "present" Christian experience.

To couch the issue only in terms of "before" and "after," however, does not exhaust Paul's purpose, which is to depict the plight of *all* who find themselves confronted with the claims of external law without the aid of God's grace in Christ. The challenge of the Mosaic law is the apostle's point of departure, but the account becomes increasingly general as it proceeds; and so it is capable of universal application. The passage is thus a traditional theme or motif—the conflict between "knowing" what is right and finding the moral capacity to "do" it—and applying this to the description of life "under the law" intended to serve as a negative foil against which to exalt the freedom and capacity brought about by the Spirit of God in Christ (8:1-16).

The passage is highly repetitive, aiming not only at the truth but also at driving it home forcefully by repeated descriptions of the self-contradictory plight of the "I." Paul depicts three situations in which the "I" finds itself in conflict in 7:14-17, 18-20, and 21-23. The first two predicaments are closely parallel:

- Each begins with a sentence with the verb "know" and mentions the "fleshly" constitution of the "I" (vv 14 and 18*a*).
- Each concludes with the same phrase blaming "indwelling sin" (vv 17 and 20*b*).
- Between the two, each states the moral dilemma in almost identical words (vv 15*b*-16*a* and 19-20*a*).

The third statement, in vv 21-23, employs fresh terminology revolving around the Greek word *nomos*. Verses 24-25 offer a climactic conclusion (vv 14-25*a*) and a retrospective summary (v 25*b*).

IN THE TEXT

(i) The Predicament: First Statement (7:14-17)

■ **14** First, the "I" confesses to being totally perplexed by its own behavior. It finds a complete split between what the "I" wills and what the "I" achieves. The only conclusion it can draw is that the "I" has lost control of the moral direction of its life, that another power has taken over—*the sin dwelling in me* (*hē oikousa en emoi hamartia*, vv 17, 20; see v 23). In this sense, Sin is my slave master.

Paul has already insisted that the Law is not sin. On the contrary, it is holy, just, and good. To these endorsements, he adds another: **We know** [*oidamen gar, for we know*] **that the law is spiritual** [*pneumatikos*] (v 14). No surviving literature prior to Romans makes such a claim for Law (Jewett 2007, 460). Nonetheless, Paul assumes that he and his readers agree (**We know;** see 2:2; 3:19) that the Law is divinely inspired, i.e., "Spirit-caused" or "Spirit-given" (Sanday and Headlam, 1929, 181).

By way of contrast, Paul concedes, **But I** [*egō*] **am unspiritual** (*sarkinos, fleshly;* see 7:5). Humans are bodily creatures of "flesh and blood," mere mortals subject to death (see 1 Cor 15:35-49). His point is not to disparage the material nature of humans in contrast to God. Rather, it is that, unaided by the Spirit of God, I am morally impotent to fulfill Law's demands. I am **sold as a slave to sin** (*pepramenos hypo tēn hamartian,* **having been sold under Sin,** Rom 7:14). Left to my own resources, I am held as a helpless captive under Sin's tyranny.

Who is Sin's prisoner? In vv 7-13 it was the Law; but here in vv 14-25 it is I. The emphatic Greek pronoun *egō,* **I,** is explicitly expressed in vv 14, 17, 20, 24, and 25. Other forms of the first person pronoun appear in vv 17, 18, 20, 21, 23, 24, and 25. It must be stressed that I am Sin's captive, not some part of me.

It is true that Paul seems to picture a cloven *egō*, engaged in civil war against itself. On one side of the battle line he identifies in v 22 **my inner being** ("my inmost self" RSV). In vv 23 and 25 the same reality is identified as **my mind**. On the opposing side in v 23 are **the members of my body**; and in v 25, **this body of death** and ***the flesh*** (see vv 18, 5; 8:3, 4, 5, 6, 7, 8, 9, 12, 13).

Nevertheless, there is but one *egō*. I may distinguish my "self" from my body ideally, but not in reality. Paul does not say, "I have flesh," but ***I am flesh.*** To be "flesh" is to be human, to be a creature, a physical part of this material world. To attach the word "sinful" to any translation of the term "flesh" as the NIV does is unwarranted. There is nothing evil about being human or material. The created order is good. It is quite another thing to worship and serve the creature rather than the Creator (see 1:25). To do so is to become Sin's slave.

The Divided State in Rom 7:14-25

What is the nature of the divided state described in Rom 7:14-25? The popular answer is that my higher desire to do right is always defeated by my divided will. My baser desire to do evil inevitably prevails. But the contest is not fair to begin with. I am unable to do what I ought to do because the Law is too hard, impossible to fulfill.

However, what Paul actually says suggests that the problem is a discrepancy between my purpose and my performance, not a battle between my better and worse self. Nor is my problem the inevitability of failure when my noble aspirations encounter Law's impossible demands (despite the tradition of Lutheran-Reformed Protestant interpretation).

Even if we accept that the "I" of Rom 7 refers universally to all humans, we cannot ignore the evidence of Paul's autobiography. Before he became a believer, he did not try to be nice to Christians but accidentally hurt them. On the contrary, his zeal for the Law led him to try to destroy the church—actions that he only later recognized as sin. His misguided attempts at obedience led him away from God and into self-righteousness.

The contrast in vv 15, 18, 19, and 21 is between my good intentions and my poor achievement. I am torn by self-contradiction. My will presents no problem; my problem is my failure to achieve what is right. "I do not understand what I do" (v 15). Pursuing righteousness, I find myself alienated from God. Seeking life, I find death. Persecuting heretics, I find them to be the Israel of God (see 1 Cor 9:1; 15:8; 2 Cor 5:6; Gal 1:12-17; Phil 3:5-8; Acts 9:1-19; 22:4-16; 26:9-18).

■ **15** So, why is it that **I do not understand what** [*ho gar . . . ou ginoskō*] **I do** (7:15; *katergazomai*, "I accomplish"; see the comments on v 8)? There is an incomprehensible disconnect between my intentions and my results. The expres-

216

sion *Ho . . . katergaxzomai,* **what I do,** employs an intensive form of the verb for working, referring to achievements or accomplishments as the ultimate result of purposeful activities. Thus, I am mystified by the unintended consequences of my actions: **For I do not do** [*prassō*] **what I do really want. Instead, I do** [*poiō*] **what I hate.** There is no short-circuit between my brain and my body. There is no contradiction between my reason and my passions. Nor is my body acting spontaneously, as if by involuntary muscle spasms. It is not that I am acting irrationally. No, I am confused and frustrated by how weak I am. What I accomplish is not what I intend.

Within a single Greek sentence, Paul uses three different verbs meaning "do" in English. Commentators differ as to whether we should find subtle distinctions between them or whether he simply introduces some welcome variety—note the six monotonous **dos** in the NIV. We proceed on the assumption that these terms are *not* simply stylistically motivated synonyms.

■ **16** **And if I do** [*poiō*] **what I do not want to do, I agree that the law is good** (v 16; see vv 12-13). How could Paul maintain that **the law is good** and also consider it a divine demand that was impossible to fulfill? Such a law might be holy (v 12), spiritual (v 14), and good (vv 12, 16), but how could it be just (v 12)? Romans 8:4 insists that God has made it possible for the Law to be fulfilled in us who live our lives out of the resources he provides.

■ **17** The answer is that the problem is not the Law; it is Sin. **As it is, it is no longer I myself that do it, but it is sin living in me** (7:17). Paul does not mean to exculpate the "I," as though it is merely the helpless puppet of some external force. The language is metaphorical. Sin has entangled its strong tentacles around me and become such a part of my "I" that I cannot break free. Sin is my slave master, to whom I have been sold and whose dictates I am obliged to obey. In the grip of Sin as an indwelling power, "I" can helplessly struggle to obey the Law, but I find no capacity to achieve what I desire.

(ii) The Predicament: Second Statement (7:18-20)

■ **18** Despite the lack of any explicit mention of Law in vv 18-20, they cover much the same ground as vv 14-17. I can **agree that the law is good** [*kalos*] (v 16), but **I know** full well **that nothing good** [*agathon*] **lives in me** (v 18). Paul apparently intends no subtle difference in meaning between the two Greek words for "good." He can describe the Law's goodness as *agathē* in vv 12-13, and his unfulfilled aspiration to obey it as **the desire to do what is good** (*kalon*) in v 18. The aspirations of the "I" remain noble, despite its frank and disheartening self-appraisal.

His point is that "I" am not good. **That is, there is no good in my flesh** [*sarki*]. The NIV rendering of *sarx* as **my sinful nature** is not a justifiable translation of Paul's word. *Sarx* is *not* our **sinful nature** (as opposed to our new nature) or our "lower nature" (as opposed to our "higher nature"). Flesh is unredeemed *humanity* under the reign or control of the Sin that entered the race with Adam's defection. Sin is the power that now *rules* human existence *apart from Christ*. John Wesley recognized that "the flesh here signifies the whole man as he is by nature" (1950, 545). "The flesh" is who I am unaided by the indwelling Holy Spirit, not something that I have.

The Translation of *Sarx*

Prior to the appearance of NIV in 1973, all standard versions of the English Bible translated the Greek *sarx* literally as "the flesh." The NIV's rendering of the word "our sinful nature" provoked a white paper from a committee of Wesleyan scholars, protesting this rendering as not a translation but a *commentary* on the text. This Reformed interpretation of *sarx* as a component of human nature reflects a Greco-philosophical rather than biblical understanding of human nature. As a small concession, the 1978 NIV simply omitted the possessive pronoun "our," leaving the text to read **the sinful nature,** with "the flesh" as a marginal footnote (in v 18 *"my flesh"*; see 8:4, 5, 8, 9, 12, 13; 13:14).

Sin indeed *resides* in the flesh (7:23-25), but the flesh is not inherently **"sinful."** It is "weak" (as in the Hebrew equivalent *basar*, 8:3), calling for the resident, indwelling power the Spirit to liberate humans from sin's power (vv 8-9). Neutrally, *sarx* is my total human nature "before" or "apart from" Christ's grace and the liberating power of the Spirit, which is the sense of 7:18 translated literally: *I know that nothing good lives in me, that is, in my flesh.* On this text Wesley comments, "The flesh here signifies the whole man as he is by nature" (1950, 545).

In v 18 Paul seems to be answering the question, "How much good dwells within me?" He answers, "Nothing good." That is, we are "totally depraved" apart from the "prevenient" grace of the Spirit, who when reigning within sanctifies us (8:1-17). Translating *sarx* as "the flesh" reflects no Socinian compromise of the gospel, as some critics of "Arminianism" think, since Arminianism presupposes God's grace in every step of our salvation. Rather, the heavily Reformed theology reflected in NIV's rendering distorts the biblical view of human nature. Our sinful condition is not substantival, it is *existential*: our religious-moral predicament as a consequence of the disobedience of the first man, "the plight of the Adamic self" (Keck 2005, 189).

The NIV's rendering of Rom 8 makes it virtually impossible to use it as the basis for a faithful interpretation of the original Greek of this important chapter. We use instead a personal translation of vv 1-17, which follows the classical King James tradition (RSV, NASB, NRSV).

For I have the desire to do what is good, but I cannot carry it out. This second statement of 7:18 repeats the point Paul made earlier. The same Greek verb describes "what I want" (*ho thelō*) in v 15 and my **desire** (*to . . . thelein*) in v 18. Likewise the same verb describes "what I do" (*ho . . . katergazomai*) in v 15 and **I cannot carry it out** [*to . . . katergazesthai . . . ou*] in v 18. *For the will to do good is there* [*parakeitai*; see v 21]*; but the accomplishing of it is not.*

■ **19** *For I do* [*poiō*] *not do the good* [*agathon*] *that I want; instead, I keep achieving* [*prassō*; see v 15] *the bad* [*kakon*] *that I do not want* (v 19). Does this tension between what I want and don't want confirm or challenge the description of "The Divided State in Rom 7:14-25" discussed above? Commentators often assume that Paul here reformulates a *topos*, a traditional motif widespread in ancient literature. An oft-quoted form of this theme is from Ovid, a first-century B.C. Latin poet:

> *My reason this, my passion that, persuades.*
> *I see the right, and approve it too;*
> *I hate the wrong, and yet the wrong pursue.* (*Metamorphosis* 7:19-20)

Epictetus (late first- to early second-century B.C. Greek philosopher) uses words closer to Paul's: "What he wants he does not do, and what he does not want he does" (*Dissertations* 2.26.4). These parallels are generally taken, however, to support the view that the divided state consists in the losing battle between weak reason and overpowering passions. If that is the case, it is certainly a different understanding than reflected elsewhere in these verses. The "I" does not **want** two different things, but only the **good**. The division is between the **good** that is wanted and the **bad** results (see 10:2).

■ **20** *If I do* [*poiō*] *what I do not want, then this is no longer my accomplishment* [*egō katergazomai*]*; rather, it is the accomplishment of the Sin that lives in me* (7:20). The human problem is not that God's expectations are unreasonably high (see vv 16-17). Nor is it base bodily passions that overpower rational decision-making. It is that human beings have been taken captive by the occupying power of Sin (see v 17).

Of course, this is only metaphorical language, and we should not objectify Sin, as if it were literally a person that might be served an eviction notice. But neither should we trivialize Sin as if it were a figment of our imagination. Jewett suggests that Sin

> is used here to refer to a cosmic force that leads people to act in certain ways. A demonic social power . . . that had infected religion . . . , had been internalized by Paul so that it "dwelled" within him and led him to act as he did. The frustration consisted not in the ability to perform the zealous deeds he felt were justified, but in the inability of such deeds . . . to achieve the good. Such zeal, in fact, had led him into conflict with the very God he wanted to serve. (2007, 468)

(iii) The Predicament:Third Statement (7:21-23)

■ **21** This third statement of the predicament of the "I" begins with a summary (*ara*, **So**, "then, consequently"; Bauer 1979, 103) of vv 14-20: **So I find** this law [*ton nomos*] at work: When I want to do good [*kalon*], evil [*kakon*] is right there with me [*parakeitai*] (v 21).

This incongruous discovery (*heuriskō*, I find) is also reminiscent of the one in v 10—"I found [*heurethē*] that the very commandment that was intended to bring life actually brought death." In both instances, this "implies a new insight that had been unavailable to Paul prior to his conversion" (Jewett 2007, 468). Here, however, the *nomos* is not the Mosaic law (as in v 22), but a "principle" (v 21 NASB). **This law,** like the law of gravity, is an impersonal and inviolable observation of how things work. The rare verb *parakeitai* appears in the NT only here and in v 18. Here it describes **evil** as **right there with me;** there, **the desire to do what is good** *is present with me.* The inescapable reality of the divided state could not be starker.

■ **22** In v 22 Paul offers two new ways to characterize the predicament of the conflicted "I." The **inner being** (*ton esō anthrōpon,* **the inner person**) seems to re- fer to what Paul calls my **mind** (*tou noos*) in vv 23 and 25 (see 2 Cor 4:16-18). Thus, in my rational seat of thinking and willing **I delight in God's law** (Rom 7:22). That is, *I joyfully agree with the Law* (Bauer 1979, 789). Or, "I share pleasure in the law of God" (see Pss 19:8; 20:5; 112:1-2; Jewett 2007, 469).

■ **23** The Law's demands are right; I would love to obey it, **but** (Rom 7:23) I must reckon with still other inescapable divisions within my human reality. Paul has already mentioned the unhappy discovery of the "law" that my every desire to do good exists side-by-side with ever-present evil (v 21). Here he clarifies this law as evidence of corollary laws, other competing realities within the "I."

I see another law [principle] **at work in the members of my body** [*melesin;* see 6:13, 19; 7:5] (v 23). The "I" detects a sinister controlling force that resides in "my" every bodily activity and ruins my every good resolve. This other law is the principle **of sin at work within my members.** Its twofold mis- sion is conflict and conquest: **waging war** [*antistrateuomenon*] **against the law of my mind** [*to nomo tou noos mou*] and *taking me captive* [*aichmalōtizonta*]. "Tak- ing captive" originated as a term used to refer to the capture of prisoners of war to be sold into slavery (see v 14). The "I" finds itself in the middle of a war zone: Sin has no intention of relinquishing its power over its hapless victims.

My mind can be a combatant on the side of right only to the extent that it is **a slave to God's law** (v 25). It is equally possible to have a mind set on what the Flesh desires (8:5). Verse 23 of ch 7 lends no support for an explana- tion of the divided state in this chapter as some kind of mind-body dichotomy or a cleft will or an internecine battle between my better and worse self (see the sidebar "The Divided State in Rom 7:14-25" above). This is no civil war in which one part of the "I" battles another. The "I" has been invaded, victimized, ravaged, and left enslaved by an alien power.

For all its sympathy with **God's law** (v 22), the "I" cannot command what happens on the field of action, where the "other law" is in control. Even the best motives of the "I" cannot determine the consequences of its actions because the intransigent enemy Sin pervades and perverts everything.

(iv) Conclusion and Recapitulation (7:24-25)

■ **24** Left to its own resources, the "I" faces a hopeless moral impasse. In despair, the "I" confesses its miserable condition: **What a wretched man I am!** But it also cries out for deliverance: **Who will rescue me . . . ?** (v 24). Throughout Rom 7 the "I" identifies its slave master most often as "Sin" (vv 14, 17, 20, 23). However, it also acknowledges its own complicity with the enemy through the "Flesh" (vv 14, 18, 25) and "myself" (v 17), thus contributing to its own distress. Here the "I" seeks rescue from **this body of death**. This could be taken (mistakenly, we think) to mean that being a mortal body, being a created thing subject to death, is the source of my defeat and despair.

Within the context of Paul's letters, this cannot be understood as reflecting such a Platonic or gnostic body-soul dualism. If it did, the solution to the predicament of the "I" would be physical death. But such a solution would be a totally unexpected concession in a letter that so clearly identifies Death as an enemy combatant intimately allied with Sin (see 5:12, 14, 21; 6:14-16; 7:5, 10, 13; 8:2; see 1 Cor 15:56). Paul does not conceive of bodily death as the welcome shedding of a body-prison, enabling escape from this material world to the realm of pure spirit. This is not Paul's anthropology.

Although Paul uses favorably the metaphor of death to Sin and Law, we should recall that it is clearly just that—imagery. What the "I" needs is not literal, but metaphorical death. "I" can appeal in the abstract for heuristic purposes to the opposition between "my inner being" (Rom 7:22) or "my mind" (v 25) and "my flesh" (margin) or "my body" (v 23). But in reality "I" am one indivisible whole. I am my body, myself. My problem is not my materiality. There is nothing wrong with the body that a new "Lord" cannot fix.

7:23-25

The impotent "I" has the same inadequacy as Law. The Law is not sinful. To be human is not to be sinful by definition. The problem of the "flesh" is the same as that of Law. It is weak (see 8:3) and under the enslaving power of Sin. "Flesh" is not sinful; it is sin's victim. Because I am flesh, I am victimized. I am helpless. I am **wretched** (7:24).

■ **25** I can cry out for deliverance, but I cannot save myself. Is there hope for a wretch like me? Will anyone or anything rescue me from myself, victim of Sin and Death as I am? Paul cannot withhold his emphatic *yes* much longer! So, anticipating the fuller answer he will provide in ch 8, 7:25*a* precedes his summarizing recapitulation (*Ara oun,* **So then**) in v 25*b* of the predicament of the "I" he has stated three times in vv 14-23. Paul's recapitulation describes the unaided human condition as a standoff in a struggle for sovereignty.

The divided state is a struggle between two masters for control of the "I." **I myself in my mind am a slave to God's law, but in the [*flesh*] a slave to the law of sin** (v 25*b*). Arminius called this "the war of laws": the law of God and

221

the law of Sin, diametrically opposed to and at war with one another. Corresponding and subordinate to the law of God is **the law of my mind** (v 23*b*); and to **the law of sin** (v 25; see v 23), the **law at work in the members of my body** (v 23*a*).

Verse 25*a* anticipates the good news of deliverance announced in ch 8. Rescue comes through the expulsion of indwelling sin (v 20) by the indwelling Holy Spirit, who enthrones a more powerful new Lord—Jesus Christ. Almost before he knows it, Paul cries out in gratitude, **Thanks be to God— through Jesus Christ our Lord!** This glorious statement is grammatically an incomplete answer to the question that has been raised, but it is not out of place. Paul merely anticipates the conclusion he will make explicit in ch 8.

"Paul cannot be speaking here of the current condition of believers, following the *simul iustus et peccator* interpretation" (Jewett 2007, 472). Clearly, the conflicted "I," the "wretched" person, in Rom 7 is an awakened sinner, struggling for deliverance from indwelling sin. To apply these verses to the normal Christian believer would be to admit that the grace of Christ is as powerless against sin as the law of Moses!

The Christian is not left to "go it alone" (*autos egō*, v 25) apart from God in a way that reflects badly on Christ. This passage can then become a "test of spirits" in the sense of an invitation to turn away from ourselves and our own efforts back to the Spirit of Christ who alone can create inner healing and the longed-for moral possibility of holiness (Byrne 1996, 230).

Romans 7:14-25 may apply most directly to the experience of enlightened Jews under the Law, but its allusions to Gen 2—3 suggest a more universal application to all sinners. Its threefold description of the human predicament applies primarily to the miserable past from which Christians have been delivered (see Rom 6 and 8).

However, it may apply equally well to the miserable present into which we may fall if we try to live the Christian life in our own strength (**I myself** in 7:25). Anyone who attempts to substitute legalism or self-reliance for moment-by-moment dependence on the grace of Christ will meet with only failure and frustration (Mitton 1953-54). Perhaps "Paul's concern in this scripture is not with a category of people but a problem of persons." It applies to all persons who have not been freed from the power of sin (Purkiser, R. S. Taylor, W. H. Taylor 1977, 293 n. 16), or, who once freed, submit again to its rule (see 6:13).

FROM THE TEXT

Romans 7 does not seem to refer to the frustration of a believer who inadvertently sins upon occasion, but to a life of total failure. In light of chs 6 and

8, one who is "a slave to sin" (7:14), who keeps on doing evil (v 19), in whom sin lives (v 20), who is "wretched" (v 24), hardly sounds like a Christian, at least nothing like the Christian life described in ch 8. This objection also challenges the interpretation of nineteenth-century Holiness movement preachers and writers who understand ch 7 as a description of the justified but unsanctified believer. This "I" hardly seems a fit candidate for entire sanctification.

Does ch 7 refer to one's preconversion or postconversion experience? The past tense of vv 7-13 clearly seems to refer to preconversion experience, but what of the present tense of vv 14-25? Does this describe Paul's personal experience at the time he was writing? Is this the normal Christian experience? Those interpreters who consider the life in the Spirit described in ch 8 as the normal Christian experience have been labeled "optimistic"; those who consider the life of unending struggle in ch 7 the normal Christian experience "pessimistic."

Optimistic interpreters understand these verses as a dramatic presentation of the story of every person under the Law. This is the diary of the enlightened sinner, who knows what God demands but finds it impossible to achieve the desired results. This is the view of early Greek-speaking church fathers, including the early Augustine; and of Arminius, Wesley, and Adam Clarke; and of many modern NT scholars, including some from the Lutheran and Reformed traditions.

Pessimistic interpreters include the fathers of the early Latin-speaking church; the medieval church including Aquinas; the Reformers including Luther; and most Calvinists. They regard the experience of being at once justified and sinful the normal Christian experience.

In a papal encyclical written for the third centenary of Francis de Sales, Pius XI quotes the early Augustine, arguing that Christians may be made perfect in love in this life, "God does not command the impossible, but in giving the command [of Matt 5:48] He admonishes us to accomplish what we can according to our strength, and to ask aid in accomplishing whatever exceeds our strength" (Peters 1956, 198-99). The position in this commentary is in the tradition of Origen (ca. 185-254) and of most of the early Greek fathers. It was the understanding of Augustine, *before* his historic debate with Pelagius on original sin.

After that debate, Augustine retracted his earlier view, arguing that Rom 7:14-25 was Paul's testimony *at the time* he wrote Romans. The only human exceptions to this dilemma Augustine allowed were Jesus and his mother Mary. This "pessimistic" view was that of most Latin fathers after Augustine, who believed the passage to be speaking primarily to *Christians.* Luther and Calvin took the same position, as do most Reformed interpreters. On this view the Christian is forever consigned to the dilemma of vv 14-25, always struggling with but never being delivered from indwelling sin. This is the prevailing view of "popular" Evangelicalism.

Dutch Reformed theologian James Arminius (1560-1609) returned to the earlier Greek view, devoting the major part of Volume 2 of his three-volume *Writings* to Rom 7, to a point-by-point argument that follows Paul's diagnosis of our sinful condition, preparatory to his treatment of the gospel's great promise of liberation from sin in ch 8. John Wesley's understanding of chs 7 and 8 derives from the redemptive promise of Christ and Adam in 5:12-21. For him, the depth of the tragedy of the fall must be attached with the heights of grace. The "optimism of grace" flows from the faith relationship with "Christ, the Victor over sin and death." Wesley understood the cry of the "wretched man" of 7:25 to be that of "the man . . . now utterly weary of the bondage, and upon the brink of liberty," the deliverance from Sin promised in ch 8 (see Wesley 1950, 537-54, for his comments on chs 5—8).

(3) Sanctification Through Christ (8:1-39)

Romans "begins and ends like a letter (1:1-15; 15:14—16:27) but its core reads like a discourse" (Keck 2005, 20). To read the Epistle thoughtfully is to be impressed from the outset that the apostle is "going somewhere" in this discourse. Paul weaves together many diverse themes as he unfolds the end-time salvation that has entered history through Christ. God's purpose and plan points steadily forward toward the return of Christ, when God will complete the final redemption, not only of humanity, but also of creation itself corrupted and frustrated by human sin.

We have now come to the heart of Romans, where justification unfolds into sanctification (8:1-17), issuing in glorification (vv 18-39). This brings the reader to the conclusion of the first major section of the letter. In laying out his soteriology, the apostle has introduced two key words: "righteousness" (or "justification") and "holiness" (or "sanctification"). As we have noted, "righteousness" is a *relational* word (3:21—4:25) with *moral* implications (6:1-23). "Holiness" is also a relational word. God invites believers to participate in his holiness. As they do, he enables them to enjoy loving fellowship between themselves and God. This, in turn, issues in neighborly love actualized through Christ and empowered by the Spirit. Holiness of heart and life consists of "pure love to God and man" (Wesley 1979, 6:509). Holy love is a consequence of the incarnate Son's total identification with fallen humanity, actualized in us as we *participate* in Christ.

Romans 7 highlights the hopeless dilemma humanity faces under Law, whether the Mosaic law or enlightened conscience (2:14-15). We know what we ought to do and even want to do it, but we are driven to despair by the realization that we remain incapable on our own of achieving the good ends we seek.

From the depths of fleshly frustration, ch 8 lifts us to the heights of spiritual fulfillment. Here, Paul explores, first, the present prospects of God's *sanctifying* grace in Christ by his Spirit (vv 1-17); and, second, the future hope of glorification (vv 18-30). The chapter closes with the conclusion of Paul's argument in chs 5—8, and in fact of 1:18—8:39 (vv 31-39), affirming his confidence that nothing we may experience is capable of separating us from God's tenacious love. This conclusion anticipates the next major section of the letter, chs 9—11, which takes on the challenge to Paul's claims about God's keeping power presented by the unbelief of Israel.

The first section of Rom 8 (vv 1-17) offers an exposition of sanctification as the fulfillment of the Law in the lives of believers through the power of the Spirit. This fulfillment is made possible because the Spirit frees believers from their enslavement to Sin and the Flesh (vv 1-8). The indwelling Spirit provides divine life (vv 9-11) and enables believers to follow his guidance and so live as adopted children of God (vv 12-17). To prepare the way for the next stage in his reasoning, Paul reminds his audience that with Christ as the model child, believers must expect to suffer on their path to glory (v 17).

In the second section (vv 18-30), Paul discusses the Spirit's role in assisting believers to survive the frustrations of the present age of suffering and death. Anticipation of the coming age of redemption involves the entire created order. The Spirit even enables us to pray consistent with the purposes of God for us (vv 18-27), specifically that God will conform us to the likeness of his Son (vv 28-30).

(a) Fulfillment of the Law Through the Spirit (8:1-17)

(i) The Liberating Spirit (8:1-8)

BEHIND THE TEXT

Romans 8:1-17 is the climax of a section that began at 5:12, as well as the conclusion of Paul's argument up to this point. It also looks ahead through open windows to the widest horizon on the letter, the promised redemption of the entire creation. The key word in vv 1-17 is "Spirit," found 15 times in this first unit of ch 8.

In ch 7, Paul has argued that Sin as an occupying power in our humanity (flesh) is more decisive than our willingness to obey (vv 12, 17, 20, 23). So dire is the situation that Paul can characterize the human self as Sin's **slave** (v 14), as a prisoner of war needing rescue from captivity (v 24).

In ch 8, the liberation from Sin "through Jesus Christ our Lord" (7:25) is proclaimed, first, by declaring it to be God's work through Christ, then, by identifying the role of the Spirit as God's power indwelling the self, enabling it to *walk* [= live] *not according to the flesh, but according to the Spirit* (8:4).

The contrast between the two mind-sets, the *mind-set* (phronēma, "disposition") of the flesh and of the Spirit, which pervades these verses, is to be understood, as in ch 7, as the tension between two competing *powers*, not two parts of the same self. Paul is not talking about the conflict between two "natures" in the human self. The human problem is that as flesh we are contested territory in the conflict between two powers vying for sovereignty over us. The contest is actually Sin vs. Spirit. However, Sin disguises itself in the attractive guise of its willing host—the Flesh—which is nothing more than humanity serving merely human ends. Deceived by the illusion of self-sovereignty, Flesh has become the host for its malignant slave master, Sin.

Sin's lying claim over the human race (flesh) had prevailed from Adam until the coming of Christ. Christ challenged and defeated Sin on its own turf—in the human sphere—as a true human of flesh and blood. The victory accomplished in his death and resurrection defeated the powers of the old age and made available the Spirit as the power of the new age, already present in Christ. The potential victory in behalf of the entire human race is experienced on a personal level as justified believers pass through baptismal waters from death to life. Freed from the old slavery to Sin, they must decide what they will do with their newfound freedom. Will they submit once again to the old slave master Sin, or will they surrender to the Lord of the new age, who died and rose again to make possible their freedom (6:1-19)?

To read the Flesh-Spirit contrast in ch 8 in terms of Greek body-soul dualism is to misunderstand the apostle completely. Paul is not setting at odds earthly vs. divine elements in the human self. Nor is this the rivalry of material vs. spiritual realities. On the contrary, the contest is between two dispositional "mind-sets" the same self may exercise toward the competing sovereigns, Flesh (acting as a proxy for Sin) and Spirit. The mind-set of the Flesh leads to death; and the mind-set of the Spirit leads to life and peace. So inveterate is the disposition of the Flesh, preoccupied as it is with its merely human interests, that it is "hostile to God," indeed incapable of pleasing God (vv 7-8).

IN THE TEXT

■ **1** The declaration, **Therefore [ara], there is now [nyn] no condemnation for those who are in Christ Jesus** (v 1), is negative in formulation, but its content is positive, expressing the gospel in the idiom of the courtroom (as in v 34). The inferential particle *ara,* **Consequently,** picks up the argument interrupted after 7:6 (see 5:18; 7:3, 25; 8:12; 9:16, 18; 14:12, 19) by Paul's discourse on the inability of Law to sanctify (7:7-25). The adverb *nyn,* **now,** marks the contrast between the old era of Law, Sin, and Death (vv 22-24; 8:2) and the era of Spirit, Freedom, and Life (7:6; 8:2).

Thanks to what God has done in Christ, the old age of **condemnation** is over. The once-guilty have been acquitted and spared from "the wrath of God"

(1:18—2:4). The acquitted are **those who are in Christ Jesus** (8:1; see 1 Pet 5:14)—those "united with" him (REB). Here, the language of participation (see 2 Cor 5:21) is linked with the forensic language of acquittal. God declares guilty sinners "in the right," that is, "justified," because by faith they share in the destiny of Christ (Rom 3:21-25), rather than the destiny of Adam (5:12-21).

Paul's language is relational. Only **those who are in Christ Jesus** have **no condemnation** (8:1). That is, only those who by faith participate in the new humanity his saving death created know this freedom. See the commentary on 5:12-21 for a comprehensive treatment of the corporate solidarity of believers and their Lord in this new relationship.

Paul considers his declaration of freedom from condemnation so important that **no condemnation** (8:1) begins his Greek sentence: *Not, consequently, now* [*is*] *condemnation to those in Christ Jesus* (a woodenly literal translation). The clarifying clause added in the KJV, "who walk not after the flesh, but after the Spirit," is absent in the early manuscripts of v 1. It was apparently inserted by a scribe, concerned that **no condemnation** might be separated from life **according to the Spirit** (v 4). Later scribes included it in the medieval texts that were the basis for the KJV. The scribe's concern was well-taken, since in popular post-Reformation Protestantism forensic justification was frequently mistakenly divorced from incorporation into Christ and transformation into his likeness. Verses 1-2 remind us that there is no such thing as mere justification, as Wesley insisted.

Condemnation is the opposite of justification (see 5:16, 18). To be condemned is to be pronounced guilty before the judgment bar of God (see 8:33, 34). It is to be doomed to death. **Therefore** reminds Paul's readers of the gospel-fact that, as a consequence of justification, God has declared Christians not guilty and given them the gift of life.

Freedom from **condemnation** is not release from feelings of doom or despair. So long as we remain in a right relationship with Christ, we are not condemned, regardless of our emotions (see 1 John 3:18-24) or distressing experiences (see Rom 8:31-39). The freedom the Spirit gives is not emotional release from the burden of guilt for past sins or guaranteed future comfort. Conscientious, committed Christians often experience feelings of guilt and suffering. Paul's concern is not with *feelings* but with *facts*. His language is legal, not psychological.

We may know the reality of release from the guilt of Sin **now**—in the present. We need not anxiously await the Last Judgment. Freedom may be ours already! Because of what God has done for us in Christ, Christians are already free from the powers of Sin and Death. We are no longer hopeless slaves to Sin and doomed to suffer its wages. When believers grasp these facts, the feeling of freedom is usually not far behind.

■ **2** Paul explains (*gar*) **no condemnation** in vv 2 and 3 as freedom from sin and empowerment to obey. *For [gar] the law [nomos] of the Spirit of life in Christ Jesus has freed you from the law [nomos] of Sin and Death. For [gar] God has done what the Law [nomos] could not do, because it was weakened by the flesh [sarx]: by sending his own Son in the likeness [homoioma] of sinful flesh [sarx], and for sin [peri hamartias], he condemned sin in the flesh* (vv 2-3).

Paul uses the word **law** three times in vv 2 and 3. In v 3 the powerless **law** clearly refers to the Mosaic law. In v 2, however, **the law of sin and death** expand "the law of sin at work within my members," mentioned in 7:23. That is, **law** here seems to describe an operative principle, not the Torah (see Jewett 2007, 480-81, for a contrary view).

It is true that Paul closely aligns Law and Sin and Death (5:12-14, 20; 7:5, 9-11, 13, 23-24). Nevertheless, Christian freedom is not release from Law as such, but only from the oppressive powers Sin and Death, which have made Law their reluctant vassal (see 5:12, 14, 21; 6:10, 13, 16, 23; 7:9-13; and the commentary on 7:21-23).

It is impossible to take **law** here as a reference to the Torah, if this implies that freedom from the Law implicitly authorizes antinomianism. This would render meaningless Paul's concern for obedience in ch 6 and for the fulfillment of the Law in 8:4 (see also 1:5; 2:13; 3:31; 9:31-32; 13:8-10).

The **law of the Spirit of life** (8:2) might be taken as a reference to the law of Moses, freed from being Sin's agent (as in 7:23-25). The obvious parallelism with **the law of sin and death,** however, suggests that **the law of the Spirit of life** similarly refers to a working principle, in this case the Holy **Spirit.** Thus, the freedom is from Sin and Death for Spirit and Life.

Admittedly, the parallelism is not exact: Paul refers to **the law of the Spirit of life** and of **sin and death** (emphasis added). Nonetheless, "the law of the Spirit," says Käsemann, "is nothing other than the Spirit himself in his ruling function in the sphere of Christ" (1980, 215). Because of his role in creation (see Gen 1:2; 2:7) and the resurrection of Christ (Rom 1:2; 8:11), he is called **the Spirit of life** (see vv 6, 10, 11, and 13; 2 Cor 3:6). The Spirit brings the freedom God sent Christ to bring into the hopeless situation described in Rom 7:14-25. He is the source of the new quality of life Christians may enjoy now and the basis for hope for resurrection life in the future (see 5:5, 10, 17, 18, 21; 6:4).

God does not condemn Christians; instead through Christ Jesus [see 6:23] *the life-giving Spirit has freed you from Sin and Death* (8:1-2 paraphrased). Paul describes human redemption using the imagery of slavery: *The Spirit . . . has freed [ēleutherōsen] you* from your former slavery to Sin and Death. See the commentary on 6:18 for a discussion of the metaphor of freedom.

In 6:16-23 Paul describes the life of sanctification (vv 19, 22) as possible only to those who, having been set free from Sin and the prospect of Death, offer themselves without reservation to God. Here, we learn that the Spirit is the divine agent of this sanctification for those who **live . . . according to the Spirit** (8:4).

Freedom from Sin is the necessary preparation for lives of obedience to God here and now (6:16-18; 7:4-6; 8:5-14). Christians still face the possibility of suffering and the certain prospect of physical death as they await with the rest of creation the future "glorious freedom [*eleutherian*] of the children of God" (v 21; see vv 18-21). However, the power of Death is incapable of separating believers from God's love (vv 35-39).

The reality of **no condemnation** (v 1) and Spirit-empowered freedom from Sin (v 2) are both experienced **in** [*en*] (v 1)/**through** [*en*] (v 2) **Christ Jesus. Those who are in Christ** are what we would call *Christians* today, a term never found in Paul's letters. Salvation is certainly **through Christ** (v 2)—the saving death of Christ is never far from the apostle's mind—but the expression here seems designed to point us back to the language of participation that dominates 5:12-21. We are reminded of the two humanities—"in Adam" and "in Christ." Because existence "in Christ" is shaped by the new humanity— Christ and ourselves in him—no longer are we defined by our old, sin-dominated existence "in Adam."

Different MSS of 8:2 have two other pronouns in the place of the singular "you" (NRSV). A few omit the pronoun entirely. The reading *hēmas* (us) is almost certainly "a secondary modification, introduced in order to make the apostle's statement apply to all Christians (as in ver. 4)." But "it is much more difficult to choose between *me* [me] and *se* [you]" (Metzger 1994, 456). The "easier" reading—**me**—may be an assimilation to the sustained use of the first person singular pronoun ("I") throughout 7:7-25. Most interpreters accept the "more difficult" reading, supported by early texts from different parts of the church, as probably original. Paul's singular *you* was perhaps used for rhetorical effect to address *each* hearer of the letter.

■ **3** Liberating humans to do the will of God requires breaking Sin's power over them. Paul begins 8:3 by explaining how (*gar*, **For**) this was accomplished: God has done this through Christ. The rest is detail; but the detail is theologically rich: ***God has done what the Law could not do, because it was powerless to assist humans to obey it. He did this by sending his own Son as a weak human being like us to save us from Sin by destroying Sin's stronghold in humanity*** (v 3 paraphrased).

In v 3 the Greek sentence begins emphatically with its direct object— *"what was impossible [To . . . adynaton] for the law"* (Bauer 1979, 19). The *nomos* here is the Torah, the Mosaic law. Paul challenges the "characteristic

Jewish view that the law provided the necessary resources for the daily walk of the people of God" (Dunn 2002a, 38A:419). Then he explains why (*en hō*, *because;* Bauer 1979, 261 s.v. *en* III.6.d) Law was impotent to free captive humanity (v 2).

Paul's claim that Law *was weakened by the flesh* succinctly rehearses the thrust of ch 7. The Law was in no position to liberate, because like humanity, it, too, was powerless and enslaved to Sin and Death (see 8:2; the comments on 7:5; and the sidebar associated with 7:18-20 on "The Translation of *Sarx*"). The subject of the sentence is **God** (8:3); but it lacks an explicit verb. Most translations and commentators agree that the omission implies that **God did** what the Law could not.

Paul offers considerable grist for later theological and christological refinements in his description of what God did to achieve the impossible, but before Paul explains *what* God did, he explains *how* he did it: **By sending his own Son** (see Matt 15:24; Mark 9:37; John 3:16-17; Gal 4:4; 1 John 4:9). Paul expresses the uniformly held early Christian conviction that the new age of salvation came through what God the Father accomplished in Jesus Christ **his own Son** (Rom 8:3). Paul's concern here is not to explain Christ's preexistence and incarnation or inter-Trinitarian relationships. As a monotheist, Paul certainly did not think in terms of two gods acting in concert (see 3:29-30). The Christ event is the activity of the one God of Israel.

God's Son was sent *in the likeness* [*homoiōmati*; see 1:23; 5:14; 6:5] *of sinful flesh* (8:3; see Gal 4:4). For Paul to have said *the likeness of . . . flesh* would have implied what became known as the heresy of Docetism; Christ would then be without real humanity. To have said "the flesh of sin" would imply Ebionism; Christ would then have been a sinner. Paul presumes that Christ assumed our humanity but not our sinfulness. His use of the term **likeness** in 6:5 and Phil 2:7 implies no illusion. The preexistent Son's solidarity with our human condition came as a result of God sending him to become one of us, actually assuming our **flesh.**

Although the word "incarnation" is not biblical, the concept certainly is. The word comes from the same Latin term as our English word "carnal," which means "fleshly." Christ came as a human being of flesh and blood. The word **likeness** does not suggest that his humanity is merely in appearance or only a clever disguise. His humanity is as real as ours. Unlike us, however, Jesus did not sin (Gal 2:17; 2 Cor 5:21). Instead, he met sin head-on, on its own turf, on its own terms, and defeated it. He is the victor over Sin, not its victim! But his victory is God's victory. Thus, the creed affirms: He *is* very God and very man (Phil 2:7; Col 1:22).

What did God do in the Christ event? *He condemned* [*katekrinen*] *sin in the flesh* (Rom 8:3). The Greek verb translated **condemned** is from the same cognate family as the noun **condemnation** in v 1. Thus, the reference is not to a denunciation of sin as evil but to a destruction of its enslaving and death-dealing power.

Rather than condemning powerless human beings, God condemned sin! He pronounced Sin's doom. So far as Christians are concerned, Sin is dead—stripped of its power, dethroned from its tyrannical rule over us, and destroyed as a controlling influence in our lives. Paul makes a similar point in 2 Cor 5:21: "God made him who had no sin to be sin for us, so that in him we might become the righteousness of God." "The death that Christ died on the cross 'in the flesh' sentenced to impotence the sin that reigned in human flesh, which could touch him only in the flesh that he had in common with all human beings" (Fitzmyer 1993, 487).

Paul's central point is not that Christ became human or that he lived a sinless life. When he says God sent his own Son *peri hamartias,* the phrase can be translated "for sin" (RSV) or "to deal with sin" (NRSV, REB) or paraphrased **as a sin offering** (NIV, NASB, HCSB, NCV). In the LXX *peri hamartias* translates the Hebrew expression "as a sin offering" (see Lev 5:6-7, 11; 16:3, 5, 9; Num 6:16; 7:16; 2 Chr 29:23-24; Ezek 42:13; and 43:19; 1 Cor 15:3; Heb 13:11; and 1 John 2:2; see Rom 3:25 and 5:9). Paul's emphasis here is on *how God used* the Christ event to condemn sin in the flesh, where it resided and reigned. Christ fully participated "in the realm of sinful flesh in order to replace it with a new lifestyle based on the Spirit" (Jewett 2007, 484).

■ **4** Romans 8:4 explains the *purpose* (*hina,* **in order that**) of God's destruction of sin in the flesh through Christ's death and resurrection: **in order that the *just requirement* [*dikaioma*] *of the Law might be fulfilled in us, who walk not according to the flesh but according to the Spirit.** The meaning of *dikaioma* is pivotal. If Paul had used the plural *dikaiomata,* **requirements,** as in 2:26 (and as the NIV inexplicably translates it here), it would have suggested that the specific commandments of the Law are fulfilled by Christ. The singular, however, refers to what the Law, in its totality and unity, rightly requires of human beings: conformity to the will and character of God—that which God's law *as such* is about.

More importantly, Paul does not claim that we "do" the *dikaioma,* but that it is *fulfilled* (*plērothē*). The passive voice makes it clear that *we* are not the agents who fulfill the Law's requirement. This seems, instead, to be a theological passive meaning that it is **God** who actualizes the Law's requirement *in us,* by the power of his indwelling Spirit. He *enables* us to **walk** [*peripatousin*] **according to the Spirit** (v 4).

The Greek verb *peripatousin* here (as in 6:4; see the commentary) employs the typical Jewish imagery of walking as a metaphor for the way we conduct our lives morally. In the Talmud, rabbinic discussions of legal matters relat-

231

ed to appropriate and inappropriate behaviors and lifestyle fall under the heading of Halakhah (Hebrew: "walk"). God enables us to live in such dependence on the Holy Spirit that we may actually obey God and live morally as he expects. Consequently, *the just requirement of the Law* may *be fulfilled in us.*

We must not forget the community context of the Law's fulfillment: *among us.* If love fulfills the Law, this can never be achieved as isolated individuals. Paul speaks of the relational fulfillment of the Law in Gal 5:14 as loving our neighbor, and in Rom 13:8 as loving one another. Love focuses on meeting the needs of others rather than being preoccupied with oneself (= *the Flesh*). Mutual love is the perfect expression of righteousness (see Matt 5:17, 43-48; Rom 5:5; Gal 5:6). "In being filled with the Spirit," Peter Stuhlmacher observes,

> the promise of Ezek. 36:26ff. is realized for those who believe, so that they are capable of returning the love of God bestowed upon them. . . . In this active love, supported by the Spirit, Christians complete the state of grace into which they were transferred through Christ. (1994, 80)

That Christ is both our sanctification and our righteousness (see 1 Cor 1:30) should not encourage passive inactivity on the part of believers. God's fulfilling of the Law's requirement in us is not about magic but about lived morality. God acts cooperatively through us, not unilaterally in spite of us. Paul clearly presumes that Spirit-empowered believers will live lives marked by obedience, righteousness, and all-inclusive love; but such are possible because of divine enabling, not because of human ability, and certainly not by individuals acting alone.

If it is possible for God to fulfill the Law in us, is this inevitable? What determines whether we obey God or disobey him? Paul explains the basis for the difference in terms of the two contrasting ways in which we may live our lives: *according to* [*kata*] *the Flesh* vs. *according to* [*kata*] *the Spirit* (Rom 8:4). The traditional translation of the preposition *kata* as **according to** assumes that its object (**Flesh** or **Spirit**) refers to the norm or standard in accordance to which we conform our conduct. "The realms of flesh and Spirit create two distinct mind-sets and modes of behavior" (Jewett 2007, 486).

An Explanation of Prepositions

It is difficult to define the precise meaning of the grammatical classification of words designated "prepositions." These little words introduce noun phrases (thus, preposition) that usually provide additional information about the action of the verb the phrase modifies. That is, most prepositional phrases function adverbially. They function to clarify the relationship between their noun objects (the words that follow them in the phrase) and the rest of the sentence. This relationship may be spatial (place), temporal (time), logical (reason, purpose), etc.

Perhaps some illustrations will help. In the sentence, "He put the book <u>on</u> the table," the prepositional phrase clarifies the place where he put it. In "He put the book <u>under</u> the table," the phrase still clarifies the place, but the location is different. In "He drove <u>in</u> haste because he had to meet the pastor <u>at</u> 10 A.M.," the second prepositional phrase specifies the time when the meeting occurred, but what is the function of the first phrase? The phrase "in haste" as a whole functions as a synonym for the adverb "quickly." The phrase "to meet," which at first glance might seem to be a prepositional phrase, is actually an infinitive of purpose.

In the sentence, "He went <u>to</u> church <u>for</u> a meeting," the first prepositional phrase identifies the place he traveled; and the second, the reason why he did so. Inspection of an English dictionary will demonstrate the complexity of the little word "for." Its meaning varies considerably, depending on its context. It does not mean the same thing in the sentences "He went to the store <u>for</u> bread" and "He went to the store <u>for</u> his wife" as it does in the previous example. To complicate matters further, consider the sentence: "He went to the restaurant, <u>for</u> he was hungry," where "for" does not function as a preposition, but as a conjunction. Small wonder many find grammar challenging!

Prepositions are notoriously difficult to translate from one language to another, in part because they identify a range of potential functional relationships between words rather than communicating a precise, singular meaning. For that reason, "definitions" of prepositions in dictionaries and lexicons are often much longer entries than those for nouns that designate a thing or a concept or for verbs that describe an action or state of being. In my dictionary, e.g., the definition of "for" is seven times as long as that of "sanctification." For all the apparent insignificance of prepositions, understanding the relationships they specify is crucial to responsible interpretation.

But *kata* has a considerably broader range of plausible meanings here. It may refer to metaphorical space—thus, to living in the realm of the merely human as opposed to living in the realm of the divine presence and power. This would be comparable to Paul's account of the two humanities in 5:12-21 who live either "in Adam" or "in Christ." *Kata* may refer to the direction toward which we orient our lives. It may describe the goal or purpose for which we live—in order to please the Flesh or to please the Spirit. It may explain the reason why we live as we do—because of the powerful influence of either Flesh or Spirit. It may give its objects adverbial force—living carnally vs. spiritually.

It seems unlikely that Paul self-consciously contemplated all of the nuances of these possible meanings of the preposition as he wrote. However, we would do well to keep them in mind, if we are to appreciate the force of the little word *kata*, which has no exact equivalent in English.

Paul continues the contrast between these two antithetical ways of living described in 8:4. The conjunction *gar, For,* introduces his elaboration in vv 5-

233

11. Paul nuances what he says in v 4 a bit differently in v 5: Here the contrast is between *those who exist* [*ontes*] *by dependence on* [*kata*] *the Flesh* vs. *those who exist by dependence on* [*kata*] *the Spirit.*

Despite the translation—**Those who live . . .** , Paul's point in v 5 seems to be less about the way we conduct our lives than about the orienting focus of our lives, our identity. Jewett notes that "the mind-sets of flesh and Spirit are radically and unalterably opposed because they derive from different starting points" (2007, 487). Paul's is in a sense an "ontological" statement, since the Greek participle *ontes* is the source of the English "ontology." Ontology is the study of what actually exists, what is real and true, as opposed to what is merely perceived to be true (which is the focus of epistemology).

Paul presumes that "being" is the basis for "doing," that our character shapes our conduct. However, this is not an ontological classification, if this is taken to suggest that "Paul envisaged two classes of humankind, created differently and forever locked into a particular character and destiny." This is "not so much a given condition as an attitude and orientation" (Dunn 2002a, 38A:425). People depend on *the Flesh* to the extent that their lives are determined by their merely human appetites and illusions. People depend on **the Spirit** when their existence is determined by heavenly appetites and realities.

The antithesis between *Flesh* and **Spirit,** which dominates this section of the letter, is presumed throughout Romans and Pauline theology (see 1:3-4; 2:28-29; 7:5-6; 1 Cor 5:5; 6:16-17; Gal 3:3; 4:29; 5:16-24; 6:8; Phil 3:3; Col 2:5; 1 Tim 3:16).

> What is in view here are two alternative and opposed drives which come to expression in the ethical character of everyday decisions and relationships. . . . For Paul, the opposition is that between two epochs . . . ; the appropriate ethical walk is the consequence of the Son's mission (8:3), and the enabling factor (the Spirit) has the character of eschatological newness. Paul sees the old epoch as characterized by an inability to live in accordance with God's will. (8:3; Dunn 2002a, 38A:424)

In the new epoch, however, the liberating experience of God's love (Rom 5:5) and guidance (8:14) empowers Spirit-filled believers to love and obey God as the Law requires.

■ **5** Those who depend on human resources alone (*the Flesh*) as the basis for their lives *set their minds* [*phronousin*] *on the things of the flesh,* while the Spirit-filled *set their minds on the things of the Spirit* (v 5). This verb *phronousin* is from the same cognate family as the noun *phronema* in vv 6, 7, and 27. Greek nouns ending in the suffix *-ma* indicate the result of the verb's action—here, the result of thinking. Our **mind-set** denotes our disposition, attitude, aim, orientation, or aspiration (Bauer 1979, 866).

■ **6** *The mind-set of the Flesh* (vv 6-7) is that of the autonomous self, the life of the "I" living for itself and out of its own resources. Paul has already demonstrated in ch 7 that to live in this way is "death" to the essential self, separation from God, and the personal disintegration and corruption that inevitably follow (see 5:12-21; 6:21, 23; 8:2).

The mind-set of the Spirit, on the other hand, aspires to please God. Those who live in this way are committed to seek the things "above, where Christ is seated at the right hand of God, . . . [a] life now hidden with Christ in God" (Col 3:1, 3). This is a life that draws its sustenance, direction, and satisfaction from God in Christ.

To set the mind on the Spirit is life and peace (Rom 8:6), God's *shalom,* "which transcends all understanding" (Phil 4:7). Peace emphasizes "the social, relational quality of mind of the Spirit" (Jewett 2007, 487), in contrast to individualistic notions of life in the Spirit, whether conceived along moralistic or charismatic lines.

This is the life of "standing grace" Paul describes in 5:1-11 (see the comments there) as the logical follow-through of justification by faith: peace/reconciliation with God and a new quality of life now and hope for resurrection life in the future (see 1:17; 2:7, 10; 6:1-13, 22-23). The life of sanctification, the end of which is eternal life, pursues the path of peace with all, both inside and outside the Christian community (6:22; see 14:17, 19; 15:13; Heb 12:14).

■ **7-8** In Rom 8:7-8 Paul offers three reasons why [*dioti,* **because**] **the mind-set of the Flesh** brings death. It **is hostile** [*echthra,* **enmity**] **toward God. It does not submit to the Law of God, indeed it cannot. Those who are in the Flesh cannot please God.** Confidence in **the Flesh** is contrary to true worship of God (Phil 3:3-6). Cranfield comments:

> Fallen man's fierce hostility to God is the response of his egotism (which is the essence of his fallenness) to God's claim to his allegiance. Determined to assert himself, to assert his independence, to be the centre of his own life, to be his own god, he cannot help but hate the real God whose very existence gives the lie to his self-assertion. (1975, 1:386-87)

Dunn adds that, as in Rom 1:18-32, "the mind-set of the flesh is the same refusal to acknowledge human creatureliness and dependence on God; to make self-satisfaction the highest priority is to reject the self-giving God" (2002a, 38A:426). Jewett notes that self-centered preoccupation with *the Flesh*

> corrupts all good intentions and relationships, bringing conflict, despair, and death. The mind of the Spirit, on the other hand, confirms God's love for the undeserving (Rom 5:5) and halts the quest for [human] honor that produces enmity with God (Rom 1:18—3:20; 5:10). . . . There is no middle ground here, no possibility of successfully combining these contrary orientations. (2007, 487)

To be **hostile** toward God is to make ourselves his enemies (see 5:10; see Jas 4:4). Although this may not express itself in overt hatred, it is the spirit of rebellion that refuses to **submit** [*hypotassetai*] **to** God's law (see Rom 10:3). Such a denial of God's right to reign is not merely an act of disobedience or insubordination but also practical atheism. While maintaining this pro-Flesh stance, people **cannot** submit to God and **cannot please** him (see 1 Cor 7:32-34; 1 Thess 4:1).

Paul does not presume that some people are innately incapable of obedience; on the contrary, their choice of life-orientation and mind-set reinforce their self-imposed status as intractable rebels. Only the revelation of the wrath and righteousness of God in the gospel has the potential to shake the confidence of those who refuse to honor God as God and give him thanks (Rom 1:18-21).

FROM THE TEXT

The source of the Christian's release from condemnation might be called (anachronistically) a Trinitarian conspiracy of human salvation. Of course, it was centuries before the ecumenical creeds articulated a fully nuanced doctrine of the Trinity. However, this passage and others certainly made the extended debates that led to the orthodox consensus a necessity. **God** the Father took the initiative **by sending his own Son** (8:3), **Christ Jesus,** as the Mediator (note **in** and **through** in vv 1 and 2), and by giving the Holy **Spirit** (v 2; see 2:29; 5:5; and 7:6).

The modalist heresy imagined that the one God merely assumed different roles as he fulfilled his various job descriptions—e.g., as if the Father legislates, the Son justifies, and the Holy Spirit sanctifies. Orthodox faith insists that salvation in all its facets is the work of God—Father, Son, and Holy Spirit. The same God who judges justifies; the God who condemns sin also sanctifies.

The church fathers of the patristic era said of Jesus: "He became what we are, that we might become what he is" (variously credited to Irenaeus, Athanasius, and Gregory of Nazianzus). The eternal Son entered into our *fallen* humanity for the sake of our salvation, so that we might "become partakers of the divine nature" (2 Pet 1:4 RSV). He assumed our *fallen* humanity without being contaminated by it. Christ did begin with the standing of unfallen Adam, but started from where we do, subject to all the evil pressures we inherit and using the altogether unpromising and unsuitable material of our corrupt nature to work out a perfect, sinless obedience (Cranfield 1979, 1:383 n. 2). The assumption of our fallen humanity is the sine qua non of our redemption, because "he could heal only what he assumed" (Gregory of Nazianzus). By his *Spirit-empowered* obedience to "Abba, Father," Jesus potentially sancti-

236

fied our human existence (see 2 Cor 5:14-15). He became a man of *flesh* that we might become men and women of the *Spirit!*

Our flesh is naturally "sinful flesh," not because it is sinful per se, but because it is tyrannized by Sin consequential to Adam's disobedience. Christ was "made in human likeness. . . . found in appearance as a man" (Phil 2:7-8). He is completely human—sin only excepted, but his existence, from the moment of his conception by the Spirit to the instant of his death, was a life in the Spirit. And "through the Spirit of holiness [he] was declared with power to be the Son of God by his resurrection from the dead" (Rom 1:4). He sanctified every stage of our existence from the womb to the tomb. He became Flesh that we might receive the Spirit! Raised by the power of the Spirit and exalted to the right hand of God, he has poured out his Spirit on believers that we might also share his resurrection glory (8:11; 2 Cor 1:22; Eph 1:13-14).

Christ's flesh in the Spirit was *holy* flesh. He was mistaken as a sinner (John 9:16) because humans "look at the outward appearance" (1 Sam 16:7). The early church applied Isaiah's prophecy to him, "He . . . was numbered with the transgressors" (Isa 53:12). Yet in his inner self Jesus was totally under the Spirit's control (see Heb 9:14).

Christ offered up his life "for sin" (Rom 8:3). By becoming "obedient to death—even death on a cross!" (Phil 2:8), he destroyed sin in the flesh (Rom 8:4). He deposed Sin from its usurped autocratic power. By his life of perfect obedience, and his victorious death and resurrection, he broke the tyranny Sin exercised over enslaved humanity. He destroyed Sin's claim and power for all who are in him, making humanity's earthly condition the scene of Sin's defeat.

Holiness, then, is our Christian heritage (1 Cor 1:30-31). Christ died and rose again, not only to make possible our pardon and acceptance with holy God, but also to pronounce the doom of Sin and Death, making possible our restoration in the image of God (2 Cor 3:18). The sanctification Christ procured is reproduced in us by the Spirit of God as we yield ourselves to him. The entire work of Christ in our behalf had as its grand aim the making of us holy—*in order that the just requirement of the law might be fulfilled in us* (Rom 8:4). Christ fulfilled the Law *for* us that it might be fulfilled *in* us. The love that moved him to obey the Father and give himself for others now empowers us, for that same love that fulfills the Law (13:8-10).

Walking according to the Spirit (8:4) is basically a matter of our *being* in the Spirit (v 5). If we are *of the Flesh* we have the mind-set, the orientation, and aspirations of *the Flesh,* those of people "without the Spirit" (1 Cor 2:14). If we are *of the Spirit,* we have the mind-set, etc., of the Spirit (see 1 Cor 2:15-16). The orientation of our lives determines our lifestyle and our final destiny, whether death or life.

It is imperative to understand that by *Flesh* Paul means the *entire human person* under the power of Sin, the mind and spirit as well as the body. John Wesley recognized that the "works of the flesh" (Gal 5:19-21)

> are wrought principally, if not entirely, in the mind, and yet they are called "works of the flesh." Hence it is clear, the apostle does not by "the flesh" mean the body, or sensual appetites and inclinations only, but the corruption of human nature, as it spreads through all the powers of the soul, as well as all the members of the body. (Wesley 1950, 697; on Gal 5:21)

To live *according to the Flesh* is not necessarily to pursue a life of sensual indulgence. It may be merely living for oneself alone. This may be expressed in making the "stomach" one's god (Phil 3:19), in inappropriately loving "the present age" (2 Tim 4:10; see Rom 12:2; 1 John 2:15-17), or in setting one's mind "on earthly things" (Col 3:2).

Simply because believers enjoy the gift of the Spirit does not guarantee that they will live **according to the Spirit.** The life of holiness requires believers to be crucified with Christ, to die to themselves (Gal 2:20) and to the world (6:14). Every rival to the unhindered reign of God in human life must be completely removed. Insofar as believers continue to live *according to the Flesh,* they rely on their own efforts, futilely endeavoring to do God's will out of inadequate human resources (see Rom 7).

Such "confidence in the flesh" is clearly misguided (Phil 3:2-3). The "wretched . . . I" of Rom 7:25 describes all who, by relying on themselves, find it impossible to please God. Left to myself (*autos egō*), I "can will what is right, but I cannot [accomplish] it" (7:18 RSV). Rebellion against God ceases when one is justified by faith. However, self-reliant believers continue to live *according to the Flesh,* suffering under "the delusion of self-sovereignty" (Millard C. Reed). Paul's last word on *the Flesh* summarizes the warning of Jeremiah: "Cursed is the one who trusts in man, who depends on flesh for his strength" (Jer 17:5). Hebrew parallelism demonstrates that Flesh refers to unaided humanity focused on itself.

We cannot say too emphatically that life **according to the Spirit** (Rom 8:4) is possible to **those who are in Christ Jesus** (v 1). The incarnate Son has introduced and modeled that life. By his death and resurrection, he accomplished liberation from **the law of sin and death** (v 2) for all, making possible life **according to the Spirit.** Only those who pursue the mind-set of the Spirit, who live to please God and love others, know what it means to be holy.

(ii) The Life-Giving Spirit (8:9-11)

BEHIND THE TEXT

This passage elaborates on the new possibility of holiness opened by God's sending his Son. "Flesh" and "Spirit" do not denote separate, competing elements of our human makeup (as in the Greek "body-soul" dualism), but instead two possibilities of human existence. The one is turned in on itself, preoccupied with human concerns, self-centered, and hostile to God. The other is oriented outward, toward loving God and others.

The same Spirit of God/Christ, who liberates believers from their slavery to Sin, empowers them to live the life of sanctification and assures its end, eternal life (6:22). Our present life in the Spirit is the basis for our future hope of the resurrection from the dead.

As Paul makes clear, living *according to the flesh*—with its fatal consequences—is still possible for believers. This is the crucial difference from the situation portrayed in 7:14-25, where it is portrayed negatively. Under the rule of Sin, exacerbated by Law, it was impossible *not* to sin. Under the new era of grace it is possible *not* to sin. *The believer has the freedom in Christ to say no to sin and yes to God—or vice versa.*

There remains, then, a tension in Christian life, and choices must constantly be made. However, it is not the fatal tension of the old Adamic era, tearing the "I" apart (v 24) with every noble intention doomed to failure; it is a constructive tension of the Christian era, opening the way to growth and life, which is sanctification.

While living *in the flesh* remains a possibility, it is not the normal life of believers. Turning to the direct second person plural address in 8:9 (see the singular in v 2), Paul reminds the Romans that they live "in the Spirit," in the sense that the *indwelling power of the Spirit* enables them to live lives of "righteousness." In 7:14-25 the root problem with efforts to achieve self-sanctification by the Law had been the *indwelling power of Sin*. In 8:1-17 the hope for full and final redemption is the Spirit of God indwelling us (vv 20-21).

What makes all the difference in the new situation is that the indwelling *Spirit* now displaces indwelling *Sin*. Three times in ch 7 (vv 17, 20, 23) Paul refers to the indwelling (*enoikein*) of Sin. This is matched in ch 8 by three references to the indwelling (*oikei en*) Spirit (vv 9, 11a; *enoikountos* in 11b).

The indwelling Spirit is the power of new life in Christ. God has made good his promise to write the Law upon the hearts of his people (Jer 31:33) and through the Spirit to grant the capacity to obey his Law (Ezek 36:26-27; see Rom 2:29; 7:6). The Christian community can live "according to the Spirit" (8:4) or "in the Spirit" (v 9 NRSV), because the Spirit lives "in" his holy church, making it the temple of God (see Heb 9:12; 10:19), the point of encounter between God and humanity.

One remarkable feature of this passage is the variety of ways in which Paul refers to the indwelling power of the Spirit: He is "the Spirit of God" (Rom 8:9b), "the Spirit of Christ" (v 9c), "the Spirit of him who raised Jesus from the dead" (v 11a), "Christ . . . in you" (v 10a). These describe the same reality.

The virtual identification of the experience of the Spirit with the indwelling Christ (for all its risk of hopelessly confusing the members of the Holy Trinity) is of utmost theological importance. It saves Christians from falling into a nonmoral, half-magical conception of the supernatural in human experience, bringing spiritual experience to the test of the historic revelation of God in Christ (Dodd 1932, 124).

The logic of this passage moves from the reality of the power of the indwelling Spirit to its consequences with respect to salvation (vv 9b-11). Those who do *not* "have" the Spirit of Christ (v 9b)—that is, who are not *indwelt* by the Spirit of Christ—do not "belong to Christ." Here the paraphrase of the NLT captures Paul's meaning precisely: Such people "are not Christians at all." They will have no share in the full provisions of the Christ event up to and including the resurrection (see 6:5, 8). If, on the contrary, Christ really does dwell within them, both full and final salvation is the assured hope of Christians.

IN THE TEXT

■ **9** In 8:9*a*, addressing living "saints" in Rome (see 1:6-7), Paul writes, **You** [emphatic *hymeis de*] **are not in the Flesh, but in the Spirit, if in fact** [*eiper*] **the Spirit of God dwells** [*oikei*] **in** [*en*] **you.** Spirit-indwelt believers, who are **not in the Flesh** (*sarx*) in the sense of 7:5 continue to live as human beings in physical bodies (*sōma*, 8:13). The contrast between Flesh and Spirit now becomes direct address, personalizing the more general description of vv 5-8.

What is the force of the preposition "in" (*en*) in the expressions **in the Flesh** and **in the Spirit**? (See the sidebar "An Explanation of Prepositions" with the commentary on v 4 above.) It cannot merely refer to two different metaphorical places. Christians do not cease to be physical beings or leave this planet when they are justified. They do not literally reside in heaven; nor are they in a perpetually inspired or ecstatic state.

Paul continues to think of antithetical mind-sets, motivations, characteristic behavior patterns, and life orientations—each determined by whether one belongs to the old age or to God (Dunn 2002a, 38A:427). Paul's understanding of the two ages and two humanities begun in 5:12 (see the commentary on 5:12-21) suggests that to be **in the Flesh** is to remain in the old age shaped by Adam's sin; whereas to be **in the Spirit** is to participate fully in the blessings of the new age inaugurated by Christ. (See the comments on 7:5 and the sidebar associated with 7:18-21 on "The Translation of *Sarx*" for Paul's use of Flesh.)

Sarx and Sōma

For Christians, Flesh is dead and deposed (8:2-11), excluded from participation in the kingdom of God (I Cor 15:50). However, the *sōma* [= body], transformed through deliverance from the dominion of the Flesh and disciplined through the indwelling Spirit, is the vehicle of the risen life. Paul uses the word *sōma* to refer to human beings themselves. He reserves *sarx* to refer to the sinister Power that lays claim to him and determines him. (Bultmann 1970, 1:201)

If Paul assumes that his hearers are already Spirit-filled, *eiper* here must have the force of "since" (Rom 8:12 NJB; see 3:30; 2 Thess 1:6), indicating "a *fulfilled* condition" (Cranfield 1975, 1:388). "If, as is also possible, *eiper* is taken as leaving open the question whether the condition is fulfilled (see esp. 1 Cor. 8:5 and 15:15), then the statement becomes more of a warning or threat" (Byrne 1996, 245). As such, this may be implicit encouragement to become Spirit-filled.

Paul certainly assumed that the Spirit was present within (*en*, **among**) the Christian community collectively (see 1 Cor 3:16). However, the shift from the second person plural personal pronoun (*hymeis*, **you all**) in Rom 8:9*a* to indefinite (*tis*, **anyone**) and demonstrative (*houtos*, **this one,** he) singular pronouns in v 9*b* suggests that Paul allows that some individuals within the church may not be thoroughly Christian. Perhaps the ambiguity of the condition (*eiper*, **if**) recognizes that not all in his audience are in the same place in their personal spiritual journey. Regardless, he reminds all that the indwelling Spirit may now exert the same controlling influence in the lives of Christians that Sin formerly did.

This is the first time in the letter that Paul uses the designation **Spirit of God** (v 9*a*; see v 14; 15:19; 1 Cor 2:11, 12, 14; 3:16; 6:11; 7:40; 12:3; 2 Cor 3:3; Eph 4:30; Phil 3:3; 1 Thess 4:8). And there is no reason to think that he has in mind a different reality when he refers simply to the "Spirit," as he has up to this point, or to **the Spirit of Christ** (Rom 8:9*b*), as he will in short order, or to the "Holy Spirit" (1:4; 5:5; 9:1; 14:17; 15:13, 16; see 1 Cor 6:19; 12:3; 2 Cor 13:14; Eph 1:13; 3:5; 4:30; 1 Thess 1:5, 6; 4:8; 2 Tim 1:14; Titus 3:5).

The language of indwelling (whether *oikeō en*, "dwells in," as in v 9*a*, or *enoikeō*, "indwells," as in v 11) denotes "a settled relation rather than the more transitory state of possession" (Dunn 2002a, 38A:428) characteristic of Israel's judges or prophets. By way of contrast, indwelling refers to a permanent, penetrative influence, possession by a power superior to oneself (Sanday and Headlam 1929, 196). "If the indwelling of the Spirit is spoken of here as that of sin in 7:17ff.," Käsemann comments, "in both cases radical possession is indicated which also affects our willing according to v. 5" (1980, 223).

Of course, this is metaphorical language. In one sense, we must insist that the Spirit does not literally inhabit the bodies of believers or the church as a body. We should certainly not think of Spirit possession as if it were comparable to popular notions of demon possession, and not only because such notions

8:9

241

are informed more by the popular media than by biblical revelation. In another sense, however, since the Spirit is omnipresent, there is no place or no one he does not occupy. So the real question is: In what sense does the Spirit indwell fully surrendered believers in a way that he does not indwell all people?

Later Jewish rabbis note that the one "who dwells in a house is the master of the house, not just a passing guest. . . . [Thus,] Paul perhaps chooses the verb [*oiken*] here to mark off the lordship which should characterize the Christian from the lordship of sin" (Dunn 2002a, 38A:428). Spirit-filled Christians are not zombies, incapable of thinking or acting on their own, but because Jesus is their Lord, they allow his Spirit to lead them (8:14). Perhaps the imagery of dwelling also echoes OT promises that in the new age God would dwell in/among his people (see Ezek 37:27; Zech 2:11; 2 Cor 6:14—7:1). In this case, indwelling refers to the empowering, sanctifying presence of God with his holy people. God is not merely present to the Spirit-filled. They are distinguished by their obedience to the Spirit, energized collectively and individually by his presence to serve one another in love.

Immediately, Paul adds, ***And if someone does not have*** [*echei*] ***the Spirit of Christ, that person is not his*** (Rom 8:9*b*). This statement amounts to saying that all Christians "have the Spirit" *in greater or lesser degree* (Sanday and Head-lam 1929, 196). One "who does not have the Spirit (whose life bears no evidence of the Spirit's sanctifying work)," says Cranfield, "is no Christian, however much he may claim to be one" (1975, 1:388).

Like Spirit-indwelling, having the Spirit "is from the language of possession. . . . Implicit is the understanding of the Spirit as a power which, working from within, manifests itself perceptibly (in word and deed) and determines the whole life of the one so possessed" (Dunn 2002a, 38A:429).

Paul's point here is not to distinguish believers who are *fully* indwelt by the Spirit—who are "filled with the Spirit" (Eph 5:18; see 3:14-21) from those who merely *"have* the Spirit" (Rom 8:9*b* emphasis added)—or who have been "given" the Holy Spirit (5:5) or "received the Spirit" (8:15). The verbs ("indwell," "fill," "have," "given," and "received") seem to be used interchangeably. Thus, there seems to be no exegetical justification for speaking of differing degrees of Spirit-indwelling. The proximity of Paul's two statements suggests that they are mutually explanatory; that is, to be indwelt by the Spirit is to have the Spirit.

Myron Augsburger helpfully suggests:

The Spirit-filled life, or Spirit-possessed life, is not one in which we have a certain amount of the Spirit, but rather one in which He possesses all of us. The Spirit-filled life is one in which the Spirit expresses Himself in us as a controlling and overflowing force. The condition is one of yieldedness on our part. We are filled with the Spirit as we are emptied of self. (1961, 39-40)

If the ecumenical Christian creeds have correctly identified the Holy Spirit as a person, there is no reason to imagine that he is dispensed piecemeal, as if there are varying degrees of Spirit-indwelling. We may not have more or less of the Spirit. We either have the Spirit or we do not. Since the language of Spirit-indwelling and Spirit-infilling is metaphorical, we must ask what reality stands behind the imagery. The underlying issue seems to be that Christians receive the Holy Spirit so that he can be the Lord of their lives. The presence of God among and within the Christian community is sanctifying, empowering, and personal.

Paul claims that the Spirit who comes through faith in Christ is **the Spirit of Christ** (v 9*b*). Therefore, the indwelling **Spirit of God** (v 9*a*) is **Christ . . . in you** (v 10). Paul here (vv 9-11) treats **the Spirit, the Spirit of God, the Spirit of Christ**, **Christ . . . in you**, and **the Spirit of him who raised Jesus from the dead** (v 11) as *experientially* synonymous. These expressions are, in effect, only different ways of describing the same experience of the one God from different points of view. In v 11 Paul clearly distinguishes God the Father, Jesus Christ, and the Spirit. However, his virtual identification of the *experience* of the Spirit with that of the indwelling **Christ** here is of utmost importance.

Paul is not speaking here of spirit possession in the sense the Corinthians seemed to understand it in their zeal for spirits (1 Cor 14:12)—as "the experience and phenomena of possession" by some anonymous and mysterious supernatural power. For Paul, however, "it was important to be able to distinguish the *pneuma theou* [Spirit of God] from other *pneumata* [spirits]" (Dunn 2002a, 38A:429).

Judaism's struggle to establish criteria for making such distinctions is evident in the accusations by Jesus' opponents that his exorcisms were performed by the power of evil spirits, whereas Jesus insisted they were by the Holy Spirit (see, e.g., Matt 12:22-32). Early Christians made Jesus the criterion of Spirit possession (Acts 16:7; Gal 4:6; Phil 1:19; 1 Pet 1:11) and Christlike love the distinguishing evidence of the Spirit's indwelling (see 1 Cor 13).

Paul's essential point in Rom 8:9 is *not* that every Christian has/is indwelt by the Spirit. It is that "only those whose lives demonstrate by character and conduct that the Spirit is directing them can claim to be under Christ's lordship" (Dunn 2002a, 38A:429). If you **have the Spirit of Christ** (v 9*b*), **Christ is in you** (v 10), and, therefore, you *are his*, i.e., you **belong to Christ** (v 9*b*). Spirit possession is about belonging to Christ (see 1 Cor 3:23; 15:23; Gal 5:24). It is not about ecstatic/mystical experiences but about being servants of the Lord.

■ **10** But if [*ei*] **Christ is in you, your body is dead because of sin** [*dia hamartian*], **yet your spirit is alive** [*zōē*, "life"] **because of righteousness** [*dia*

243

dikaiosynēn] (Rom 8:10). Like the *eiper* of v 9, the *ei* of v 10 might be translated as either "since" or "if." One's translation depends on whether or not Paul considered his hearers to be fully Christian. Clearly, Paul assumes that Christ indwells believers (2 Cor 13:5; Gal 2:20; Col 1:27); although he writes more often of believers being "in Christ" (Rom 8:1).

Given the language of mutual indwelling, **Christ** living **in you** should not be misunderstood as a personality invasion any more than the Spirit's indwelling is. This is the language of participation in the new age and the new humanity, as in 5:12-21. "In Christ . . . everything old has passed away; . . . everything has become new . . . so that in him we might become the righteousness of God" (2 Cor 5:17, 21 NRSV).

To the extent that the crucified and risen Christ actually is your Lord— morally transforming your character and governing your conduct, the invisible Christ continues to be visible and active in *your* life. *He* lives in you as you live no longer for yourself but for him (see Rom 14:7-9; 2 Cor 5:14-21).

The conviction Paul articulated earlier in Gal 2:20 seems to be in the back of his mind as he continues. If so, he writes, **your body is dead because of sin** (Rom 8:10; see 7:24), precisely because Christians have been baptized into Christ's death and so are dead to sin (6:1-11); and, **your spirit is alive because of righteousness** (8:10), because through Christ's resurrection we, too, may live a new kind of life (6:4; Jewett 2007, 491).

Dunn (2002a, 38A:431), however, takes Paul's reference to the dead body here as a literal reminder of human mortality due to Adam's sin. Full redemption awaits the second coming and the final resurrection. The rule of physical death will not be finally ended until then (1 Cor 15:26). He also understands "the spirit" (*to . . . pneuma*) to refer to the Holy Spirit, who is the source of our present life as believers. Twice in Rom 8:1-11, Paul notes that the Holy Spirit is the life-giving Spirit (vv 2 and 11).

This interpretation is possible. Greek manuscripts did not distinguish between lowercase and uppercase letters, and the personal pronoun **your** is only one plausible interpretation of the Greek article (*to* = *the*) here (Dunn 2002a, 38A:431). But this interpretation "does not do justice either to the introductory 'but if Christ is in you . . . ,' or to the theme of new life which dominates Rom. 8" (Jewett 2007, 491).

Rather than **because of righteousness,** the Vulgate translates the Greek prepositional phrase "because of justification" (*propter justificationem;* see the REB: "because you have been justified"). Either rendering is acceptable (see 5:21). Paul insists in ch 6 that Christians are obligated to offer their lives to "righteousness leading to holiness" (v 19; see vv 15-19). Here, he spells out this truth in terms of the ministry of the **Spirit.** Chapter 6 presents the *conditions* to be met for a life of righteousness/holiness; ch 8, the ministry of the Spirit as the divine agency for creating "righteousness leading to holiness" (6:19). Verse 22 similarly associates freedom from sin with sanctification and its end, eternal life.

■ **11** Here also, Paul proceeds to the eschatological significance of the Spirit's ministry: *If the Spirit of the one who raised Jesus from the dead dwells in you, the one who raised Christ from the dead will also give life [zōopoiēsei] to your mortal bodies through [dia] his Spirit who indwells you* (8:11). Abraham believed that God was able to overcome the "deadness" of his reproductive possibilities (see *zōopoiountos*, "gives life," in 4:17). Christians similarly "believe in him who raised Jesus our Lord from the dead . . . for our justification" (vv 24-25).

Through our participation in Christ, what was true for him will be true for us. Our faith not only looks *back* to the raising of Jesus from the dead but also looks *forward* to the raising of our **mortal bodies** (Keck 2005, 204). Paul's resurrection hope indicates his expectation that believers will die before the second coming of Christ and the resurrection (see differently 1 Cor 15:51; 1 Thess 4:15-17). Significantly, "salvation will be completed not by escape from the body but by redemption of the body (v 23)" (Dunn 2002a, 38A:444-45).

Paul places his confidence in the future resurrection of believers entirely on their present experience of the indwelling Spirit of God, *who raised Jesus/Christ from the dead.* Quite obviously Paul treats as synonymous the Spirit *dwells in you* (*oikei en hymin*; see also 8:9 and the comments there) with the Spirit *indwells you* (*tou enoikountos autou pneumatos en hymin*). It also appears that Paul is willing to identify the Spirit with God, who raises the dead (Acts 3:15; 4:10; 13:30; Rom 4:24; 6:4; 10:9; Gal 1:1; Eph 1:20; Col 2:12; 1 Thess 1:10; 1 Pet 1:21).

God vindicated Jesus' personal righteousness—he was "obedient to death" (Phil 2:8; see Rom 5:19)—by raising him from the dead. His resurrection was, then, the outward sign of his "justification" (4:25) by God. Believers, however, have no such "righteousness" (v 24); it is as sinners that we are grasped by God's grace. However, "in Christ" (8:1) the indwelling Spirit fulfills in us the faith-acquired righteousness necessary for our final salvation.

Paul is confident that the God who was faithful to Jesus will raise our **mortal bodies** (v 11) **because of righteousness** (v 10), created by faith and preserved in us by **his Spirit, who lives** in us (v 11). God, who has intervened at such great cost to create righteousness (vv 3-4), will complete the salvation he has begun through the resurrection (v 11; see 5:1-11)!

FROM THE TEXT

Believers are set free from indwelling sin (7:19-20) so as to become a fit "dwelling in which God [may live] by his Spirit" (Eph 2:22; see 3:16-19). The indwelling of Christ for which Paul prays is "so deep and great as to constitute a new arrival, and remain where He so arrives not as a Guest, precariously detained, but as a Master resident in His proper home" (Moule n.d., 128).

Even with the Spirit of God permanently residing and reigning in believers, our "mortal bodies" remain. The Flesh is destroyed, but the body is assured a glorious future, organically one with the living presence of the Spirit of God (Rom 8:11). The body, once defiled, is now the habitation of the Spirit, the very temple of the Triune God. The same Spirit who unites us now to Christ will "be somehow the Efficient Cause of 'the redemption of our body'" (Moule n.d., 215; quoting v 23).

(iii) Led by the Spirit (8:12-17)

BEHIND THE TEXT

In stark contrast to the dark background of captivity to Sin and Death under Law in 7:7-25, Paul has celebrated the liberty and life the Spirit brings to believers in 8:1-8 and 9-11. He now offers a note of friendly admonition, before continuing the "flesh" vs. "Spirit" antithesis. He brings the entire moral and eternal consequence of these two ways of living to a close, offering his hearers in v 13 the stark choice between "death and life," echoing Deut 30:15-16, and promising **you will live,** echoing Hab 2:4 and the theme of the letter: "The righteous will live by faith" (Rom 1:17; see comments there).

Paul frames his implicit exhortation in the indicative mood as a statement of fact—**we have an obligation** (8:12). His hearers' indebtedness to the Spirit for the life and liberty he has made possible calls for a response. What they should do is **put to death the misdeeds of the body** (v 13). Paul's reminder in vv 14-17 is that Christians are children of God because they have **received the Spirit of *adoption*** (v 15; see Gal 4:6-7).

IN THE TEXT

■ **12** The introductory *ara oun,* **So then,** as frequently in Paul (see Rom 5:18; 7:3, 25; 9:16, 18; 14:12, 19), signals an important conclusion based on what he has just said (8:12). He addresses his hearers as brothers and sisters for the fourth time in the letter to reinforce his friendship with these as-yet-largely-unknown fellow believers (see 1:13; 7:1, 4; 10:1; 11:25; 12:1; 15:14; 16:17). He drops the direct second person plural ("you") address sustained throughout 8:9-11, to assume again the first person plural ("we"), used frequently in 1:5—7:14, but not since. However, in 8:13-15*a*, he briefly resumes the second person plural. Paul reminds his hearers of their shared obligation: **We are debtors.** As those redeemed by Christ at great cost and indwelt by God's Spirit, we owe our lives to God.

Although there are no imperative verbs in ch 8, the cohortative functions as an implicit exhortation. Paul includes himself in his indirect appeal for appropriately living out the life in the Spirit. That encouragement is required demonstrates that the possibilities of grace outlined in vv 1-11 are not automatic.

Paul first reminds his readers that we owe nothing *to the flesh* [*sarka*]*, to live according to the flesh.* To offer anything to the Flesh would only return us to our former slavery and death from which the Spirit set us free (on *the flesh,* see 6:12-14, the comments on 7:5, and the sidebar "The Translation of *Sarx*" with the commentary on vv 18-20; on *according to the flesh,* see the comments on 8:4 and the sidebar "An Explanation of Prepositions").

■ **13** Returning briefly (vv 13-15*a*) to the second person plural ("you") to address his hearers directly, Paul explains first why they owe nothing to the Flesh: *For* [*gar*] *if you live according to the flesh, you will die.* Paul uses the verb *mellete* (lit. "you are about to") with the infinitive *apothnēskein* ("to die") as a paraphrase of the simple future. This variation brings home the certainty of the consequences: *you are destined to die* (see Bauer 1979, 501; s.v. *mellō* 1.b). If you allow Flesh to dominate your lives again—death—here, of course, eternal death—will be the certain result.

Paul explains negatively that we owe nothing to the Flesh, but he never states positively to whom we are indebted. However, the implications are clear enough. We owe our Christian lives to the Father who justified us at the incalculable cost of his Son's life, and who gave us his Spirit that we might be set free from Sin to live lives of freedom (vv 1-11). Paul explains the consequences of acknowledging our obligation by refusing to pay any homage to our old slave master. In doing so, he comes close to equating the Flesh with the **body.**

He writes: *But if by the Spirit* [*ei de pneumati*] *you put to death the deeds of the body* [*tas praxeis tou sōmatos*]*, you will live* [eternally] (v 13). Paul probably casts the exhortation in the negative rather than the positive to make it more forceful. The instrumental dative of *pneumati* suggests that the Spirit brings "about for those 'in Christ' the fulfillment of 'the righteous requirement of the law' (8:4)" (Byrne 1996, 246). This does not eliminate the need to cooperate with the Spirit in putting **to death the misdeeds of the body** (v 13) with its impulses.

Paul knew the challenges presented by the necessity of ongoing life in this present age, despite our participation in the age to come. He wrote the Corinthians, "I beat my body and make it my slave so that after I have preached to others, I myself will not be disqualified for the prize" (1 Cor

9:27). All saints are "spiritual athletes" who are crowned only after successfully contending (see Heb 12:1-3, 14-17).

Despite Paul's negative formulation, his purpose is positive. He wants us to understand that we should live **by the Spirit** (Rom 8:13). This obligation expresses itself in a life of disciplined obedience. The Spirit empowers us to refuse to allow Sin to rule our desires (6:12), so that we need not offer the parts of our body as instruments/weapons of unrighteousness (v 13). This is what Paul means by putting **to death the deeds** [*praxeis*; see *prassō* in 7:15 and 19] **of the body** (8:13). Paul's allusions to ch 6 suggest that his positive intention is that we should offer ourselves in obedience to God as instruments/weapons of righteousness for sanctification (6:13, 19).

First, Paul implies that holiness is expected of all believers: **We are debtors** (8:12). Christian holiness is not just the special interest of the few who accept "the counsels of perfection"—spiritual ascetics. It is the sacred and binding debt owed by *all* the children of God to separate from sin and be holy to God. As Christians, we owe a debt we are able to pay, but only *in the Spirit*. Once we were morally bankrupt, totally resourceless. Now we still owe God— and with the Spirit's assistance, we are sufficient. We are able to fulfill our moral obligations, because the one who demands also immeasurably gives. Christ is our life; his Spirit dwells within us; we have "the riches of grace" from which to draw.

Second, holiness calls for Christian discipline in the power of the Spirit. *If you live according to the flesh,* Paul warns, *you will die, but if by the Spirit you put to death the deeds of the body, you will live* (v 13). Death is the inevitable result of either self-gratification or self-reliance—gratifying the flesh (6:23) or trying to live by fleshly resources (7:7-25). Even though we are *not in the Flesh but in the Spirit* (8:9a), we are still in the body (*sōma*).

By the term "body" Paul means the physical organism, of course; but he means more. Indeed, *sōma* ("body") "is the nearest equivalent to our word 'personality'"—"the whole person" we are (Robinson 1952, 28). We can exercise bodily self-control in the power of the Spirit (Gal 5:22-23).

The *deeds of the body* we must put to death involve psychological and physical impulses—tendencies of the psyche (to rationalize, overcompensate, etc.) and the instinctual desires and drives of our common humanity. Since such impulses reside beneath the level of consciousness, they may be considered morally neutral. However, they may lead to sin, thus, they must be controlled and subjugated by the power of the Spirit. If we *repress* or deny their existence, we only deceive ourselves, but if by the Spirit we acknowledge and surrender them to God, he will give us victory over them. The inward stirring of such subconscious impulses are very real forms of temptation but need not lead to sin (Sangster 1954, 235-36).

■ **14-15** In Rom 8:15 Paul warns against the danger of falling back (*palin*, **again**) into legalism (ch 7) through the excessive exercise of discipline (vv 12-13). The "spirit" we have received is not one of "slavishness" (*douleias;* see Gal 5:1) or **fear** (*phobon*) (Rom 8:15a; see vv 1-4 and Gal 4:1—5:1). This warning aside, the major concern of Rom 8:14-17 is the promise of eternal life (*zēses-the*, **you will live**) mentioned at the close of v 13. Paul develops this in terms of the privilege we have as we follow the lead of the Spirit as adopted children of God (*huioi*, v 14; *huiothesias*, v 15).

Verse 14 asserts the fact of filial status for all who are led by the Spirit; vv 15-16 ground this reality in believers' experience of the Spirit; v 17 moves from "divine filiation" to our heritage as God's children and co-heirs with Christ—both cruciform suffering and resurrection glory.

Paul rounds off the implied exhortation in vv 12 and 13 with the promise that putting **to death the deeds of the body** through the Spirit leads to eternal life. The basis for (*gar,* **because**) this is that **those who are led by the Spirit of God are sons** *and daughters* **of God** (*huioi*, "sons," v 14). That Paul in vv 16 and 17 employs the gender-inclusive term *tekna*, **children,** as equivalent to *huioi* in v 14 justifies translating as **sons** *and daughters* in v 14. This filial metaphor (current in the Greco-Roman world; see Acts 17:28) reflects both the Roman practice of adoption (Rom 8:15 margin; see Gal 4:1-7) and the OT language of Israel as God's children (Exod 4:22; Deut 32:5-6; Isa 1:2; Hos 11:1).

Our status as **sons** *and daughters* of God (see 2 Cor 6:18) is a hidden thing (see 1 John 3:1-3). The only visible *evidence* is to be found in obedience, as we **are led** [*agontai*] **by the Spirit of God** (Rom 8:14). To understand Paul's thought here we must consider the meaning of *hosoi* and *agontai*. The correlative pronoun *hosoi* means "as many as" or "whoever." Obedience is expected of all Christians, regardless of where they are in their walk of faith. Since justification and sanctification are inseparable in the divine economy (see 6:15-19), the *lowest* degree of obedience expected of us as God's **children** is *the highest* degree of which we are capable at any moment.

The present passive verb *agontai* means "are being led." In Gal 5:18, being led by the Spirit is parallel to living by the Spirit (v 16) (*peripateite*, "walk" in NASB; *zōmen*, "we live" in v 25). The Spirit actively influences our lives to the extent that we are willing to be guided into active obedience. Paul "evidently understood the Christian life as an integrated balance between moral effort (v 14) and yielding to deeply felt inward compulsions (see Gal 5:16, 18, and . . . [Rom] 12:1-2)" (Dunn 2002a, 38A:450).

The Spirit offers moral direction, enabling us to demonstrate the fruit of "love, joy, peace, patience, kindness, goodness, faithfulness, gentleness and self-control" (Gal 5:22-23). Byrne translates Rom 8:14: "All who are *shaped* by the

Spirit of God are sons of God" (1996, 252). The ministry of **the Spirit of God** is directed toward *conforming believers* "to the image of his Son, in order that he might be the firstborn within a large family" (v 29 NRSV).

■ **16** Our responsiveness to his moral leadership in shaping our lives is one evidence that we are God's children. Another, inner, subjective evidence is the witness of the Spirit that **testifies with our spirit,** guaranteeing here and now **that we are God's children** (v 16). The preposition **by** (*en*) may also mean "in," "in the presence of," "with," "in communion with," "because of," or "with the help of" (Bauer 1979, 258-61. See the sidebar "An Explanation of Prepositions" with the commentary on v 4). It is **by** the Spirit that **we cry,** *"**Abba,** Father"* (v 15; see Gal 4:6-7).

The verb *krazomen,* **we cry,** is an emotionally intense cry (Bauer 1979, 447), like that of Jesus in Gethsemane. That Paul should cite the Aramaic term *Abba,* "Father," in a letter to a largely Gentile audience may suggest something of the impact the memory of Jesus' reluctance to face the cross had on early Christianity. "'*Abba,* Father,' he said, 'everything is possible for you. Take this cup from me. Yet not what I will, but what you will" (Mark 14:36). He did not relish the prospect of suffering any more than we.

Paul identifies the cry *"**Abba,** Father"* as **the Spirit himself** bearing witness with (*symmartyrei,* **testifies with,** *co-testifies with*) our spirit that we are **God's children** (Rom 8:16). Thus, the witness is *dual.* Since our sense that we are children of God is frequently threatened, perhaps even submerged, by the trials sometimes besetting our present life in Christ, the *"Abba,* Father!" brings confirmation and support to the sometimes faltering conviction of individual believers.

The cry, *"**Abba,** Father!"* seems to be typical of the religious and liturgical life of the early Christian community. Paul mentions it in Romans, addressing a community he did not found, as well as in Gal 4:6-7, one he did. In this address to God, echoing the cry of Jesus, we seem to encounter the prayer-life of early Christianity, which resisted absorption into Greek. Paul closely linked his experience of the Spirit and the risen Christ (see Rom 8:9-11; 1 Cor 15:45). Perhaps, he also believed that the Spirit-inspired cries of Christians continued their Lord's own characteristic address to the Father (see esp. Gal 4:6: "the Spirit of his Son").

The Spirit believers have received (Rom 8:15*b*) enables them to be confident that they enjoy filial status (*huiothesias*) in the family of God. In the Greek-speaking world of Paul's day *huiothesia* (see v 23; 9:4; Gal 4:6; Eph 1:5; not in the LXX) referred to "adoption," a widespread practice in the Greco-Roman world. Thus, rather than **Spirit of sonship** (Rom 8:15), the translation ***Spirit of adoption*** is preferable. Since God does not literally beget biological sons and daughters, "adoption" is an appropriate way to refer to the status of believers as children of God. The Spirit does not merely make us aware that we are children of God; he is responsible for our new status.

■ **17** The word "adoption," *huiothesia* (lit. "son-effecting"), originated in a well-established practice of Roman law, uncommon or unknown among Jews (Keck 2005, 206), by which a man formally designated someone other than his physical offspring to be his "son," his heir-designate. That God's *adopted* children are his **heirs** (*klēronomoi*), indeed **co-heirs** [*synklēronomoi*] **with Christ** (v 17), is a reminder that we have no right to our new status. We are children solely because of the Father's decision—through an act of sheer grace.

While rare in Jewish practice, behind Paul's use of the term *huiothesia* stands a broad Jewish tradition of Israel, especially eschatological Israel, as children of God (Byrne 1996, 250; Jewett 2007, 398). In 9:4 Paul mentions *huiothesia* among the privileges of ethnic Israel. In Christ, both Jewish and Gentiles believers have received the Spirit who attests that Christians enjoy the filial privileges of the eschatological (= last-days) people of God.

The images of adoption and inheritance comprehend all the eschatological blessings promised Israel, including God's promise designating Abraham the "heir of the world" (4:13). The promise stands open to all believers—Jewish and Gentile alike (vv 16-17a). Male and female alike are **children of God** (*tekna theou;* 8:16). Thus, all Roman believers are **heirs of God and fellows heirs with Christ** (v 17a).

The filial status of Christians leads naturally to the conclusion that we are *heirs as well.* According to 4:13-14, Abraham was "heir of the world," because God justified him by faith, rather than by "works of the law." Whether Jews or Gentiles by birth, by faith in Christ all Abraham's heritage (vv 9-17; see Gal 3:6—4:7) become **heirs of God** (Rom 8:17a). The provisions of adoption, granting nonchildren the legal status of children, also gave them the full privileges of inheritance. Thus, "every promise and possession once granted to Israel are now granted in a new and symbolic sense to each and every believer and to each believing community" (Jewett 2007, 501).

God's adopted **children** are his **heirs,** and since Christ is uniquely God's Son (v 3), they are also co-heirs with Christ (v 17a; see v 29). Because Christ is uniquely the Crucified and Risen One, Paul immediately reminds us that our status as God's children is contingent upon (*eiper,* **if**) sharing **in his sufferings in order that** [*hina*] **we may also share in his glory** (v 17b; see 2 Cor 4:10; Phil 3:10).

Paul's insistence that these **heirs** are also **co-heirs with Christ** (Rom 8:17a) places this "inheritance" on a solid christological basis. The destiny of believers is through their union with the crucified and risen Lord, who as the "firstborn" (v 29) is the primary Heir. Our union with Christ is not unconditionally guaranteed. As Christ's path to resurrection and glory was through his obedient suffering, so is ours. Our promised heritage will be ours only *eiper*, "if in fact" (or "since"; see the comments on v 9) **we suffer with him** (*sympaschomen*).

Our suffering with him gives us the confident hope of sharing also his glory (*syndoxasthōmen*). Thus, Paul returns to the motif of suffering that was the context of his initial affirmation of hope in ch 5, esp. vv 3-4. The same mysterious conjunction of suffering and the hope of resurrection glory becomes the main theme of the rest of this chapter (8:18-39).

For Paul, the risen Christ as the "last Adam" (1 Cor 15:45) is heir-already-in-possession of his inheritance (Phil 2:9-11). Believers are heirs-in-waiting, who enjoy their status solely in virtue of their union with Christ. In 1 Cor 3:21b-23 Paul states that "all things" belong to Christians in that they "belong" (see NRSV) to Christ. Union with the Last Adam prepares them to enter into that lordship of the universe. This early Christians following Jewish tradition—based on Gen 1:26-28 and Ps 8—took as representing God's original design for human beings.

Life in the Spirit imparts both present and future benefits. Jewett summarizes the thrust of Rom 8:1-17 in these words:

> While walking according to the flesh was a matter of the perverse quest to earn and retain glory at the expense of others and in opposition to God, walking by the Spirit brings one into participation with the dishonored, crucified Lord whose glory was granted as a gift from the God of glory (Rom 6:4; see also Phil 2:9-11). By sharing suffering with the dishonored Christ, believers receive the promise of a divine reversal, sharing in his glory. (2007, 503)

FROM THE TEXT

The Christological Basis of Holiness. Paul asserts that "God has done what the law, weakened by the flesh, could not do: sending his own Son in the likeness of sinful flesh and for sin, he condemned sin in the flesh" (Rom 8:3 RSV). Sanctification of our human nature is not done by Christ *external* to himself; rather, it takes place *internally* in the very flesh and blood of the man Jesus (Noble 1999, 33-43).

Christ's life, before his ministry and death, was not just a standing where unfallen Adam had stood without yielding to the temptation to which Adam succumbed. He started from where we start, subject to all the pressures we inherit and using the unpromising and unsuitable material of our corrupt nature to work out a perfect, sinless obedience (Cranfield 1975, 1:383 n. 2). The Son assumed our *fallen* humanity, since "He could only heal what he had assumed" (Gregory of Nazianzus, and others).

As Origen noted, we human beings have "the flesh of sin," but the Son had the "likeness of sinful flesh." He came in a form like us in that he became a member of the sin-oriented human race; he experienced the effects of sin and suffered death, the result of sin, as one "cursed" by the law (Gal 3:13). Thus, in his own person he coped with the power of sin. Paul's use of the phrase *sarx hamartias* denotes not the guilty human condition, but the proneness of humanity made of flesh that is oriented to sin. (Fitzmyer 1993, 485)

The assumption of our fallen humanity is, therefore, essential to our sanctification, as the church fathers insisted. Jesus was enabled to resist temptation, not by some immanent conditioning as the Son of God, but by his human obedience through the enablement of the Spirit.

> Thus from a perfectly holy life of Jesus there proceeds a conspicuous condemnation of sin; and it is this moral fact, the greatest of the miracles that distinguished his life, which the Holy Spirit goes on reproducing in the life of every believer and propagating throughout the entire race. (Godet 1883, 300-301)

For the Son, sanctification is accomplished because he "was conceived of the Holy Spirit, born of the Virgin Mary" (Apostles' Creed). For us, it is only because we are regenerated and sanctified by the Holy Spirit who comes through him. "He became what we are, that we might become what he is" (paraphrasing patristic fathers).

The Sanctifying Spirit. George Croft Cell perceptively observed that John Wesley's theology brings together the Protestant conception of grace and the Catholic conception of holiness (1935, 359). Albert C. Outler points out that "the 'catholic substance' of Wesley's theology is the theme of *participation* —the idea that all life is of grace and all grace is the mediation of Christ by the Holy Spirit" (cited in Collins 1997, 20). Like Luther and Calvin before him, Wesley views grace as the undeserved favor of God. However, it is also divine empowerment to live the life of sanctification.

Wesley viewed salvation as consisting of "two grand branches," justification and sanctification, integrated in and mediated through Christ by the Holy Spirit:

> The title "holy," applied to the Spirit of God, does not only denote that he is holy in his own nature, but that he makes us so; that he is the great fountain of holiness to his church; the Spirit from whence flows all the grace and virtue, by which the stains of guilt are cleansed, and we are renewed in all holy dispositions, and again bear the image of our Creator. (1979, 7:486; sermon "On Grieving the Holy Spirit")

Spirit Baptism and Entire Sanctification. Wesley considered the promise of baptism with the Holy Spirit in Acts 1:5 to be for "all true believers, to the end of the world" (1950, 393, on Acts 1:5). He insisted, however, that this baptism is *corporate*. According to 1 Cor 12:13, it initiates believers into the body of Christ. It is corporate because "the gospel of Christ knows of no religion, but social; no holiness but social holiness" (Wesley 1979, 14:321). Spirit *baptism*, promised in the Gospels and fulfilled at Pentecost, is commanded in the NT letters.

John Fletcher (1728-85), Wesley's chosen successor, was unequaled as a saint and eminent theologian. In Fletcher's more dynamic and flexible theology of Spirit baptism, the expression is used frequently, but not in any consistent manner (see Bassett and Greathouse 1985, 2:238-44). Fletcher distinguished between believers baptized with the Pentecostal power of the Holy Spirit, and believers not yet filled with that power. The former are entirely sanctified; the latter are not (Tyerman 1882, 411).

Wesley objected to Fletcher's teaching that by receiving the Holy Spirit, believers were entirely sanctified. He was uncomfortable with the equation of Spirit baptism and entire sanctification, which he understood to entail freedom from all sin and perfection in love (1979, 5:125; sermon "The Witness of the Spirit"). Lawrence W. Wood's argument that the mature Wesley accommodated Fletcher's terminology (1996, 31, 1:125) has not persuaded most Wesley scholars.

Methodist missionaries who came to America in the early nineteenth century, however, were inclined more toward Fletcher's holiness terminology than Wesley's. They preached Spirit baptism in *individualistic* terms, as a believer's *personal* "Pentecost." This departure from Wesley appears to be the bridge over which the Holiness message passed into modern Pentecostalism.

The Witness of the Spirit. Wesley's interpretation of Paul's statement in Rom 8:16—"It is the Spirit himself bearing witness with our spirit that we are children of God" (RSV)—emphasizes a joint witness between the Spirit of God and the human spirit (or conscience). The witness of God's Spirit in Wesley's classic phraseology

> is an inward impression on the soul, whereby the Spirit of God directly witnesses to my spirit, that I am a child of God; that Jesus Christ hath loved me, and given himself for me; and that all my sins are blotted out, and I, even I, am reconciled to God. (1979, 5:115; sermon "The Witness of the Spirit")

The witness of the human spirit, which follows, is an *indirect* witness or testimony that we are children of God. Wesley believed this witness is given, not only to those who are born of God in the "lower degree" of the new birth but also to those who are also "perfect" in Christ. With reference to *any* stage of personal holiness, he sees the direct divine witness *preceding* the indirect witness of our spirit (see 1979, 5:115).

Wesley applies Rom 8:16 to "perfection" as the *highest* stage of Christian experience. This passage defines the essence of the Christian ethic in terms of the *loving* obedience of "children of God" who from their hearts cry out sincerely (1979, 8:288-89), with Jesus in Gethsemane, *"Abba*, Father!" in the power of their risen Lord.

The Paradox of Sanctification According to Barth and Wesley. Karl Barth argued strongly for "the reality of sanctification" as "the problem of obedience," in an important essay "The Holy Spirit and Christian Obedience," which resonates with what may be called Wesley's "paradox of perfection." Barth insists that Christian obedience can be understood only as the work of the Holy Spirit. "In the secrecy of faith" it is characterized by repentance and faith. Paradoxically, it is still *our own faith.* Faith is not without works; nor, justification without sanctification. Faith "becomes concrete as the gift of the Holy Spirit, in the reality of sanctification," for "faith cannot stand alone: it is always in this and that action self authenticating. . . . So far as the Holy Spirit is in the action, he is especially the Spirit of holiness."

Thus "only in the Holy Spirit is it decided whether it is obedience and not disobedience. . . . The Holy Spirit is absolutely and alone the umpire with reference to what is or is not Christian life." Our sanctification is real, but our obedience is a problem we cannot solve, since it depends "utterly and alone upon God." (Barth 1993, excerpts from 32-58 with endnotes.)

If we take into account the qualifications made to his doctrine by the mature Wesley in his "Plain Account of Christian Perfection," we are struck by the similarity of his and Barth's ideas of sanctification. Fundamental to Wesley's teaching on the topic is the distinction he makes between "the perfect law" of love (see 1 Cor 13) and "perfect love" (defined by Wesley as "pure love to God and man"). Even those who are perfect in love, Wesley admits, "fall short of the glory of God" (Rom 3:23) and are, therefore, "justified freely by his grace . . . that came by Christ Jesus . . . apart from observing the law" (vv 24, 28).

Such a distinction is necessitated by Wesley's doctrine of "actual sin." Primarily, sin is "every voluntary breach of the law of love . . . and nothing else" (1931, 5:322). Yet, after his delineation of "the perfect law of love," Wesley urges, "You who feel all love, compare yourselves with the preceding description . . . and see if you are not wanting in many particulars" (1979, 11:418; in his "Plain Account of Christian Perfection"). Wesley rejects any notion of *sinless perfection.*

Wesley's standard definition of Christian perfection is salvation from *known* sin—from its *power* in the new birth and its *root*—affections contrary to love (1979, 6:489; sermon "On Patience")—in entire sanctification (1979, 6:509; sermon "On Working Out Our Own Salvation"). Christian perfection is *Christ-centeredness, total Christ-dependency.* Wesley acknowledges:

The holiest of men still need Christ as their Prophet, as "the light of the world." For he does not give them light but from moment to moment. The instant he withdraws, all is darkness. They still need Christ as their King; for God does not give them a stock of holiness. But unless they receive a supply every moment, nothing but unholiness would remain. They still need Christ as their Priest, to make atonement for their holy things. Even perfect holiness is acceptable to God only through Jesus Christ. . . . But if I should be left to myself, I should be nothing but sin, darkness, hell. . . . (1979, 11:417; "A Plain Account of Christian Perfection")

Barth and Wesley both acknowledge the *darkness* into which those who know "the reality of sanctification" sometimes find themselves in their attempt to distinguish temptation from sin. Both agree that at such times our only hope is the grace of God and the Holy Spirit, who alone determines what Christian living demands.

What comes to light—when we compare Wesley's and Barth's views—is *the paradoxical nature* of the Christian life. When probed to its depths in the presence of the holy God, we cast ourselves on him who gave his Son to die for us. For Wesley, it is the anomaly of *perfection*; for Barth, it is the problem of *obedience*. For both, the answer is *not* theological speculation but childlike *faith* in Christ alone. Barth's reference to the Holy Spirit as the divine "umpire" may be more helpful than Wesley's metaphor of witness. We stand between God's judging Word and strengthening presence in temptation and trial.

(b) The Spirit and the Hope of Glory (8:18-30)

(i) The Spirit Helps (8:18-27)

BEHIND THE TEXT

In 8:18-39 Paul returns to the hope of glory held out for believers despite the sufferings of the present time mentioned in 5:1-11. He also repeats a series of key terms found there: love (5:5, 8; 8:35, 39); justify (5:1, 9; 8:30, 33); glory (5:2; 8:18, 21, 30); hope (5:2, 4, 5; 8:20, 24); suffering (5:3; 8:35); save (5:9, 10; 8:24); and patience (5:3, 4; 8:25). In 8:18-30 Paul "provides the climactic elaboration of the themes of creation, corruption, and glorification" in 1:18—3:20 "as well as the themes of Adam, suffering, and glorification announced in" 5:1-21 (Jewett 2007, 505).

In 6:1—8:17 Paul grounds our hope of sharing the glory of God in the replacement of the Law by the Spirit, who creates and preserves in Christians a righteousness that opens the way to salvation and eternal life. In vv 18-27 a further role of the Spirit emerges. In the context of present suffering, the Christian's experience of the Spirit becomes the supreme pledge of future glory (anticipated in 5:5). As the conclusion of 8:12-17, v 17 also serves to introduce the theme of vv 18-30, providing a smooth transition between the two.

The Spirit assures us of our status as **God's children** and **co-heirs with Christ** (vv 16, 17), but v 17 cautions that as followers of the Crucified and Risen One, we must expect to **share in his sufferings** so that **we may also share in his glory.** In 8:28-30 Paul emphasizes that God's **purpose** to share his glory with his human creation will be achieved as he conforms them to **the likeness of his Son.**

Paul's argument proceeds in stages: in vv 19-22 **creation** groans; in vv 23-25 **we** groan; in vv 26-27 **the Spirit himself . . . groans.** In vv 28-30, through predestination, justification, and glorification to the image of Christ, God will lead many sons and daughters to glory. Paul sees each stage as an index of hope. The cumulative effect of the divine plan is to bring human beings to "glory," following the risen Lord.

The *groaning* of the nonhuman creation, with the hope of its redemption, is singular in Paul's writings. In Wis 16:24 and 19:6, however, personified "creation" transforms itself in favor of the "sons" of God (= Israelites). In Rom 1:20 Paul, echoing Wisdom, speaks of "creation" as the entire nonhuman world (see Isa 65:17). God's future purposes for creation can only be expressed poetically and metaphorically.

The fate of the created order is bound up with that of humanity. With the human fall, it also fell (Gen 3:17-19). Thus, when God's plan for human redemption is fulfilled, creation will be restored (Isa 11:6-9; Ezek 34:25-31; Hos 2:18; Zech 8:12; see Greathouse 1998, 44-45, 51).

Paul presupposes in Rom 8:35-39 that the final vindication and salvation of the elect will be preceded by a time of greatly increased turmoil and suffering. Such is the idea behind the **creation . . . groaning as in the pains of childbirth** (v 22), while it awaits the final deliverance. (Following Jer 30:4-7 and Isa 13:6-8, Jewish rabbis referred to this difficult waiting as "the birthpangs of the Messiah." See Lyons 1985, 214-15 n. 140 for the evidence.) Sufferings of the present time are not a threat to salvation but a sign that the longed-for deliverance is at hand.

In addition to the groaning of creation as a ground for hope, Paul points to the parallel groaning of believers. Creation groans for believers; believers for themselves. Behind the "groaning" of believers lies their longing for salvation stimulated by the Spirit; the gift of the Spirit is the **firstfruits** of their redemption (v 23). Believers possess fully the privilege of divine **adoption** (v 23). When their bodies are redeemed, they will be **revealed** as **the sons *and daughters* of God** before the assembled universe (v 19; see Heb 2:10-13).

In this hope, Paul affirms, **we were saved** (Rom 8:24). The mention of salvation as a past event and already present reality is striking. Paul generally reserves "salvation" to the final age. Here the sense seems to be that the hope we have is so secure that with it we are *already* "saved." We are *no longer* what we once were, but *not yet* what we shall be—the theme of the rest of this chapter. Christian "hope" is not mere wishful thinking—"pie in the sky by and by"; it is a *confident expectation based on Christ's resurrection*, resting on the faithfulness of God to make good the final installment of salvation already pledged through the Spirit.

Our Christian existence, thus, has three temporal dimensions: past, present, and future. It is based on the foundation that has been laid, Christ (1 Cor 1:30). It lives in the present by the power of the Spirit and reaches out to full redemption in the future. Since he has dealt with the first two, Paul now turns to the third, our hope for the future.

The immediate link in the preceding section is Rom 8:15, where Paul speaks of *the Spirit of adoption.* He realizes that our adoption is incomplete. Our status as God's children is now *concealed*, obscured by our body of humiliation, but at the end of this age, when our Lord returns (see 1 Thess 4:13-18), our adoption will be *revealed*. What we now see is adoption as children of God as a fact of Christian experience. The Spirit is the firstfruits of that coming disclosure (see 1 John 3:2).

The Children of God in This Age

The apocryphal Wisdom of Solomon presents the righteous as victims of the plots of the ungodly, who make their lives miserable because they call themselves children of God (2:13, 18) and consider God their Father (v 16). The Sage describes their undeserved suffering as serving a disciplinary function, to demonstrate their worthiness of God's blessing of immortality (3:4-5)—"the faithful will abide with him in love" (v 9 NRSV); "they will receive a glorious crown" (5:16 NRSV).

The popular early second-century Christian apocalypse, the so-called Shepherd of Hermas, vied for canonical recognition. It is now considered a part of the Apostolic Fathers. Its third Similitude concerning deciduous trees during the winter illustrates the early Christian understanding of the present age of suffering and its connection with the as-yet undisclosed status of the righteous as children of God. The trees' shed leaves make the various species indistinguishable. Just so, the righteous and sinners cannot easily be recognized now, for this age is "winter for the righteous" (Herm. *Sim.* 3:8; 60:8).

IN THE TEXT

■ **18** What shall we do now, between the suffering of the present and the awaited future glory? Paul describes the interim period, showing how Christians can take courage from the prospect of glory and through the assistance offered by the Holy Spirit to those who suffer. Paul assumes a cost-benefit perspective: **I consider that our present sufferings are not worth comparing with the glory that will be revealed in us** (v 18).

The construction translated **will be revealed** is no simple future tense. As in v 13, *mellousan* ("it is about to") with the aorist passive infinitive *apokalyph-thēnai* ("to be revealed") conveys a note of confident certainty: *the glory that will certainly be revealed in us soon.* However, if *mellousan* modifies *doxan*, **glory,** which immediately follows it, Paul refers to the future glory (see Gal 3:23; Jewett 2007, 510).

When Paul writes, **I consider** (*logizomai*; Rom 8:18), he means, "This is my considered opinion." The **present** age is the period during which our **sufferings** occur. It is "this age" or "this present age" in contrast to "the age to come" (see 3:26; 12:2; Gal 1:4; Eph 1:21, where the "world" translates *aiōn*, which is properly rendered "age").

Godet notes the significance of this truth for universal Christian experience: "As to the spirit we are in the *age to come*; as to the body, in the *present age*" (1883, 313). In this age Christians share in the sufferings of Christ (2 Cor 1:5; Phil 3:10; Col 1:24); only in the age to come will we fully share in his resurrection glory (see Rom 8:17). Despite the pretensions of the Roman imperial cult that Augustus had launched a golden age, Jewett notes that Roman believers "had already experienced harassment and deportation and [their] everyday life as members of the Roman underclass was anything but idyllic" (2007, 509).

Paul insisted that "despite the illusions of the Roman civic cult, the originally intended glory of the creation shall yet be restored, including specifically the glory humans were intended to bear," but only in the future (Jewett 2007, 510). **Sufferings** belong to this present age, between the advents of our Lord. **Glory** belongs to the age to come.

The prepositional phrase **in us** (*eis hēmas*) may also be translated "to us," "of us," or "for us" (see the sidebar "An Explanation of Prepositions" with v 4). Paul anticipates that the revelation of the Lord Jesus at his coming from heaven will cause him "to be glorified in [*en*] his holy people and to be marveled at among [*en*] all those who have believed" (2 Thess 1:10). The **glory** that is promised will not only **be revealed** to us but will transform us (see 2 Cor 3:18; Phil 3:21)—our resurrection bodies will be a glorious spectacle to behold (see 1 Cor 15:42-57).

Glory

Paul uses the word *doxa*, **glory**, with its LXX force as a translation of the Hebrew *kabod*. It is an abstract noun describing a quality possessed by a person or thing that metaphorically "shines" or "has great weight." The verb form ("to glorify"

259

or "give glory") involves recognizing and praising one who possesses glory. It is not to give something he or she does not already have, but only to acknowledge it.

We use the underlying imagery of glory regularly in English, although we seldom use the term itself outside of religious settings. For example, we might refer to an unusually intelligent person as bright or brilliant, a job well done as a shining performance. Or we refer to celebrities as stars or bright lights, speak of an important student leader as a big man on campus, or speak of the use of power and influence as throwing one's weight around.

This is the language of honor and recognition. It was crucial in an honor-shame society like the ancient Mediterranean world that those who possessed glory should receive honor. To fail to give honor was to disgrace the person instead. But who is qualified to decide who or what is deserving of recognition as glorious? Our view of glory and how we assign it discloses our value system. Should we glorify might or meekness? Do we glorify violence or peacemaking? Do we praise God or human prowess? Are we to honor the rich and famous or the righteous and faithful?

The glory of God is a major theme of Romans, where forms of the Greek root *dox-* (*doxa*, "glory"; *doxazō*, "I glorify") appear more than 20 times (1:21, 23; 2:7, 10; 3:7, 23; 4:20; 5:2; 6:4; 8:17, 18, 21, 30; 9:4, 23; 11:13, 36; 15:6, 7, 9; 16:27). We make no attempt here to treat the many references to "glory" elsewhere in the Pauline corpus, much less throughout the NT (where it appears at least 235 times). Interested readers should refer to the standard biblical-theological dictionaries for a more thorough discussion.

The apostle's aim in Romans is to promote the glory of God (15:6-7), i.e., to urge people to recognize God as God and to praise and thank him (1:20-23). But he also uses "glory" to describe human relationships. His basic presupposition is that humans are created in the image and likeness of God and are to live to acknowledge that God alone is worthy of honor (16:25-27). Fallen human beings, however, are preoccupied with created things instead of their Creator (1:20—2:3). We all, therefore, stand desperately in need of redemption that only the Creator can provide, "since all have sinned and fall short of the glory of God" (3:23 NRSV; see vv 21-30).

The "glory" to be restored describes the manifest perfection of God in his goodness, saving grace (1:23; 3:7, 23, etc.), and power (6:4). That "Christ was raised from the dead by the glory of the Father" (v 4 NRSV) asserts that God's action of raising the crucified Jesus demonstrates God's glory. Glory also fittingly describes the splendor of the resurrection body of the Lord. The eschatological revelation of God's glory will result in the resurrection and recognition of those human beings who gave God the glory due him. Regardless of how important or unimportant they seemed to other people, God's recognition will be the ultimate honor.

The final revelation of glory will also encompass the transformation of corrupted, groaning creation, which now "waits with eager longing for the revealing of the children of God" (8:19 NRSV; see vv 18-25 NRSV). Restored to its pristine state, the natural creation will provide the glorious stage on which previously unsung "stars" will enjoy not only unbroken fellowship with the one true God but also appreciative recognition from him for their faithfulness.

■ **19** Despite the literal translation of Rom 8:19—*For the eager expectation* [see Phil 1:20] *of the creation waits patiently for the revelation of the sons of God,* Paul seems to mean that *"the eagerly awaited creation"* (Bauer 1979, 92) patiently waits. Paul either assigns to *the creation* (*tēs ktiseōs*, v 22; see 1:20) a level of intelligence unrecognized by most human observers or employs personification to stress the universal longing for God to reveal his glory.

Jewett takes Paul to imply "that the entire creation waits with baited breath for the emergence and empowerment of those who will take responsibility for its restoration" (2007, 512), but he insists that Paul refers not merely to the eschaton but also to the missional advance of the gospel.

As the children of God are redeemed by the gospel, they begin to regain a rightful dominion over the created world (Gen 1:28-30; Ps 8:5-8); in more modern terms, their altered lifestyle and revised ethics begin to restore the ecological system that had been thrown out of balance by wrongdoing (1:18-32) and sin (Rom 5—7). (2007, 513)

That **the sons** [*huiōn*] **of God** in 8:19 (see v 23) are called "children [*teknōn*] of God" in v 14 (NRSV) justifies a more gender-inclusive translation. **The creation** (v 19) is depicted as an audience on the edge of its seat, anticipating the drawing of the final curtain. The root meaning of the word *apokalypsis,* "revelation," is unveiling. It remains to be seen who all will participate in the final curtain call of the ongoing drama of human salvation (Dunn 2002a, 38A:470).

■ **20** What part of created reality does Paul envision awaiting this revelation of God's **sons and daughters** (*huiōn*)? We may exclude angels, for they are apparently not subjected to vanity and the bondage of corruption (vv 20-21). Satan and demons must be excluded, for they cannot be imagined as awaiting a revelation that will seal their doom. The children of God are not included, for they are expressly distinguished from the rest of **creation** in this verse. Unbelievers are not included, for they have no such expectation. **The creation,** thus, must mean the natural order, the nonhuman creation, cursed as a consequence of Adam's sin (Gen 3:17). Paul's object in mentioning the natural order is to emphasize the certainty of future salvation for Christians.

Although Paul's primary concern is not with creation for its own sake, his bold imagery prompts further explanation in Rom 8:20-21. **The creation was subjected** [*hypetagē*] **to frustration** [*mataiotēti;* v 20; see 1:21; Eccl 1:2]. It was forced to submit to the experience of *"emptiness, futility, purposelessness, transitoriness"* (Bauer 1979, 495). The **frustration** is that creation has malfunctioned; it does not play the role God designed it to have in his original creation (Dunn 2002a, 38A:470).

Paul does not say explicitly who corrupted and destroyed the created order, but that this was done **by the will of the one who subjected it** (Rom 8:20), points to God's judgment pronounced on human sin, which affected wholly innocent plants, animals, and the ground (Gen 3:14-20).

Creation suffers because human beings foolishly refused to live in dependence on God. Instead they perverted their God-given responsibility of dominion (1:21) into exploitation and self-aggrandizement. Jewett suggests that Paul's first readers may

> have thought about how imperial ambitions, military conflicts, and economic exploitation had led to the erosion of the natural environment throughout the Mediterranean world, leaving ruined cities, depleted fields, deforested mountains, and polluted streams as evidence of this universal human vanity. (2007, 513)

The created order was not corrupted through any fault of its own; it is involved in the fatal defection of humankind. However, this curse upon nature, though arising from human rapacity, was imposed upon it by the Creator. This subjection of the natural order was not **by its own choice** (Rom 8:20) nor its responsibility.

Paul lends no support to gnostic notions of the material world as innately evil. Human sin created the problem, but the rest of creation suffers the consequences as well. God uses crippled creation to contribute to the self-destructiveness of sin, so that he can eventually restore creation to its proper function as a suitable environment for human life as he originally intended it to be (Dunn 2002a, 38A:471).

The creation was subjected **in hope.** Since creation is under the control of God, it has never been without **hope.** The world as we know it is not "the best possible of all worlds." It shares in the misery and purposelessness of human sinful existence, but since it was not enslaved by its own will, God reserves a **hope** in its behalf. In fact, God has already begun to reverse the curse by subjecting the creation to the rule of the new Adam—Christ, instead of to the first Adam, who proved to be an unworthy master (Ps 8:6; 1 Cor 15:27; Eph 1:22; Phil 3:21; Heb 2:5-8; 1 Pet 3:22). "The Christian perspective is determined not by the frustrations of the present, but by its future hope" (Dunn 2002a, 38A:476). The hope of creation is for the total reversal of the ancient curse.

As Paul uses it, **hope** is not merely wishful thinking or optimism in desperate times. As faith oriented to the future, it is the believer's confidence that God will fulfill his promises firmly based on the already experienced reality of God's love (see Rom 5:1-11 and the commentary). The **hope** of creation is that it will share in human redemption. In the mystery of God's eternal purpose the two go hand in hand and are inseparably united. "Just as God, on the day of resurrection, will give man a body that corresponds to the new aeon of glory, a 'spiritual body,' so He will create a corresponding new cosmos, 'new heavens and a new earth'" (Nygren 1949, 332). Paul probably has in mind the fulfillment of prophecies like those in Isa 11:6-9; 65:17, 25; and 66:22 (see *Jub.* 1:29; *1 En.* 24—25; 91:16-17; *T. Levi* 18:10-11; 2 Esd/4 *Ezra* 13:26; *Sib. Or.* 3:744-45, 750-51, 788-95; Acts 3:21; Rev 21).

■ **21** The specific content of this hope is that **the creation itself will be liberated** [*eleutherōthēsetai*, "set free"/"delivered"] (Rom 8:21). Although Paul insists that freedom from sin is a privilege Christians may enjoy in this present age (see the commentary on 6:20-23), the progressive losses associated with our mortality is another matter. Believers die! And before they do, they generally experience diminished capacities (see the allegory on aging and death in Eccl 12:1-8). The substance of the freedom creation yet awaits is deliverance **from its bondage** [*douleias*, "slavery"] **to decay** [*phthoras*, "*ruin, destruction, dissolution, deterioration, corruption*" (Bauer 1979, 858)].

The hoped-for liberation of the natural order, personified as enslaved to the power of Death, will allow it to experience ***the freedom*** [*eleutherian*] ***of the glory of the children of God.*** Paul exuberantly piles up one genitive (of) phrase after another, making his meaning as uncertain as his eager anticipation is certain. "Paul's premise is that humans and the creation are interdependent and that human fulfillment is contextual and cosmic" (Jewett 2007, 515).

Perhaps the apostle expects "The General Deliverance" (sermon on Rom 8:19-29 in Wesley 1979, 6:241-52) to so renovate creation as to allow it to enjoy the same **glorious freedom** that **the children of God** will in the new age. ***The freedom of the glory*** is equivalent here to deathlessness, the gift of immortality (see Rom 2:7; 1 Cor 15:53-54). Just as resurrected believers will never die, sustained as they are by "the Tree of Life" (Rev 21:1-4; 22:1-5), decay will never spoil the new creation. The Christian hope does not call for escape from the created order, but for a thorough restoration of the original creation to its Creator's design.

Isaiah's prophecy predicting the new heaven and earth is preceded by the analogy of labor pains (66:7-9, 22). These are anticipated in **the present time** (*nyn*, "now"; Rom 8:22; see 3:21; 7:6; 8:1) by the natural order, struggling even now to be delivered from its bondage. In vv 22 Paul asserts a confidence shared by his audience: **We know that the whole creation has been groaning** [*systenazei*, "groaning together"; see Job 31:38-40; Isa 24:4-7; Hos 4:1-3; and 4 *Ezra* 7:1-4]. This groaning is occasioned by **the pains of childbirth** [*synōdinei*; see Isa 13:8; 21:3; 26:17-18; Jer 4:31; 22:23; Hos 13:13; *1 En.* 62:4; Mark 13:8; John 16:21; 1 Thess 5:3].

■ **22** Despite Roman pretensions that the emperors had launched the golden age (see Jewett 2007, 517), Paul insists that creation's groaning continues **right** up to the present time (Rom 8:22). **Not only** the natural order**, but we ourselves, who have the firstfruits of the Spirit, groan** [*stenazomen*, "sigh"] **inwardly as we wait eagerly** [*apekdechomenoi;* see v 19] **for our adoption as sons** [and daughters], **the redemption of our bodies** (v 23). Paul's hope sees behind the world's suffering the universal longing for salvation promised in the gospel.

The collective **groaning** of the creation, like our private **groan,** is occasioned by the **present sufferings** (v 18) and other undesirable circumstances of this age (see Job 31:38; Isa 24:4; Jer 4:28; Hab 3:10). These occasion an inward longing for the glorious future Christians can sample but even Spirit-filled believers cannot yet fully experience (see 2 Cor 5:1-5).

Like **the pains of childbirth,** our cries of agony are not plaintive expressions of hopeless despair. Instead, they look forward to the joy that will come with the birth of the new age and with it resurrection bodies (see Mark 13:8; John 16:20-22; Acts 2:24; 1 Thess 5:3; Rev 12:2). The Christian hope is not for escape from the created order but for redemption comprehensive enough to include all of creation.

The **firstfruits** (*aparchēn*, the "first installment" or "down payment") **of the Spirit** is the foretaste of our heavenly glory, the anticipation of our future redemption. The Spirit is that foretaste (a genitive of apposition), not something the Spirit gives or does (a subjective genitive). It should also be recalled that the Jewish feast known as Pentecost in the NT was known as Firstfruits in the OT (Exod 23:16; 34:22; Deut 16:9-12), which probably explains why Acts 2 makes a point that this was the day when the Spirit was first outpoured on believers (Dunn 2002a, 38A:473).

In two other letters Paul conveys similar teaching about the Spirit using *arrabon*, which means "pledge" or "earnest" (see 2 Cor 1:22; 5:5; Eph 1:14). In modern Greek *arrabon* is employed for an engagement ring, as the pledge and promise of future marriage. The indwelling Spirit is the believer's assurance of God's glorious, better day. *Aparchē*, however, is an even stronger metaphor. The **firstfruits** are the early, *specimen crop* of the **glory** (Rom 8:18) offered to God as a thank offering (e.g., Exod 22:29; 23:19; Lev 23:10; see Rom 11:16; 16:5), representing the full harvest, which will be ours when Christ returns. As the grapes of Eschol, brought back by Caleb and Joshua from the land of Canaan, were meant to whet the appetite of the Hebrews for the Promised Land, so **the Spirit** offers us a foretaste of the new promised land.

Paul's discussion of the resurrection in 1 Cor 15 appears to echo in the present passage. There, in vv 20 and 23, he refers to the resurrected Christ as the "firstfruits" of the dead, but he is also "the last Adam, a life-giving spirit" (v 45). More importantly, in v 44 Paul identifies the full harvest of the sown "natural body" as "a spiritual body" that will "bear the likeness of the man from heaven" (v 49). The gift of the Spirit is the firstfruits we already possess; the "new creation" and eternal life (2 Cor 5:17; see Gal 6:8, 15) of the resurrection body are what we eagerly await.

■ **23** Meanwhile *we eagerly await our adoption* (Rom 8:23), just as the creation awaits our revelation as the children of God (v 19). The two are functionally equivalent: both refer to the unveiling of our true selves as children of God clothed in our resurrection bodies. Thus, **adoption** (*huiothesian;* see v 15) here must refer to the full *revelation* of our status as **the sons and daughters of God** (vv 14 and 19).

The indwelling Spirit assures believers that we have already been adopted into God's family: *By the Spirit of adoption* [*huiothesias*] . . . *we cry, "Abba, Father"* (vv 15-16). Adoption is another of the already-but-not-yet realities of the Christian life. Only when Christ returns will there be a public proclamation of this glorious fact before the whole world (v 19; see 1 Cor 15:50-51; 2 Thess 1:5-12; 1 John 3:1-3).

The resurrection will effect **the redemption** [*apolytrōsin,* "setting free," "liberation"; see Rom 3:24; 1 Cor 1:30; Eph 1:7, 14; 4:30; Col 1:14] **of our bodies** (Rom 8:23), not their elimination. Paul does not look forward to some kind of bodiless spiritual existence, but to the transformation of "our lowly bodies" (Phil 3:21).

Redemption is another way of referring to **the glorious freedom** (Rom 8:21) *from Death* the new age will bring, significantly not freedom from our bodies. Bodily redemption is the *third* gracious work of our salvation (justification/regeneration/initial sanctification being the *first* work of grace; entire sanctification, the *second*). Believers **wait eagerly** (v 23) for the final stroke of bodily redemption **in hope** (vv 20 and 24).

■ **24** Paul's sequence of verb tenses in vv 23 and 24 is striking: **In this hope** (v 24; see 4:18) for **the redemption of our bodies** (v 23), i.e., the future resurrection from the dead, **we were saved** (v 24). This is one of those rare times when Paul speaks of salvation in the aorist tense as a completed action (contrast Rom 5:10; 13:11; 1 Cor 3:15; 5:5; 1 Thess 5:8).

■ **25** For the present, our salvation remains in prospect only; it is not a finished work, for we have not yet been resurrected. And so we press on (see Phil 3:7-21). *We were saved in hope* only. We do not yet have [*ou blepomen, we do not see*] what we hope for (Rom 8:25).

Simple logic undermines Roman imperial claims that the golden age had dawned, but Christians, despite ongoing suffering and death, do not despair. Instead, they hope. **Who hopes for what he already has** [*blepei,* "sees"]? (v 24). And so, for now, **we wait for** [*apekdechometha;* see vv 19 and 23] **it patiently** [*hypomonēs,* "with perseverance" NASB; see 5:3] (8:25). Final salvation remains contingent upon our perseverance in faithful waiting in the present. Paul's ambitious plans to evangelize Spain make it clear that such waiting does not entail passive resignation to the status quo. Instead, he presumes that believers will persist in good works (2:7; 5:3-4).

■ **26** It is not only **hope** (8:20, 24, and 25)—future-oriented faith—that sustains us in our present suffering and decay; **the Spirit helps us in our weakness** [*asthenia*] (v 26; see v 3). We, **in the same way** (v 26) as the rest of creation, are subject to the **bondage to decay** (v 21); and we **groan** for **redemption** (v 23).

Our **weakness** encompasses the whole array of human infirmities: the racial effects of sin in our bodies and minds, the scars of past sinful living, our prejudices that sometimes hinder God's purposes, our neuroses that bring emotional depression and cause us at times to act "out of character," bodily and mental deterioration due to illness and the passage of time, our temperamental idiosyncrasies that trouble us and others, and a thousand faults to which our mortal flesh is heir. Here Paul particularly mentions our inability to pray (v 26).

We are weak because "we have this treasure in jars of clay to show that this all-surpassing power [which transforms us into God's 'likeness with ever-increasing glory' (2 Cor 3:18)] is from God and not from us" (4:7). Because we are not finally redeemed we *all* continually "fall short of the glory of God" (Rom 3:23*b*), but the Spirit actively **helps** us (8:26), thereby making us strong (see 2 Cor 12:10).

In the NT the Greek verb *synantilambanetai,* **helps,** is used only here and in Luke 10:40. In the latter passage, Martha complains that her sister Mary's failure "to help" left her to do all of work alone (see LXX occurrences of the verb in Exod 18:22 and Num 11:17). The Spirit, however, comes to our aid, shares our burdens, participates in our suffering, and gives us the strength we need to persevere (Bauer 1979, 784).

The Spirit helps us under the trying circumstances of unrelieved suffering and the prospect of death, by enabling us to pray as we should. **We do not know what we ought to pray for, but the Spirit himself intercedes for us with groans that words cannot express** [*alalētois,* "unspeakable"] (Rom 8:26). Some consider Paul here to allude to Spirit-inspired charismatic prayer within the community, involving so-called glossolalia. However, in 1 Cor 14 the gift of tongues, as Paul understands it, is a medium of praise, not intercessory prayer. It was thought to be the spoken language of angels (13:1), not inarticulate confusion and frustration.

If the "groans" of suffering Christians involved audible expressions, they would seem to refer not to unintelligible words but to inexpressible feelings (Byrne 1996, 271). The word translated **groans** here (Rom 8:26; as in vv 22 and 23) refer to "sighs too deep for words" (v 26 NRSV). Our experience of being unable to communicate our heartfelt but inexpressible longing for redemption evidences our solidarity with the rest of groaning creation (see v 22; Dunn 2002a, 38A:478).

Perhaps Paul's point is that because we do not know **what we ought** [*katho dei*, "in what way it is necessary"] **to pray** and can only sigh, **the Spirit himself intercedes** [*hyperentynchanei*, "super-prays"] **for us** (v 26). Sometimes "sufferings" (v 18), "frustration" (v 20), "bondage to decay" (v 21), "weakness" (v 26), and ignorance (**We do not know**) make it difficult, even impossible, for us to pray for ourselves, much less for others. Our problem is not just a failure to find the right words to say; it is that we do not even know what we want or need. When we cannot ask God for the help we need, the Spirit asks in our behalf. He knows **what we ought to pray for** (v 26), because he knows both **our hearts** and **God's will** for us (v 27).

The impersonal verb *dei*, **ought,** here as almost always in the NT refers to what must be done to conform to the will of God. So how can we pray that his will might be done? We sometimes do not know God's will for ourselves; but the Spirit does. God has a purpose for his creation and for his people (see vv 28-30), and the Spirit helps us pray consistently with it.

■ **27 And he who searches** [*eraunōn*, "examines" or "investigates"] **our hearts knows** [*oiden*] **the mind of the Spirit, because the Spirit intercedes** [*entynchanei*, "prays"] **for the saints in accordance with God's will** [*kata Theon*, "according to God"] (v 27). What does the divine investigation of our hearts entail? Twice in John's Gospel (5:39 and 7:52), the same Greek word is applied to the careful study of the Scriptures. The parallelism between searching hearts and knowing minds suggests that both involve intimate insight into the inner person.

And who **searches our hearts** (Rom 8:27)? In Rev 2:23, the risen Christ asserts, "I am he who searches [*eraunōn*] hearts and minds." In 1 Cor 2:10, however, Paul identifies the Spirit as the one who "searches [*erauna*] all things," i.e., who knows "the deep things of God" and humans (see 1 Cor 2:11-16). Here, however, the one **who searches our hearts** is God as distinguished from the Spirit.

It is uncertain what OT passages may have echoed through Paul's mind as he wrote (see e.g., Deut 8:2; 13:3; 1 Sam 16:7; 1 Kgs 8:39; 1 Chr 29:17; 32:31; 2 Chr 1:11; 6:30; Pss 17:3; 26:2; 44:21; 139:1-2, 23; Prov 15:11; 17:3; 20:27; 24:12; Jer 11:20; 17:10). But he is hardly the only NT author (Luke 16:15; Acts 1:24; 15:8; 1 Thess 2:4; 1 John 3:20) to insist that God alone knows/searches/tests/looks at human hearts. That God knows what we are thinking and can even make sense of our inner confusion is not a troubling thought to Paul; it is a source of relief.

The Spirit does not leave us voiceless before the God who knows us more intimately than we know ourselves (1 Cor 4:1-5); he takes our inexpressible confusion and prays in our behalf. In Rom 8:26 Paul says that **the Spirit . . . intercedes for us;** but in v 27, that **the Spirit intercedes for the saints.** This is a reminder that we are God's holy people (see 1:7 and the comments there). It seems more likely that Paul refers to Spirit-inspired intercession that weak humans articulate in prayer than about a heavenly conversation in which the Holy Spirit must inform the Father of needs we cannot articulate. Thus, the Spirit helps us pray as God would have us pray, consistent with his intentions for us. This anticipates what Paul is about to write in vv 28-39, where he also will add that Christ intercedes (*entynchanei*) for us as well (v 34).

FROM THE TEXT

Wesley recognized that even "perfect" Christians "fall short of the law of love" and "transgress the very law they are under," therefore "need the atonement of Christ" as well as "the direct witness of the Spirit," when it is impossible for the conscience to distinguish temptation from sin (1979, 11:417-19; "A Plain Account of Christian Perfection"). Thus, an intellectually honest understanding of "entire sanctification" must be placed within the framework of "this present time" (v 18), which is characterized by "weakness." We are "no longer" what we once were, but we are "not yet" what we shall be. The *tyranny* of the Flesh as a power is ended, and we may enjoy the sanctifying presence of the Holy Spirit; but the *weakness* of our flesh—our humanity lingers. Thus, even those who claim to be Spirit-filled and entirely sanctified may confess with Paul, **The life I now live in the flesh, I live by the faithfulness of the Son of God, who loved me and gave himself for me** (Gal 2:20). "If we are faithless, he will remain faithful, for he cannot disown himself" (2 Tim 2:13; see 1:9; 2:1-6).

Furthermore, the Spirit-indwelt must always confess with Paul, "I know that nothing good dwells within me, that is, in my flesh" (Rom 7:18 NRSV). Apart from Christ I am flesh, a mere mortal, only human. In Wesley's words, we have "no stock of holiness"; whatever holiness we enjoy at any moment is in us by his indwelling Presence. As Jesus says, "Apart from me you can do nothing" (John 15:5). To see this is to understand "our" holiness as wholly *his* work.

In Philippians Paul puts this in a broader perspective. "It is God who works in [us] to will and to act according to his good purpose" (2:13). In view of "the resurrection from the dead" (3:11), we must confess that even those who are "perfect" (*teleioi*; see 1 Cor 2:6, 15-16) are not yet "perfected" (*teteleiomai*, Phil 3:12). Our bodies await final redemption (Rom 8:23). Nevertheless, **we are confident of this, that the God who began a good work in us will continue to perfect it until Christ Jesus comes again** (Phil 1:6, paraphrased).

In view of the paradoxical nature of Wesley's doctrine of Christian perfection, it has been described as "imperfect perfection" (see the discussion of Barth's dialectical understanding of obedience in the From the Text section following the commentary on Rom 8:12-17). But to deny the possibility of being truly sanctified, because we are still finite creatures subject to the limitations of an earthly existence, is to miss something essential to NT Christianity. The full truth is not gained by removing the tension between the two poles ("perfect"—"not yet perfected") but rather by holding the two truths with equal emphasis. Only thus does Christian experience flower into the likeness of Christ promised us "from the Lord, who is the Spirit" (2 Cor 3:18; see 1 Cor 15:45).

(ii) God's Eternal Purpose Consummated (8:28-30)

BEHIND THE TEXT

God not only listens to the ineffable cries of the Spirit, who assists the praying of Christians, but also hears them pray. God also sees to it that their very lives—their aspirations, their sufferings, and all they do—contribute to the good of those who pray in this way.

Here Paul introduces a formal affirmation of Christian destiny, the basis for the hope he discussed in vv 17-27. Apart from the gospel, all human beings had sinned and continually "fall short of the glory of God" (3:23). Now through the gospel God has manifested his righteousness and salvation in Christ Jesus among the Gentiles and reveals how his plan of salvation destines all justified believers for a share of glory in his presence. All are called in accordance with the divine plan of salvation. As this plan unfolds in reality, it orders all things in conformity with it.

It seems that Paul has finished his discussion of the role of the Spirit in Christian life in 8:27 and moves on to the place Christians play in the plan of salvation conceived of old by God the Father. However, v 28 is textually problematic; it is entirely possible that the Spirit could be the unexpressed subject of the verb here. We cannot be sure whether the discussion of the Spirit's role comes to an end with v 28 or v 27. It is certainly a transitional verse to what follows in vv 29-30. But before we consider the interpretation of v 28, we must note its textual challenges.

The Text of Rom 8:28

A few early and important Greek manuscripts and translations of Rom 8:28 have the reading *synergei ho Theos* ("God works with"), but the vast majority of the surviving manuscripts—early, late, and diverse in origin—have the shorter reading, omitting the subject entirely. Since the verb "works with" seems to imply a personal subject, early editors of the text may have added "God" as a "natural explanatory addition" (Metzger 1994, 458). One important and very early manuscript also has *pan*, "everything," instead of *panta*, "all things." Two interpretive complications remain, even if we accept the shorter reading.

First, Greek verbs do not require explicit subjects, since they take personal endings that presume a pronominal subject. Thus, *synergei* means "he/she/it works." But who/what is the antecedent of the implied pronoun? It appears that some early copyists presumed that this subject was "God," but is it likely that Paul would have written, "(God) works with all things for good to those who love <u>God</u> . . . ," rather than, ". . . to those who love <u>him</u>" (emphasis added)? The last explicit subject in the main clause of v 27 is the one "who searches the heart," presumably God. The verb in the subordinate clause that follows has no subject—"because [he] intercedes for the saints," but it is almost certainly the Spirit, the explicit subject of a nearly identical verb in v 26—"the Spirit intercedes"—but if God is not the subject of the verb, who or what is?

Second, because, unlike English, word order is not decisive for communicating meaning in Greek, Greek nouns and pronouns have inflectional endings that indicate their functions within sentences. Unfortunately, the nominative and accusative forms of neuter nouns and pronouns are identical. Thus, it is impossible to be certain whether *panta*, "all things" (or *pan*, "everything"), is the subject or direct object of the verb. If it is the subject, the translation could be: "We know that all things work together for good" (NRSV; see KJV, NKJV, ASV, ESV, NAB). But, if it is the direct object, the translation could be: "We know that in everything God works for good" (RSV; see NASB, NCV, NIV, NJB, NLT, TEV).

Another possibility, rare among the standard English translations (NEB), remains: the Spirit could plausibly be taken to be the subject. After all, what would prevent the same indwelling Spirit who "helps us in our weakness" (v 26) and "intercedes" for us (vv 26 and 27) from also working in all things for our good? This would certainly contribute to an even smoother transition from the theme of vv 18-27 to that of vv 28-30.

In 8:28-30 we encounter for the first time the mention of "predestination," which Paul will mention again in ch 9. His references to this topic in these chapters have led to numerous unresolved controversies within the church. Average readers seem to ignore that what Paul asserts here is stated from the *corporate* perspective (as also in chs 9—11). That is, he says nothing about God micromanaging and determining the destinies of individuals, but only about God's plans for the community.

Controversies over predestination began with Augustine's debate with Pelagius on the subject. It resumed with the systematizing of John Calvin's doctrine of election. The debates these views sparked continue to our day, often distracting interpreters of Romans from the indisputably central thrust of these chapters. Although it is not a major preoccupation of ch 8; Paul's treatment here seems to offer the key for making sense of the teaching he initiates in setting forth his understanding of God's plan of salvation.

Paul begins this unit of the letter by affirming that everything that happens to Christians in their earthly life is somehow governed by God's gracious providence. Nothing in this life can happen to ultimately harm Christians; all of these things can contribute to the destiny to which God has called them—that they should **be conformed to the likeness of his Son, that he might be the firstborn among many brothers** (v 29).

Verses 28-30 serve as the climactic conclusion of vv 18-30. Throughout the passage, Paul's perspective has widened step by step, bringing us to this survey of God's eternal purpose. The present age is not the first, as its comparison with God's new age might suggest. Just as the present age is to be followed by eternity, it has already been preceded by eternity. Only when we view our present existence set in God's eternal purpose, which extends from eternity to eternity, do we get the right and fullest perspective.

From the vantage point of eternity, **all things** (v 28) that come to Christians in this life—even the sufferings of this present age—somehow serve God's purpose. Superficially, "our present sufferings" (v 18), our present anonymity (v 19), our "frustration" (v 20), our deteriorating and dying bodies (vv 21, 23), our groaning and waiting (v 23), our disciplined perseverance (v 25), "our weakness" (v 26), and our difficulty praying (vv 26-27) would seem to hinder God's purpose for us.

But, in fact, everything that seems to frustrate God's purpose comes to serve its accomplishment. As a result, nothing can ultimately harm the Christian. Even the full onslaught of the powers of destruction (see vv 35-39) belongs only to the age that is passing away (see 1 Cor 7:31). They, too, contribute to God's good purpose for those who love him.

IN THE TEXT

■ **28** We know in Rom 8:28 (see v 22) stands in contrast to "we do not know" in v 26. *We* may not know how to pray for the will of God, but "he who searches our hearts knows" and helps us to pray to that end (v 27). *God* knows his plans; and we know all we need to know—that he loves us, as evidenced by his gift to us of the Holy Spirit (5:5; 8:31-38).

Speaking from common Christian experience, in v 28, Paul, therefore, connects what he has just written and what he is about to write. The Spirit assures us that we are God's children, destined to share his glory (vv 12-17) and that God's love for us (vv 37-39) is far more indestructible than our **love** for him could ever be (v 28).

The NIV follows a small but significant group of textual witnesses that preserve **God** (*ho Theos*) as the subject of the main verb in the *hoti* (**that**) clause in v 28—**in all things God works for the good of those who love him**. It would be possible to defend this translation based on contextual considerations, even if the words *ho Theos* were not an original part of Paul's sentence (see the sidebar in the Behind the Text section above).

If *ho Theos* is the subject, the verb *synergei* (**works**) must be taken in a transitive sense: ***God causes all things to work together.*** The *syn-* verb prefix presupposes that God cooperates with others to accomplish his purpose. Paul's point could be that God exerts his authority to override "divergent and even antagonistic factors so that despite themselves they collaborate for the ultimate good of those who love God" (Wood 1963, 126-27). Paul's sentiment, but not his wording, seems to echo Gen 50:20 (see Josephus, *Ant.* 1:14).

Since Rom 8:27 already refers to collaboration between God the Father and the Holy Spirit in prayer, Paul's point could be that the two also cooperate to work for our good. This would corroborate a Trinitarian reading of the passage. However, it seems more likely that Paul emphasizes the divine-human partnership—that even under adverse circumstances God works synergistically with those who love him to accomplish his good purpose for them.

The NIV's translation disguises one significant challenge to its interpretation of the passage. Whether or not the nominative (subjective) form of **God** (*ho theos*) appears in the original text, the accusative (objective) form of God (*ton theon*) does. Thus, a more literal translation of the Greek text would require: ***God causes all things to work together for the good of those who love God*** [emphasis added]—not simply **who love him,** which we would expect if God were the subject. This problem would be removed if we were to take the Spirit as the implicit subject: ***The Spirit causes all things to work together for the good of those who love God*** (see Jewett 2007, 527).

If we were to accept as original the manuscripts that omit *ho theos*, we may still suppose that **God** is the implied subject. However, the ambiguity of the grammatical case of **all things** (*panta*) would allow it to be construed as the subject of the verb. This is the basis of the NRSV translation (a return to the earlier approach of the KJV): "all things work together for good for those who love God."

Despite modern notions of inevitable progress (Dodd 1932, 138), the natural law of entropy suggests that things tend to fall apart. It might also be objected that **all things** would seem to include every *thing* that exists—personal and impersonal, animate and inanimate, sensible and insensible, events as well as objects, and bad things as well as good. Many such things do not independently or of themselves actually do anything, but this does not deter Paul in vv 19-23 from using personification to suggest what is literally implausible—creation groaning, watching, waiting, and enslaved.

It would never have entered Paul's mind that **all things** just work out on their own in some mechanistic or magical way; he is discussing divine providence. Although God may act anonymously and invisibly in the only apparently coincidental events that transform life's tragedies into triumphs, it is God who acts. The death of Jesus did not just work out for the best after all; God intervened, disrupting the normal course of events to vindicate his faithful and obedient Son by raising him from the dead. Regardless of how we translate the verse, Paul almost certainly takes for granted "that all things work together for good" (NRSV) only because of God.

The knowledge that everything that comes our way may serve God's good ends for us is the property, first, of **those who love** God (*tois agapōsin ton Theon*). Paul only rarely describes Christians as those who **love** God (here and in 1 Cor 2:9; 8:3; see Eph 6:24). He usually prefers the verb "believe" (or the noun "faith"). This is the first appearance of the verb **love** (*agapaō*) in Romans; the noun *agapē* has appeared in 5:5 and 8; and the adjective *agapētos* ("beloved"), in 1:7.

There does not seem to be a single instance in Paul where the noun *agapē* ("love") clearly means our love for God. *Agapē* for Paul, as for John (1 John 4:10, 16), is primarily the love of God revealed in sending his Son (Rom 5:5-8; see John 3:16). Love is **the love God shows us in Christ Jesus our Lord** (Rom 8:39). Here, however, Paul speaks of the love Christians have for God. The rarity of such expressions should not be taken to suggest that Christians do not love God (see Matt 22:37-38) or "our Lord Jesus Christ with an undying love" (Eph 6:24); clearly, they do.

"The idea of loving God is untypical of Greco-Roman religiosity, while being characteristically Jewish" (Dunn 2002a, 38A:494). Pious Jews characteristically referred to themselves as "those who love God and keep his commandments" (following OT precedent, e.g., Exod 20:6; Deut 5:10; 6:5; 7:9; see in the apocryphal Sir 2:15-16; and in the NT, 1 John 5:2) (Dunn 2002a, 38A:480). Here, Paul uses only the first part of the formula, **those who love God,** as a designation for those we would call "Christians" today (a term Paul never uses).

Love for God is more than an emotional response—it is the devotion of one's total personality to God (Matt 22:37-38, citing Deut 6:4-5). It is the loyalty of Job, whose love for and service of God were not for selfish reasons (Job 1:9-12; 2:4-10). It is the devotion that says, "Though he slay me, yet will I trust in him" (13:15 KJV). Adam Clarke notes that **those who love God** are those "who live in the *spirit of obedience.*"

The conviction that God/the Spirit makes **all things** work together **for the good** is also the privilege of those **who have been called** [*tois . . . klētois;* see the comments on 1:1, 6] **according to** [*kata*] **his purpose** [*prothesin;* see 9:11; Eph 1:11; 3:11]. Of course, the two different designations do not refer to different groups but to the same Christian people described from different perspectives. Christians **love** God, but this is not why **all things** work together **for** our **good.** The reason is not found in us but in God's objective, eternal **purpose** (see Isa 46:10); and it is in this **purpose** that the ultimate assurance of salvation rests.

■ 29 In designating Christians as those who **love** God, Paul views the Christian life subjectively; but in referring to them as **called according to his purpose,** he moves to the objective plane of the divine plan. From this he proceeds with a series of sentences that have been called the most objective in the NT: **For those God foreknew he also predestined to be conformed to the likeness of his Son, that he might be the firstborn among many brothers** [and sisters]. **And those he predestined, he also called; those he called, he also justified; those he justified, he also glorified** (Rom 8:29-30).

Predestined to Christlikeness

Romans 8:28-30 contains the essence of Paul's understanding of predestination, governing everything on the subject in both Romans and the remainder of the NT. Predestination is the belief, born of saving faith in Jesus Christ, that God has already decided upon the final destination he intends for Christians. It is that we will "be conformed to the image of his Son, in order that he might be the first-born within a large family" (v 29 NRSV). Predestination is the free and love-motivated choice of God, but it is certainly not arbitrary.

God acted with foresight to provide all of the ways and means necessary to lead all who would believe to salvation as they follow the Spirit's guidance (vv 14, 27). Predestination is the primordial triune conspiracy of love that caused God the Father to send his Son to die for us and to give us his Holy Spirit to give us access to God (Eph 2:18) and to lead us to the planned destination: Christlikeness (see Eph 1:4, 5-6, 13-14).

"These are mighty affirmations which are closely knit together," Nygren comments, "and stretch *from eternity—through time—to eternity*" (1949, 339). "Before the creation of the world" God purposed to create a holy people in Christ (Eph 1:4). That eternal purpose is fulfilled in time when God calls and justifies persons and is consummated in eternity when he finally glorifies them. Thus, the whole scheme of redemption—from election to final glorification—is utterly in God's hand. There is no place for either chance or arbitrariness, for it is all the purposeful activity of the God who reveals himself as holy love.

Chapter 9 deals in detail with divine election, but the doctrine is introduced here. Election means calling. This is an invitation, not an ultimatum. This is a divine initiative, not coercion. This is orchestration, not foreordination. It is a plan, not a script. "All this is from God, who reconciled us to himself through Christ" (2 Cor 5:18).

God's will has absolute priority in both creation and redemption. That God has "chosen" to create the cosmos is the reason things exist. That God has "chosen" to make us humans in his creaturely image is the ground of our existence as human beings. That God has loved us from "before the creation of the world" and has "chosen" us in Christ is the explanation of our salvation. This is surely the meaning of **foreknew**—God "fore-loved" and "fore-chose" us *in Christ*. Our election is *in Christ*, who is **the firstborn among many brothers and sisters** (Rom 8:29). Christ is the Elect—God's chosen one; we are elect in him (Eph 1:4; see 2 Thess 2:13; 1 Pet 1:2). God's eternal "decree" is that we shall be saved through faith in Christ (John 3:16). This will become increasingly clear in Rom 9 (see commentary there).

The meaning of **foreknew** (*prōegnō*) should be governed by the biblical use of the word "know," which is very marked and clear. (See the sidebar "Biblical Knowledge" with the commentary on 7:7.) It describes the "knowledge" of marriage (Gen 4:1, 25 NRSV). It is used to set forth God's election of Israel: "You only have I known of all the families of the earth" (Amos 3:2 NRSV; see Rom 11:2); "It was I who knew you in the wilderness" (Hos 13:5 RSV). To the reprobate on the Day of Judgment Christ will say, "I never knew you" (Matt 7:23). God's foreknowledge is, thus, his elective love, his purpose to create a people for his possession and fellowship.

We must keep in mind that we are not here dealing with a rigidly thought out and expressed deterministic philosophy but with a profound religious conviction (Barrett 1957, 170), so that the best commentators on this passage may not be the great theologians but the great hymn writers of the church.

Those who **love God** (Rom 8:28) are the *community of believers* chosen to enjoy his salvation—the "large family" (v 28 NRSV) that resembles his Son (v 29), not select individuals he has arbitrarily singled out to love. This community is the creation of "the God who gives life to the dead and calls things that are not as though they were" (4:17). Our redemption is not the outworking of fickle human purposes or self-initiated choices; rather, it represents the outworking of God's eternal purpose. Confident of this, we take heart in the knowledge that God is working in all things for our good.

Foreknowledge and election issue in predestination, and predestination means that our God-fashioned destiny is that we may be **conformed to the likeness of his Son.** The image/likeness is not something the Son has but who he is. The Son perfectly reveals God the Father (2 Cor 4:4-6; Col 1:15), in whose image and likeness humans were first created (Gen 1:26-27); and so he is the model of perfect humanity. His life of faithful obedience, his willingness to accept undeserved suffering, and his vindication by resurrection are among the aspects of the Son that make him the exemplary pattern for Christians (see Heb 2:6-10). Conformity to Christ is

> a process of transformation that begins in baptism, in which an old self is buried and a new person arises out of the water to live henceforth in Christ, who was himself the image of God. The transformation is cur-

rently manifest, at least in part, as believers cooperate with the Spirit to achieve the good (Rom 8:28); to restrict the bearing of this passage to future transformation in the resurrection overlooks the significance of the aorist verbs and the context of current suffering. (Jewett 2007, 528)

God's Elect

> He knew about them and by knowing and thinking about them he gave them their purpose—both in advance, i.e., by himself, in the power of almighty mercy which existed before the world (Eph. 1:4). While they were yet deaf he called them by his word, while they were yet ungodly he told them, in the hearing of the whole celestial creation, that they were righteous, while they were subject to temptation he clothed them with his own glory. (Barth 1959, 104-5)

Christ is at once "the image of God" (2 Cor 4:4; Col 1:15) and the image of our humanity (see 1 Cor 15:49). In the God-Man, Christ Jesus, we learn who God is and what humans are and ought to become according to their true nature. The process of metamorphosis by which we are gradually changed into the *imago Dei* is the work of sanctification through the Holy Spirit. "But we all, with unveiled face, beholding as in a mirror the glory of the Lord, are being transformed [*metamorphoumetha*] into the same image from glory to glory, just as from the Lord, the Spirit" (2 Cor 3:18 NASB).

8:29

When the sanctifying process is finally complete—when we have experienced "the redemption of our bodies" (Rom 8:23; see vv 11 and 23)—"we shall be like him, for we shall see him as he is" (1 John 3:2). For now we are "conformed [*synmorphizomenos*] to His death" (Phil 3:10 NASB). When we offer our bodies as living sacrifices to God, he transforms [*metamorphousthe*] us by renewing our mind (Rom 12:1-2). When the new age comes in its fullness, we shall finally be **conformed** (*synmorphous*, 8:29) to the body of Christ's glory (Phil 3:21).

Predestined (*proōrisen*) means "marked out beforehand" (only here and Eph 1:5, 11; see Acts 4:28; 1 Cor 2:7 in the NT).

> A parent who, before his child is old enough for a trade, predestines the boy. He *marks out beforehand* a path in which he designs him to go. The purpose, whether carried out or not, is predestination. . . . Before they were born, and therefore from eternity, God resolved that believers should be made like His only begotten Son. . . . Predestination is simply a purpose; and by no means implies the inevitable accomplishment of that purpose. (Beet 1885, 256-57)

In Rom 8:29 we have returned to the thought of a new humanity in Christ (see 5:12-21). Only here the picture of Christ as the eldest in God's redeemed family, **the firstborn** [*prōtotokon*] **among many brothers *and sisters.*** He who is the Son of God by *nature* (8:3, 32) is the Heir of God. God's children (vv 14-15) are "co-heirs with Christ" (v 17) of his predestined glory.

Colossians identifies Christ as "the firstborn over all creation" (1:15) and "the firstborn from among the dead" (v 18; see Rev 1:5). By virtue of his role in creation and his resurrection from the dead, he is the primary heir in the family (Rom 8:17). He is the prototype of the new humanity (see Heb 1:1-6).

Israel is God's "firstborn" in Exod 4:22; Sir 36:17; and 2 Esd 6:58. For Paul Christ provides the norm for defining the people of God rather than ethnic Israel, anticipating Rom 9—11. Clearly, God's concerns are corporate, not just isolated individuals. Predestination concerns the church, not individual persons. Paul's evangelistic plans for Spain reflect God's purpose to enlarge his family of Christ's brothers and sisters so that all who will believe may be a part—Jews and Gentiles, men and women, Greeks and barbarians. If inclusion in God's family were merely a matter of his choice, there would be no need for preaching the gospel.

■ **30** Planned in eternity, predestination is, according to 8:30, accomplished in time: **And those he predestined, he also called**—i.e., in conversion (see 1:7; 9:11; 1 Cor 1:26-31; 7:18; Gal 1:6; Col 3:15; 1 Thess 1:4-10; 2 Thess 2:13-15). God's call is not to salvation, "at least in the sense of final salvation, but simply to become Christians" (Sanday and Headlam 1929, 217).

Called implies a summons or invitation of God (see Rom 10:13-17) and the Spirit (John 6:44). **Those he called, he also justified** (Rom 8:30), because they responded in faith to his call. Justification here comprehends both justification and sanctification, the entire process of salvation from its outset to its consummation.

With justification Paul has reached the present; but so sure is he of the purposes of God that he describes the future in the aorist tense, used to speak of events as completed actions: **Those he justified, he also glorified.** (See the sidebar "Glory" with 8:18.) Those humans who refused to glorify God (1:21) not only dishonored God but also disgraced themselves. In a striking reversal, God will honor those who glorify him; and he does so already in the present age (2 Cor 3:18).

Future glorification, however, remains contingent on continuing faithfulness to God (see 1 Cor 15:1-2), or more specifically, suffering with Christ (Rom 8:17). Paul does not say here, nor anywhere else, that precisely the same number of persons are called, justified, and glorified. He does not deny that one-time believers may through unbelief be cut off from the community of salvation (see 11:20-23) and so forfeit their special calling and their future glorification. Neither does he deny that many are called and never justified (see 10:21).

Paul's central concern is to affirm the *method* and order of salvation: God leads us step-by-step toward glorification. This is "not a quantitative limitation

8:29-30

of God's action, but its qualitative definition" (Barth 1933, 346). This is "the final statement of the truth that justification, and, in the end, salvation also, are by grace alone, and through faith alone" (Barrett 1957, 171). (For a point-by-point exposition of Rom 8:29-30, see Wesley's sermon "On Predestination"; 1979, 6:225.)

FROM THE TEXT

In these verses Paul applies to all believers the idea of "election" so central to the self-understanding of Israel, and the church, as the people of God. Behind the existence of all who are "in Christ"—Gentiles as well as Jews—stands the eternal "choice" of God. Behind them also stands the plan or design that God has formed in their regard.

Paul defines "predestination" in christological terms. The entire section (vv 18-30) draws to a close the "christological proviso" of v 17. It is as those who have suffered with Christ that believers will be glorified with him and share his inheritance. Paul does not have individuals principally in mind; he is applying the scriptural privilege of election to the Christian community composed of believing Jews and Gentiles. The perspective is positive and inclusive, indicating that God's will is to bring all his children to the fullness of humanity, **conformed to the likeness of his Son** (v 29).

Whether or not some individuals fail to be included is not the point here. Implicit in the description of God's plan for human beings is the place of Christ, as risen Lord and "last Adam" (1 Cor 15:45). As such, Christ models for the new humanity, the original design of the Creator according to which human beings "image" God before the rest of creation (Gen 1:26-28; Ps 8:5-8). In this role the first Adam failed; and unbelievers also tragically fail to fulfill their calling.

Paul's doctrine of predestination says nothing about an arbitrary selection by God of certain people to be saved and of others to be lost. This would not be loving foresight and preparation, but vicious capriciousness. Likewise, Paul lends no support for notions of predestination as salvation based on merit known beforehand, as if God chose to save only those he knew in advance would believe in Christ. This would be nothing more than salvation by works. Predestination is not about persons but about God's **purpose.**

Paul understands predestination as God's well-conceived plan to save the church—all those who become a part of the "large family" of adopted brothers and sisters of Christ. It is not about individuals; it is about just one individual—Jesus Christ, God's beloved Son. In him God has provided the wherewithal for all to be saved, but he has chosen not to act coercively. He does not impose his will, he invites us to collaborate (***work together***). Only those who accept the invitation by faith and so align themselves with God's plan will have a part in the achievement of his purpose.

God foreknew, but his foreknowledge comes, not through an intellectual vision of timeless reality or the perception of events before they become historical realities, but in the context of personal relationship with his people. Standing in personal relationship to God, the NT community believes that its entire history, from beginning to end, is known by God, and from that same standpoint perceives that all human history is encompassed within the divine purpose.

God's knowledge is all-inclusive in the sense that nothing escapes his personal lordship. Divine foreknowledge does not mean that history is scripted in advance or that the human choices are causally determined by God. It springs out of the experience of the Christian community's relation to a personal Lord whose personal will governs its life from beginning to end, enfolding "all things" in such a way that these things "work together for good for those who love God, who are called according to his purpose" (Rom 8:28 NRSV).

And what is God's eternal purpose? That those whom he loves and who love him might "be conformed to the image of his Son, in order that he might be the firstborn within a large family" (v 29 NRSV). To foreknow is to fore-love. It is to take the risky initiative of loving the weak, the ungodly, the unrighteous, the sinners, in an effort to make enemies friends (5:6-11). Distorted Reformed notions of predestination have led Wesleyans to refer instead to prevenient grace.

Paul announces this understanding of divine foreknowledge and predestination in the prescript of Romans: "The gospel [of God was] promised beforehand through his prophets in the Holy Scriptures, regarding his Son" (1:2-3; see Matt 1:22-23; 2:5-6, 15, 17, etc.). The apostolic church believed the foreordained purpose of God was disclosed in the life, death, and resurrection of Jesus Christ. According to the primitive kerygma, Jesus was betrayed and crucified "by God's set purpose and foreknowledge" (Acts 2:23; see 4:28). Viewing Jesus' career from the perspective of faith, NT writers discern in these events the *prevenient* purpose of God.

The NT affirms that the Elect One (Luke 9:35; 23:35) was purposed as the means of salvation from the beginning. Jesus Christ, God's beloved Son, was "destined [*proegnōsmenou*] before the foundation of the world, but was revealed at the end of the ages for your sake" (1 Pet 1:20 NRSV; see John 17:24). The sovereign saving activity of God's grace in Christ was manifested in Christ Jesus, who is the expression of God's eternal purpose. Christ is the Elect; the church is elect in him. This takes us back to Paul's delineation of the two humanities in Rom 5:12-21. Those in Christ are elect, i.e., called to salvation, called to be saints (1:7), but whether we align ourselves with Adam or with Christ is not a matter of our divinely determined destiny, but of our responsible decision.

8:28-30

The church is bound together by its divine calling. Salvation is traced back beyond anything human and temporal, to the eternal purpose of God, which spans history from beginning to end and has its center in Christ Jesus. We are "predestined to be conformed to the image of his Son, in order that he might be the firstborn within a large family" (8:29 NRSV). It is all to the praise of the glory of his grace (16:25-27). The grace that predestines us is the sovereign Lord's prevenient grace.

Prevenient grace is the grace of God that goes before any decision we make. However, predestination is not only about what God does behind the scenes to draw us to Christ but also about the free grace that gives us the freedom to make responsible choices. And it is about the keeping grace in which we stand as those justified by faith (5:1-2). Pauline predestination is not an abstract concept. It concerns God's decision to take the initiative: to love us before we even had a thought about him, to remain faithful to the faithless, to offer forgiveness to the unrepentant, to justify the ungodly, and to sanctify the unholy. Such relentless grace will prevail; God's love will not let us down (v 5; see Phil 1:6).

Predestination affirms that God plans in advance and that he acts purposefully to achieve these plans. God knows where he wants his creation to go and how he wants it to get there. He has assured the success of his plans by taking the initiative in Christ to provide the more-than-sufficient means to the final destination he has in mind: Christlikeness, i.e., **to be conformed to the likeness of his Son.**

"The eternal decree," says Wesley, is this proposition: "'He that believeth shall be saved; he that believeth not shall be damned.'" "According to this, all true believers are in Scripture termed elect, as all who continue in unbelief are so long properly reprobates, that is, unapproved of God, and without discernment touching the things of the Spirit" (Wesley 1979, 10:210; "Predestination Calmly Considered"). "The Lord is," we must meanwhile always remember, "not wanting anyone to perish, but everyone to come to repentance" (2 Pet 3:9). "Indeed, God did not send the Son into the world to condemn the world, but in order that the world might be saved through him" (John 3:17 NRSV).

From the ultimate perspective, therefore, the sovereignty of God is the sovereignty of *holy love*—that of "the God and Father of our Lord Jesus Christ, who . . . chose us in him before the creation of the world to be holy and blameless in his sight. . . . in accordance with his pleasure and will—to the praise of his glorious grace, which he has freely given us in the One he loves" (Eph 1:3-6).

(c) The Coming Victory of God's Love (8:31-39)

BEHIND THE TEXT

Romans 8:31-39 concludes vv 1-30 and, as such, chs 5—8. Thus, it also brings to a close the body of the letter to this point (1:16—8:39). Jewett notes numerous terminological and conceptual parallels between 5:1-11 and 8:31-39: justification (5:1, 9; 8:33); suffering (5:3; 8:35-37); God's love (5:5, 8; 8:35, 39); Christ's death (5:6, 10; 8:34); salvation from wrath (5:9; 8:31-34); Christ's resurrection (5:10; 8:34); and rejoicing in God (5:11; 8:31-39) (2007, 535).

Romans 8:31-39 functions like the peroration to a speech, drawing together previously discussed motifs and building to a crescendo. Paul sweeps his readers along, combining theology and emotional appeal. His rhetorical questions contribute to the overall effect, as their implicit answers draw the readers into this remarkable celebration of confidence, whatever befalls them. The paragraph begins with ten increasingly longer rhetorical questions, all in the future tense (vv 31-36). The remainder consists of Paul's confident assertions (vv 37-39).

Throughout vv 31-39 "Paul has taken over cherished themes of Israel's self-consciousness as the people of God and applied them without restriction to Gentile as well as Jew" (Dunn 2002a, 38A:499). This forces discerning readers to ask, "But, what about Israel?" Thus, Paul's conclusion serves also to introduce the next major section of the letter, chs 9—11.

IN THE TEXT

(i) Rhetorical Questions (8:31-36)

Rhetorical questions technically do not require answers; their answers are implicit in their formulation. Here, however, Paul's penchant for diatribe style leads him to pile question upon question, challenging every potential misunderstanding to assure that his hearers find his gospel manifesto totally persuasive.

■ 31 The opening question is phrased so as to signal a shift in the discussion: *So what shall we say about these things?* (v 31). *These things* refer back specifically to 8:1-30. The formulation of the question, *Ti oun eroumen*, "So what shall we say," however, has been (and will continue to be) a recurring feature of Paul's diatribe style throughout (4:1; 6:1; 7:7; 9:14, 30; see also 3:5, where the *oun*, "so," is missing). Paul is not actually expecting answers from his hearers, but only calling attention to the importance of what follows.

The first, open-ended question sets in motion a series of follow-up questions. The second asks, **If God is for us, who can be against us?** (8:31b). The protasis (if-clause) here is not a true condition. Paul's "If" obviously means "Since." That God is **for us,** *hyper hēmon,* i.e., on our side, acting on our behalf (see Mark 9:40; 14:24; 2 Cor 13:8), sums up Paul's argument since Rom 3:21, with his announcement of the revelation of God's justifying righteousness in contrast to the revelation of his judging wrath in 1:18—3:20. God proves he is for us supremely in the gifts of Christ and the outpoured Spirit (see 5:5-8; 8:27).

The question is framed so as to elicit an unequivocal answer, which does not need to be stated explicitly: "No one!" Paul echoes the OT when he exults, If the one true God (3:30), the Creator, is on our side, what possible difference does human opposition make (see Pss 56:9; 118:6-7; Isa 50:9)? Since God will prevail against all challenges (Rom 3:1-8), so will those on his side. Paul claims Israel's basis for confidence in God for the mixed church consisting of Jews and Gentiles.

■ **32** The third question begins by amplifying upon what **God** has done to prove he **is for us.** Only then does Paul ask, **How will he not also, along with him, graciously give us all things?** (8:32*b*). By first reminding his readers of what God has done, Paul's rhetorical question leaves open only one possible response. He focuses on the saving significance of God's saving gesture in Christ, stated both negatively (**not**) and positively (**but**) for rhetorical effect: **He who did not spare** [*ouk epheisato*, "did not withhold"] **his own Son, but gave him up for us all"** (v 32*a*).

The positive formulation probably echoes Isa 53:6, 12, as Paul rehearses what he has written repeatedly in the letter: God **gave him up for us** (in Rom 3:25—"God presented [Christ] as a sacrifice of atonement"; in 4:25—God "delivered [him] over to death for our sins"; in 5:8—"God demonstrates his own love for us in this: While we were still sinners, Christ died for us"; in 8:3—God sent "his own Son . . . to be a sin offering"). What is unusual here is the addition of the universal **all** to the formulation—Christ died for Jews *and* Gentiles (1:16; 3:9, 22; 4:11, 16; 5:18; 10:4, 12-13; 11:32), weak *and* strong (14:15).

The negative formulation—**He . . . did not spare his own Son**—is widely recognized as echoing Gen 22:16, in which God commends Abraham for his willingness to sacrifice Isaac: "You . . . have not withheld your son, your only son." Jewish rabbis found the Aqedah, the sacrificial binding of Isaac, a demonstration of the faithfulness of Abraham. Although Paul makes no reference to this in ch 4, where Jews might have expected it, he does so here. Perhaps, "Paul indicates that Abraham's offering of his son serves as a type not of the faithfulness of the devout Jew, but rather of the faithfulness of God" (Dunn 2002a, 38A:501). Jewett notes other OT (2 Sam 18:5; 21:7, 9) and nonbiblical parallels, which lead him to dismiss a specific allusion to Abraham (2007, 537). Regardless, because God has already done what he did not require Abraham to do, it is unthinkable that he would not grant believers everything (see Rom 5:9-10).

Paul asks, **How will he not also, along with him, graciously give us all things?** (8:32*b*). Again this summarizes what he had previously written: **With** [*syn*] **him** summarizes our solidarity with Christ in 6:1-11 and our status as "co-heirs" with him in 8:17 [where there are three *syn*-compounds]. **Will . . .**

graciously give (*charisetai;* only here in Romans) echoes "the gift" (*charisma*) of 5:15 and Paul's repeated emphasis upon grace (*charis;* see 3:24; 4:16; 5:2, 15-21; 6:1, 14, 15). The hyperbolic **all things** (*ta panta*) is deliberately open-ended. If God would give his Son for us, there is nothing he would not give (1 Cor 3:21-23).

God not only vindicated his crucified Son by resurrecting him from the dead but also made him Heir of all creation (see Rom 11:36; 1 Cor 8:6; 15:27-28; Eph 1:10-11, 22-23; Phil 3:21; Col 1:6-17). Since God has already given us his beloved Son, is there anything he would withhold from Christ's suffering brothers and sisters? No answer to such a question is necessary: Of course not. After all, we are "heirs of God and joint heirs with Christ" (Rom 8:17 NRSV). "The one crucified for the sake of others thus shares and shapes the churches' sovereignty over the world" (Jewett 2007, 539).

■ **33** The second series of follow-up questions in vv 33-35 return to the theme of opposition raised in v 31, **Who can be against us?** Certainly not God. The rhetorical questions—**Who will bring any charge** [*enkalesei*] **against those whom God has chosen** [*eklektōn theou,* **God's elect/chosen people**]? (v 33) and **Who is he that condemns** [*katakrinōn*]? (v 34; see Isa 50:7-9)—are normally taken to refer to the Last Judgment. Jewett, however, proposes that Paul may have in mind the mutual impugning of weak and strong believers in Rome, which the apostle urges them to abandon in 14:1—15:13 (2007, 540). The verb *enkaleseō,* used only here in Paul's letters, appears elsewhere in the NT only in Acts (19:38, 40; 23:28, 29; 26:2, 7) as a technical term used for legal accusations.

The expression **God's elect,** used in the OT to refer to Israel (e.g., 1 Chr 16:13; Ps 105:6; Isa 45:4), is here applied to all Christians, both Jews and Gentiles. In Rom 5:16 and 18 the noun *katakrima,* "judgment" or "condemnation," describes the consequences of Adam's transgression. In 8:1 Paul insists that because of Christ, Christians are not subject to condemnation; on the contrary, Christ condemned [*katekrinen*] Sin. In 14:3, 10, 13, and 22-23 Paul explicitly challenges his Roman audience to stop condemning one another (see 1 Cor 6).

Paul answers his own rhetorical questions, but it is not clear whether his answers are contradictory statements or rhetorical counterquestions that expect "No" answers. Versions and commentaries disagree. **Who will bring any charge . . . ? God who justifies?** (Rom 8:33). The implied answer is clearly, "Impossible! The One who justifies sinners [4:5; see 8:30] would never bring charges against those he has acquitted." If we translate the response, **It is God who justifies,** Paul implies that it really doesn't matter who accuses us, since God acquits us. Thus, his main point remains unaffected by punctuation.

■ **34** Similarly the answer to the question, **Who is he that condemns?** (v 34*a*), may be a rhetorical question or an assertion: **Christ Jesus, who died—**

more than that [*mallon de*], who was raised to life—is at the right hand of God and is also interceding for us (v 34*b;* see 1 Cor 15:3-4; 2 Cor 5:15). Christians have been released from condemnation because of their solidarity with Christ (Rom 8:1).

Since Christ, the Judge's right-hand man (2:16; 14:10; 2 Cor 5:10) is our elder brother, as part of his family (Rom 8:12-17) we have nothing to fear from him. *Mallon de* indicates that the Crucified One is now to be recognized as the Resurrected One; and this is decisive here, as the next two clauses indicate.

That the risen Christ is **at the right hand of God** reflects widespread Christian appeal to Ps 110:1—"The LORD says to my Lord: 'Sit at my right hand until I make your enemies a footstool for your feet.'" Jesus' resurrection was also his exaltation (see Matt 12:35-37; Acts 2:33-35; 5:31; Rom 1:4; 1 Cor 15:24-27; Eph 1:20; Col 3:1; Heb 1:3, 13; 8:1; 10:12; 12:2) to a position of honor and authority—the significance of **the right hand** in antiquity.

In his exalted status as Lord, Christ not only reigns but **is also interceding** [*entynchanei*] **for us.** According to Heb 7:25, Christ, our great high priest in the heavenly sanctuary, "always lives to intercede" (*entynchanein*) for us. The verb *entynchanō*, "intercede in prayer," similarly describes the help the Spirit offers us in our weakness in Rom 8:26-27. This is not surprising, since he is the Spirit of Christ (v 9).

If Paul's answer to his question in v 34—**Who is it that condemns?**—is an assertion, **Christ Jesus . . . ,** his point is that whoever might condemn Christians must recognize that Christ "pleads our cause" (REB). If the answer is another rhetorical question—Would Christ condemn us?—the answer elicited is certainly, "Never!"

■ **35** The next follow-up question leaves behind the heavenly courtroom at the Last Judgment to face the present reality of earthly threats: **Who shall separate** [*chōrisei*] **us from the love** [*agapēs*] **of Christ?** (v 35). Paul's answer consists of a list of seven possibilities, which can only be understood as counterquestions.

Except for **sword,** each of the dangers he lists had already been faced by Paul himself (see 1 Cor 4:10-13; 2 Cor 11:23-29; 12:10), although he does not mention that here. He speaks from experience. If Christian tradition about the execution of Paul by beheading is correct, he would also experience the sword.

The number seven in the Bible is "perfect" in the sense that it is all-inclusive. These seven troubles offer Paul a means of being comprehensive without being exhaustive. These are only representative of the potential threats Christians may face. None of these threats alone nor all of them together can bring an end to our experience of Christ's love. He keeps on loving us. **The love of Christ** must be a subjective genitive, referring to the love he demonstrates for us.

The verb *chorizō*, **separate,** conveys the sense of deprivation—being apart from or without something. Paul's essential point is that no imaginable suffering, not even death itself, can deprive us of the certainty that Christ loves us. Because we live in a fallen world, many of the threats the apostle mentions still face persecuted Christians in various places. However, Paul does not have in mind only the suffering people face because they are believers; **persecution** is only one of the threats he mentions.

There is no reason why we might not add to his list such contemporary threats as cancer, Alzheimer's, terrorism, etc. Even so, the relative comfort of Christians in the affluent West should not let us forget that Paul has in mind the corporate suffering of the Christian community around the world. Because we are part of the whole church, we must see a threat to one as the problem of all (see 1 Cor 12:26).

Since Paul's list responds to the question <u>Who</u> **shall separate us . . . ?** (Rom 8:35, emphasis added), each of the threats he mentions is personified as a personal power. The first two, **trouble** and **hardship,** are listed in 2:9 as consequences of doing evil (see Deut 30:15—31:22). However, these are experienced not only by evil-doers but also by all as a part of the great end-time tribulation now in motion—"the sufferings of this present time" (Rom 8:18 NRSV).

The Greek word *thlipsis*, **trouble** here, has a wide range of possible translations. It is an expected, although always unpleasant, experience of believers (e.g., in 5:3 it is translated "sufferings"; in 12:12, "affliction"; in 2 Cor 1:4, etc., "tribulation" KJV; and in 2 Cor 8:13, "hard pressed"). However, it may, nonetheless, become the occasion for divine comfort (2 Cor 1:4-7). The Greek word *stenochōria*, **hardship,** describes the experience of being crushed and confined by difficulties, darkness, and despair.

Persecution (*diōgamos*) refers to sufferings of various kinds for religious reasons (Mark 4:17; 10:30; Acts 8:1; 13:50; 1 Cor 4:12; 2 Cor 4:9; 12:10; 2 Thess 1:4; 2 Tim 3:11). **Famine** (*limos*; see 2 Cor 11:27), however, refers to the experience of hunger due to natural disasters, war, etc., often associated with the tribulations of the last days (see Matt 24:7; Rev 6:8). **Nakedness** (*gymnotēs*) results from deprivation of clothing due to poverty and disaster (see 2 Cor 11:27; Jas 2:15; see 1 Cor 4:11-12; 2 Cor 6:10; Phil 4:11-12; 1 Thess 2:9). **Danger** (*kindynos*) describes anything that places life and health at risk (see 1 Cor 15:30; 2 Cor 11:26). **Sword** (*machaira*) refers by metonymy to "violent death," whether by murder, execution, or war (see Matt 10:34, 38-39; Acts 12:2; Heb 11:34, 37; Rev 13:10).

■ **36** The **sword** and the threat of martyrdom remind Paul of Ps 44:22, which he quotes in Rom 8:36. Although the psalm referred originally to Israel's suffering at the hands of its enemies and later rabbis applied the passage to the Maccabean martyrs, Paul finds in these lines language suggestive of Christian suffering (see v 18; 1 Cor 15:31; 2 Cor 4:10-11). He considers such suffering the normal, inescapable, expected, even divinely ordained experience of Christians (see 1 Thess 3:1-5).

As a lengthy rhetorical question, Paul implies that nothing in his seven-fold list of threats can separate believers from Christ's love for them. He can rejoice in his sufferings because they allow him to participate in Christ's suffering (Phil 3:7-11; Col 1:24; 1 Thess 1:6-7), provide an occasion for knowing Christ's strength despite his weakness (2 Cor 12:1-10), and increase his dependence on God alone as the one who raises the dead (1:8-11). Paul reflects the biblical tradition of the righteous suffering defended at length in the book of Job: suffering does not necessarily indicate divine disfavor.

(ii) Confident Assertions (8:37-39)

■ **37** In vv 37-39, Paul offers the definitive answer to all his rhetorical questions from vv 31-36. Suffering does not threaten to undermine our experience of the love Christ has for us. We suffer, *but* we conquer nonetheless. In fact, we will be glorified only if we suffer with him (v 18). No [*alla*, "but"], **in all these things we are more than conquerors** [*hypernikōmen*, "super-victors"] opens Paul's rhetorical climax (v 37).

Paul identifies God/Christ (see v 39; 5:8) alone as the source of our triumph: "We overwhelmingly conquer" (NASB) **through him who loved** [*agapēsantos*] **us.** The aorist tense of the verb **loved** emphasizes God's supreme demonstration of love in the death of Christ (8:31-32).

■ **38** Verses 38-39 list nine things that will be unable to **separate us** from God's love **in Christ** (v 39). **I am convinced** [*pepeismai*, "I am in a state resulting from having been persuaded"] employs the perfect passive to emphasize Paul's unshakable conviction (v 38; see 2 Tim 1:12). Theologically, our victory is cosmic in scope (see Eph 6:10-18). Of the nine threats, all but **powers** (*dynameis*; see Matt 24:29) are listed in four pairs of contrasting realities that transcend the historical threats Paul lists in Rom 8:35.

Each pair refers to polar-opposite realities. That is, **neither** this **nor** its opposite can prevent us from achieving final salvation. The list mentions **death—life** (the givens of creaturely experience; see 8:35-36; 14:7-9; 1 Cor 3:22; Phil 1:20), **demons** [*archai*, **rulers**]**—angels** (earthly and heavenly beings; see 1 Cor 15:24; 2 Cor 11:14; Eph 1:21; 3:10; 6:12), **present—future** (fatalistic temporal realities; see 1 Cor 3:22), and **height—depth** (cosmic dimensions/astrological forces). Finally, to be exhaustive, Paul adds **nor anything else in all creation** (better, "nor any other created thing" NASB).

■ **39** Because **anything else** excludes all except God, there can be no doubt: NOTHING WHATSOEVER *can* **separate us from the love of God that is in Christ Jesus our Lord** (Rom 8:39). This indestructible bond convinces Paul that we may be, that **we are,** super-victors, for God's love expressed in Christ is invincible! (see Keck 2005, 219-23). Nothing can exclude us from final salvation, because it finally depends on him, not us. Jewett suggests that "this formulation has the function of relativizing all of the powers; they are all creatures, just as humans are, and no creature has the power to contend with God" (2007, 554).

FROM THE TEXT

At this stage in Romans, Paul emerges in a new light. So far he has written as a learned teacher, dazzling us with his unfolding of the gospel of Christ. Here, he mounts the pulpit and calls for our response. "What shall we now say to all these things?" We are not being asked to *talk about* them but to *respond* appropriately.

Our answers to Paul's questions are determined by our confidence in the truth of the gospel and the faithfulness of Christ. **Who shall separate us from the love of Christ?** We can only answer, "Nothing or no one!" The decisive battle has already been won, in the death and resurrection of our Lord. None of the lingering insurgent forces resistant to the new regime, despite their disruptive power, can separate us from God's love or hinder us from ultimately sharing in the lordship of the universe he won on our behalf. "In Christ" (8:1, 9-11) we are grasped within by the passionate love of God and drawn totally into the fulfillment of the Creator's design for us already revealed in the risen Lord.